To Dad
1959
Rosemarie

THE
DARK
SUMMER

By the same author

THE DARK SUMMER

.

An Intimate History of the Events

That Led to World War II

GENE SMITH

Collier Books

Macmillan Publishing Company

New York

Collier Macmillan Publishers

London

Collier Books
Macmillan Publishing Company
866 Third Avenue, New York, NY 10022
Collier Macmillan Canada, Inc.

Library of Congress Cataloging-in-Publication Data
Smith, Gene.
    The dark summer: an intimate history of the events that led to
World War II/Gene Smith.—1st Collier Books ed.
        p.   cm.
    Includes index.
    ISBN 0-02-037390-2
    1. World War, 1939–1945—Causes.   2. Europe—Politics and
government—1918–1945.   I. Title.
D741.S64   1989
940.53′112—dc19   89-479   CIP

Macmillan books are available at special discounts for bulk purchases
for sales promotions, premiums, fund-raising, or educational use.
For details, contact:

Special Sales Director
Macmillan Publishing Company
866 Third Avenue
New York, NY 10022

First Collier Books Edition 1989

10 9 8 7 6 5 4 3 2 1

Designed by Jack Meserole

Printed in the United States of America

I predict there would be another world war within a generation if no pains were taken to prevent it. Every woman should weep for the child at her breast who when he grows to manhood will have to go forth to fight.
—PRESIDENT WOODROW WILSON, 1919

If war is fated to be, then it will be. But history will say that the world was mad.
—AMBASSADOR SIR NEVILE HENDERSON, 1939

It all seemed quite different, afterward.
—FORMER FOREIGN MINISTER JOACHIM VON RIBBENTROP, 1946

Author's Note

On the afternoon I submitted the photographs for the picture section of this book, my last important duty toward its production, I strolled up New York's Fifth Avenue to the home of the German cultural organization located in the Goethe House. I had eaten a delightful sushi and sashimi luncheon with my editor in one of the myriad Japanese restaurants that dot Manhattan—places unimaginable in the New York or Berlin or London or Paris of the days with which this book concerns itself. Chicken chow mein was then generally accounted the most exotic food acceptable for presentation to the public—and I remember schoolyard stories of what the sly Orientals *really* put into the dish.

Culinary tastes and perceptions are not the only things that have changed since those now long gone and lost days before the war. I remember Fifth Avenue as a two-way street with double-decker buses open on the tops during warm months; I remember the New York Yankees supreme in baseball and Joe Louis winning every fight. In the background one heard the radio news broadcasts to which one's parents listened. We had an automobile with a radio, quite notable in the summer of 1939, and I remember my parents listening to it hour after hour over Labor Day in our summer place. Several times the car battery went dead and someone from the village had to come and get the motor started. I suppose jumper cables for ordinary motorists did not exist in those days.

I do not remember the first thing of what the radio speakers had to offer about the events in London, Moscow, Berlin, Warsaw. If I bothered to listen, which I doubt that I did, preoccupied as I was with other more pressing matters, I immediately forgot what was said. In this I presaged the actions of future generations. For who today recalls Beck and Smigly-Rydz of Poland, Lord Halifax of Great Britain, Daladier, Molotov, Joachim von Ribbentrop. Even Adolf Hitler, a man after all born of woman, a human being, has come to be regarded really as a horror-movie or comic-book character. One sees the symbol of his movement on paperback books in the drugstore rack: embossed swastikas on the covers of spy novels or sci-fi thrillers. Indeed, I have been amused during the three years I have worked on this book to inquire of friends their knowledge of why the Second World War came about. Only an amazingly small percentage can offer an exact description. For the others it had something to do with Czechoslovakia. The Sudetenland, wasn't it? Or that city in Poland. An astonishing number tell me someone was shot somewhere— a prince or archduke or something, wasn't that it? The Munich Conference. Hitler's hatred of the Jews. And Pearl Harbor. The Japanese bombed it—that's why the war in Europe began.

I entered the Goethe House. A photographic exhibition had attracted me there. A cache of pictures taken by Robert Capa had recently come to light. They were of Berlin the summer of 1945, a couple of months after the guns fell silent on the Continent. Here were the sights of the last act of the fall of the doomed way of life that was Europe between the wars. A civilization had come to an end, empires and swords and monocles and bat-wing collars and an American army in the thirteenth or fourteenth rank of the world's military forces. Here were the gravestones— the bombed and shelled Berlin wherein half and more of the apartments were uninhabitable, half and more of the schools gone. Ruins, the trees in the park cut down for fuel, people lining up at a hydrant for water, women massing together to push a wagon, toppled and smashed statues of Prussian kings, the dazed German soldier in the torn, old uniform of his broken array— the bottom line, as we say.

I had handed in a manuscript, and then the accompanying pictures, for a book on why the war broke out: the diplomatic Notes, the diary entries, the private conversations and impressions, what the statesmen said and the people thought. How splendid the gallant Polish cavalry was! (Until the Panzers and Stukas came.) How sad Unity Mitford, on whose physical relationship with the Leader the world speculated; how debonair Sir Nevile Henderson, KCMG, who wrote so well of his failed mission to save the peace; how tragic—how very tragic indeed—Prime

Minister Chamberlain with ever-present memories of his cousin Norman, dead on 1914–18's Western Front; how confident the French in their Maginot Line. All gone now. King George with his conquered stammer, Roosevelt, von Rundstedt, the mild Joseph Stalin with his pipe, Lord Gort, Gamelin. All gone. Capa's Berlin pictures remain.

I left the Goethe House. Who in the summer of 1945 could have conceived the fashion in which a few short years later the photographer would die? That he would in 1954 step on a land mine in a place so remote and little known that its existence was then known to even a smaller percentage of people than those of my friends who really know how the Second World War began, and why? That from what the Paris of the 1920s did and did not do, from old von Hindenburg's fatal decision, from the hesitations of Halder and Canaris, from the doings of Admiral Sir Reginald Plunkett-Ernle-Erle-Drax, from, not least, the voice of a Reich chancellor and Leader crying, "My German men and women!" there would come, as on a direct line, a war with land mines waiting to kill Capa in the place called Vietnam?

The First World War is fought and gives birth to the Second; then the empires fall and Europe declines and the actors on the edge of the stage, Russia and America, move into the spotlight. They face off, and from their competition comes Korea and then Vietnam and Capa's land mine; and I go out into the sunlight of a spring day on Fifth Avenue, the Goethe House's security lock clicking behind me, into that which we all share whether we will it or not, that which we call the March of History.

THE
DARK
SUMMER

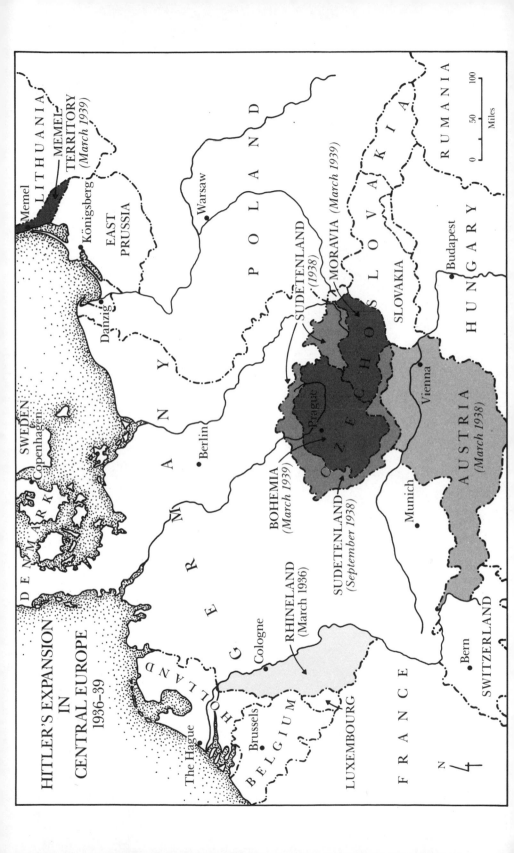

HITLER'S EXPANSION
IN
CENTRAL EUROPE
1936–39

DENMARK

Copenhagen

SWEDEN

Memel

LITHUANIA

MEMEL-
TERRITORY
(March 1939)

Königsberg

EAST
PRUSSIA

Danzig

Warsaw

POLAND

G E R M A N Y

Berlin

SUDETENLAND
(1938)

MORAVIA (March 1939)

C Z E C H O S L O V A K I A

SLOVAKIA

Budapest

RUMANIA

0   50   100
Miles

HOLLAND

The Hague

Cologne

RHINELAND
(March 1936)

BOHEMIA
(March 1939)

Prague

SUDETENLAND
(September 1938)

Munich

Vienna

AUSTRIA
(March 1938)

HUNGARY

Brussels

BELGIUM

LUXEMBOURG

F R A N C E

Bern

SWITZERLAND

N

ONE

DAYLIGHT comes early to Moscow during the warm months and stays long, and of a late August afternoon the sun stands high over the horizon even with the long half-twilight of the North's summer solstice at hand. Moscow was in the midst of a heat wave.

The people's commissar of foreign affairs—Mr. Molotov to the Western diplomats and Comrade Molotov to his own people—stepped into the office of the general secretary of the Central Committee of the Communist Party of the Union of Soviet Socialist Republics. The general secretary was known as the Gensek to many of his subordinates, Joseph Vissarionovich to some, Koba to those who had known him long before, Comrade Stalin to most and the Great Leader, the Great Teacher, the Leader-Father and Brain, Heart, Strength of the Party and the People in the newspapers and wall posters, Stalin the Sun of Our Lives, the Beloved of Our Souls, the Vozhd, the Boss. He was mild-mannered, wryly humorous, given to the use of homey peasant sayings. He liked to have his associates in for four-hour-long self-serve dinners at his villa outside Moscow, the chairs for the table of which he drew up himself and at the head of which he did not sit. Afterward the men would drink and smoke and sing along with records put on the phonograph by the Vozhd's own hand. The people's commissar for war, Voroshilov, a lover of the opera, sang the best. Sometimes Stalin, the name he had given himself deriving from "steel," desired more active entertainment. "When Stalin says dance," reasoned the rising young official Nikita Khrushchev, "a wise man dances." Awkward, chunky and pudgy as he was, Khrushchev squatted on his haunches and kicked out his heels to a Ukrainian folk song.

Patient, unhurried, methodical, always speaking in a low voice, Stalin did not forcefully offer opinions or give orders at Kremlin meetings. Endlessly smoking cigarettes or more usually his English pipes, he listened silently as subordinates put forward views. At the end he would mildly say he was inclined to agree with this comrade and disagree with that one. What the first had suggested was done.

He was no political theorist and no intellectual of the type that had taken Marxism, the product of Western European thought, and with it made the Revolution in half-Asiatic Russia. Lenin's mind was of unlimited power, and Trotsky was the greatest orator of his day and a dynamic writer also, and other leaders climbed glittering peaks. But Stalin, bland, silent, patient, was in the days of the Tsar an almost invisible middle-level member of the Bolshevik Party. He was indistinguishable from many who ran clandestine meetings denouncing Nicholas II and all his works, tried to instigate strikes, distributed seditious literature and wrote statements to be printed on cheap paper by printing presses concealed in back rooms. Saying they were appropriating money stolen from The People, these revolutionaries robbed banks and post offices. They used false names and false addresses, assassinated officials, threw bombs. Caught and convicted on one charge or another by the secret police, Bolsheviks routinely went to remote Siberian prison camps.

Off and on Stalin served eight years in jail or in exile, sitting or fishing and setting traps and reading and waiting. He then rejoined the movement to which he had belonged since leaving at the age of nineteen the seminary his pious mother in Tiflis in Georgia had selected for him. He had absolutely nothing to do with the hurricane that carried away the Tsar, and little more role to play in the coup that put the Bolshevists at the head of a nation comprising more than one-sixth of the world's surface.

No crusader and no tribune, for the Party had enough of those, Stalin worked from the first days of Bolshevik supremacy upon the organization and distribution of power. The legions of the Tsar's officials had been driven away and had to be replaced, and to the installation of petty officials in distant places he brought a command of detail and a plodding intensity. He put men into jobs and they became indebted to him. Behind the scenes, in the hidden, conspiratorial manner he had learned in the days before the Revolution he accumulated masses of debts owed.

The dynamics of power as the Party became the State involved him, not the messianic cries of the comrades who sought to bring their creed to all the world. The Red Army swept into Poland on its way to putting the Red Flag flying in the capitals of every nation in Europe and then, defeated, swept back. The White Armies loyal to the memory of the dead Tsar came aided by the West in an attempt to strangle the infant in its crib, to stamp upon the egg before it matured. And Stalin appointed men to the chairmanship of the local committee in little towns a thousand miles east of the Kremlin.

For two and a half years Moscow was without running water, and naked bodies that lay about waiting for the thaw so that they could be buried were stripped of their clothing, and carrion crows and bugs and lice came. A ward politician grown greater, he built his political machine.

Lenin died, wondering at the last, it is said, if he owed to the Russian people a terrible apology. For the system did not seem to be working. Everything that was done, the Revolution had said, was done for the workers and peasants—for The People. But uniformly, save for the small ruling group of the Party and State, Russia suffered horribly. There was no food. There seemed also no food for the mind, and for the great, thrilling rally cry, "Workers of the world unite! You have nothing to lose but your chains!" there was substituted a centralized enormous bureaucracy. Officialdom was everywhere. Without an official's permission, the peasant could not dream of killing the pig that was no longer his but the property of the State, and at every puddle in the road stood a policeman ordering you not to wet your boots.

One did not find the Trotskys working with the petty officeholders and their forms and stamps, for the Trotskys had far greater things on their minds: the Revolution that must yet come to France and then topple the king of England, the end of capitalism, the triumph of Marxism and of the spirit of the dead god Lenin, now embalmed and lying in mystical glory in a vast sepulcher atop which the Soviet leaders stood as they reviewed the May Day parade. But France and the king did not fall nor capitalism disintegrate, and soon Trotsky was gone first from Moscow and then out of the country itself to lead a wandering existence until an assassin drove an alpine ax into his head in Mexico.

It was Stalin who sent Trotsky away, Stalin in concordance with Zinoviev and Kamenev; they maneuvered together to oust him. Then with Rykov and Bukharin he worked against Zinoviev and Kamenev. All four had been pallbearers for Lenin. When the first two were gone, he put the second two against a wall and shot them. Bukharin had been the editor of *Izvestya* and the man who had heard Lenin's last words, a remark about Bukharin's dog. Lenin's widow protested the execution and the general secretary in his Caucasian accent, which he never lost when he spoke the alien Russian language, told her to keep quiet or he would appoint someone else to be the official widow.

All revolutions have purges. The conspirators conspire against one another. Robespierre died under the guillotine. Danton died under the guillotine, Saint-Just also. But they died when their revolution was still going on. Stalin's purges took place when he was ten years in power and the volcano's lava had cooled. The purges began with the assassination of one of his cronies in Leningrad in 1935. The killer's associates were arrested. The associates had associates. The secret police came for them.

The thing gathered momentum. A plant had failed to meet its assigned quota. The failure must have been due to sabotage. The head of the plant was taken. His subordinates. The families. The friends. They were spies, saboteurs, terrorists, anti-Soviet agitators, counterrevolutionaries, White Guards, Trotskyites, wreckers. Men who had joined the Bolshevik Party before the Revolution were found to be secret tsarists. Their wives were arrested also. The marriages had been arranged by the anti-Soviet forces menacing the State of the Workers and Peasants.

Shot by the Vozhd's orders were his best friends, who had eaten with him at night and sung with him and danced to his records. He shot Bela Kun, who headed the brief Communist government of Hungary; he had the members of the Central Committee of the Communist Party of Poland called to Moscow for consultations and shot them to the last man; he shot the Communist leader of the German Parliament, who had fled Hitler. Nondenunciation of an agent of international imperialism became a crime, which meant that anyone who heard a joke told about Stalin and failed to report the incident became an accomplice of the one who told the joke.

Mostly there were no trials. When legal proceedings were instituted, they were based entirely upon confessions in the medieval fashion discarded in the West hundreds of years earlier. No proof of the truth of the confession was required. Why the confessions? Who could say. It was a good Bolshevik's duty to do what the Party ordered. The Central Committee elected at the Sixth Party Conference in 1927 consisted of twenty-seven people; by the 1930s seventeen of them were still alive. Stalin shot them all. Twelve members of the first Soviet government lived in 1937. Stalin killed eleven of them. He himself was the twelfth. They were deviationists, British spies, provocateurs, monarchists, right-Trotskyites, Japanese spies, German spies, enemies of The People, oppositionists, hirelings of the world bourgeoisie, agents of the international reactionary capitalist class. The Soviet ambassadors to Poland, Japan, Turkey, China, Romania, Finland and Bulgaria were called home and shot. The doctors and servants and chauffeurs of the dead followed them.

"He was and now he is no more" became a common Russian expression; all officials, Nikita Khrushchev remembered, were "temporary people." Then the Gensek would look at you. "Then it would be your turn to follow those who were no longer among the living."

It was the most common thing for a man to be accused of plotting against the State, tried in a matter of five minutes, condemned and shot. The next day the prosecutor who brought the case and the judge who pronounced the verdict would be taken into custody and given the same treatment. The Gensek's old housemates from Siberian exile of tsarist days were imprisoned to his perfect indifference. It meant nothing. He remained as he had always been, untheatrical, serene, more Oriental in appearance than his pictures indicated—"I am an Asiatic," he often remarked—and walking into a room with a slow and rather flowing manner that made people think of a great pockmarked and yellow-eyed cat of the jungle seeking new prey. If he had any viewpoint regarding those he sent to death and imprisonment, it was that it did not much matter if a man was innocent if by his punishment he served to cow others who might be guilty. Russia and the Vozhd needed to go forward. What is the death of a thousand today if it assures the life of one hundred thousand tomorrow? Communism was at war with the world. In a war there are casualties.

His secret agents of the NKVD were the unsheathed sword of the Revolution, the combination of no official's safe unknown to them and to him. He slew the NKVD head, Yagoda, and Yagoda's first team, and the second and third and fourth and nth team and installed Yezhov. Then he shot Yezhov and replaced him with Beria, who said, "Listen, give me someone for one night and I'll have him confessing he's the king of England."

The Gensek lived an hour's drive out of Moscow at what everybody called the Nearby Dacha. Essentially he existed in one room, sleeping on a sofa made up as a bed. The dining room table was piled with books, papers, documents. There was a soft rug and a fireplace. Those were his only luxuries. He liked to see things growing, and by the twenty-first day of August 1939, when People's Commissar for Foreign Affairs Molotov came into his Kremlin office, things were in season—the cherries, vegetables and tomatoes and the blooms. In the area of the Nearby Dacha were little summerhouses, some open to the sky, platforms with tables and chairs and wicker lounges. He liked to roam among them for hours, stopping for a moment to do a little gardening. The executed Bukharin had been a frequent visitor, bringing his animals and children.

"Everyone had a good time when he was around," remembered the Vozhd's daughter, Svetlana. She was not with her father that August, but down at Sochi on the Black Sea. On the eighth of the month he wrote her that he did not plan to come south that year. "I'm busy. I can't get away. My health? I'm well. My spirits are good. I miss you a bit, but you'll be coming soon. I give you a big hug, my little sparrow." He signed as his daughter's "wretched Secretary, the poor peasant J. Stalin."

In later years she wondered about the endless executions and the deportations of peasants who declined to do as ordered by the State, whose Party her father headed. When convinced that someone he had known and trusted for years had turned against him and thus become an enemy of The People, she decided, the past ceased to exist for him. He would wipe it out with a stroke. "He couldn't go back. He couldn't even remember."

Svetlana was twelve that summer. Her mother had shot

herself in 1932 after an argument with her father about the sufferings of millions of people forced to perform almost inhuman feats under the threat of instant death so that the Soviet Union could have plants, factories, dams, hydroelectric installations.

Mornings around ten the Gensek got into a big American Packard equipped with bulletproof windows and doors and with two identical cars sandwiching his, or with his car at the front or in the rear. The pattern was randomly changed each day. He drove down the suburban Mozhaisk Road and through the long Arbat Boulevard. Police stood along the sidewalk and NKVD men in leather jackets went up and down on motorcycles. No one who had not been meticulously checked out was permitted to live in the buildings fronting the roadway. He went through a gray, drab, unpainted Moscow, dreary and dilapidated and monotonous, parkless and empty of color, a desert of stones whose people clung like bunches of grapes to the dull brown streetcars that were the principal means of transportation.

Almost all of "the former people," those who had counted before the Revolution, were gone by August of 1939, dead or scattered to Harbin or London or New York or Paris, where lived Cyril Romanov, "Tsar before God and the conscience of humanity," according to his backers, who had spun out the years of exile by telling credulous ears that Trotsky and Stalin had belabored each other with vodka bottles in a brawl, that the peasantry was in revolt, that White officers were gathering an army to march on Moscow, that the monarchy was to be restored to its old glory.

Such of the former people who had stayed were by 1939 so beaten down as to be unrecognizable, and gone with their identities were the massed military bands of Imperial Russia, the picked men of the crack regiments of the Empire, whose hussars carried long-tipped cavalry lances and wore uniforms very similar to those of the Guards regiments of the Tsar's look-alike first cousin, George V of England, and the latter's son George VI. Gone were the clicking spurs, long dresses and parasols, family livery, the French and English governesses of the former ruling classes, their footmen, their glow and pomp and their elaborate restaurants and shops. The elegant details of their town houses had since the Revolution been only a nuisance with no function and their churches were ill-suited to their new uses, which were to be hospital, school, apartment building or stable. The city was unsmiling, poorly dressed, gray and sad.

Stalin drove into the Kremlin, a conglomeration of eight centuries of Muscovite architecture, churches, palaces, barracks, wide streets, spacious squares surrounded by a wall a mile and a half around. In its gilded and marbled halls reposed what the world since the Middle Ages had put as gifts before the feet of the Tsars: gold-embroidered garments, Persian rugs, silver that Elizabeth of England sent to Ivan the Terrible, the wedding dress of Catherine the Great, coronation coaches, jewel-encrusted swords, saddles, uniforms. In the vast St. George's Hall, where more than three thousand people could comfortably dine, the enormous crystal chandeliers were still in place, and the marble wreaths celebrating long-ago victories. He was not interested in these things of former glory. He kept a tiny apartment for Svetlana in what had been servants' rooms, and he himself worked from a similarly modest office.

His people, the Russian public, saw him almost never, and then only as a vague figure reviewing parades once a year atop Lenin's tomb. Those who saw his Packard passing through the Mozhaisk Road had learned to turn away so as not to be caught staring. For a member of the NKVD might come up to ask why they stared. He was compared to Ivan the Terrible, building upon the bones of thousands, but mainly it was said of him that he was most like Nicholas I, the Iron Tsar. Yet even the most powerful Romanov had had to consider his soldiers. The Vozhd had no worries about officers making palace revolutions. In the spring of 1937 he had named the operating chief of the Red Army, Marshal Mikhail Tukachevsky, as Soviet representative at the forthcoming coronation of George VI of England. On May 3 his documents had been sent to the British Embassy in preparation for the trip to London. The next day the British were told reasons of health made it impossible for the marshal to attend. Five weeks later it was announced that Tukachevsky had been arrested on charges of treason.

"Lenin's gendarme of the Revolution," Tukachevsky had been impetuous and reckless against the White admiral Kolchak in the north, and against the White general Denikin in the south cool, precise, determined. Upon his victory or loss to either hung the fate of the Revolution. He won both times. Then he had moved into Poland with big sweeping, arched movements covering hundreds of miles. He had been compared to Napoleon even after his 1920 offensive against Poland failed. In 1935 he and four others were made marshals, the first Russians to hold that rank since Kutuzov, who defeated Napoleon a century and a quarter earlier. As head of the Red Army under Stalin Tukachevsky became the first soldier in the world to experiment with paratroop drops. He worked on rockets, jet engines for planes, new types of pontoon bridges, runners under cannons and howitzers for winter warfare. The day after his arrest was made known, the Kremlin announced he had been shot.

Dying with him were two more of the five marshals of the Red Army, sixty out of the sixty-seven corps commanders, 136 of the less than 200 divisional commanders, 221 of the less than 400 brigade commanders. They were all named as spies in contact with unfriendly powers, they had sabotaged the Red Army, they had plotted to restore capitalism. Of the nine officers who sat on the tribunal that sentenced Tukachevsky, seven were within weeks standing before firing squads. A total of thirty thousand additional officers perished. Tukachevsky's wife and brother died in prison; his daughter and four sisters were arrested under the charge of being members of the family of a traitor to the native land. Women he had been involved with were sent to Siberia. No one was left to dream of menacing the Gensek with military insurrection. No one was left to rally the Party against him. He was the army and the Party and the State. He was Russia. Around four o'clock on that afternoon of August 21, his people's commissar for foreign affairs came into his room. In the presence of Westerners Molotov—so he had titled himself long before, the name deriving from the word for "hammer"—was a stubborn man woodenly repeating and repeating any point he wished to make. The desk in his office sat atop a raised dais from which he looked down upon the West's ambassadors as they sat with papers balanced on their knees while they took notes. There was a conference table with chairs around it in the room, but he never invited them to sit there with him on an equal level. With the Vozhd Molotov was quite different, lighting his cigarette for him, stooping to pick up any papers he might drop, rising like a schoolboy to answer questions. The two men spoke for a short time and Molotov went out to order the placing of a call to the German ambassador asking him to come to the Kremlin.

Count von der Schulenburg's car arrived at around five in the still-brilliant summer afternoon. Molotov spoke with him briefly. Molotov handed von der Schulenburg a brief letter he was to telegraph out at once, signed by the Gensek and addressed: *To the Chancellor of the German Reich, Mr. A. Hitler.*

TWO

TWO TIME ZONES to the west of Moscow lay Warsaw, capital of Poland the miracle country, Polonia Restituta, Poland, which after a century and a quarter of death had returned to life. Poland had been a great united country when Joan of Arc was trying to unify France. Poland had been a great Continental power when the Germanies were a conglomeration of petty duchies, baronies, princedoms and city-states. It had been Poland that in the seventeenth century repelled the Turk and in doing so became the savior of western Europe. Then, weakened by its rapacious nobility bereft of the slightest sympathy for their peasants and interested mostly in raising armies to war upon one another, Poland began to lose its strength.

The three adjoining powers each took a slice of the country in 1772. There came a second partition and then, in 1795, a third. Poland vanished from the map and Ivan Ivanovitch, most miserable, filthy and greasy of soldiers in Polish eyes, ensconced himself in the king's palace at Warsaw with his soot and stains and samovar. In the throne room of the royal castle on a hill overlooking the Vistula at Krakow, where the kings of Poland had received envoys of defeated Russians or Germans, Austrian soldiers slept on straw mattresses. In the third section of the former country, Frederick the Great in one century and Bismarck in another attempted to Germanize the inhabitants. They succeeded no better than did the Tsar and the Tsar's governor-general in attempting Russification, though the teaching of Polish was made a capital offense, for which hundreds of teachers paid with their lives, though Cossacks knouted Polish patriots in the wake of an 1863 uprising and made order reign in Warsaw by a massacre that shocked the world.

Even divided and under foreign rule the country would not die. Catholic Poland saw itself as the true follower of Christ wedged between Lutheran Prussia and Orthodox Russia. Poland was the edge of Europe holding back Asia. In every city of the Continent émigré Poles spoke of the day when Poland would be free and true to herself. They were considered romantic, idealistic, fanciful, heroic and ultimately slightly ridiculous in the single-minded, hopeless spirit of rebellion that possessed their souls.

Poland was more than their country, it was a religion, and it became their historic vice to believe that the affairs of the world revolved about Poland. A well-worn joke had it that a teacher asked his international class to write an essay on the elephant. The British student fresh from India wrote, "How I Shot My First Elephant." The Frenchman: *"L'Éléphant et Ses Amours."* The German produced a five-volume work entitled "Introduction to a Monograph on the Study of the Elephant." The Russian retired with a bottle of vodka and emerged with a slim philosophical inquiry: "The Elephant—Does It Exist?" The Pole, the story went on, inevitably wrote: "The Elephant and the Polish Question."

In early 1918 President Wilson in Washington proclaimed his Fourteen Points, which outlined what America considered must emerge from the vast and terrible carnage of the Great War. The Thirteenth Point was that an independent Poland be established. At the Versailles Peace Conference a year later the pledge was made good, although Wilson was shocked at the demands of the Poles. He had asked them what they wanted, he said, and they showed him a map of half the world. That much they could not be given, but after 123 years of what they in their proud Hotspur fashion considered servitude, their country was reestablished. Three empires had had to die that Poland might live— the German, the Russian, the Austro-Hungarian; resurrection in the midst of such death had about it, they said, a quality to be called holy. Their first act was to reduce to a sea of mud Warsaw's Orthodox Cathedral of the Holy Trinity and the palace of the Russian governor-general.

The ashes of Russian suzerainty were not yet cold before the army of New Poland attacked almost all of the country's neighbors in an attempt to bring back the old Poland of the sixteenth century, when it had been six times the size of the territory assigned to it at the Peace Conference. Speaking of a Poland that would extend from the Baltic to the Black Sea and saying they would add to it an overseas empire of colonies, the Poles fought with Czechoslovakia over Teschen, with the Lithuanians for Vilnius, with the Ukrainians for Lvow, with irregular bands of German soldiery along the entire frontier to the west.

Their greatest advance was into Bolshevik Russia, against whom, they said, they were more than ever the last bulwark of the West and of Christianity. Their cavalry, that Polish light horse that had always been their chief weapon in their flat riders' land and that they in their romantic fashion entitled the immortal garland of Polish history, swung forward hundreds of miles and flung away Lenin's peasant masses. Then, fatally extended, the Poles were forced back. An army of Russians poured upon Warsaw. A long semicircle of their campfires could be seen from the city. Wolves' eyes gleaming, Poles said.

Their leader was Joseph Pilsudski, a fierce-eyed man with giant mustaches falling away from his lips. On August 6, 1914, four days after the first shots of the Great War were fired by and at the Germans, Pilsudski, on his own, with no governmental backing from anyone, invaded Russia in the name of Polish freedom. His force consisted of some 170 men led by eight cavalrymen, five of whom had horses. The other three carried saddles. Each of the infantrymen bore several rifles for expected recruits to the cause. The Russian colossus threw them back. But Austria outfitted two brigades of 2,500 men each for Pilsudski, and he led what he called the Polish Legion back into Russia. To his men he was the Commandant and those who served with him never called him anything else.

With the end of the Great War and the establishment of New Poland Pilsudski threw off the left-wing political ideas with which he had flirted in the past. A group of Socialists called upon him and addressed him as Comrade. He replied, "Gentlemen, I am no longer your comrade. In the beginning we followed the same direction and took the tramway painted Red, but I left it at the station Poland's Independence. You are continuing your journey as far as the station Socialism. My good wishes accompany you, but be so kind as to call me Sir."

By then the Commandant embodied Poland, dashing and theatrical as he was, and gallant and exhilarated by danger. When in the summer of 1920 the Russian wolves appeared at the gates of Warsaw he gathered boys, students, volunteers. Disdaining to put the Vistula between himself and the enemy, he sallied out, found a weak point in the Russian order of battle, pierced the Red Army, rolled it up and with daring night rides and cavalry charges harried it back into Asia.

The world had trembled at the Bolshevik advance upon Poland. All the foreign diplomats in Warsaw save the British ambassador and the Vatican's representative, the future Pius XI, packed and fled. Had Lenin taken Warsaw, he would have owned a Poland that bordered disordered and revolutionary Germany and Austria. The Red Army without doubt would have taken those two countries, and uprisings in northern Italy would have followed. Soon the Red Flag might have flown in Paris and then leaped the Channel to London. It was what the Bolsheviks confidently expected. They had thought it a matter of months before their doctrine ruled the entire Continent. The battle in which Pilsudski turned back the seemingly unstoppable tide of Bolshevism merged with Asiatic fire and sword was accounted the most significant event in the world's history since the outbreak of the War in 1914: the Miracle of the Vistula.

To the conquerers of Russia and of Bolshevism their great victory was final proof of the messianic destiny that God had ordained for Poland. Their grandiloquence laughed at for a century and more had carried them through. A nation of knights and chivalrics had subdued fate and leaped into prominence in Europe and the world, fulfilling, its citizens said, what the Almighty wished. When their representative to the League of Nations in Geneva came into a room, there was that in his attitude that made the journalists think he was proclaiming, "Make way for Poland. Poland is here!"

Yet what was Poland? Across the great dead-flat plains, which were a featureless swamp for much of the year and a dustbowl at other times, were sprinkled wretched peasant villages so poverty-stricken that if a girl got hold of a pair of silk stockings, it was esteemed a community event. Lodz, a city of six hundred thousand had no sewer system. The family cow or pig, if there was one, slept in the same room as its owners. The houses, tiny, with thatched roofs, sat in seas of soupy mud or vanished in swirls of dust. The children had rickets. Sorcery, invocations, the evil eye were believed in by the majority of the population, and the few foreign visitors who ventured down the unspeakable roads found all about them paganism mixed with Christian concepts, and superstitions worthy of the Dark Ages.

The country was overpopulated, for there was no industry at all—a Thermos bottle or a needle had to be imported—and working the land could not produce sufficient income to support the thirty million inhabitants. There was typhus, dysentery, tuberculosis, malaria, lice, bugs. The Jews lived a life apart from the Catholics, dressing entirely differently and not even speaking the language, although they had been there a thousand years. One saw them in their miserable, segregated, primitive villages or heading for the town square on market day, one Jew pulling the shaft of a cart loaded with brass or tin or horsehair for a sofa, others pushing, all of them unshaven and spattered with mud. The barefoot peasants hated them; they hated and feared their world.

Atop this backward place sunken into a time the West had long ago passed, there reigned a nobility immersed in memories real and fancied of the great past, when Poland had ruled central Europe, when great-great-grandmother sent her laundry to Paris in a coach accompanied by postilions. Accustomed to peasants wiping their mouths to kiss Master's hand, completely feudal in their outlook, believing in the ancient Slavic rule that the law applies only to the weak, the paper-thin upper crust of the social structure clicked its heels and carried in hundred-year-old horse carriages evening dress to weekend parties. Their footmen dressed in patched knee breeches and ancient buckled shoes, and in their stables grooms standing at attention proffered battered silver salvers from which a carrot might be selected for a favorite horse.

Job-seeking in the new government was their passion, that and politics. For all the courtly manners that found them addressing one another as "Mr. Colleague," with "Mr. Banker" and "Mr. Merchant" used for followers of those professions, the gentry of resurrected Poland impressed foreign visitors as backstabbers competing for position with brutal viciousness. It was required that only half a dozen men should meet in a tavern, Pilsudski said, and they would declare themselves a political party in whose ranks resided the only honest men in the country. Despite a constitution, real democracy and parliamentarianism were looked at as the West's toys dropped for show on barren ground.

Those of the gentry who did not seek office found their place in the army that had beaten Russia and that outnumbered by far the force permitted Germany by the regulations of the Versailles Treaty. One almost fell over officers in their smart uniforms in the streets of Warsaw, so numerous were they. The soldiers put their faith in the horsed cavalry of sabers and lances with colored pennants fluttering from their tips. Eventually they all but took over the political leadership: the Government of Colonels.

It required massive taxation to support legions of officeholders and majors and lieutenant colonels, who did not wear mere decoration ribbons but the actual medals that clanked when they walked. There was never any pretense about taking what money was possessed by those Jews who had risen to the status of cattle dealer, middleman or shopkeeper. It was openly decreed by the government that there were three million too many Jews in Poland anyway. But while they were there they could pay the bills. Ten percent of the population, they paid one-third of the taxes. Those who had any money were within a few years taxed out of existence and reduced to hopeless poverty.

It was an unavoidable social transformation, officials of the League of Nations concerned with minorities were told. Concomitantly the number of Jews permitted in the universities was strictly limited, as were the places in the classroom where they could sit, and participation in the professions of doctor or lawyer or journalist was strongly discouraged. Other minorities living under the flag of the White Eagle were given similar treatment— Lithuanians, Ukrainians, Germans.

Gallant New Poland had been intended to form a *cordon sanitaire* against Asia and Bolshevism, to be France's gendarme on the Vistula, standing fast in the rear of Germany, and to reward the idealism of generations. It came to be seen as a chauvinistic monster running amok in the name of romantic nationalism, a place governed by unstable men with absurd ideas of their importance in the world.

"And then there are the great powers," French Foreign Minister Louis Barthou said in a speech given before a group of Polish leaders. He paused. "And Poland. Poland, we all know, because we have been told so, is a great power." He paused again. "A very, very great power."

Above arrogance and dirt and incredible roads and boundless ignorance a tiny crust of society existed to give form to the claim that Poland was a repository of Western values and Western culture and grace. It existed almost entirely in Warsaw, the most European of European capitals because it was the last, beyond which dwelt the East, dreaming of the Vistula and Krakow's spires and Silesia's coal mines, waiting only, the Poles said, for the fires of civilization one day to die down. The city was magnificent. In the spring it foamed with white and purple lilac, lime trees, magnolia. From circles cut out of the pavement around the trees pansies and geraniums bloomed. There were sidewalk cafés with tables reserved for groups of the artists, poets and writers of gay and cosmopolitan Warsaw. Afternoons from noon until one, horse equipages paraded along the Aleje Ujazdowskie, lined on either side with clipped hedges of high beech trees and a broad sidewalk flanked by grass borders. The Bristol and Europejski hotels had chambers like mansion drawing rooms, with immensely high ceilings, double windows, vast mirrors held by heavy gold frames; and the people in the restaurants and barrooms below indulged in subtle flirtations and held light and delicate, imaginative conversations.

This elite segment of society looked to Paris for their inspiration, ate elegant food cooked in the French style in their homes furnished with Steinway pianos, Oriental rugs, bathtubs descended into by three or four marble steps, mahogany bookshelves to the ceiling in the library and potted palms and ferns in the corners of the dining room. They went to outdoor theater and ballet performances in the Lazenki Gardens. They met for afternoon tea dances in high-windowed places with maroon and gilt wallpaper. Outside electric tramcars of nickel and glass and pale blue paint rumbled by. At diplomatic dinners the guests in full dress went into dinner past heralds and trumpeters playing on long silver instruments. Cavalrymen with drawn swords stood at the doors. Conversations at table were carried on in several languages. It was all lightness and charm and high sophistication. No British or French traveler failed to note the extreme hothouse atmosphere.

From modest quarters at the Belvedere Palace Marshal Joseph Pilsudski, the George Washington of Poland, ruled the country through his Government of Colonels. Not to have been in his legion that fought against the Russians, never to have earned the right to address him as Commandant, was to insure a limited future. Pilsudski possessed insights unknown to most men. He knew that there were those in Germany who felt and said that Poland was a season-state that would bloom for a short time and then die. Two months after Adolf Hitler came to power in 1933 Pilsudski massed five army corps on his western frontier and suggested to the French that he and they march on Berlin. The French declined. Pilsudski elected not to go it alone, and concluded a ten-year nonaggression pact with the Germans.

Pilsudski was old. In 1935 he fell ill. One night it became clear the end was coming. He asked for his foreign minister, Joseph Beck. The ex-colonel came from a dinner in his white tie and tails and star and cordon of his Order of Polonia Restituta. "Aren't you chic, my boy? And how are you?" Pilsudski said. They talked for a while and the Commandant offered a last warning against Russia. "Myself," he ended, "I don't think that I can do anything more." His funeral was attended by massed horse regiments, booming guns, bands, eulogies beginning, "Thou, beloved remains."

Joseph Beck as foreign minister and as man impressed people as both subtle and supple, as evasive, sinuous and even sinister. His face was masklike. What he said was said in a tortuous way, devious, circumspect, impossible to pin down. Telling Britishers his medals were the equivalent of so many Victoria Crosses, he moved in a flurry of smart aides, smoking cigarettes in a holder, wearing a monocle and saying of himself that there was only one Colonel Beck. Of Adolf Hitler he offered the opinion that the man had power and charm and a flair. "But he is not Colonel Beck."

His policy was what New Poland's had been since its rebirth in 1918. He presented neighboring Lithuania with a twenty-four-hour ultimatum to hand over some of its territory and saw Lithuania bow. When Hitler dismembered Czechoslovakia under threat of leveling Prague with air attack, Beck, like a carrion fish swimming in the wake of a shark, helped himself to some Czech territory. (When Beck did so, Hitler remarked that the Poles were tough. "Pilsudski would be pleased.")

For Russia and for Germany alike Poland professed the deepest contempt. When spoken to of the strength of his two neighbors who might someday attack, the army chief Marshal Smigly-Rydz* could reply, "Just let them try. The Polish army

*Born Edouard Rydz, he served in the legion under the alias "Smigly"—nimble. After the War he called himself Rydz-Smigly. In 1936 he changed to Smigly-Rydz.

will be in Berlin *and* Moscow in no time. Poland is invincible."

But on January 4, 1939, Foreign Minister Beck had a disturbing talk with Adolf Hitler at the German leader's mountain home at Berchtesgaden in southern Bavaria. Beck noticed that Hitler never looked at him directly but kept his eyes on the ceiling of the room, the walls and the floor as he talked for hours. His thoughts wandered as he conducted his monologue, but where in the past he had spoken to Beck of Polish-German relations by saying, "I would like . . . ," he now said, "It must be." Always before, Beck told German foreign minister von Ribbentrop the next day, he had left Hitler's presence with a feeling of optimism. He did not have such a feeling now.

He returned to Warsaw, where three months later, in April, he received Romanian foreign minister Grigore Gafencu. In Gafencu's eyes Beck had always seemed a "flexible cavalier" of "nonchalant, feline graces" characterized by an "imperturbable smile and haughty self-composure." His "romantic transports were not without grandeur." But Beck had changed since his talk with Adolf Hitler. Gafencu found him no longer so certain of his undertakings as he had been in the past. There was something of a furtive nature to eyes in "which there shone a glint of fever." His long, elegant hands seemed nervous. There was an unusual pallor to his face.

The summer of 1939 arrived. In the hot August sun the peasant women in bell-shaped skirts and colored kerchiefs around their heads gathered and bound the swatches of the harvest the men had cut, and on the way back along the dusty roads into the villages knelt before wooden shrines with fresh flowers always before them. On August 15 pilgrims carrying crosses and banners came to Czestochowa, the Lourdes of Poland, to pray before the picture of the Virgin Mary for the Feast of the Assumption. It was the hottest and driest summer anyone had ever seen. The ruins of a bridge over the Narew blown up by the Russians in 1920 as they fell back after the Miracle of the Vistula stuck higher into the air than anyone could remember. Certain European events hung over Poland that August, even before the people's commissar for foreign affairs spoke in Moscow with the Vozhd and then sent for the German ambassador.

The American-born Princess Virginia Sapieha attended a party at the countryside castle of a nobleman who had his own orchestra made up from his stable boys. On a warm night they played marches from the Imperial Russian Court, and then Strauss as the guests danced on the lawn. It came to her when the party ended that people were suddenly different to one another, as on the last night on shipboard when passengers who had viewed one another with reserve threw confetti and popped balloons because on the morrow a new life would begin. She and her husband went to the new race club just opened in Warsaw. There were two pavilions seating several thousand people. The clubhouse was almost all glass, with flower-decked terraces and roof gardens, the best course in Central Europe and comparable to Longchamps—this, she thought, in a country in which only moats and drawbridges were needed for a complete return to medieval days. Poland had, she thought, no schools, no hospitals, crumbling roads—and its great racetrack for its great Polish horses.

"In autumn it will be lovely out there," said her husband. "That is, if nothing happens."

That was the phrase, she thought to herself, that suddenly that summer was used to modify every plan. They returned to their country seat in Upper Silesia six miles from the German frontier, where a visiting relative who usually slept until lunch got up early to say good-bye to her when she went off on a trip.

"Why did you get up?" she asked him. He looked at her silently. "Because, otherwise, we might not meet again," he said.

"What a funny notion," she said. Something caught at her throat.

THREE

YOU ASK ME how I feel about the French army," the general said. "I believe that the French army is of greater intrinsic value than ever in its history. Its armament is of the first quality, its fortifications are of the first order, its morale is excellent and its leadership outstanding."

Maxime Weygand was esteemed to know. Always at Marshal Ferdinand Foch's side in the Great War, Weygand had stood with Pilsudski as head of the French military mission to Poland during the Miracle of the Vistula. Though he said the great victory over the Russians was solely due to Polish valor, there were those who said it could never have been done without his guidance.

Ten days after he had spoken, the French army marched in Paris in the greatest display since the Victory Parade of 1918. Down the Champs-Élysées came the soldiers of the homeland and overseas possessions in the magnificence of their uniforms and their drill. It was the 150th anniversary of the storming of the Bastille, July 14, 1939. Past packed crowds came the glittering bayonets of the Zouaves in red fezlike hats, the *tirailleurs* from Algeria and Morocco in baggy blue trousers, horn-blowing Senegalese, the Foreign Legion in white-topped kepis, the infantry, the *chasseurs* and marines and the fortress troops at the Maginot Line. Tanks and motor-drawn guns rumbled past, planes roared overhead.

Then the crowds increased the volume of their cheers, for swinging down the great avenue, glorious in scarlet, bands and pipers heralding their appearance, came detachments of Great Britain's Brigade of Guards, whose streamers told of momentous

21

battles at Agincourt and Waterloo against France, and of supreme victory with France after the Somme and Ypres. For two
and a half hours in the drizzle to the sound of rolling drums and
trilling fifes the troops continued, France's chief of staff Maurice
Gamelin and Britain's chief of the Imperial General Staff the
Viscount Gort standing side by side at the salute.

The great display of military might was at least partially an
answer to a parade held three months earlier, on April 20, in
Berlin. "Please invite a number of foreign guests for my fiftieth
birthday, and among them as many as possible cowardly civilians
and democrats to whom I shall show the most modern of armies," Adolf Hitler told Foreign Minister Ribbentrop. The day
dawned clear on the Continent and across the Channel. "Lovely
spring day," His Majesty's permanent under-secretary of state
for foreign affairs, Sir Alexander Cadogan, wrote in his London
diary. "Hitler's birthday! I arranged that H.M. should not
wish him 'Happy Returns' (as we don't want any of them!) but
only 'congratulations' on his fiftieth birthday—blast him!" In
Berlin the British military attaché, Colonel Frank Noel Mason-
Macfarland, looked out the window of his drawing room. He saw
swastika banners going up on plywood columns flanking the
Charlottenburger Chaussee, running from the column celebrating the German victory over France in 1870–71 to the Branden-
burg Gate.

"Easy rifle shot," he said to a friend, pointing at the saluting-
base where Hitler would stand. "I could pick the bastard off from
here as easy as winking, and what's more I'm thinking of doing it."

Ewan Butler, the friend, while agreeing the act would be a
blessing to mankind, felt called upon to utter conventional words
of disapproval. "Besides, think of the backlash when they discovered that he'd been potted by a British officer!"

"Oh, I know," Colonel Mason-Macfarland said. "There'd be all
hell to pay, of course, and I'd be finished in every sense of the
word. Still, I doubt if they'd declare war, and with that lunatic
out of the way we might be able to get some sense into things."

"It's certainly an idea."

"Yes. Bloody awful one, of course, but I'd be prepared to do
it, if the worst came to the worst."

But Mason-Macfarland held his fire. For more than three
hours the German Wehrmacht pounded down the pavement with

the newest medium artillery, heavy antitank guns, ultramodern antiaircraft weapons, mortars, howitzers, and regiment after regiment of infantry, motorized and on foot, the whole accompanied by the joyful fanfares of trumpets and the clangor of metal, which bid to shatter the nerves. Representatives of a three-million-man army passed in review. Six years earlier when Hitler took power, the German army consisted of one hundred thousand men, its size limited by the Versailles Treaty. Overhead in the cloudless sky roared bombers and fighters of the German air force's 4,500 planes. Six years earlier by the terms of the Versailles Treaty there had been no planes.

"Thank God for the French army!" exclaimed the British politician Winston Churchill when Hitler took office. Then the force that was the descendant of La Grande Armée stood supreme in the Continent and in the world, able to occupy at will any part of Germany it chose to march into—as it did the Ruhr in 1923 when the Germans were slow with the reparations intended to compensate the French for the damage suffered on their territory in 1914–18. In 1939, even as the Germans marched for the Leader's fiftieth birthday, the army of the Third Republic was the largest in the world. But many of its allies were gone. Czechoslovakia, with its defense line facing the Germans and its great Skoda armaments plant, was German. Vienna was German.

All along the German frontier and to the east and down the Danube, each day more terrified of resurgent Germany, cowered the weak Successor states of the Austro-Hungarian Empire, destroyed by the Great War—Austria, Romania, Hungary, Yugoslavia. Cowering with them were Bulgaria and Turkey, and the Baltic republics of Latvia, Lithuania and Estonia.

In Russia there was an army whose officer corps lay in unmarked graves dug for them by Joseph Stalin. Only Poland commanded a force estimated to be of any value. France's ally England possessed little military strength, and what she did possess was scattered all over the world. In 1914 the German emperor had referred to England's "contemptible" little army; committed to action against him, it had been all but wiped out in one month. England was hardly stronger now. There was little to back up the beautifully uniformed Brigade of Guards square-bashing in the Champs-Elysées and swinging their arms up to nose level in parade-ground heroics.

The strength of European democracy was gone with the once-strong position of France united with its allies, its arrangement meant to contain Germany on the east while France held her in the west. The War to Make the World Safe for Democracy, fought from 1914 to 1918, had brought in its wake Nazism to Germany, Fascism to Italy, Communism to Russia and authoritarian states everywhere else save for Scandinavia. Democracy must be destroyed, Hitler had written in *My Struggle*. (It had been composed in the prison into which he had been thrown after staging a ridiculous *opéra bouffe* attempt at revolution in 1923. A line of police fired a single volley and destroyed his revolution.) Democracy had been destroyed. France must also be destroyed, he had written.

But between that aim and its fulfillment stood the five-million-man army of the Republic. It was an army in whose uniform 1.4 million men had died in the Great War, with five million wounded or missing. A third of the men between the ages of eighteen and twenty-eight were killed. From that immense bloodletting, which left families without sons to till the soil, and daughters who would never marry, a great pacifism had come to France. Children did not play at war games. Their parents would not permit it, nor their aunts, whose husbands-that-might-have-been lay forever young in Picardy or along the Meuse. The tactics of the army itself were entirely defensive in nature. Cadets at the military schools trained to defend a hill, a river, a railroad, a village, but never to attack.

Along the frontier facing Germany stood the embodiment of defense: the Maginot Line. It was like an endless fleet of battleships sunk six stories deep into the earth, with turrets of from thirty to three hundred tons that rose up at the touch of a button ready to throw a salvo before sinking down for reloading. Below were staircases, galleries, tunnels, barracks, engine rooms, hospitals, diesel engines for electricity and ventilation, airtight doors that would keep out poison gas, stores of food, water, ammunition. Telephone wires buried under fifteen feet of concrete connected the fortresses. No single foot of ground was not open to bullets from double machine guns firing out of revolving turrets. The land was kept clear of any trees or even a bush that might offer the slightest protection to the Germans if they came.

The Maginot Line resembled an elongated and gigantic version of that great fortress complex at Verdun, which in the Great

War broke and then bled the enemy white and cost them three hundred thousand casualties. It was one half of the French response to the cry for security above all other things. The other half had been the lost French group of client states that ringed Germany on the east. Now only Poland was left.

France had had one great chance to arrest the course of events three years before the Bastille Day parade of 1939. By the terms reached after 1918, the Rhineland dividing Gaul and Teuton was forever to be free of German soldiery. There were to be no troops there, no forts or fieldworks. The Germans could neither launch an attack nor defend against a French one.

In 1936, against the advice of his generals who knew that Germany's army in the first stages of rebuilding could never hold the French for a moment, Hitler ordered a move into the Rhineland. With unloaded weapons, for it would have been impossible to fight, the Wehrmacht walked in. For the first time in almost two decades German uniforms appeared in Cologne. It would have taken but a flick of France's finger to eject them, but France did not lift that finger. Years later the president of the Republic, Albert Lebrun, was asked by the American diplomat Robert Murphy why the French had not moved.

"But we were just too tired," the president said.

They had not always been too tired. The 1920s had been glorious for France. The world came to Paris. When the Duke of Westminster, immensely rich and one of the premier noblemen of England, asked Gabrielle (Coco) Chanel for her hand in marriage, she declined because, she said, "There have been several Duchesses of Westminster. There is only one Chanel." When the Grand Duke Dimitri asked her, she turned him down also. To be ranked with Mainbocher and Schiaparelli and Coty, to be the couturier who had dismissed the pre-War trailing flounces, tiered trains, gussets, garters, corsets, whalebones, false hair and brassieres, to be one who dressed the *Gratin,* the upper crust of the 16th Arrondissement, was a far higher world position than to be an English duchess or the claimant to the throne of the Romanovs.

Artists and writers came to the Left Bank in the twenties; there was brilliant music, exhibitions, brilliant talk, food, excitement. Every man had two countries—his own and France. Happiness was defined by the Germans as being as happy as God would be if He could be in France. The Riviera was jammed with foreign tourists in the season, as were Deauville and the Loire valley.

Foreign affairs vanished from the French consciousness in the 1920s. Diplomats held conferences—in Locarno, in Stresa, at Rapallo, at the League of Nations in Geneva—and emerged with a jumble of pacts, treaties, conventions, agreements and disagreements on reparations and disarmament. For the most part the citizenry of France did not care. It was a matter for politicians. Only let them bring peace and security. That was their job. They would do it. What really mattered was to live the life bought and paid for by the great sacrifices of the War, to have the August vacation, the car, the radio, the new styles.

Then, in far-off New York, the stock market crashed. The tourists went home and did not come again. Trade with the outside world dried up. The solid franc began to slide in value. The government cut back. Business slowed. Agriculture fell into a hole from which it seemed unable to emerge.

Artificially important to Europe and the world for ten years— because of revolution for Russia, defeat for Germany, disarmament and isolation in England and abandonment of international obligations in America—France in the early 1930s began to feel the earth falling away from under its feet. The Depression hit home, and simultaneously an astonishingly vigorous new regime replaced the Weimar Republic in Germany. The glorious days and the feeling of a wonderful new life that had followed The War to End War had promised a new era of French supremacy. Now it was slipping away. They had thought that an eternally powerful France would dictate the affairs of a Europe bowing to a new Napoleonic, imperial nation. But suddenly French culture and French wines and French glamour were at a discount. France began to doubt herself.

She was not the first nation of the post-War world to do that. Out east past Germany in the wreckage of the Austro-Hungarian and Russian and German empires there had existed since 1918 a ramshackle structure of weak little countries mutually suspicious of one another, puny and insecure heirs to the destroyed political systems whose death had given them life but whose disappearance in clouds of artillery fire and killing along the Eastern Front had taken away stability, tradition, the ways of a millennium. What had replaced the vanished Imperial and Royal Highnesses and their understood old polished ways and centralized governments and discipline and accepted rule was base and despicable.

Out there, out east, the uprooted had learned to cheat and lie and smuggle across the new borders, to intrigue against one another for petty advantage, to embargo one another's goods, to make propaganda and to assassinate, fight undeclared wars, to depart completely from the path that a score of earlier generations had traveled and to find in the earthquake of 1914–18 and its aftermath justification for all that a previous code had disdained. Pauperized, overcrowded, poor, prejudiced, stratified, the Europeans on the other side of the Rhine, including Germany, learned to forgo the use of good solid silver coins in favor of shabby banknotes of monstrously high denominations, to live in surroundings mean, drab, chaotic, to live in armed bankruptcy with the wall hangings in shreds and the furniture covers filled with holes.

Tinseled tin soldiers declared their adherence to high aims in which the simplest soul knew they had no faith, and in the name of patriotism wiretapped telephones and threw into prison their political opponents. To lie was nothing in the wake of the destruction and upheaval the War had brought, to spy and cheat was less. Older people remembered what in every country came to be known as the Good Old Days, but younger ones without memory had nothing by which to judge anything since the War but the ugly and destructive present, the disintegration and decay and, above all, a frightful hopelessness. They had lost the track.

Alone in Europe, save perhaps for isolated Scandinavia, France had emerged strong from the War. But in the 1930s the demons from the other side of the Maginot Line crossed over it and came with their curse to the very heart of civilization. France slid downhill with terrifying speed. Nothing held. The process came to a climax on February 6, 1934, when a restive crowd gathered in the center of Paris. A wretched swindler, one Serge Alexander Stavisky, had died in mysterious circumstances. For years Stavisky had lived unbothered by the law, bribing politicians, buying up newspapers to push his fraudulent stock issues, consorting with officials of the police on his payroll. Now he was dead, and all over Paris people said the police killed him to silence a mouth that could tell of corruption in the Cabinet, the army, the intelligence services.

All the opposing concepts that arise in fragmented societies of the type that followed the ordered life of before-the-War were found in the crowd: monarchists pledging allegiance to the Royal Pretender, the Duc de Guise, whom they referred to as "King Jean"; Communists calling for a Soviet France and singing "The Internationale"; Socialists who hated Moscow; Fascists who looked to Italy for their model; French followers of Nazism. United only in their hatred of the democratic France of the Republic and in their longing for the happiness of a better past that was gone to be replaced by the deteriorating cheap present, they began over-turning and burning cars and throwing rocks at streetlights. Shop windows buckled in.

The horsed members of the Garde Républicaine moved up and found people carrying sticks to which razors were attached. Slashed horses reared in the air. When their riders toppled off, the mob fell upon them.

One hundred thousand people surged through the Place de la Concorde screaming they would hang the elected representa-tives of France meeting in the Chamber of Deputies across the Seine. Baton and saber charges failed to halt them. Shots began to sound. Thirty people dropped mortally wounded, but the mob came on. Desperate appeals for police reinforcements and troops went out. Suddenly France appeared to face not a riot but an insurrection.

The forces of the Republic fell back steadily until only a thin line held the bridge to the Chamber of Deputies. One thousand policemen were out of action and the rest exhausted by six hours of fighting. Messengers were sent to tell the Deputies to clear out. The mob was about to break through. In an instant the Chamber was deserted by men fleeing for their lives. Outside the sound of potential revolution was terrifying. A colonel organized a line of horsemen and charged, and at last the mob broke. The Chamber was safe. For days more sporadic rioting broke out. Then it faded away. Had there been a leader to take charge, or had the crowd invaded the Chamber, the Republic would have fallen.

After that, France was not the same. The Chamber formed two investigative bodies to look into the Stavisky affair and the events of bloody February 6—the first was popularly dubbed the "Thieves' Committee" and the second the "Murderers' Commit-tee"—but little resulted. Pus poured from the wound of February 6. The level of political discourse fell to abysmal levels. It was nothing for the newspapers to refer to the premier as a blackguard, his ministers as curs, the judges as corrupt, the police as scoundrels, the entire civil service of the accursed regime as composed of cads, cowards, degraded bandits. Even in the glorious twenties men talked of a cascade of ministries, with governments frequently changing; now it became a massacre of ministries. Premiers lasted, on an average, three months. Then they left office to reappear a ministry or two later.

Politicians would do anything to hold power if only for a moment, and to get power back when they fell. France held her leaders to be contemptible. A famous cartoon showed a hostess telling her servants that two deputies and a minister were expected for dinner that night; the servants must be sure to count the spoons carefully. Behind one another's backs the leaders intrigued. Promises that could never be kept were made and were disbelieved. Their mistresses negotiated backstairs on their behalf. Schemes, plots, corruption, bribes filled the atmosphere of the round-robin of men standing for nothing beyond their own personal advantage.

Overcharged and superheated, the leaders of France concentrated on keeping their political aims alive and on getting into the next government. There was no time to give to running the country or to the study of important subjects, and it was difficult to put into effect any decisions reached. When Paul Reynaud and his adviser the junior army officer Charles DeGaulle proposed the creation of a mobile strike force based on tanks, the innovation was voted down mostly for fear that it might be utilized to stage a coup d'état. (The representatives of the Left voted against it on the grounds that such an elite force was against the tradition of an army representing The People.) Had it existed in 1936 it could have effortlessly evicted the Germans from the Rhineland.

In the dreary days of the 1930s, of strikes, lockouts, the hardening of class lines—"Better Hitler Than Blum" was a catchphrase of the Right during the brief premiership of the Left politician Léon Blum—of anti-Semitism, street battles and riots, uniformed gangs on the style of Italy and Germany, there vanished all the classical thirst for glory that had once possessed eternal France. "But we were just too tired."

The Germans marched into the Rhineland and France did

nothing. The Italians used mustard gas and machine guns against virtually unarmed natives in Ethiopia and France did nothing. The Germans took Austria and Czechoslovakia and France did nothing.

The faithful of many faiths in Paris viewed their opponents as the representatives of the anti-Christ, and it became a commonplace for those who hated the Republic to refer to it as *La Gueuse*, the slut. The French refought the Dreyfus Affair with its anticlerical ring. They cursed Science and the Machine that took men's jobs, or perhaps the bankers, capitalism, the foreigners who stole French markets and French greatness. Those who had never accepted the Revolution of 1789 cursed those who snarled at the mention of the ancien régime, and the air was filled with talk of "action," coup d'état, class war, throwing the deputies into the Seine and stringing them up from lampposts. There was no forward motion in France, no one in command, no forceful thinking. The Indian Summer of French greatness had come.

The last remnants of the France of glory and dominance and hope were dying by then, in the 1930s, the *grandes horizontales* and dandies of the Second Empire grown old, the silky and scented *belle époque* pre-War courtesans who had given way to fake silver-foxed modernities.

Another world had passed away, Clemenceau, Foch, Joffre, Briand, who had tried to make a lasting peace with Germany, Ravel, Anatole France. Time was, of course, bound to take them all, but time brought something else to replace what they represented. It was the belief that the world committed suicide in 1914 but the dying took long and that now in the 1930s the last breath was about to be drawn, that there would come the reign of the hollow men in a world confronted by psychic tuberculosis and a syphilis of the soul.

Perhaps the War had brought a vacuity of spirit that was not a German or Italian or Russian disease, but a European one, even as the Revolution of 1789 had not been a French experience but a European one. Perhaps the dawn of civilization had been the Renaissance, with the Age of Reason and the liberal experience the high noon; and perhaps night was coming on now, a doomed twilight for the gods rationalism had worshiped that would be followed by descent into blackness and death for ancient cultures. The winding sheet of the European race was woven, wrote the historian Frederick Schuman, and the Kingdom of Death was upon the Continent. The damned would bring faggots to the stake at which they must die, the doomed and the damned, to experience the domain of Death to the end of the world as they knew it and beyond.

"The newspapers fill me with despair," the sacristan of Sens Cathedral told the British writer Sir Philip Gibbs. "Are we all mad? Have our statesmen no sanity—and our young men—and those politicians in Paris?" Gibbs was on a tour of the Continent to talk with whomever he came across in a string of countries. It was 1934. The War had been over for sixteen years.

"It is inconceivable that such a horror should come again," said the sacristan. But from the sickness of a disordered civilization there had arisen exactly that possibility: that a crash more terrible than even Wagner foretold was coming, a war in which civilization before quitting its home would destroy all its possessions.

"We cannot stand the strain of another war," a woman who kept a newsstand in Geneva told Gibbs. "It will let loose the beast in mankind."

"The whole world is mad," said an old gentleman at a Vienna dinner. "It was the War which drove us all insane."

"We are, of course, all mad," a Hungarian lady told him. "There is no sanity in the world. It is terrible. Everybody is talking of another war—after that last one which ruined us all. It's as though we were all doomed by such frightful destiny. What is the meaning of it all—this life?"

Gibbs went back to England. "That is the astounding and alarming phenomenon of life in Europe as I have seen it on this journey," he wrote. "There is no belief in the chance of peace, although all peoples desire it."

His trip terrified him, Gibbs wrote. That Europe of church bells sounding for worship and feast days for six hundred years past, of old towns with houses elaborately decorated by scenes done by master painters long ago, was all physically intact. But the soul? His most terrible memory was of the Geneva workmen he found building the new Palace of Nations to house the League. "We're not building a palace for the League," one told him.

"What then?"

"A new hospital for the wounded of the next war."

In the summer of 1939 the roses planted before the graves were in their twentieth year of blooming along the four hundred miles of the Western Front from Switzerland to the North Sea. *Mort pour la France.* Mixed with the French cemeteries were those of the British army, more than 150 of them in Ypres alone, hundreds more at other places along what had been the British zone. It was the proud claim of the Imperial War Graves Commission that every man who died for Great Britain and the Empire, for King and Country, had his name written somewhere on a memorial. Either there was a stone saying he was known to be buried in a particular cemetery, or believed to be, or his name was written on one of the great arches across France and Belgium erected to the missing. Or there was an individual stone at the head of a grave with a name on it.

One of the known graves was of an officer from the great industrial city of Birmingham. He had devoted his time before the War, and much of his substantial fortune, to helping young people of the slums get an education and a start in life. He had personally financed the immigration of many boys to the Colonies, where he had obtained work for them. He had been reported missing in December 1917. His body was found and buried in February 1918 under a stone saying Captain Norman Chamberlain, Grenadier Guards. He had been a cheerful, graceful man carrying his considerable intellectuality lightly. His cousin Neville never forgot.

FOUR

THE PRIME MINISTER was the second son of one of Victorian England's greatest figures. His father, Joseph Chamberlain, apostle of the expanding Empire, Imperialist of Imperialists, had coined the slogan "Trade follows the flag." As secretary of state for the Colonies he had worked to bring British might and British rule to the ends of the earth. The proconsul in remote China and the Resident in deepest Africa reported to him, and no Thin Red Line troopship could depart for punitive expedition service on the Northwest Frontier without his consent.

Joseph Chamberlain's first wife died in childbirth. He married her cousin, who met the same fate. Twice a widower before he was forty, with a total of six children from both women, he buried himself in his work. There was a big house in Birmingham with vast hall, stained glass and inlaid woods, flower houses and ponies and governesses, but it was always understood that there must be no noise when Father was working on a Parliamentary speech. At table his train of thought must not be disturbed by too much conversation.

Joseph Chamberlain represented no ancient aristocratic line, but the new burgeoning commercial drive of the industrialists and businessmen and men of property making Great Britain and her Empire supreme upon the earth. Second only to Lord Salisbury in the government, he was not of the type of the other Cabinet officials nor of the Foreign Office men of country seats built three hundred years earlier and filled with old silver and family portraits. He was very much of Birmingham, for whom it was said there was an eleventh commandment: *Thou shalt keep a balance sheet.* Birmingham was the iron and coal and manufacturing that had won England the Empire and made her rich. Birmingham stood for Trade. With it went a social conscience, contributions to charity and good works.

The colonial secretary had two sons, one by each of his wives. His first son was Austen, very clever and very promising. The father early on decided that Austen would follow him into public life. The second son, Neville, younger by six years, considered perhaps not quite so clever or promising, would see to the family fortune made in the iron screw business. The girls Joseph Chamberlain would provide with dowries; they would marry and give him grandchildren.

Austen went to Rugby and did very well there. Neville stayed at home and grew up exclusively in the company of the sisters and a variety of cousins, with whom he rode, swam, fished. He had been five when his mother died at twenty-eight, and he retained of her nothing but dim memories of a sea holiday in Wales. One of his father's sisters, Aunt Clara, ran the house. He was a slender child, pale, shy in the presence of strangers, deeply involved in the study of natural history. He kept lists of birds and insects and had a great interest in plants and flowers. At twelve his father sent him off to Rugby to follow in Austen's footsteps.

The school was a disaster for Neville. All British institutions of the type by long tradition did nothing to discourage the bullying of younger students—it built character—and in his case it got out of hand. He was from the very start kicked around and humiliated by the other boys and it never stopped. At the end of his first semester he returned home and flung himself into his aunt's arms. It was too emotional a gesture, too noisy, not in keeping with Birmingham's businesslike ways. He always remembered her reaction: "Neville, your cap's crooked." He vowed to himself that he would never kiss her again.

Lonely and always desperately unhappy there, he managed to get through Rugby. He was never to visit it after graduation, never even to see the school except from a passing train. He lived for vacations, when he and his sisters and cousins put on theatricals, and he got up at dawn to make notes on the squirrels and bird songs. His family was rich at a time when the rich had squads of servants and the most luxurious manner of dressing and eating and traveling, and Great Britain and British ways set the standard of the world. It was very pleasant. That life of family and old retainers in the big, peaceful, prosperous house was quite sufficient for his needs and he mixed almost not at all with anyone not of his immediate circle.

After Rugby there was no question of sending Neville to Oxford or Cambridge despite the development of a precise mind that was expansive enough to have a great knowledge of music, particularly that of Beethoven, of Shakespeare, and of novels and foreign languages. Joseph Chamberlain's viewpoint did not encompass sending his second son off to study history or the classics and instead Neville studied metallurgy and engineering. There followed an apprenticeship with a firm of chartered accountants. Austen by then was helping the father with Parliamentary campaigns and being introduced to the great of the realm.

Joseph Chamberlain married for the third time. His new bride was very young, around Austen's age, and American. On a trip to the States to visit her family the couple stopped in Montreal. There they met the governor of the Bahamas, who had formerly been in hemp manufacturing in the Philippines. In the Bahamas, the governor said, a fortune in hemp was waiting to be made from the sisal plant, which, he said, could be grown there.

The colonial secretary had spent his public life speaking of how the Empire must ever expand. This seemed an opportunity to put his ideals into practice. He and the two sons visited the Bahamas and were told that the world's best hemp could be made there. They traveled on the island of Andros through a wild tropical place almost entirely uncivilized and filled with strange birds, clouds of mosquitos, wild horses, flamingos, exotic plant and bird and animal life of every sort. The father put up money and delegated his younger son to go out and produce plantations.

Neville was twenty-one. It was 1891. He hired eight hundred natives, cleared swamps, burned off thousands of acres of ferns, vines, creepers, built a railroad seven miles inland and a long jetty into the sea, lived in a hut and fought off the ants and scorpions and centipedes. He wore out a pair of boots each month clambering about on the rough soil, got soaked through several times a day by quick, passing storms. There was no town and few roads on the dot in the ocean where he was all but king, and Boss and Mistah Chimblin to all. The natives mixed Christian ritual with Obi worship and suffered from leprosy and consumption. He sent to England for medicines he administered to them, and goods for a shop he set up. He was their magistrate and adviser. He got blisters from a poison-wood tree, the skin coming off and leaving the flesh raw. The nearest neighbor even remotely his social equal was half a day's trip away.

Neville built himself a house, got a sailboat in which he could run over to Nassau to mix with other edge-of-the-Empire pioneers, stayed up late over his accounts, created a magnificent garden with wonderful flowers and tubs of plants. During the day he was filthy and shabby but in the evenings he dressed and never degenerated with liquor or native women as did many of the settlers on Andros and other islands. He opened a bank for his employees and closed the squalid grog shops where they had drunk their wages away.

He made his house pleasant with vases and curtains and photos and artwork sent out from England, and took great pleasure, as he always had and always would, in his dogs. Then and always he had enormous energy and intellectual curiosity, and in his spare time he studied algebra and worked on his German. When the native engine drivers failed to show up for work, he ran the locomotive himself.

Chamberlain spent six years in the tropics, visiting England annually. At the end he knew Andros was never meant for cultivation of the sisal plant. The land wasn't right. In 1897 he had to admit he was licked. He went home to talk it over with his father and then came back to sell everything. His father had lost fifty thousand pounds.*

His people sobbed when they bade him good-bye and thanked him for the way he had treated them, and he returned to Birmingham heartsick and depressed. But in later years he came to esteem his hard years at the edge of the Empire, saying he had learned much there—self-reliance, discipline, responsibility.

Back in a Birmingham at the peak of its heyday commenced with the Industrial Revolution, he entered into the manufacture of copper and brass. He built up his company, absorbed other ones. He got into the manufacture of cabin berths for ships, riding his high bicycle to his plants and taking the night train at a moment's notice to clinch a contract. He was extremely generous with his workers and was proud all his life that his plants never had a strike. He improved technical processes, gave bonuses on

*Some quarter of a million in 1890s dollars, the equivalent of several millions today.

increased output, instituted a pension scheme and built company infirmaries. He made back his father's lost fifty thousand pounds and more.

Tall, slim, meticulously turned out, Neville Chamberlain followed the High Victorian merchant tradition of shrewd business dealing mixed with philanthropic endeavors. He worked very hard at setting up Birmingham University and became the moving spirit of a new general hospital with many modern services. His lifelong interest in music found expression in his successful campaign for a city orchestra supported by tax money. His cousin Norman Chamberlain, fifteen years younger, the son of a brother of his father, was always by his side.

Ten of Neville Chamberlain's relatives had filled the office before him when he became Lord Mayor of Birmingham. Feeling that health is ruled by housing and that housing is made up of many strands including wage standards, employment and transportation, he created town planning programs that demanded open spaces, good roads, zoning, modern sanitary arrangements. Birmingham became a model for the whole country. In 1911, when he was forty-two, he married Anne Vere Cole. She was nearly twenty years younger than her serious, earnest husband, and a complete contrast to him, gay, laughing, fun-loving.

Her brother Horace was one of the great practical jokers of England. Given to outfitting himself as the Sultan of Zanzibar with his friends serving as his entourage, he and they with skins dyed brown and gorgeously attired in robes and turbans would be received by the mayor of Cambridge, who gave them a scroll of welcome and a dinner in the Town Hall. When a friend married, Cole was likely to hire a beautiful woman to rush up to the bridegroom, fling her arms around him and scream, "Always remember that when *she* grows weary of you, I shall be waiting!" He filled suitcases on his honeymoon with horse manure, which he dumped on the central square of Venice where no horse had ever been. (People came from all over the city to wonder how it had happened.)

No more contrasting type could have been found than the former Miss Cole's new husband, for in middle age Chamberlain remained what he had always been, the most solid and level-headed of men. England's coin rang good on the counters of the world, England was the world's ironmaster and the world's shipbuilder, the world's banker and the workshop of mankind. Men like him had made it so by their hard work and good business and attention to detail and to quality. With his concern for business matters and his local philanthropies, the teaching of Sunday school, he appeared the most provincial of men. He was not. Before and after his marriage he traveled widely, to the Continent, Africa, India, the United States and Canada, always taking notes on everything he saw and writing long accounts in his diary. Well read in many fields, he had almost professional knowledge in subjects far removed from the image he presented of a sober, upstanding business leader. He knew long passages of Shakespeare by heart, knew china and antiques and art and modern fiction. In the family circle he could unbend and do imitations and mimicry but outside it he was quite different.

Chamberlain's wife and relatives realized that his formal and reserved manner with the world covered an overwhelming bashfulness. Perhaps it was the early loss of his mother, the remote and busy father, his relationship with Aunt Clara, the anguished days at Rugby and the isolation of the years at Andros that formed an aloofness perhaps the residue of a life of emotional impoverishment. Without Mrs. Chamberlain he would never have gone far in politics, for it was agony for him to meet people. A dinner party of more than six or eight forced him into himself and made him tight-lipped and short, almost harsh. He knew no small talk and was incapable of offering a cheery greeting, but he remained a figure of admiration in Birmingham for his honesty and regard for the right and the truth as he saw it. But to all but a tiny circle he appeared the most unlovable of men.

Norman Chamberlain, his cousin, was his conduit to the world in many situations, for Norman would talk to people as Neville never could. So when the War came and Norman went into the Grenadiers, his cousin deeply missed him. He had always counted on Norman near him, he said. It would be hard to envision a future without him. He was never to recover from the shock of Norman's death on the Western Front and for the rest of his life never spoke of him without the deepest emotion. The only book he ever wrote was a privately printed memoir of his dead cousin, written, he said, so that succeeding generations of the family would know what they had lost. But even when writing his tribute he was unable to let loose, putting his thoughts in constricted and cold phrases. As soon as the fighting ended in France, he went to seek Norman's grave, and found it surrounded by shell holes, other graves, dead stumps of trees.

"Nothing but immeasurable improvements will ever justify the damnable waste and unfairness of this war. I only hope that those who are left will never, never forget at what sacrifices these improvements have been won," Norman had written home in one of his last letters. In 1919 the dead captain's cousin Neville took his seat in Parliament.

He was fifty years of age, appealing in his matter-of-fact manner of precise speaking and reasoning when contrasted with the men who had taken England to war with bombast of England's glory and honor, and who now spoke of making England "a home fit for heroes to live in," so the phrase went. Such sentiments so expressed were now accounted cant and demagoguery, exactly the opposite impression given when Mr. Chamberlain of Birmingham spoke in his emotionless manner, emphasizing points with the fingers of his left hand tapping on the upheld palm of his right, his pince-nez held in that hand. He was determined, he told his family, to aid in the building of a lasting memorial of social legislation for those who had fallen, Norman and another cousin, Johnny, and the myriad of others.

He displayed no interest in foreign affairs—that was his half-brother's affair. Austen had fulfilled their father's plan and was His Majesty's secretary of state for foreign affairs, the moving spirit of the Locarno Pact meant to insure European peace forever, and a Knight of the Garter as a reward for his work.

Neville concentrated entirely on domestic issues, becoming postmaster general in 1922, then minister of health, then chancellor of the exchequer. Very vigorous, very efficient, analytic, methodical, concrete, definite, he never wanted to let anything slide but always sought direct action. He worked on matters concerned with broad-reaching social reform in the England of after-the-War, housing, pensions, health insurance, infant welfare, slum clearance. All who saw him respected him for his quick understanding of complex issues and his ability to suggest remedies.

Yet in the House of Commons and in the Cabinet Chamberlain was as far from being personally popular as he had been in Birmingham, for he struck his colleagues as cold, austere, remote. His clothing was curiously old-fashioned. Long after the styles had gone on he wore the dress of the Edwardian Age, usually appearing in a black tailcoat and stiff wing collar and looking, people said, like an undertaker who only lacked black gloves and top hat with broad band of mourning. With his long head and thin features he was compared to a forbidding-looking crow, and his unmelodious voice completed the simile.

He was aware of the bleak impression he made. "If I had not previously met the person who addressed us from the screen," he wrote of himself as seen in a newsreel, "I should call him pompous, insufferably slow in diction and unspeakably repellent."

But there seemed nothing he could do about it. What emotions light or heavy he owned were revealed mostly in letters to his sisters, which he churned out at a rate of at least one a week. The House of Commons could hardly believe it when Chamberlain, speaking of a maternity services bill, referred to his mother, choked up and appeared to be on the edge of tears.

As chancellor of the exchequer he saw England through the Depression. His colleague Winston Churchill said his work had saved the country from bankruptcy. Masterful and resourceful and never showing fatigue, he dictated tax policies and steered the allocation of funds, never lacking, however, the energy to continue his private interests. At the height of a desperately serious financial crisis readers of *The Times* letters column could discover that he had the previous morning spotted a gray waterwagtail in St. James's Park.

His prime minister in those years was Stanley Baldwin, dear and staunch old Stan, on whose election posters was written "Safety First." Baldwin gave Chamberlain power and trusted him and kept him close at hand at all times, but there could never be any real understanding between them. Baldwin was the comfortable country Englishman raised to high estate, smoking his pipe and radiating the supposed virtues of an avuncular and tolerant John Bull. He did as little as possible. The former prime minister David Lloyd George said of him that he was a miser of power, collecting and hoarding but never spending it. The member of Parliament Leo Amery looked at Baldwin during sessions of the House of Commons and decided that Baldwin was studying his colleagues only as interesting specimens of humanity, looking at a speaker "probably to wonder why on earth he had wanted to get into Parliament or what he was like at home."

The prime minister was capable of breaking off conversations in a baffling manner, or by remarking on the beauty of the scenery. He made the "most deplorable impression" on Chamberlain once in Cabinet, Chamberlain wrote in his diary, when during an important meeting he passed an open note across the table to Winston Churchill. On the note was written:

MATCHES
Lent at 10:30 A.M.
Returned?

Baldwin had an almost pathological indifference to foreign affairs. When the Italian dictator Mussolini invaded Ethiopia in 1935, Baldwin explained to a friend why he had not closed the Suez Canal and sent the Royal Navy to interdict the Italian supply lines across the Mediterranean, a simple enough task: "I want it to be said of me that I never sent a single Englishman to die on a foreign battlefield."

"But, Prime Minister," said the friend, "don't you see that you are piling up troubles for the future that will kill a million Englishmen in the next war?"

"That is a problem for my successor."

When a short time later the Germans entered the Rhineland and Baldwin was asked if he would support a French police action to drive them out, his reply was that if even one chance in a hundred existed that to do so would bring Britain to a war, he could not do it. He bestirred himself only to remark to Anthony Eden, Sir Austen Chamberlain's protégé and successor as foreign secretary, that perhaps Britain should do something about getting on good relations with the New Germany of Adolf Hitler.

"How?"

"I have no idea. That is your job."

Baldwin's forte was handling the British public. Despite the efforts of his chancellor of the exchequer the Depression took hold, as it was bound to do, as it did all over the world. But by being what he was more than what he did, Baldwin by his homeliness kept banked the fires of class hatred and desperation that might have flared and given birth to the sinister forces rising everywhere across the Channel. The knights and second sons of lords who otherwise largely composed the government might not have done half so well.

When in 1936 the new King Edward VIII let it be known that he wished to marry an American woman who had two previous husbands still living, it was Baldwin who knew intuitively that the British public would never stand for having such a queen. It was Baldwin who eased the king out with no constitutional crisis and no King's Party arising to rip apart the social fabric woven over centuries. King Edward abdicated for she whom he had titled "The woman I love," and merciless London wits said he had given up being admiral of the fleet in favor of becoming third mate on an American tramp.

His brother the Duke of York cried when he learned he was to be king. "Awful, ghastly, dreadful," he told his mother, Queen Mary.

"Dickie," he said to Lord Louis Mountbatten, "this is absolutely terrible. I never wanted this to happen."

But happen it did, and smoothly enough, largely thanks to Baldwin. Having seen King Edward VIII out and King George VI in, Baldwin prepared to retire and go off to get his earldom and be a country worthy in Worcestershire.

The chancellor of the exchequer in no way shared his chief's indolence or indifference to foreign affairs, but he made no claim to being an expert on matters overseas. Once he sat with his brother and Anthony Eden over dinner in his official residence at 11 Downing Street saying little while Sir Austen and Eden discussed Czechoslovakia and Austria. When he ventured a remark, Austen said, "Neville, you must remember you don't know anything about foreign affairs."

Neville smiled wryly, Eden remembered, and said that this was rather hard on a man at his own dinner table. "Austen made one of his sweeping, deprecatory gestures, half apologetic, and went on in his way."

The opposite of the Colonel Blimp type of Britisher who felt and said that wogs began at Calais, Chamberlain nevertheless had no great trust in the French and a distaste for the former enemy on the other side of the Rhine. "On the whole I loathe Germans," he wrote his sisters after a Black Forest vacation in 1930. Three years later Adolf Hitler came to power. His violence and ruthless persecutions horrified and baffled the logical and businesslike chancellor of the exchequer. "A lunatic," he wrote his sisters. "Half mad." That England in response to Hitler inaugurated a slight program of rearmament enraged a man who knew how dearly the money was needed for more socially beneficent purposes. "What a frightful bill do we owe to Master Hitler, d—n him!" he wrote his sisters regarding the taxes he had to impose for new military equipment.

When Hitler's crony Joachim von Ribbentrop came to London as ambassador to the Court of St. James's, Chamberlain estimated him as "stupid, so shallow, so self-centered and self-satisfied, so totally devoid of intellectual capacity." The chancellor of the exchequer was in a unique position to make an assessment with which few would disagree. The new ambassador had sought a home for rent in London and had found Chamberlain's was available while its owner lived in his official residence at 11 Downing Street.

"Did I tell you that we had let Eaton Square to Ribbentrop?" Chamberlain wrote his sisters. "Amusing, considering my affection for Germans in general and R. in particular."

Ribbentrop became Chamberlain's tenant in early 1937. In May of that year the landlord left 11 Downing Street, but not to reclaim his home. Stanley Baldwin was stepping down from the post of His Majesty's First Minister and, as Winston Churchill said, Chamberlain was "the one man to whom at this juncture the high and great function should be confided."

Neville Chamberlain took office fully feeling himself up to the task in which he felt he should have been preceded by his father and brother. But Joseph Chamberlain had never quite made it, and Austen was dead a year. He wrote his sisters that the traditional usage of the phrase "kissing hands" when the king offered the prime ministership confused him. Was it to be taken literally? On May 28 he went to George VI and emerged as leader of Great Britain and the Empire. He was sixty-eight. It was said of him then and history would repeat that he was sincere, honest, forthright, filled with the very best of intentions, a logical and well-meaning and intellectual gentleman. Hitler was waiting.

FIVE

IN AUGUST 1933 the town clerk of Eferding, Austria, opened an envelope and read:

My dear Kubizek,
    I have only just been shown your letter of February 2. In view of the hundreds of thousands that I have received since January this is not to be wondered at. So much the greater was my pleasure to receive news of you after so many years and to have your address. I should be very glad—once the period of my hardest struggles is past—to revive once more with you those memories of the best years of my life. Perhaps you could come to visit me. With all good wishes to you and your mother, I remain, in memory of our old friendship,
                                        Yours,
                                        Adolf Hitler

    It was positively miraculous, almost beyond the bounds of belief, August Kubizek said to himself, that his boyhood friend in Linz and roommate in Vienna had risen to be chancellor of Germany. He certainly had not shown much evidence of being a future political leader during their teenage years more than a quarter of a century earlier. Then his interests had been almost entirely confined to things artistic. He had never been without a sketchbook, and a substantial proportion of his money was spent on attendance at musical performances. That was how the two boys met, in the standing-room area of the Linz opera house, in 1904. Kubizek himself, always "Gustl" to his friend, never thought of anything but music. Forced to work as his father's assistant in the family upholstery shop, he spent every spare minute practicing on his viola or trumpet.

Shy and passive, Gustl was entirely dominated by his friend. Adolf determined the destination of Sunday outings in the countryside, the subjects to be discussed, and, finally, the education Gustl should receive, and indeed that there should be an education at all. That stemmed from Adolf's visit to Vienna when he was seventeen. "Well, I have safely arrived and am going around everywhere," read his first postcard. "Tomorrow I am going to the opera, *Tristan*, and the day after, *The Flying Dutchman*. Tonight Stadt-Theater. Greetings, your friend, Adolf Hitler." There followed a card showing the stage of the Hof Opera House with the writer's opinion of the decor. He found the gold and velvet overdone, appropriate only when swelling music complemented it. "Greetings to your esteemed parents. Adolf H." He returned to provincial Linz determined to get back to the capital for good. And Gustl must come with him. They would live together. He, Adolf, would enroll in Vienna's Academy of Fine Arts, and Gustl would go to the Conservatory.

For Adolf the plan was reasonable. He had money enough from his late father's estate and pension—the father had been an Austrian customs official. To convince the workaday Kubizek family that their son should leave the upholstery shop for the study of music was another question. Adolf got the job done. "What extraordinary eyes your friend has!" Gustl's mother said. There was something burning in them. Perhaps it was that, and his throbbing voice and intensity, that convinced Gustl's parents. They gave their consent. Adolf went on to look into living arrangements. It was early 1908. "Dear Friend, Am anxiously awaiting news of your arrival. Write soon so that I can prepare everything for your festive welcome. The whole of Vienna is awaiting you."

They lived together in a little room near the West Railroad Station. Gustl went to classes at the conservatory, was accepted as a viola player in the school orchestra, studied conducting. It was quite different for Adolf. He had presented himself at the Academy of Fine Arts believing, he said later, that it would be child's play to gain admittance. He was rejected. He could not believe it. He spoke with the director, who told him he was not equipped to be a painter. Perhaps he might try the School of Architecture. When he went there, they told him entering students had to be high school graduates. As he had dropped out of school without graduating, it would be impossible for him to be taken on.

He told no one of his failures but read, sketched, went to the opera. His mother at home fell ill. Word came that she was dying. He went to her. His Vienna roommate visited during her last hours. "Gustl," she whispered, "go on being a good friend to my son when I'm no longer here. He has no one else." She had always been devoted to Adolf. He was not like her, not like the rest of the family; he was, she always said, different from them. Her funeral took place just before Christmas. Her son rejected Gustl's offer to come to dinner on Christmas Eve but went out into the night and wandered for hours. New Year's he spent with Gustl and his family sitting silently at the table.

Back in Vienna, his money running out, bitter at the academy and the world, he raged so wildly that his roommate began to think he was unbalanced. He cursed the Czechs and Magyars and Slovaks and Jews of cosmopolitan Vienna, cursed the rich, the Hapsburgs, the Church, the politicians, everybody and everything. At the end of the school year in the early summer of 1908 Gustl went home to Linz to see his parents. Adolf stayed in their room, writing now and then. He had been to see *Lohengrin*. He had caught a cold. In the fall Gustl came back. He had expected Adolf to meet him at the train, but when he arrived, Adolf was not there. He went to their room.

The landlady said, "Don't you know that Herr Hitler has moved out?"

Gustl knew no such thing. Where had he gone? "Herr Hitler didn't tell me."

But surely he had left a message for his friend, a note?

"No, Herr Hitler didn't leave anything."

Bewildered, Gustl took up his studies. Adolf would get in touch. But he did not. On a visit back to Linz Gustl went to Adolf's half-sister to learn where he was. She did not know. She had not heard from him in months. Gustl went back to Vienna, still hoping that Adolf would turn up. He never did.

August Kubizek spent four years at the Vienna Conservatory, graduated, got a position as an assistant theater conductor. After a couple of years he was offered a better job in the capital of Carinthia province, Klagenfurt. His duties were to commence in the summer of 1914.

But that summer, the most beautiful in memory—or so it seemed to those looking back in later years—a youth fatally ill with tuberculosis raised a pistol as the car carrying the Austrian heir to the throne passed through a street in Sarajevo. "Is Your Imperial Highness hit?" asked a fellow passenger and the Archduke Francis Ferdinand repeated three times "It's nothing" before telling his wife, also hit and toppled over in his lap, that she must live for their children's sake. Blood bubbled out of his mouth.

His death brought an Austrian ultimatum to Serbia, Notes from other Powers, additional ultimatums, mobilizations, declarations and eventually the Great War. Along with the other millions upon millions it swallowed up August Kubizek. "My youthful dreams disappeared in the fire of the Russian batteries when I experienced my baptism of fire on the Galician front. This was not the music I had dreamed of."

Kubizek survived despite wounds and sickness. But the tiny and poverty-stricken Austrian Republic that emerged after the War offered few opportunities for conductors of music. He went to be an employee of the town of Eferding. He married and had sons. Music was still his first love and over the years he built up a little amateur orchestra and a string quartet and choral society. Through the twenties he heard mention of a German politician with the same name as his vanished friend, but it was simply a coincidence of names, he reasoned, for he had long before decided that Adolf had probably died in the War. Then one day in a bookstore window he saw a copy of a Munich magazine. On the cover was the face of his friend grown sterner, more mature, more manly, but hardly any older. "The well-known Nationalist Socialist orator, Adolf Hitler."

Kubizek went home and got out the old letters and postcards and pored over them. But there did not seem to be any point in contacting his onetime roommate. Their boyhood friendship had been based upon a common interest in art and music, and all that was gone. Kubizek did not write until Hitler became chancellor. Five years later the German army marched into Austria. Kubizek went to the chancellor's hotel in Linz. He showed his old letters and postcards to the guards and was led in. Thirty years had gone by since last they met.

Hitler came into the hotel foyer. "Gustl!" They held each other's hands. "You are just the same as you always were," Hitler said. "I should have recognized you anywhere." They talked for an hour about Linz and Vienna, about the musical performances

Kubizek was putting on in his little town. "It's really necessary that we should meet more often," Hitler said. "As soon as it's possible I will send for you."

A year later came an invitation for attendance at the Richard Wagner Festival in Bayreuth. Kubizek had never had the opportunity to go before. It was his dream to do so. He saw four Wagnerian operas at the festival. When it was over he was asked to Haus Wahnfried, the home of Wagner's daughter-in-law. Hitler was there. To Kubizek this house, once Wagner's home, was a holy place. It was the thrill of his life to be there with the friend of his youth and his lost dreams. Together they went into the garden and to a high wrought-iron gate. Hitler opened it. They stood before Richard Wagner's tomb.

They talked with Winifred Wagner and her son Wieland, the Master's grandson, and Kubizek spoke of something from the long ago. They had been to see Wagner's *Rienzi*, he said, back in Linz when they were boys. Something of the story of Cola di Rienzi's rise to be the tribune of the people of Rome who brought order from chaos had caught at the teenager Adolf Hitler. Usually talkative after a performance, he had upon this occasion been silent.

The boys climbed a high hill. Adolf began to speak. He had a mandate, he said, to lead people as Rienzi did, out of servitude to the heights of freedom. Gustl was bewildered. Until that moment Adolf had never spoken of being anything but an artist. Now he said there was a special mission that would one day be entrusted to him and to him alone. Kubizek did not know what to think. It was three in the morning when they parted in front of Kubizek's home. Hitler turned and headed again for the high hill.

"Where are you going now?" Kubizek asked.

"I want to be by myself."

They never mentioned the occurrence again until nearly thirty-five years passed and Kubizek spoke of that night to Winifred Wagner. He had thought that perhaps the Reich chancellor had forgotten but he had not. "In that hour it began," Hitler said.

•

He had gone from their little room, alone, to a cheaper little room. He told his landlady he was studying to be a writer. From there he went to a still cheaper room, infested with bugs and with walls always damp. He lived on the tiny pension paid to him by the State because he was an orphan. It would buy him a loaf of bread and two pints of milk a day. His sleeves raveled at the edges and the lining came out of his coat. His shoes went down at the heels. Pale and with sunken eyes he left his last room and went to sleep on the benches of the Prater, Vienna's great park. When it rained he hid in cellars or under an archway.

Cold weather came and he went to what was called warming rooms. Men sat up all night at packed tables there, slumped over. No talking was allowed. A little thin soup and a slice of bread were the fare, provided by charity organizations. In the mornings the tramps who landed there were kicked out onto the sidewalk to beg or steal or do what they could to earn a few pennies. He shoveled snow, carried travelers' bags at the railway stations. His hair grew long, he had a beard.

Adolf Hitler finally reached the House for Men on the Meldemannstrasse, the absolute bottom of the heap of the capital of the great Austro-Hungarian Empire. No one with an income of more than a dollar a day was allowed there. He easily qualified. By then he was wearing an old coat. That was all. He had no shirt, no underclothing. He was literally in rags, greasy and dirty, his shoes falling apart. He got a job doing construction work, but his talkativeness irritated the other men. They told him to get going or they would throw him off the scaffold. He quit the job.

When he had a few pennies he went into the Home's kitchen and cooked himself a concoction of rice and milk mixed with sugar and chocolate. One Reinhold Hanisch, a drunkard and bum, heard him refer to himself as a painter and asked if he painted houses. Indignantly Hitler explained that he was an artist. Hanisch saw an opportunity to make a little money. Let Hitler paint some pictures and he, Hanisch, would peddle them. They would split the proceeds. So he went to work producing copies of other men's work or street scenes or buildings or trees. Never any human figures. Hanisch took the pictures to bars and told drinkers these were the works of a sick and starving artist. If a prospective customer hesitated, Hanisch coughed in his face, knowing he would be given a little something so that he would leave the painting and get out.

The two kept at their enterprise for half a year or so. Then they argued over the disposal of a Hitler painting of the Austrian Parliament building. Hanisch said he had sold it for fifteen

crowns, less than four dollars, and had given Hitler his rightful
share, seven and a half crowns. Hitler said it was worth more
and went to the police and complained. He took on another agent,
an old-clothes dealer. The man was unable to peddle a single
painting.

He drifted along selling his work to little shopowners who
wanted something to put in their windows. He made crude posters to be tucked in piles of merchandise—pictures of soap or
candles, one for Teddy's Perspiration Powder. He did not work
steadily, often knocking off for a week at a time and going back
to it only when his slight store of money was gone. He sat at
cafés eating cream cakes and reading the free newspapers the
proprietor supplied, or hung around the charity soup kitchens.

In Vienna's underworld of drifters and down-and-outers he
made no friends, formed no close relationships. There never was
another Kubizek. Yet he knew a good many men of the warming
rooms and soup lines. They uniformly regarded him as unbalanced because of the wild spurts of feverish words that would
suddenly come pouring out of him. He could sit numbly silent
in a corner for hours but then without warning be up shouting
that the Catholic priests were despoiling people or that the Imperial Hapsburgs were unfit to rule German-speaking men. Or
he talked of how he would improve airplane design and invent
a new method of finding underground sources of water. The
others laughed at him or told him to shut up, but he waved his
arms and shouted until the porter came in to order the disturbance ended.

For five years he lived in this fashion, never getting a regular
job. To do so would mean that he had become a simple wage
slave trapped in a dull, workaday existence, not a student and
thinker and artist temporarily in poor circumstances. In 1913 he
left Vienna as a result of never having registered for his military
training. Lost in the depths of the great metropolis he was a
draft-dodger who with luck might never be apprehended by the
authorities. But if he were, a prison term could await. He went
to Munich to live the same life as before, making a few pennies
from his paintings and arousing in the few Germans who came
to know him the same reactions as he had in the Viennese: they
thought him an unbalanced crank given to sudden fits against
supposed enemies.

Behind him the slow Austrian police system listed him as a

draft-dodger. He was traced to the Home for Men, where it was found that he had gone to Munich. The aid of the German authorities was sought, and a policeman went to the home of a poor tailor in the slums and arrested the tailor's boarder. The Austrian consular officials saw a thin, ragged, undernourished twenty-four-year-old who begged for a chance to explain. He wrote a long letter to the Linz police, who had originated the search for him, telling them of his poverty, of how for years he had hardly earned enough to pay for a place where he might sleep. "I had no other friend but care and want, no other companion but everlasting insatiable hunger. I never learnt the meaning of that fine word Youth. Today after five years the tokens are still with me in the form of chilblains on fingers, hands and feet. I most humbly request that this letter may kindly be taken into consideration and sign with great respect, Adolf Hitler, artist."

He was sent across the border to the nearest Austrian military post. Army doctors there declared him too weak to serve. He went back to Munich and was there a year later when the War came. He greeted it joyfully. He would be a soldier for great Germany, the Germany of Wagner's operas, the legends and myths. One of the millions feeling a part of something greater than themselves, he rushed with the youth of all the nations of Europe to the recruiting stations.

An infantry private well dressed and eating regularly for the first time in years, he underwent two months of training and then with his regiment joined the German forces facing the British in Flanders. Under intensive fire that decimated its ranks, his formation was committed to the hellish first battle of Ypres. It was the beginning of two years of uninterrupted fighting for him, and his world became the mud and trenches and misting rain of lowlands Belgium. He made an excellent soldier, brave and willing. He did not complain as others did and was respected for his ability.

Yet his fellows found him strange. Unlike them he was not interested in getting leave or finding girls. He did not smoke or drink. Sometimes, exactly in the fashion of his days in the Home for Men in Vienna, he sat silently, sunk in thought, his head in his hands. Then suddenly he ran about excitedly saying Germany was being betrayed, that victory was being stolen by scum behind the lines.

He got an Iron Cross, First Class, and a leg wound the recovery from which took five months in a hospital. In early 1917 he was back at the Front, a lance corporal, the equivalent of private first class in other armies. In the spring of 1918 he was caught in a chlorine gas attack. A blinded man, he was sent to Germany in a hospital train and was slowly recovering in Pasewalk when an army chaplain came in to say the War was over. Tears came into the half-seeing eyes. He had found a home in the German army. He had served contentedly, never protesting when passed over for promotion by officers who considered him too unstable and eccentric to be placed in any kind of command position. Now the German army lay prostrate in the dust.

In the spring of 1919, his eyesight restored, Lance Corporal Hitler, still in his shabby uniform, went back to Munich. He was thirty. He stayed on in the army, living in a barracks and wondering what to do with himself. He went into an army political instruction course whose aim was to remind the troops that they had been betrayed by the November criminals who signed the Armistice, that Germany would yet find its place in the sun, and that whoever worked against that goal was evil. He did not need reminding. In the thin faces and sunken eyes of a people half-starved by the Allied blockade during the War and the hopeless poverty afterwards he saw his own past. In the hope of Germany's rising he saw his own hopes.

He seemed well suited for the job of an undercover spy reporting to his military superiors on political developments in a Munich aflame with all kinds of movements, each of which, whether its participants knew it or not, aimed to restore the feeling of well-being and stability that had vanished in 1914. A hundred little groups came springing from the ground—for the Republic replacing the fled Kaiser, against the Republic, peaceable, violent. Political schemers, Bolsheviks, idealists, dreamers, ideological murder gangs, the army wished to keep tabs on them. He was one of many spies told to go about in civilian clothing.

In September 1919, he was sent to look into the doings of a little crew that, like all the others, called itself a party. It held its meetings in a Munich beer hall. The night Hitler came for the first time he found a gathering of twenty-five people. The treasury of the German Workers' Party contained seven and a half marks—between $1.75 and two dollars. The speakers addressing the tiny group were vaguely in favor of German greatness and a better break for the workingman. Hitler listened and went away. A few days later he received a postcard inviting him to another meeting. He went to a cheap beerhouse, which he found completely empty. He walked to a little side room, looking for the meeting, and, opening a door, found four men sitting under dim gaslight. A few days later he received an announcement that he had been enrolled in the Party. He had not applied, but now he was Party Comrade Number Seven in what would soon be called the National Socialist German Workers' Party—Nationalsozialistische Deutsche Arbeiterpartei—Nazi, for short.

•

He got up. There were thirty-four people. He began to talk. Versailles Treaty. November criminals. Stab in the back. Communists and Jews. Germany's glory and Germany's shame. Down with the Republic. Germany would rise again. The voice rose and fell and then rose again to an almost hysterical screaming note, the r's rolling and the Austrian accent thickening. The hands shot out, pointed, clenched into fists. German arms and German culture, German right and German might. Yet this heroic people was being gnawed at by traitors, war profiteers, pornographers, cheats, liars, thieves, foreigners.

They must go, all of them. There was only one way, that of the knife. Scum, vermin, dogs. Away with them, let Germany be clean. Then the Poles would be chased away, and the Lithuanians. Then the French would be put to flight. England's face would be ground into the dirt and the Americans would be taught to stay on their side of the Atlantic, mongrel-race niggers. As he talked his eyes seemed to cloud over and then light up. Passion lived in every word, each screaming cry that German blood would conquer yet, that the will of the German race could not be denied. Victory would come over the swine who ruled Germany, those of the accursed Republic, traitors, cowards! It would come, it would come!

Spittle collected at the corners of his mouth, and a lock of hair fell over his forehead. Kill the Jews, drive them out, down with the priests who debased the people, the pure German people, the sons of Siegfried and daughters of Brunhilde, the greatest warriors and makers of the finest music the world knew now ground under the heels of their betrayers. Filth. Pigs. Hang them. Cut out their hearts. Awaken, Germany! Take up your place in the sun! Germany awake! Germany awake!

He sat down. The people in the tiny room were electrified. He had them. He saw it. I can speak! his heart cried to him. Fourteen years later he was chancellor. Chancellor then, and the Führer, the Leader, he went to Haus Wahnfried in Bayreuth and with Gustl Kubizek to Richard Wagner's grave. It was August 3, 1939.

"There was a preponderance of military personalities present," Kubizek remembered, "and it struck me that the general situation was very strained, in particular with regard to Poland."

SIX

THE GERMANY whose chancellorship Adolf Hitler assumed on January 30, 1933, had since the War sustained shocks no other country ever knew. The people had gone to battle united and confident. He now knew no parties but only Germans, the Kaiser had told them in 1914, saying also that the troops would be home before the leaves turned in the autumn. There were a few glorious weeks of advance in the west followed by a four-year purgatory of body- and soul-killing motionless, stalemated trench warfare. In the east an advance could be sustained, but the conditions were frightful and ultimately nothing was gained.

Encircled and blockaded, starving, their weak satellites falling away, the Army of a Thousand Victories threw in one last western offensive in the summer of 1918. It was halted by the last-gasp Allies and the oncoming Americans. That was the end. Everything fell away. The liege lords tumbled from their thrones, Highness and Majesty signed abdications, the Kaiser fled to Holland. The army marched home in good order, but home had changed. Miniature civil war swirled about, armed mobs, political assassinations. The blockade continued and children died as the Allies waited for the Germans to sign the Versailles Treaty.

There were to be no negotiations. Germany must sign away colonies, must cede indisputably German territories to its neighbors, must agree to never having more than a tiny military force, must agree to pay immense reparations, must accept all guilt for the War. More children died. People fainted in the streets from hunger. Germany signed the treaty.

The Weimar Republic, which followed the reign of Wilhelm

55

II, had a constitution drawn up by theorists and professors that created what was uniformly called the freest country in the world, where every minority had a voice and every need was offered remedy. Germany had been a country of which it had been said that leadership consisted of officers of the Guards yelling orders, a society where every man had a stipulated place and stipulated social rights and obligations. Now the new politicians had substituted a democracy more complete than England or America knew.

In some ways it was wonderful. The Republic lacked the collapsed order's tradition, splendor, ceremony, but it opened the gates for an explosion of creative display unknown in German history. Ancient forms in music and art and architecture were swept away, remnants of the buttoned-up, stiff-necked, failed past, and replaced by a flood of exciting new output, including the most innovative cinema in the world. Life, free and vibrant, was also overheated and supercharged.

"Anything that gave hope of newer and greater thrills," Stefan Zweig remembered, "anything in the way of narcotics, morphine, cocaine, heroin, found a tremendous market; on the stage, incest and parricide."

Berlin became the Babylon of the world. Along its principal avenue, the Kurfürstendamm, strolled powdered and rouged young men, and for a young girl "to be sixteen and still under suspicion of virginity," Zweig wrote, "would have been considered a disgrace in any school of Berlin at that time; every girl wanted to be able to tell of her adventures, and the more exotic, the better."

Yet it all lacked footing. Germany's currency had been stable and powerful before the War, as were her rules and her institutions. But when in 1923 the French army marched into the Ruhr Valley, Germany's premier industrial district, to enforce payments on the war debt to the former Allies, the mark completely collapsed. Nothing similar had been seen in history. Traditionally it had taken four marks to buy a United States dollar, but day by day the value dropped so that soon it took a hundred marks to buy a dollar, a thousand, a million. The price of a meal doubled as one ate. Government printing presses ran all night to print new bills, all for stupendous amounts but all virtually worthless. It took a billion marks to buy a dollar, ten billion. A government bond purchased a year before would not buy a ride on a streetcar. A pension given for a lifetime of service would not buy a postage stamp. People were paid their wages with wa-gons full of currency. The price of an egg was four billion marks, the previous value of all the real estate of Greater Berlin.

In such a situation all values and faith and hope vanish. The last trailing ends of the staid old Fatherland of set ways came unraveled. A generation and a country that had undergone war, starvation, defeat and dishonor now faced such a destruction of values as to make the earthquake complete. There now existed the direst poverty. Those of the middle class impoverished by the hideous inflation competed in begging alms with crippled or blinded veterans of the War who dragged themselves about in pushcarts or on crutches with tin cups in their hands, still in their tattered uniforms. Past their ranks moved limousines owned by the newly enriched, profiteers in currency speculation escort-ing their new mistresses of the old aristocracy, or at least of the formerly self-respecting classes that had made Wilhelmenian Germany strong.

There was always something of a temporary feeling to Wei-mar Germany. The Republic was always something in the nature of a frantic interlude between acts. There was much that was sinister in the air beyond economic distress and artistic creativity, the average, everyday woman wearing too much makeup, the leather-booted prostitutes carrying whips and soliciting men in monocles and dress-for-dinner bat-wing collars. No sensitive vis-itor came away without feeling that the new music's ticky-tacky beat was played for a doomed and corrupted masquerade ball.

Then came the Depression. No country was hit harder than Germany. The foreign loans dried up. There were no jobs and no food, every index was down, there were seething lines of un-employed at the soup kitchens and on the breadlines. From the ranks of those who had never recovered from the War, who car-ried it in their blood, who though they lived yet had died in 1914–18, there came new recruits for the two parties massing in the streets and fighting the police and one another: the Com-munists and the National Socialists. Hitler had always said it would come to this.

Now the birds were coming home to roost, Adolf Hitler cried to ever-growing crowds at Nazi rallies. A chancellor ruling by special emergency powers fell to be replaced. His replacement fell. Hitler went from meeting to meeting shouting that the Weimar Republic had rotted Germany's values and asking the

German people to give him their votes and their destiny. He would give them back their future.

The decision lay in the hands of President Paul von Hindenburg. To him Hitler was "a Bohemian corporal" fit perhaps to be postmaster general so that he could lick stamps bearing the president's portrait.* He warned Hitler to moderate his words and actions. He and his followers were too intolerant of opposition, too noisy, too undisciplined. The excesses against the Jews, the illegal acts, the violence, showed that the Nazis were a group out of control. Hindenburg raised his hand and stuck out a finger in imitation of a revolver and said, "Herr Hitler, I will shoot!" But in the end he could not shoot. He was too old to start a civil war, he said. Just before noon on January 30, 1933, Hitler was sworn in as chancellor.

There was a constitution, there were safeguards, there were restraints. But in an amazingly short time all was thrust aside. Within a year, everything of Weimar was gone. Posters announced it un-German for women to paint their faces; makeup vanished. The unions were no longer needed, said the new government; they were done away with. By far the greatest number of the clergy and the business leaders, the university faculties and students, supported the Hitler government. With the utmost brutality the Leader crushed a segment of his coterie that he said, held overly radical views and in addition sought to take over the army. After that the officer corps went along with the new regime.

The New Germany was on the march. Prior to Hitler there had been squads of spiritual healers in Germany—Doctor for Suffering of the Soul, read their cards and stationery. They vanished, no longer required by a people finding self-forgetfulness in a common effort to rise with their nation. For the first time since the War, Germany seemed at one with itself with the exception of those elements, a small percentage of the population, whom the new regime proscribed. Few bothered with their fate. Everyone else was enrolled in the service of the nation and the Leader. There was after a year hardly a breath of dissent anywhere. "The will of the Führer is the will of the German people!"

The Depression slipped away, or appeared to, vanquished by better world economic conditions and by government spending

---

*Old and failing when he met Hitler, Hindenburg took remarks about his bohemianism to mean that he was born there.

for roads, for youth camps, reforestation projects. And for arms factories. There was no great pretense about the violation of the Versailles Treaty, which had been meant to disarm Germany forever. Anyone who spent a Sunday in the park was likely to see platoons of Boy Scouts with wooden guns practicing squad tactics.

But it was absurd and dangerous, the Leader said, his country agreeing with him, that the greatest Power in Central Europe should have to resort to transparent subterfuges while remaining effectively helpless and presenting an invitation to others to attack it. He took Germany out of the League of Nations and the great Disarmament Conference, saying what was true, that the world that had promised in 1918 to disarm had instead rearmed. (There was not much market for plowshares during the Depression; swords paid better.) New Poland was a ferociously bellicose country. France had a mighty army. Just weeks after his accession to power Czechoslovakia, Romania and Yugoslavia had signed a military pact. Was Germany alone, Hitler asked, to remain defenseless?

He appealed for a rise in the level of the German army from the paltry one hundred thousand men allowed by the Versailles Treaty, and to allow a shorter period of service for enlisted men. (By the terms of the treaty they served twelve years, which meant there would be no rotating groups of men going through and returning to civilian life to form a standing reserve.) France would not consent. He said he would limit the armaments permitted Germany if other nations did the same, even to throwing away his last machine gun. France, with her memories of 1870 and 1914, had received the same requests and offers from Hitler's Weimar predecessors. She could not agree then and could not now.

In March 1935, two years in office, arguing that the conditions of 1918 could not dominate the world forever, Hitler publicly repudiated Part V of the Treaty of Versailles and announced that Germany would introduce universal conscription aimed at producing an army of thirty-six divisions, three hundred thousand men. The former Allies sent protesting Notes. But was the world to go to war for this? Because Hitler said with admitted justification, "We are not to be treated as shoeshine boys!"?

France reacted by rearranging a pact with Russia under which each nation pledged to come to the aid of the other in the event of unprovoked aggression. Czechoslovakia negotiated similar terms with Russia. The answer to the enlargement of the German army was that Germany was encircled. But Hitler had accomplished what no German before him had done: he had breached the Versailles Treaty.

A month after Russia made the two treaties with France and Czechoslovakia Hitler asked for and got a naval treaty from Great Britain. It limited a German shipbuilding program to a fraction of that of Britain, but it again went beyond what Versailles had decreed. Was the League of Nations to mobilize an army? When one of its main supporters, the premier sea power of the world, had willingly acquiesced in the establishment of the German navy on a new basis? And when the chancellor spoke so of peace?

"The blood shed on the European continent in the course of the last three hundred years bears no proportion to the result of the events," he told the Reichstag. "In the end France has remained France, Germany Germany, Poland Poland and Italy Italy. If these states had applied merely a fraction of their sacrifices to wiser purposes the successes would certainly have been greater and more permanent. No war would be likely essentially to alter any distress in Europe. The principal effect of every war is to destroy the flower of the nation. Germany needs peace and desires peace.

"Whoever lights the torch of war in Europe can wish for nothing but chaos. We, however, live in the firm conviction that in our time will be fulfilled not the decline but the renaissance of the West. That Germany may make an imperishable contribution to this great work is our proud hope and our unshakable belief."

The speech was hailed everywhere. It would have been out of the question for the League of Nations to have taken any action against Germany after that. Soon the impotence of the League to do anything significant in any case would be entirely revealed, for when in the fall, in October 1935, the Italian army invaded Ethiopia, spokesmen for the League talked and denounced and protested, but did nothing. Benito Mussolini had calculated on the League's failure to act by observing the fashion in which it had met Hitler's violation of the Versailles Treaty armaments clause.

Mussolini had been in power for thirteen years by then. Dynamic, a great speaker, a splendid physical specimen, intellectual, well-read and psychologically discerning, he had taken a poverty-stricken agricultural nation with no coal, no steel, no oil, and turned it into what was viewed as a first-class Power. He had been condescendingly unimpressed by Hitler when they had met in Venice the preceding year. "I don't like the look of him," he muttered to his aides when Hitler's plane landed to disgorge an ill-at-ease man in a soiled raincoat ruinously contrasting with the magnificent plumage of his host's Fascist uniform. "A talkative monk," Mussolini declared upon closer acquaintance.

They had nothing in common. Hitler was uninterested in food, in drink, in sports, in women. Mussolini told his intimates that all that involved Hitler was talk, talk, and talk some more. That had always been Hitler's way, as others had long before discovered. Completely discarding the rules of conversation that permit the other party or parties at least occasionally to voice an observation, he monopolized the floor for what his associates estimated to be 80 to 90 percent of the time, offering his thoughts on religion, history, art, philosophy, actors and actresses, his past, his struggle, his plans. The monologues went on each night into the early hours of the morning, listeners struggling to keep awake.

His talk was always vague save for when he discussed military statistics and equipment, of which he had a great knowledge, or architecture, his memory for details of which was phenomenal, extending to the recall of the exact placement and size in every room of any building whose plans he had ever seen.

On other matters he was never definite and never precise but always given to the use of generalities. He had been that way with Gustl Kubizek back in Linz and in Vienna long before the War, and stayed that way in prison after attempting the revolution that the Munich police put down with a volley of rifle fire. ("This last half hour, while I was resting," he told a visitor to his cell, "I invented a new machine gun and a contrivance for bridge-building, and composed a piece of music in my head.")

To Mussolini Hitler was a welcome newcomer on the international scene in the sense that the German was the Italian's lesser disciple as dictator of an authoritarian state. And he had shown the League could be flouted with impunity. Responding to Hitler's example and saying in his flamboyant, bombastic manner that after a lapse of fifteen hundred years a new Empire was rising upon the storied hills of Rome, Mussolini mercilessly deployed modern weaponry against the primitive and entirely unindustralized Ethiopia. His planes dropped mustard gas upon natives armed with spears. The burning rain, they came to call it. His planes machine-gunned them and his aviator son permitted himself to speak of the remarkable beauty as seen from above brought about by a heavy bomb dropped upon a village of thatched huts: it was like a flower opening, a sunrise. Ethiopia's emperor Haile Selassie, the Lion of Judah, the descendant of the Queen of Sheba, driven from his country, went to the League of Nations in imperial robes. "God and history will remember," he said. King Victor Emmanuel of Italy added a new title: Emperor of Ethiopia.

The slight disapproval by the League and the world in the face of invasion and slaughter had its effect in Berlin even as Hitler's doings regarding rearmament had had their effect in Rome. In March 1936, the German army marched into the Rhineland, that section of German territory that was by the terms of the Versailles Treaty to be free of troops and fortifications for a distance fifty miles into Germany. France's Marshal Ferdinand Foch had said after the War that the area must be ceded to France, that if it were not, then the four years of battle had been in vain and what was called the Peace would prove instead a twenty-year armistice. His plea was not granted by the Powers meeting at Versailles. The demilitarization of the Rhineland was the best the French could get. It was a mainstay of the system they had set up to assure themselves security from invading Germans.

But a part of their system was the recently ratified pact they made with Russia. Hitler said it was because of that treaty that he had to move. He must assure that his west was safe because of the danger from the east. He had pledged himself to keep the Rhineland demilitarized—but now, he said, the alliance of France with Asiatic Communism released him from his promise.

The troops were received with flowers and tears of joy by the populace. Priests blessed them. To evict them would be the work of a moment for the French army, and indeed the German rifles were empty—this was a parade, not an invasion—and to do so would likely topple the Leader from power. There was the question of who would follow him. Someone who did not speak so feelingly of peace, perhaps, or a German Lenin who would, in association with Moscow, bring Stalinism into the heart of Europe. That the Germans were only walking into their own back garden became a commonly used expression in London, and in any case they were only doing what every other country in the world could freely do: move its own troops about in its own indisputable territory. It was not a matter of taking foreign lands by fire and sword.

The troops stayed, and Adolf Hitler became the most loved German in history. No one had ever known such acclamation. He had taken a profoundly dispirited and disordered country, no other citizen of which so brilliantly expressed its malaise—it was the German people who gave him his voice and his vision, he said, it was their need and their want that formed the words that came from his mouth—and he had made this people and this country whole. To the rest of the world he seemed a miracle worker.

Britain's prime minister of the later War years came to visit the Leader six months after the Rhineland move and upon his return to his hotel, his daughter laughingly flung up her hand and cried, *"Heil Hitler!"* David Lloyd George replied, "Certainly, *Heil Hitler!* I say it too, for he is really a great man."

They had held a friendly talk. Hitler gave him an autographed portrait, for which Lloyd George had asked permission to place on his desk next to those of Wilson, Clemenceau and Foch. The former prime minister wrote a newspaper article terming Hitler the George Washington of Germany and said to intimates, "He is a great and wonderful leader. He is a man who cannot only plan, but can put his plans into execution. He is the savior of Germany."

The British statesman was received at Hitler's residence at Berchtesgaden in Bavaria, fifteen miles from Salzburg, Austria, where he had a house with a magnificent view of the mountains ranging over into his former homeland. Lloyd George would have seen the splendid main drawing room and inviting terraces, but one member of the household he would have never met. Eva Braun had been an employee of a photographer, Heinrich Hoffman, when she came to Hitler's notice. (Hoffman had been an early follower of the Leader. Hitler once mentioned to Hoffman that he had been in Munich's Odeonsplatz on the day Germany's declaration of war was read out to an enormous crowd in August 1914. Hoffman remarked that he was there, too, taking pictures. He went back to his files and found a crowd scene that included a clear shot of a thin young man waving his arms in happy excitement.)

Eva Braun had known Hitler since 1929. For two years she had a rival for his attentions in his niece, Geli Raubal, the daughter of his half-sister Angela. Geli was nearly twenty years younger than her uncle but she became, and remained, the love of his life. In 1931 after a violent argument with him—she had been with another, younger, man; she wished to study singing in Vienna—she shot herself with his revolver.

A day or two after the funeral, driving to a Nazi Party conference, he stopped with his aide Hermann Goering at an inn, where at breakfast he refused to eat a piece of ham. "It is like eating a corpse," he told Goering. He never ate meat again. His transformation was instantaneous, said the wife of his aide Rudolph Hess. "He ate meat before that. It is very difficult to understand or explain." Henceforth he lived on vegetables and cereals, pastries, zwieback, honey, ketchup, mushrooms, yogurt.

Eva Braun became his mistress, and when he was named chancellor, there was always a place near him for her. But no one must know. He was consecrated to his people, he said, and must stand alone, a monk devoted to his god and his duty, which was to lead Germany to deliverance from evil. Mother of the German People, so she mockingly titled herself, she had to stay in her room when visitors came. She was a cheerful, simple, athletic, pleasantly likable girl whose lover gave her modest gifts, inexpensive costume jewelry.

It was another woman whose relationship with the Leader was the focus of the world's speculation. Unity Valerie Mitford, the daughter of Britain's Lord Redesdale,* had been a student at a Munich finishing school. While she was having a bite at the Osteria Bavaria, a small artists' restaurant Hitler favored, her statuesque figure and blonde hair caught the eye of some of Hitler's associates. She was asked if she spoke German and her affirmative answer brought an invitation to sit down. She became an adornment of the group around the Leader.

"Next to my wife, Miss Mitford is the most beautiful Nordic woman I have ever seen," said Hermann Goering. (His wife, the former actress Emmy Sonnemann, was physically so much the embodiment of Miss Germania that the Polish princess Virginia Sapieha, meeting her at a German Embassy dinner in Warsaw, professed herself "surprised, when she started to speak, that she did not utter the Walkyries' battle-cry.")

*And sister of the renowned writers Jessica and Nancy Mitford.

Within a short time Lord Redesdale's daughter, mistakenly called Lady Mitford by the Germans when she was in fact the Hon. Unity Mitford, was being described by the newspapers of the world as the future Frau Hitler. Her devotion to Nazism was unlimited.

"Ordinary people in England have no idea of the Jewish danger," she wrote the editor of a German publication. "It is to be hoped that in England too we shall be victorious over the world enemy, in spite of his cunning. With German greetings, *Heil Hitler!* Unity Mitford. P.S. If you should happen to find room in your paper for my letter, please print my name in full. I do not want my letter initialed U.M. for everyone should know that I am a Jew-hater."

"Bobo" to her friends and family during her childhood, lonely, big, strong, good-looking, perhaps not too smart and therefore very much in the shadow of her brilliant sisters, she found a sheltering home in Nazism, as did millions of German women. When the British newspapers, delicately speculating upon the nature of her physical relationship with the Leader,* reported that she flew a swastika from her British-licensed car, she began to receive hate mail. She told Hitler she feared for her life, and he gave her a 6.35 Walther pistol she carried everywhere. She became, in the words of the London *Daily Express* Munich correspondent, "the most dangerous woman in Munich." More than one German owed her his life, wrote Ernest Pope, "his life in Dachau Concentration Camp." Her victims were Germans who criticized the Leader to Englishmen and were overheard.

Adolf Hitler, she said, was destined to be the Emperor of Europe. She herself was described as the honorary princess of the annual Nuremberg Nazi Party celebrations. Wearing her golden swastika badge, the only one issued to a non-German, its obverse inscribed with the initials A.H. in the writer's hand, she stood on the platform with other notables and reviewed an assemblage that had grown from a handful at the first Party conference in 1927 to a days-long gathering of hundreds of thousands. Each year's session had a theme. In 1936 it was the menace from Russia and its Communism. "Bolshevism must be annihilated," Propaganda Minister Joseph Goebbels told the massed members of the Party, the Hitler Youth, the League of German Girls, the army formations. The Party philospher Alfred

*Probably none.

Rosenberg said Russia was controlled by Jewish interests trying to awaken "the underworld in all nations to march against European culture and the holy traditions of all peoples."

Hitler himself dreamt aloud in his speech of what he could do if "I had the Ural Mountains . . . Siberia . . . the Ukraine." Communism to him was "this destructive Asiatic *Weltanschauung*** striking at all values. I will not have this gruesome Communist international dictatorship of hate descend upon the German people." He signed an agreement with Japan against the plague and pestilential disease of the Communist International: the Anti-Comintern Accord. Italy soon became the third partner.

•

A month after the rally Joachim von Ribbentrop went to London to take up his post as ambassador to the Court of St. James's. Most of those around Hitler had never graduated from high school and few of them had any knowledge at all of foreign countries. To them, noted Hitler's architectural adviser Albert Speer, anyone who went to Italy on a two-week vacation qualified as an international expert. The new ambassador stood alone in his backround in foreign affairs. Born Joachim Ribbentrop, he came from five generations of army officers. As a teenager he dropped out of school and went to Canada, where he knocked around working in bridge construction and as a bank clerk and cub newspaper reporter before returning to Germany when the War came. He reached the rank of first lieutenant and then with the Armistice went into selling wines and liquors.

Good-looking, a performer in amateur theatricals, a fine skater, card player, violin and tennis player, he attracted the attention of the daughter of the eminent sparkling-wine producer Otto Henkell. Married to her, rich from her money and what he made from his purchases and sales of spirits in several countries, he had himself for a financial consideration adopted by an aunt who had his name, but prefixed by the "von" symbolic of nobility, or at least of a family once identified with the ownership of land. He was past thirty at the time. With his new "von," which remained an important social asset in the Germany of the thirties, he moved easily in Berlin society. Just before the Nazi accession to power he joined the Party and made his expansive home available to Hitler for important meetings. Thereafter he functioned

* Worldview.

as a foreign policy adviser on the basis of speaking French as well as English, and because he had been to Paris and London many times.

Ribbentrop was not a pleasant man. His language to subordinates was filled with excited shouts that they were oxen, dunderheads, idiots, idlers, halfwits. He was quite different when dealing with the Leader and in fact, said General Carl Heinrich von Stulpnagel, "His idea of foreign policy is this: Hitler gives him a drum and tells him to bang it, so he bangs the drum loud and strong. After a while Hitler takes the drum away and hands him a trumpet; and he blows that trumpet until he's told to stop and play a flute instead. Just why he's been banging and trumpeting and fluting, he never knows and never finds out."

His debut in London was not an auspicious one. Received by King Edward, the new ambassador flung up his hand and shouted, *"Heil Hitler!"* The newspapers reported that his fingers quivered inches from the end of the king's nose, and a member of Parliament suggested in the House of Commons that His Majesty's ambassador at Berlin be instructed to bawl out "Rule Britannia!" when next he was received by the Leader. The new German ambassador never recovered from the gaffe. When he found himself at a dinner seated next to Margot Asquith, daughter of the former prime minister H. H. Asquith, she said to him in the frank fashion that characterized her, "You are the very worst ambassador that Germany has ever sent to this country."

"Do you really think so?"

"Yes. You have absolutely no sense of humor, or you would not have given the Nazi salute when you were presented to the king."

Ribbentrop passed over the question of how properly to greet royalty and concentrated on the charge that he was not facetious. "You are quite wrong. I have a great sense of humor," he said, adding in an improbable aftermath, "You should see me and the Führer rolling on the floor together at Berchtesgaden and roaring with laughter after one has made a joke."

He was not tactful. "Even here one cannot escape this Jewish music," he said after hearing a Mendelssohn piece performed in London. Nor did he seem intelligent. The Czech diplomat Jan Masaryk told a Spanish Embassy party that he had "seen many foolish things and listened to many misplaced speeches," but that never had he heard "anything so inept, so arrogant or so senseless" as a talk he had heard Ribbentrop deliver on the dangers of Bolshevism. It was the ambassador's favorite subject. "The activities of the Communist Party in various parts of the world seem to obsess him to the exclusion of all other considerations," wrote the British foreign secretary, Anthony Eden.

When Ribbentrop "anxiously" asked about the situation in England, Eden replied there were virtually no Communists in the country save for those created by the would-be British Führer, Sir Oswald Mosley. Married to Unity Mitford's sister Diana, a hereditary baronet, rich, charming, dynamic, Mosley had been considered a rising young man in the 1920s. Then he commenced his flirtation with radical concepts, which finally found him head of the British Union of Fascists rigged out in Nazi-like uniform and holding provocative meetings in Jewish districts. His following was always minuscule and he was regarded as a police, not a political, problem.

Ribbentrop did not understand why Eden said Mosley's outlandish behavior was the only thing that could make Communists of Englishmen. The concept seemed to leave him baffled. Eden tried to explain and found it fruitless to make clear to this ambassador something of the political views of the people on whom he was supposed to report to Berlin.

Prime Minister Chamberlain, from the first time he met the tenant of his Eaton Square home, considered him a hopeless fool and hardly saw him as a reliable conduit to Hitler. Nor could he be considered a good source for insight into Hitler's thinking, the content of which was far from clear to the British leader. Few Englishmen had ever spoken to the Führer, and Lloyd George could not be consulted because of a long-standing enmity between himself and Chamberlain. Eden, it was true, had spent some time with Hitler when passing through Berlin in 1935. They had discovered that in July 1916 Captain Eden had been opposite Lance Corporal Hitler across a few hundred yards of French no-man's-land.* Hitler traced their positions on a menu card. Eden got the impression of a man with a consuming hatred of Communism.

The former king of England now titled the Duke of Windsor had soon after his abdication and marriage toured Germany and

---

*When Eden told Churchill he had faced Hitler over the firing line, Churchill groaningly inquired why in God's name Eden hadn't "shot the bastard."

been received at Berchtesgaden, but it was unlikely that any observations of his would be of value to Chamberlain. He was pathetically happy that at dinner parties the German place cards identified his wife as Her Royal Highness, which would never happen in England. Thus he saw all of Germany through rose-colored glasses. Twice at least he gave the raised-hand salute and its accompanying *"Heil Hitler!"* In any event, he had exiled himself from England because of his family's refusal to give his wife the prized HRH and so was not available for consultation.

It was therefore a welcome event when in late 1937 the lord president of the Council, Viscount Halifax, late viceroy of India, received an invitation to the International Hunting Exhibition in Berlin. It came from Hermann Goering, the famed sucessor of the Red Baron, Baron von Richthofen, as head of a flying group when Richthofen was shot down. Goering had been an early adornment of the Nazi Party and upon its accession to power and with German rearmament became chief of the country's air force. He held numerous other positions, including chief huntsman and game warden of the Reich, and it was in that capacity that he extended his invitation to Lord Halifax, a great hunter and the master of the Middletown Hounds, despite the handicap of being born with only one hand.

With Chamberlain's consent and indeed at his urging Halifax went off to Germany to be entertained by Goering at his country home, Karinhall, a magnified and glorified modern re-creation of an ancient Teutonic log hut. He impressed Lord Halifax as a combination of great schoolboy, modern Robin Hood, film star, gangster, landowner, Party stalwart and head gamekeeper.

There followed an invitation for the English visitor to call upon the Leader at his Bavarian hideaway, "Berchtergarten, or whatever the place is," Halifax wrote Eden. On a snowy November day he drove up the mountain road to the Leader's home accompanied by the German foreign minister, Baron von Neurath, and Sir Ivone Kirkpatrick of the British Embassy, who would act as interpreter. Their car halted before the house. Immensely tall, Halifax looked through the bottom half of the automobile window accessible to his eyes and beheld a pair of black patent-leather shoes of the type worn in the evening in London, and a pair of black-trousered legs. He took the wearer to be a footman, and getting out of the car prepared to pass him by, perhaps handing him his hat to hold, when the hoarse whisper of Foreign Minister von Neurath stopped him short: *"Der Führer, der Führer!"*

Recovering, he made his salutations and they went into the house where Hitler showed him around. They settled down at an inconveniently low table and through Sir Ivone Kirkpatrick's translations began their conversation. Something was said about the recent weather. "The weather," Hitler said. "The weather prophets are idiots. When they say it's going to be fine, it always rains and when they foretell bad weather, it's fine."

The subject of the recent hunting exhibition in Berlin came up. "I can't see what there is to shooting," Hitler said. "You go out with a highly perfected modern weapon and without risk to yourself kill a defenseless animal. Of course Goering tells me that the pleasure lies not in the killing, but the comradely expedition in the open air. Very well. I merely reply: if that's the case let's spare ourselves all bother and make a comradely expedition to a slaughterhouse where in the greatest comradeship we can together kill a cow." He sat back with an angry gesture.

Laboriously dragging up a new subject to discuss, Kirkpatrick offered something about airplane travel. "Only a fool will fly if he can go by train or road," Hitler responded. His attitude, Kirkpatrick thought, was that of a spoiled and sulky child. Halifax appeared bewildered. Mention was made of his viceroyship of India. "Shoot Gandhi," Hitler suggested. If that did not calm down the situation, shoot a dozen leading members of the Mahatma's Congress Party. If that was not sufficient, shoot two hundred more, and so on "until order is established." Lord Halifax would be surprised how easily the natives would then fall into line.

The British nobleman, Kirkpatrick saw, was completely at sea. He was an English country gentleman, a public school man, a High Church aristocrat. He had spent his life surrounded by those of similar background and his contacts with persons of a different class were confined to discussions with workers on his estates. His entire upbringing in the secure Victorian and Edwardian England of his years of development worked against the idea, the very conception, that such a person as Adolf Hitler could exist, schooled in the slums and soup kitchens and warming halls of Vienna and fueled by the tense and disordered and neurotic world of Weimar Germany, and still less that such as he could rule a great Power. Halifax turned to the purpose that had brought him to Berchtesgaden: his desire simply to discuss matters and see how relations between Germany and England could be brought into harmony.

His host began to denounce the critical view the British press took of him and to say obstacles were repeatedly being put in his way by the Western Powers. "Political ambitions which I have never entertained are attributed to me!" he shouted. Foreign Minister von Neurath looked ill at ease. They went about in circles, Halifax saying there was always room for amicable solutions, Hitler declaiming that Germany was the victim of the world's ill will, two men speaking different languages in every sense, two men from different worlds.

The Britons left, Lord Halifax thinking that they had not understood each other at all, that Hitler was bewildering, but if savage and uncouth also sincere, a German who sought the best for his country. They would have to live with him, the English and French and the rest of the world, he reported to Neville Chamberlain.

That view accorded with the prime minister's own concepts. "If we could sit down with the Germans at a table, and pencil in hand go through all their complaints and other claims, this would greatly clear up relations," he said to the Soviet ambassador to the Court of St. James's, Ivan Maisky. To the Russian, Neville Chamberlain was the embodiment of the class enemy, a representative of that capitalism whose aim, although sometimes concealed by bourgeois good manners, was ultimately the destruction of Communism and the Workers' and Peasants' State. Chamberlain was to Maisky a man whose political horizon did not rise above that of "a provincial manufacturer of iron bedsteads," yet he was at the same time sinister and reactionary and a willing instrument of dying historical ideologies ready for the ash bin.

"So the whole problem was one of sitting down at a table, pencil in hand!" Maisky thought to himself. "How simple!" He saw Viscount Halifax as representative of the same view and similarly deceptive, a slow-moving man speaking in a low, calm voice, always with a pleasant smile, but fatally limited by his class outlook. Maisky wondered exactly what Halifax had discussed with Hitler at Berchtesgaden and decided the visit had been made for the English peer to tell the German dictator that the door to Russia was open to him, that he had the blessings of the British ruling class to be their agent in the destruction of Communism. To the Russian that ruling class was, as another observer said, "the well-connected and the well-endowed, Eton and New College, Downside and Balliol, White's and Brooks', grandpa's country houses, mama's brewery shares"; it was the luxury, the golfing and bathing and eating and drinking of the Cliveden Set, that group that gathered at the palatial country estate of Lord Astor and his American-born wife, Lady Nancy. Hating the Soviets, hating progress, evil and degraded and degenerate, Maisky reflected, it would be natural for all they represented to espouse any policy that did looked to unleash Adolf Hitler upon the East.

SEVEN

I N 1933 when Hitler came to power the Germany army had forty-two generals and in the street one passed people wearing the little bronze broken-rifle pin, which represented membership in the Never Again War movement. Five years later there were more than four hundred generals and the pins were gone.

Few of the generals were Nazis. Many were titled, fifty out of the 187 officers on the General Staff. Traditionally from the upper classes, heirs of the old aristocratic military hierarchy of the Prussian king and the German emperor, booted and besworded and bespurred, a group that had always held itself aloof from politics and the government of the day, a state within a state, the officer corps might appreciate Nazi largesse, but Nazism's chief was to the generals what old Field Marshal von Hindenburg had termed him: "a Bohemian corporal." Hitler might employ his remarkable memory to good effect when quoting pertinent passages from Clausewitz, von Moltke and von Schlieffen, but after five years of National Socialism he remained socially outré to the monocled "vons" in uniform. The armed forces remained the only important faction of Germany that had not been completely integrated into the National Socialist State.

In December 1937, a month after Lord Halifax went home from his Berchtesgaden visit, the great War leader Erich Ludendorff died. His funeral oration was delivered by Field Marshal Werner von Blomberg, minister of war and commander in chief of the armed forces. He was a pleasant man a distance removed from the traditionally harsh Prussian soldier, an idealist almost

73

boyishly enthusiastic about the knight-errantry of the soldier's profession and the appeal of gentlemanliness in war.

When the services were over von Blomberg asked the Leader if they might speak for a moment. A widower for five years, the field marshal had recently met a woman he wished to make his second wife. But she was not, he told Hitler, from the stratum that might have been expected to furnish a prospect for the position of First Lady of the German army. She was his young secretary, a Fräulein Erna Gruhn.

Social differences in the New Germany, Hitler said, did not have the importance of days past. He offered his blessing. In January 1938 the wedding took place, Hitler and Hermann Goering serving as the two principal witnesses. The bridal pair went off to Italy for a honeymoon.

They were still away when a member of the Berlin police vice squad looking through a stack of confiscated pornographic pictures came on one that showed a woman naked save for a string of pearls. The picture was shown to a superior who looked, turned pale, sat down and gasped, "Good God, and the Führer kissed that woman's hand!"

"One cannot tolerate the highest-ranking soldier marrying a whore," said the chief of the general staff, Ludwig Beck. It was suggested to von Blomberg that he shoot himself to wipe out the disgrace. He declined to do so, but submitted his resignation and went into retirement to live quite happily with the bride who had been a registered prostitute in several German cities plus a dealer in the traditional dirty postcards.

The obvious candidate to succeed to the posts of war minister and commander in chief was Colonel-General Freiherr Werner von Fritsch, the operating head of the army. He was an ice-cold, formal, conservative soldier's soldier who had no time for the rougher elements of the National Socialist German Workers' Party and was capable of publicly offering harshly sarcastic appraisals of their type and ways. He had the distaste for labor unions, Catholicism and the Jews of a nobleman member of the Prussian officers' caste. At the same time he believed that the German army was the custodian of honor, decency, rectitude, tradition. He would certainly stand against any Party domination of the army.

Von Fritsch was a lifelong bachelor. So were many Nazis, including Adolf Hitler. But no other bachelor had leagued against him the forces of the Gestapo's Heinrich Himmler in association with Hermann Goering. Hitler was presented with a completely false file that purported to show that Colonel-General von Fritsch was a homosexual who for years had been paying blackmail money to an ex-convict who knew his secret. The charge was absolutely what von Fritsch termed it: "A lot of stinking lies!" Brought up in a world where a reserve lieutenancy meant as much socially as a councilorship of state, he was taken before the Leader to be confronted with a sleazy denizen of the Berlin underworld, a convicted thief and embezzler, who said that he had caught the colonel-general participating in a homosexual act with one "Bavarian Joe"—no other identification offered—in a dark alley near the Potsdam railroad station. Von Fritsch refused to dignify the statement with a rebuttal.

To Adolf Hitler, a personage whose very being was talk, the silence was an admission of guilt. Saying he had lost confidence in the generals, he made himself the replacement of the fallen von Blomberg. War minister and commander in chief of all branches of the armed forces, he had reduced the German military of traditional independence to a functionary of the ruling Nazi Party. As its new head he relieved sixteen high officers known to be critical of Nazism of their commands and transferred forty-four others to less than desirable posts.

Von Fritsch demanded and got a military court of honor to hear his case. It commenced sitting on March 30, 1938. Before the day was over its hearings were hastily suspended. Its members had more important things to do elsewhere.

•

The first paragraph of *My Struggle*, the book Hitler had written in prison after his failed coup of 1923, said that one day Germany must unite with Austria. "Common blood belongs in a common Reich." He had believed that even as a boy growing up in an Austro-Hungarian Empire controlled by German-speaking men but contaminated in his view by Magyars, Czechs, Slovaks, Romanians, Jews and Italians. With the end of the War, Austria had been severed from her great holdings to become a tiny body with a giant head, the city of Vienna. The country was left with no way to exist and sank into a lost existence of poverty and mourning for the great past, the Empire, the music and art, the tinkling waltzes, the Good Old Days. No one could visit Vienna and see gigantic railroad stations serving as the terminuses of short suburban runs, or the government buildings rivaling those of London made almost pointless, and not believe that history had been unkind to Austria. Affiliation with Germany, *Anschluss,* seemed the only answer for a pathetic and bewildered country made almost the ward of the League of Nations because it was helpless when left to its own limited resources.

But the Powers who had won the War forbade *Anschluss.* It was Austria that had after all made the War, it was from Vienna that the Note to Serbia went out after the assassination of the Archduke Francis Ferdinand. Austria must pay. In addition it would be unwise to permit Germany to enlarge itself even to the limited extent that amalgamation with Austria would offer. And so, bleak and worn and hopeless, once-glittering Vienna and its tiny hinterlands made their way through the twenties and early thirties as best they could.

In 1934, with Nazi connivance, Chancellor Dollfuss was assassinated. Hitler was poised to go in and take over the country. But Benito Mussolini moved four Italian divisions to his border with Austria and kept them there. No German invasion took place.

Yet the souls of many in both Germany and Austria cried out to one another. Was it not logical, people asked, that they merge? Among those who asked, none did so more fervently or with more affirmative an answer than Adolf Hitler. Vienna was the great prize of his youth that he had so signally failed to win. There he had all but starved, there he had been paid pennies for shoveling snow in front of a hotel to make a dry passage for the Archduke Charles, who became the last emperor of Austria and king of Hungary. By his will Nazi sympathizers across the border were given arms and money. They blew up buildings, cut communications, rioted in the streets. In February 1938, Hitler asked the dead Dollfuss's successor, Kurt von Schuschnigg, to come to Berchtesgaden and discuss "points of friction" between the two countries.

The son of a general of the old Empire, a good Catholic, mannered and intelligent, von Schuschnigg arrived and, shown into the Leader's second-floor study, three thousand feet above sea level with views of the mountains, remarked that it offered a beautiful vista. And what delightful weather they had been having lately.

"We did not gather here to speak of the fine view or of the

weather," the Leader said. He began to denounce Austria. He was tired of Austria's attitude toward Germany. Throughout history it was one uninterrupted act of baseness and treachery. It must reach an end.

But he could not agree, Schuschnigg said, that Austria's activities showed no positive contributions.

"Absolutely zero," Hitler said. "I am telling you, absolutely zero."

Von Schuschnigg tried to speak of Austrian cultural contributions, of how Beethoven selected Austria as his residence, but the Leader cut him off. "That's as may be," he said, "but I am telling you once more that things cannot go on in this way. I have a historical mission and this mission I will fulfill because Providence has destined me to do so. Who is not with me will be crushed."

But exactly what did he want, Schuschnigg asked? Whatever was desired would meet with Austria's cooperation. "We will do everything to remove obstacles to a better understanding."

"That is what you say," Hitler said. He raised his voice and said that Austria had fortified her border with Germany. That was not friendly. He did not like that. "Listen, you don't really think you can move a single stone in Austria without my hearing about it the next day, do you? I have only to give an order and in one single night all your ridiculous defense mechanisms will be blown to bits. You don't seriously believe that you can stop me for half an hour, do you?"

Austria was isolated, he continued. Herr Schuschnigg had better understand that. He was alone. Italy would do nothing: "I see eye to eye with Mussolini." England? "England will not move one finger for Austria." As for France, she could have stopped Germany with ease at the time of the move into the Rhineland. "Now it is too late for France."

To the business at hand. "I will give you once more, and for the last time, the opportunity to come to terms, Herr Schuschnigg. Think it over, Herr Schuschnigg, think it over well. I can only wait until this afternoon."

But what, exactly, did he want?

"We can discuss it this afternoon."

They went to lunch. The menacing air vanished and at the table the Leader talked about how he would build the greatest skyscrapers in the world. "The Americans will see that Germany

is building bigger and better buildings than the United States."
Architectural plans had always been a preoccupation of his since
taking power: a new Berlin railroad station with a basin of water
larger than twenty football fields in front of it, a new air force
building with the largest staircase in history and acres of forest
and gardens on its roof, a Great Hall in Berlin into which the
United States Capitol would fit with room to spare and with seating for 400,000 persons, a new chancellor's palace one hundred
and fifty times larger than the one that served Bismarck.

After the meal Hitler left the Austrian chief. A chain-smoker,
Schuschnigg had not been allowed to smoke in the Leader's
presence; now he quickly got out his cigarettes. For two hours
he cooled his heels, sitting with a single aide. Then he was handed
a list of what the Leader wanted from Austria: a Nazi war minister, a Nazi finance minister, a Nazi minister of the interior with
full control over the police, forgiveness for all Nazis imprisoned
after Chancellor Dollfuss's murder, close cooperation between the
German and Austrian armies, and economic assimilation of the
latter by the former. He must sign at once.

But it would mean the end of his country's independence,
Schuschnigg protested. He was taken in to see Hitler again.

"There is nothing to be discussed," the Leader said. "I will
not change a single iota. You will either sign it as it is and fulfill
my demands within three days, or I will order my army to march
into Austria."

The ruination of his country hanging in the balance, Schuschnigg said he could not guarantee compliance with such
demands.

"You have to guarantee it!" the Leader shouted.

"I could not possibly," Schuschnigg got out.

Hitler appeared to lose all control and all restraint. He rushed
across the room, flung open the door, and at the top of his lungs
shouted, "General Keitel!" His principal military aide came running up.

Hitler swung around to face Schuschnigg. "I shall have you
called later!"

Schuschnigg sat alone with his aide, who whispered that it
would not surprise him if they were both locked up in a cell
within the next five minutes. After a while they were taken in to
see Hitler again. Schuschnigg signed Austria's death warrant. He
went back to Vienna and did what he had been ordered to do.

Freed from all restrictions and smiled upon by a police force now under Nazi control, mobs ripped down the country's flag and ran up the swastika in its place.

Panic seized Austria. No one was safe. Heads got broken, things stolen. Suddenly SS uniforms adorned with skeleton heads appeared on one's neighbors. There was a rush to get across the borders into Czechoslovakia or Hungary. Schuschnigg's authority and his government were crumbling. He stiffened and decided to make a last attempt to save Austria from Germany and Germany's Leader. He announced a plebiscite, an election in which all voters would be asked to vote yes or no on whether they wished their country to remain independent. The announcement of the forthcoming plebiscite, set for March 13, was made on the day that the military court sitting in judgment of Colonel-General von Fritsch commenced its deliberations.

Schuschnigg's announcement threw the Leader into a frenzy. He could not dream of risking a yes majority, still less endure Schuschnigg's defiance, or what Hitler regarded as defiance. He ordered a march on Austria for the twelfth. The court of honor broke up as its members rushed to join their units. On the eleventh, at five-thirty in the morning, Schuschnigg was awakened to be told that the Germans had closed the border. All rail and road traffic had been halted. German troops were reported forming on their side of the frontier.

Schuschnigg got up and headed for his office, pausing only to stop at St. Stephen's Cathedral, the greatest church in Austria. Kneeling, he prayed for a moment and then crossed himself and went out. At his office he learned that the police could no longer be relied upon to support him in any way. Even his army was a question mark. Very well. He would call off the plebiscite. Anything to prevent a German invasion. Word of the cancellation was sent to Berlin.

It was no longer enough. Hitler replied that Schuschnigg must resign the chancellorship in favor of Austrian Party Comrade Arthur Seyss-Inquart. A telegram from Berlin went out to Seyss-Inquart. As soon as he took over he must request the immediate dispatch of German troops to put down disorders in Austria.

Schuschnigg complied with Hitler's orders. Outside his office mobs were running through Vienna's streets: *Sieg Heil! Sieg Heil! Heil Hitler! Hitler!*

Schuschnigg went on the radio to say he was yielding to force:

"We are not prepared even in this terrible hour to shed blood."

Standing five paces from the spot where Dollfuss had been shot, he ended his talk: "God save Austria!" The next day the German army poured over the frontier.

With them came the Leader. He crossed the border on one of the exact spots where long ago his father had served as a customs official. Almost with his entry Seyss-Inquart's government voted to dissolve itself in favor of becoming a province of Germany. In a moment the Austria of great history became a German administrative subdivision. Heir to the Imperial Hohenzollerns of Germany, heir now to the Imperial Hapsburgs of Austria, Hitler went to the Vienna he had left twenty-five years earlier as a penniless vagabond and stood where the emperor had stood. Parades and flags greeted him, that and the knowledge that the SS was whipping thousands of Jews to their new work of cleaning public latrines and German army barracks. Former chancellor Kurt von Schuschnigg was carted away and put to cleaning SS toilets with a towel that he was then forced to use on his face.

France was in one of her perennial political crises and for the moment without a government as Austria and its seven million subjects and its army and strategical position became a part of Germany. There was nothing France could do. Mobilize? Fight? To liberate a people who had greeted their blood brothers with cheering and tears of joy in what the Germans called the Battle of Flowers, the Flower March?

To the English the reports from Vienna were stomach-turning. The political and literary figure Sir Harold Nicolson met an Austrian who told him of how the Nazis rounded up people in the Prater, the city park, separated the Jews, made them strip off their clothing and forced them to walk on all fours in the grass. Old Jewish ladies were forced to get up in trees and chirp like birds. It made Nicolson ill.

But what was England to do about it? "The hard fact is," Prime Minister Chamberlain said, "that nothing could have arrested what has happened—unless this country and other countries had been prepared to use force."

Use force? As long ago as 1932, six years earlier, Stanley Baldwin had told England what another war meant: "No power on earth can protect the man in the street from being bombed.

Whatever people may tell him, the bomber will always get through. The only defense is in offense, which means that you have to kill more women and children more quickly than the enemy if you want to save yourself." In the summer of 1936 a group of members of Parliament brought in a Royal Air Force officer who told them what he would do to London if he were the head of the German air force and a war broke out: He would conduct raids at hourly intervals. His first planes would carry incendiary bombs, his second wave an hour later would spray the city with poison gas and his third would drop high explosives. Then he would pour on more incendiaries and more gas. At the same time he would mount minor raids against other cities to disperse British air defenders. ("This picture did not promote cheerfulness," observed the Labor MP Hugh Dalton.)

On March 16, 1938, four days after Hitler crossed the border and went to Linz and his reunion with August Kubizek, Winston Churchill said to a group of friends that England stood to lose everything by not taking a strong stand on Austria, but that if England did so, "London will be a shambles in half an hour."

Harold Nicolson wrote in his diary, "If we provoke Germany now when our defenses are in a pitiable state she will or may destroy us utterly. And if we do not oppose her she will become so strong that we cannot face it." It came to him that perhaps England was on its way to being less than a Holland, for the Dutch at least had an empire while England soon might not. If England were to feed the German alligator with fish from other ponds, Nicolson asked himself, would the day come when Germany would demand fish from British ponds and be found too powerful to be denied?

Such thoughts and the prospect of such a destiny could not escape the thinking of Prime Minister Chamberlain. Armed conflict to him was an abomination. "War wins nothing, cures nothing, ends nothing," he said. "In war there are no winners but all are losers." He had realized that with the rise of Mussolini in Italy and Hitler in Germany he must rearm England, but the idea appalled him, the waste, the unproductive squandering of resources.

Always so emotionless in public, dry, cold, a man so obviously of logical and reasonable solutions, Chamberlain could not prevent his voice from deepening whenever he spoke of war. Be-

yond material expenditures he was possessed by the memory of
his cousin Norman, dead with the other one million Normans
that 1914–18 had cost the Empire.

War was unthinkable, madness. "We pass no judgment here
upon the political systems of other countries," he said. "And yet,
do not forget that we all are members of the human race, and
subject to like passions and affections, and fears and desires. There
must be something in common between us if only we can find
it."

Chamberlain had spent his life in building enterprises, in developing things. "An ancient historian once wrote of the Greeks,"
he said, "that they had made gentle the life of the world. I can
imagine no nobler ambition for an English statesman than to win
the same tribute for his own country."

As chancellor of the exchequer under Stanley Baldwin,
Chamberlain's closest friend in the Cabinet had been Foreign
Secretary Anthony Eden. A gap opened between them when
Chamberlain ascended to the prime ministership. Eden knew no
less of the War than Chamberlain—more. He had fought through
the four years at the Front, had lost two brothers and a brother-
in-law. The world he knew, he said, had been destroyed. He had
derived from his losses the belief that any threat must be opposed not with understanding arrangements, but with a counter-
threat. He had for a long time placed his hope in the League of
Nations.

But time had forced him to conclude that a happy destiny
for England and the world was not to be found in the forlorn
halls of the palace along the shores of Lake Geneva. The League
had done nothing when Mussolini went into Ethiopia and nothing when Hitler went into Austria.

Eden began to think in terms of alliances. Not everybody
agreed with his view. Alliances had brought the great catastrophe of 1914, engagements and agreements to help that resulted
in the presenting of checks once blank but later filled in for pay-
ment. In a Cabinet meeting Eden could not help reading a note
atop a pile of papers written by Coordinator of Defense Sir
Thomas Inskip: *"Eden's policy to line up the U.S.A., Great Britain
and France, result war."* Inskip sat directly on Eden's left. He turned
to him. "I swear to you, Tom, that if we can really get this lineup
there will be no question of war. You will then see how the

dictators behave themselves for the first time." Inskip shook his head sadly.

The prime minister could be more forceful with the foreign secretary, telling him to "go home and take an aspirin" when Eden excitedly said England must not "court" Hitler and Mussolini, must not "pursue" and run after them. Chamberlain was far too reasonable, Eden thought, too willing to see the other side, too willing to agree. When the two sat with Italy's ambassador, Count Dino Grandi, talking about Ethiopia, one statement of the Italian more outrageous than the last in Eden's view, Chamberlain appeared to nod his head so encouragingly that "in the end it would almost seem that we had invaded" the African nation.

The final break between prime minister and foreign secretary came in the midst of the Austrian crisis. A private message had been received at 10 Downing Street from President Roosevelt. He had it in mind, he wrote Chamberlain, to call for a conference in Washington. It would deal with disarmament, access to raw materials, adherence to the laws of warfare and possible territorial adjustments. Eden was away on vacation on the French Riviera. To Chamberlain the President's idea appeared to suggest an ill-prepared meeting that in days was supposed to solve all the problems that had never yet been solved in the twenty years since the War.

Chamberlain had never thought much of the Americans. It was always best to expect nothing but words from them, he said to intimates. It was their President Wilson who had been the great sponsor of the League of Nations, the Parliament of Man meant to inaugurate a new era of reason in the world. Wilson's own United States Senate had voted not to join, and since then the Americans had withdrawn entirely from European affairs and were fervently isolationist. The Senate in 1935 had passed neutrality laws with ironclad rules to keep the country out of any possible European war.

Now Roosevelt was thrusting himself forward. What was the point? To comply with his suggestion would be for Chamberlain to cut across the lines he was pursuing with Count Grandi aimed at exploiting the differences between Italy and Germany and separating Mussolini from Hitler. He did not call Eden back from France to discuss Roosevelt's letter but instead asked the permanent under secretary of state for foreign affairs, Sir Alexander Cadogan, to discuss it with Chamberlain's closest associate, Sir Horace Wilson.

Sir Horace Wilson had been the government's chief industrial adviser, a post calling for the ability to negotiate disputes between employers and trade unions. His professional life had been spent ironing out difficulties and making compromise arrangements. His approach to such matters was not unlike that of Neville Chamberlain, who, when he became prime minister, assigned Wilson an office next to the Cabinet Room overlooking Horse Guards Parade. The adviser talked with Cadogan and gave it as his opinion that the conference suggestion should be rejected. Word was sent to Washington.

Eden returned from France and found out what had happened from Cadogan. He rushed into Wilson's office. "You damn fool!" he burst out.

"I beg your pardon, Minister," Wilson returned. "Is something amiss?"

"Roosevelt's message! Don't you see how vital it was for us to accept?"

"Oh, that. Surely you wouldn't have taken that seriously, would you, Minister? Woolly nonsense, you know, just woolly nonsense."

Eden resigned. A telephone call to the out-of-office Churchill gave him the news. To him Eden stood for that British strength of character that yet was sufficient to face down the impulses rising across the Channel past France and on the Rhine and in Central Europe. Now Eden was gone. Churchill was renowned for his ability to sleep whenever he wished and never in his life had he trouble dropping off at night. That night he lay awake seeing terrible phantoms.

"I watched the daylight slowly creep in through the windows, and saw before me in mental gaze the vision of Death." Lord Halifax came in as foreign secretary.

•

That summer of 1938, the king and queen of England paid a state visit to France. They were overwhelmed by the reception they received. Waving and cheering crowds stood along the line of the railroad from Boulogne to Paris. In the streets of the capital when they arrived at a new station built for their coming they were greeted with tremendous display. For the first time in centuries France was completely free of suspicion of perfidious Albion. Throughout Paris the royal couple were met with rapturous cheers.

By 1938 King George had almostly completely cured himself of the stutter that had blighted his life. It had begun when as a child who was a natural left-hander he was forced to write with his right. It had made him a diffident man always willing to stand in the shadow of his elder brother. All through the years of Edward's Prince Charming period, the future king always "Bertie" to the family—had been in the background as Duke of York. Speechmaking was an ordeal and a terror for him. He was chiefly identified with his Duke of York's Camp, where each summer from 1919 onward four hundred boys, half from the preparatory schools of the rich, half from mines and factories, spent a week at play and games. He was at ease with the boys in his camp, singing special songs with them and leading them on hikes. He set up his camp as a response to the War, in which he had become the first royal prince of Great Britain in centuries actually to come under enemy fire and to see men of all classes fight and die together. As a midshipman on the battleship *Collingwood* he copied in his diary his father's telegram to Sir John Jellicoe on the outbreak of the War: "I send to you and through you to the officers and men of the fleets of which you have assumed command the assurance of my confidence that under your direction they will revive and renew the old glories of the Royal Navy, and prove once again the sure shield of Britain and her Empire in the hour of trial."

That night his father wrote in his diary, "Please God it may soon be over and that He will protect dear Bertie's life."

The midshipman was ill with a potentially life-threatening problem on the eve of the Battle of Jutland, the greatest sea engagement of the four years. The doctors wanted him put into a hospital. His father the king ruled that even if it cost his life he could not be ashore when the fleet sailed to meet the enemy. Prince Albert fought the battle through from one of *Collingwood*'s forward turrets and then had an operation.

His brother Edward's abdication seemed a disaster for him. He had never dreamed of being king, but with his wife and two little daughters, the Princesses Elizabeth and Margaret Rose, took up his duties. His modest ways and appealing family made him a sympathetic figure, but something else fueled the wild cheering the French gave him in July 1938. (Few failed to note that the last state visit a British monarch paid France was in 1914, just before the War came.) After a giant review the visitors repaired to Versailles for a concert. As they listened to the music, waves of planes of the French air force flew overhead, casting fleeting shadows on the sunlit walls and drowning out all else with their motors. It seemed to both the king and queen that those sights and sounds would remain rooted in their memories ever afterward.

Neither they nor Churchill with his broken sleep was the only person in Europe to feel the future pressing on him, that summer. Outside the heavily curtained windows of the former palace that housed the United States legation, chancery and minister's quarters in the Mala Strana quarter of Prague, the diplomat George Kennan sensed that "a Europe seething with fear and hatred and excitement danced its death dance all around us." It seemed to him that dancing about him were strange beings, "demonic powers that history had now unleashed."

But who and what were they who danced over Czechoslovakia and over all Europe? It was not simple. It went back to ancient racial hatreds originating in the Dark Ages, to tribal superstitions and feuds, to lands won and lost long before and then won and lost anew, to blood, to what one saw in oneself and in one's children, to prides and contempts, to what one believed right and pure, to death in battle—in the end to my people! My ways! My tradition! What I am!

In Czechoslovakia there existed, to be sure, the Czech and the Slovak, but also the Ruthenian, the Magyar, the Croat, the Pole, the Jew, the Slovene—and the German. The country was Austria-Hungary in miniature but created as a tribute to the Versailles Treaty concept that the War was fought for the self-determination of people, the right to live undominated by those of what Europe had called for a millennium not another nationality or ethnic group, but another race.

Kneeling on the floors of the French palaces where they had their headquarters in 1919 the victors of the War—Clemenceau, Wilson, Lloyd George, Orlando—had sketched on great maps the new Europe that would permit those of one blood to live free of the pressures of those of another. But it was not easy for them to arrange that accommodation, for inextricably intermixed were villages and regions inhabited by people of differing blood and filled with mutual distrust and often hatred.

The border of Czechoslovakia facing Germany was outlined by the peacemakers of 1919 along the Sudeten Mountains. The high ridges formed a natural physical division, a cutoff point. On one side was Czechoslovakia. On the other, Germany. But in Czechoslovakia's Sudetenland lived 3.5 million people who, although they had never been part of Germany, spoke German. They did not mix with and never had mixed with the Czechs. A German-blood girl did not marry a Czech boy. In the days of the Austro-Hungarian Empire the Sudetenlanders had identified with the German-speaking Viennese overlords. The Versailles Treaty suddenly made them a minority in the new Czechoslovakia, a land dominated by the Czechs. Along their ridges, now the property of a country ruled from Prague, the Czechs built fortifications as powerful as those of France's Maginot Line. The bunkers and casemates pointed toward Germany, the spiritual home of the people among whom they were placed.

For twenty years the German-speaking citizens of Czechoslovakia mulled over their fate. Then there arose the New Germany and that New Germany took over what was left of the Austria of old. Their brothers had gone home, said the Sudetenland Germans. They too began to think of a family reunion with that country of their language, their ways, their blood. The Fatherland was calling them, they said, with a voice centuries older than the new name of Czechoslovakia.

In Berlin the Leader looked eastward and saw protruding into his lands the elongated shape of Czechoslovakia. An artificial state set up by Versailles as a fortress to block Germany on its east. An aircraft carrier whose fields could hold Russian bombers. A Slavic state holding in thrall those Germans who were his brothers.

Adolf Hitler was essentially a stop-and-go personality, an artistic individual given to long periods of lazy inaction and endless discussions of the Bavarian King Ludwig III and the music of Wagner, the speculated-upon dreams of his Alsatian dogs, diet recipes, Greek temples and the speeds of cars. Behind the dreary monologues ideas took shape, faded away, came back. Coming back ever more strongly as the warm months of 1938 arrived was his concept of what he believed he owed to his compatriots, his brothers, in the Sudetenland. It was a characteristic of his that he could dream up possible atrocities or plots, horrors or threats. (*My Struggle* abounded with visions of crooked-nosed, kinky-haired Jews seducing Brunhilde-like German virgins.) In time he would believe that his dreamings were all true.

That there were brawls and disturbances between Czech- and German-speaking people in the Sudetenland was a fact of life; but in the spring of 1938 by the orders of Propaganda Minister Joseph Goebbels, who had listened to Hitler's dreams, the German newspapers became filled with accounts of Czech soldiery firing upon Sudetenlanders, crushing them with tanks, plundering their homes and laying down poison-gas barrages. Czech gangsters in the uniforms of the state police were behind everything, the papers said, they and the Czech leader Edvard Beneš.

Hitler read the enormously exaggerated descriptions of minor incidents, or of those existing only in Dr. Goebbels's mind, and forgot that they had originated in his own visions and that by his orders the separatist movement was financed from Berlin, that German money paid for the signs of BACK TO THE REICH in every Sudeten town. Like the Austrian Nazis, whose staged disturbances helped to drive von Schuschnigg from power, it seemed to him that the suffering Sudetenland Germans called out to him. He brooded over their plight and on the temerity of the Czech leader who so tormented them.

President Beneš saw to his thirty-four splendidly equipped divisions. Czechoslovakia was not the typically sleepy, dusty, bug-ridden, provincial backwater typical of the old Empire's holdings, but a modern industrial state that had been the power-house of Austria-Hungary. It was also the only democracy that had ever existed in the history of Central Europe. The people were behind their president. He had other additional cards to play. Russia's commissar for foreign affairs, Maxim Litvinov, had asserted several times that the Soviets would come to Czechoslovakia's aid if Germany attacked her, provided France did so first. And Paris had repeatedly said that France would honor her commitment given in 1925 to come to Czechoslovakia's aid against Germany if needed.

But would it ever come to that? And if it did, the French asked one another, was it really necessary to kill three million French soldiers in order to keep three million Germans under Czech domination? The equation did not add up. Perhaps it might have made sense to go to war over the German reoccupation of the Rhineland two years earlier. Now the Rhineland was at least partially fortified. Was France to assault it on behalf of an Austria or a Czechoslovakia? To make war for peoples who wished to join their brothers, who asked to go home in the name of the self-determination that the Versailles Treaty itself had said was the right of all peoples?

In late May, alarmed by reports of German troop concentrations on his frontiers, Edvard Beneš partially mobilized his army reserves. As a response to a threatened invasion it was a logical move. But there had been no threatened invasion, and Germany was able to prove it. Yet there lingered in the world's consciousness the impression that Beneš had forced Hitler to back down, that the mobilization trumped Hitler's card.

Hitler would never forgive Beneš for what the world thought he had done. He wanted the Sudetenlanders and there was logic to his desire: they were German. Now he saw the world think of him as a bluffer who had thought of an invasion and had been scared off. His prestige was now in question. He reasoned in his fury that Beneš had done that to him. Czechoslovakia *was* Beneš. "It is my unshakable will that Czechoslovakia shall be wiped off the map!" he shouted to a group of his officers and aides. "It is my unalterable decision to smash Czechoslovakia."

The Leader was the Leader to his military adviser General Wilhelm Keitel, commonly referred to as *Lakeitel*—lackey—behind his back. One did not argue with him. The operating head of the army, General Walther von Brauchitsch, it was said, listened to everything Hitler said, hitched up his collar a notch higher and told himself, "I am a soldier. It is my duty to obey." Ribbentrop, brought back from England to be foreign minister, was so much an echo of his master as to remind those who saw him of the hysterical woman afraid of her husband who took to her bed when he looked sideways at her. Goering, although believing and saying that Ribbentrop was a "criminal fool," nevertheless said that if the Leader ordered an attack on anyone, he, Goering, would fly the first plane against the enemy, if Ribbentrop sat next to him.

None of those close to Hitler would oppose him. It was not in them. Yet there were a few soldiers and diplomats of an older Germany who began asking themselves where the Leader was taking their country. One such was Franz Halder, the chief of staff. Colonel-General von Fritsch, found innocent of the charge of homosexual doings when his court of honor reconvened after the Austrian occupation, but given no duties, told his friends that Hitler was now Germany's destiny for good or evil. Halder wished to believe otherwise. In conjunction with the head of military intelligence, Admiral Wilhelm Canaris, Halder began with the greatest care to sound out others about the idea growing in both men's minds: to remove Adolf Hitler from power before he launched Germany into a new war. But Halder came from three hundred years of German officers. Rebellion did not come easily to him.

The summer of 1938 arrived. The German papers continued to fill their columns with stories of atrocities against German-speaking citizens of Czechoslovakia. A handful of policemen putting down a village demonstration became transformed by the German press into legions of monsters brutally suppressing men and women who only wished to express their beliefs and affiliations. Beneš declared martial law in certain areas and was described as a tyrant unleasing a terror comparable to that of Joseph Stalin.

It came to Neville Chamberlain that a frontier incident a thousand miles from Downing Street across the borders of half a dozen countries might bring about a conflict between Czechoslovakia and Germany, which would automatically bring into effect the French guarantee to Czechoslovakia, followed by the Russian commitment based on that given by the French. In an instant Central Europe would be engulfed in a fire that must reach to England and produce Chamberlain's ultimate nightmare: the million-man British Expeditionary Force to the Continent, which would pay again the price of its 1914–18 predecessor. Was he, he asked himself, destined to take the Empire into war for Czechoslovakia, to ask Australia and the West Indies and the Indian army to go into battle to prevent the absorption of the Sudeten Germans into the Reich?

The British ambassador to Berlin, Sir Nevile Henderson, saw the very concept of such a catastrophe as complete madness. Long before, as a boy at Eton, he had almost drowned. He was unconscious on the bottom of a backwater of the Thames when another student, diving down by happenstance, brought to the surface what he took to be a dead body. Henderson often asked himself why God had chosen to spare him. He had gone into the diplomatic service and then into the Foreign Office. He had served in posts in Russia and Tokyo and Paris and Belgrade and Constantinople and Buenos Aires, the model of a well-born and well-off British diplomat given to polo, balls, bridge, hunting, tennis, always immaculately turned out depending upon the occasion and always when in street clothing with a fresh red carnation in his buttonhole.

He had been in the Argentine when Stanley Baldwin's foreign secretary, Anthony Eden, had sent him a cable offering him Berlin. Eden had never met him but Prime Minister Baldwin had heard, so he told Eden, that Henderson was a good man and a good shot. And he had done well in Yugoslavia, getting close to the autocratic and dictatorial King Alexander. The two most recent ambassadors to Berlin had all too obviously detested Hitler and Nazism. The Leader in turn had described one as a "cretin" and the other as a hopeless drunkard. Perhaps Henderson would be more sympathetic to the German autocrat and dictator. Henderson took the post believing that the reason God had saved him from drowning was now made clear. He had "been specially selected by Providence with the definite mission of, as I trusted, helping to preserve the peace of the world."

He had always felt Germany was badly treated at Versailles and had many justifiable complaints. He also felt good fellowship among high officials was of the greatest importance in smoothing away difficulties between countries. So thinking, he put himself out to get on good terms with the leading men of the German government. When the British newspaperman Ewan Butler, who would later listen while the military attaché Colonel Mason-Macfarland discussed shooting Hitler, first met Henderson, the ambassador asked him if he came to Germany with an open mind. Butler replied that he would do his best to file impartial reports and to judge things on their merits.

"Good, good!" the ambassador said. "I can assure you that if you keep an open mind, you will find whatever prejudices you may have come here with will disappear. Hitler? A constructive genius, a constructive genius! People come here and tell me that Goering is a butcher. Absolute rubbish! I went shooting with him only last week." (His predecessor, Sir Eric Phipps, chatting about sports with Goering and learning that the latter had been out shooting the previous day, was capable of inquiring, "Animals, I presume?")

Believing that it was necessary to become "disagreeable to the

Czechs" in the interests of European peace, and that they were a pigheaded race and that Edvard Beneš was "not the least pigheaded among them," Sir Nevile Henderson filled his reports to London with suggestions that Prague be forced to be reasonable. Through informal and secret approaches Chamberlain had received word that there was a small opposition group in the German government and army, but he discounted the possibility that its members would take action against Hitler. It seemed far wiser to come to some sort of accommodation with the Leader.

Chamberlain sent Lord Runciman, an industrial leader, to mediate on the dispute between the Czechs and their German-speaking subjects in the Sudetenland, but in a short time Runciman found there was nothing for him to mediate. The Sudetenlanders had been told by Berlin to pile one demand on another and to keep demanding new concessions far and beyond any offered. In the second week of September the Nuremberg Party rally got under way with the Czech problem as its focus. "This miserable pygmy race is oppressing a cultured people," Goering told a rally assemblage. Hitler said that the Czechs would give justice to the Sudeten Germans or that their real Fatherland, the German Reich, would see to the matter. Riots and uprisings followed in the mountains along the border. The Czech government sent in troops. Things were getting very ugly.

Neville Chamberlain was an activist, a doer. He saw a world apparently tied to a satanic timetable, marching toward another Somme and another Passchendaele, another Verdun, and worse: cities in ruins, bacterial death and death from air-dropped gas bombs and perhaps the death of institutions and law and of the West's civilization and the West itself. He held no illusions regarding Adolf Hitler. "Is it not positively horrible to think that the fate of hundreds of millions depends upon one man, and he is half mad?" Chamberlain wrote his sisters on September 3. But an attempt to save the peace, to save the world, must be made.

He wrote Hitler on September 13, "In view of the increasingly critical situation, I propose to come over at once to see you with a view to trying to find a peaceable solution. I propose to come across by air and am ready to start tomorrow."

Two days later, in his Edwardian clothing and carrying a rolled umbrella, the prime minister stepped out of a plane at the Munich airport to the rolling of drums and the universal acclamation of humanity. The savior of Peace, the reincarnation of St. George fighting the dragon of another War, he had for the second time in his life gone up in an airplane and sat for seven hours in an unheated twin-motored British Airways Electra 191 bumping its way through the clouds to the most southeastern point of Germany, where at Berchtesgaden Hitler waited.

"Good man," President Roosevelt cabled in what he said was the shortest message he had ever sent anyone, and Prime Minister Eamon De Valera of Ireland said, "This is the greatest thing that has ever been done."

With the prime minister were his adviser Sir Horace Wilson; William Strang, a Foreign Office expert on European affairs; a Scotland Yard detective; and a civil service secretary. Sir Nevile Henderson came to Munich to meet them. They got on a special train and traveled three hours to the town of Berchtesgaden, where they spent twenty minutes freshening up at a hotel. Automobiles were waiting at the door. They headed up the mountain road to Hitler's residence, Chamberlain riding with Ribbentrop, and the other Britishers in another vehicle behind. The road was lined on both sides with black-uniformed and jackbooted SS troops slapping their hands on their rifles as they came to the salute. Sir Horace Wilson had spent his professional life conducting labor-management negotiations in surroundings very different. It came into his mind that perhaps they would never get out of this alive.

Hitler was waiting on the steps of his home. He looks like a tailor's assistant, Wilson thought to himself. The commonest little dog without one sign of distinction, Chamberlain thought. "You would never notice him in a crowd and would take him for the house painter he once was."*

They were introduced to Goering and General Keitel. All seated themselves around a large, circular table and tea was served, very weak and with too much milk in it. Outside, rain was coming down and mists rose from the valleys below.

"I have often heard of this room, but it is much larger than I expected," Chamberlain offered.

"It is you who have big rooms in England."

"You must come and see them sometime."

"I should be received with demonstrations of disapproval."

"Well, perhaps it would be wise to choose the moment."

*Hitler never was a house painter.

They spoke through Hitler's interpreter, Paul Schmidt. "This business of the Sudetenland isn't really our affair, you know," Chamberlain said. "We are only interested in it because of Great Britain's interest in the maintenance of peace."

It was a pacific statement. But Hitler swept by England and England's wishes and began to denounce the Czechs, his voice rising and falling. "Let me make it clear that I am determined to solve this problem one way or the other," he said harshly. "It can no longer be tolerated that a minor country like Czechoslovakia should treat the great two-thousand-year-old German Reich like an inferior!"

"Look here," Chamberlain said. "I am a practical man." Surely something could be worked out. Perhaps the German minority could be resettled in Germany itself. Something like that.

Hitler got up and began beating his right fist into his left hand. Germany was a land of heroes, he told Chamberlain. "She will take the hero's way. I tell you that the Czechs are inhuman horrors and cowards at heart. It surely cannot be wrong to go to the aid of our brothers when they are being treated with such brutality by these worthless people." Resettlement of the German minority would not do. The entire Sudetenland region, encompassing all of Czechoslovakia's defense line, must become part of Germany. That was all he had to say. Take it or leave it.

Chamberlain considered. Perhaps that was best, he said. He would go back to London and consult with his Cabinet and the French. To amputate part of another country, and that the sole democracy of Central European history, and simply give it away was, he reflected, a hard thing to do. But how to weigh that against a possible war that would kill millions? They had been together more than three hours. Chamberlain took his leave. They agreed to meet again in a few days and Hitler said, "Next time you come I will meet you halfway. I don't like a man so much older than myself to have the fatigue of such a long journey."

Chamberlain had seen a hardness and a ruthlessness in the face of the man opposite him, but the last remark showed, he thought, that there was another side to someone who in other respects acted like a gangster. It would be worth trying to cultivate the other side. He went to Berchtesgaden's Grand Hotel and to dinner and bed.

That night the Munich-based reporter for the London *Daily*

Express, Ernest Pope, looked through the glass doors of a private dining room in the hotel and saw, drinking champagne, Ambassador Sir Nevile Henderson with the inevitable red carnation in his buttonhole. He was surrounded by men from the German Foreign Office. Henderson was following his practice of actively socializing with the representatives of the government to which he was accredited, of being persona grata and well liked, a sympathetic individual open to good fellowship. He had always said that was more important than the writing of dispatches home. State Secretary Dr. Otto Meissner stood with him. The Englishman and the Germans were laughing as they drank.

A week previous at the Nuremberg rally the reporter Pope had seen Meissner kick an SS bodyguard down the steps of the Deutscher Hof Hotel because the man was slow in getting out of Meissner's way. As he looked at him with Henderson, the image of the cat with the mouse came into Pope's mind. If Meissner could be so brutal to one of his own men, what lay ahead for a member of the British Foreign Service—or the British prime minister—if *he* got in the way?

In the morning Chamberlain flew back to London and a series of Cabinet meetings. "The alternatives are not between abject surrender and war. Acceptance of the principle of self-determination is not an abject surrender," he told the Cabinet. He said Hitler had assured him that he had no designs upon any part of Czechoslovakia peopled by non-Germans. He only wanted the German-speaking citizens of the Sudetenland in his Reich, they and the lands they inhabited. Chamberlain felt it was the only thing to do. There was much about Hitler that was repellent, the prime minister said; he appeared to lack all morality and humanity and was in fact "an inhuman brute" of a type he had never met before. ("Uncouth and certainly not the kind of fellow one would like to go around the world with on a two-wheeled bicycle," he remarked to Lord Halifax.) Yet he appeared to the prime minister as someone who could be depended upon to keep his word once he had given it.

The leaders of the French Republic came over from Paris. They agreed that it was more than painful to pressure the Czechs into giving up the land holding their defensive fortifications. Some sort of protective guarantee would have to accompany the pressure. Its nature was hashed over. No communications were held with the Czechs. Meanwhile German headlines screamed that women and children were being mown down by Czech armored cars with machines: NEW CZECH MURDERS OF GERMANS.

Finally the Czechs were given the Anglo-French decision: the Sudetenland must go. Prague rejected the idea. It was a mutilation, they said, an abandonment. The French and British ministers to Prague were told to step up the pressure on Beneš. They did so, pitying him. He capitulated.

Chamberlain flew to a rondezvous on the Rhine to give Hitler the news. They met in a conference room of the Godesberg Hotel, and the British prime minister told the German Leader that everything was arranged. All that he asked for at Berchtesgaden one week previously was his.

There was a slight pause when Chamberlain finished speaking. "I am extremely sorry but that will no longer do," Hitler finally said. He pushed back his chair, folded his arms, crossed his legs and scowled.

Chamberlain was appalled. He had done what the Leader demanded, had pressured the Czechs into giving up their lands. What more was desired? In return Hitler began to shout of Czechoslovakian treachery. He must place his troops inside Czech territory immediately. There was no time to discuss exactly how much land Germany would take. He would not go into technicalities. But the troops must be in Czechoslovakia by the first day of October, a week in the future.

There were black circles under his eyes and his body jerked with a nervous twitch. The German army would take the Sudetenland, and all Czechs there of non-German descent must leave at once, taking nothing with them, not their furniture or the family cow, no machines, nothing. In addition the claims of Germany's ally Hungary, Czechoslovakia's neighbor on the south, had to be taken into consideration. It might be necessary for the Czechs to yield some land to the Hungarians.

Chamberlain retired to his rooms in a hotel across the Rhine. Messages flew back and forth between the prime minister and his Cabinet in London and between himself and Hitler across the river. With Nevile Henderson at his side Chamberlain paced along a wide balcony. The next day he met again with Hitler. He was presented with a statement that Germany could no longer wait until October 1. The Czechs must get out by September 26. The two men wrangled. Finally Hitler said he would go back to the October 1 deadline.

Chamberlain headed back toward London, feeling that the differences between Hitler's demands at Berchtesgaden and his demands at Godesberg were relatively minor. His plane flew above the Thames toward the British capital and, looking down, he imagined a German bomber pilot following the same course. "I asked myself what degree of protection we could afford to the thousands of homes which I saw stretched out below me."

He found his Cabinet had stiffened against Hitler and Germany. Hitler's completely uncompromising attitude, his tone, his manner, all were not acceptable to many of the men. There was a point beyond which they were unwilling to go in pressuring the hapless Czechs. Lord Halifax in particular had rethought the situation and come to feel that no more pressure should be put on the Czechs. The facts should be laid before them so that they might make their own decision. But that might mean fighting, and fighting would find Britain, thought Secretary of State for War Leslie Hore-Belisha, in the position of a man who took on a tiger before loading his rifle.

They had in the French. "Like a barbarian," Premier Edouard Daladier told the Britishers, "I have been ready to cut up this country without even consulting her and handing over three and a half million of her population to Hitler. That has not been an agreeable task for me. It has been hard, perhaps even a little dishonorable. But I have felt that this was better than to begin again what we saw twenty years ago. Now the situation changes. The Anglo-French proposals are bad enough, but where are we to stop? I cannot agree to the Godesberg demands."

The German deadline was a week away. The Czechs were asked if they would accept the new demands. They rejected them. They had their fortifications. They had their alliances. They had their thirty-four well-equipped divisions. Many people in England supported the Czech attitude. If there was going to be a war, the war talked about ever since 1919, when a famous cartoon showed the peacemakers of Versailles pausing to listen to the cry of a baby who wore a banner identifying him as a member of the military class of 1940, then let the war come now rather than later.

Neville Chamberlain was not in the group accepting that idea.

He called in Sir Horace Wilson. "Here. You are to take this to Hitler."

He gave Wilson a letter saying he was his personal envoy with full powers to negotiate. He gave him another letter. It said the Czechs could not accept Hitler's demands and that the British could not advise them to do so. There was a third letter saying that if Hitler marched and France went to the rescue of Czechoslovakia, England would have no choice but to back France up.

Wilson flew to Berlin. That afternoon, September 26, at five in the afternoon, he was received by the Leader, First Secretary of the British Embassy Sir Ivone Kirkpatrick and Ambassador Sir Nevile Henderson accompanying him. It was a lovely autumn day. The streets of the German capital were filled, Wilson saw, with men in uniform. He was shown into the Leader's study, where Hitler sat on a sofa by his desk adorned with a piece of sculpture showing a sword half out of its scabbard. Walking to him, Wilson tried to keep his eyes level with those of his host and not to blink. He sat down on the sofa next to the Leader, their knees almost touching, and handed his letter of accreditation to Hitler's interpreter, Paul Schmidt.

The Leader smiled as it was read aloud. Wilson gave the interpreter the second note, which said the Czechs could not accept the German demands. Hitler interrupted before two sentences were finished, jumped up from the sofa, wheeled around and shouted at Wilson, "So! That settles it! Now I will really smash the Czechs!"

Waving his hands over his head, he marched toward the door. Wilson and Henderson tried to soothe him. Let there be a meeting between the Germans and the Czechs to talk things over. A British representative would attend to try to talk the Czechs into being reasonable.

"What do I care about British representation?" Hitler shouted. The interpreter Schmidt had never seen him so out of control. "The old shit-hound must be crazy if he thinks he can influence me in this way."

Sir Horace Wilson was profoundly shocked. Nothing in his training had taught him to deal with a head of state who would allude to Neville Chamberlain in such a fashion. "If Herr Hitler is referring to the prime minister," Wilson said, "I can assure you that he is not crazy, only interested in peace."

"The comments of his ass-kissers do not interest me," Hitler shouted. "All that interests me are my people who are being tortured by that dirty —— Beneš! I will not stand it any longer! It is more than a good German can bear! Do you hear me, you stupid pig?"

A madman, Wilson thought to himself. But a madman who controlled the German bomber fleet. He thought of his third note, the one saying Britain would have to go to war if France decided to fight for Czechoslovakia. It was in his pocket. He thought of having Schmidt read it aloud. But to do so? If I say what I'm supposed to say now, Wilson thought to himself, it might just send him over the edge and then we're really in for it. He did not take the note from his pocket. Instead he tried to persuade Hitler to pull back from saying the final, definitive word. But Hitler was shouting that he would not wait until October 1. He would give the Czechs two more days to come to terms, that was all. They must accede to his terms within that time or face German army steel. "Take your pick!"

Wilson left. That night Hitler addressed a mass meeting in the Berlin Sports Palace, pouring scorn and hatred upon the Czechs and their leader, Beneš. "The decision now rests with him. Peace or war!" Either Beneš would give freedom to the Sudeten Germans "or we will come and fetch that freedom for ourselves."

The next day Sir Horace Wilson called again and forced himself to read out Chamberlain's third letter. "I must request you, Chancellor, to take note of the following communication: 'If France, in fulfillment of her treaty obligations, should become actively involved in hostilities against Germany, the United Kingdom would deem itself obliged to support France.' "

Hitler's voice rose to a furious pitch. Few could hear that tone without feeling fear, without wondering if he were about to leap forward or throw something, his ink bottle perhaps. "If France and England want to unleash war, they can do so. It's a matter of complete indifference to me. I am prepared for all eventualities. So next week we'll all find ourselves at war with each other." It was his last word to Wilson.

The next day workmen began digging trenches in London's parks for protection against air raids, and antiaircraft guns were mounted. Chamberlain was told the capital had only sixty fire pumps and that one week's intensive bombing would burn the city to the ground. Rumors had it that old sheets were being collected for use as makeshift coffins; there was an insufficiency of the real thing for what might be coming. Experts estimated the first day's raids would kill six hundred thousand persons and injure 1.2 million more. The Royal Navy was sent to its war stations and the reserve fleet mobilized.

From Paris the American ambassador, William Bullitt, sent a message to President Roosevelt describing a meeting he had held with Air Minister Guy La Chambre. The Frenchman told him France had six hundred battle aircraft and Germany sixty-five hundred. "The minister for air said that it was certain that the German planes would be able to bomb Paris at will." Every one of France's few planes would be needed for use by the field army. "There would be no planes for the defense of Paris. The destruction of Paris would pass all imagination. No protection whatsoever against the large-sized German bombs except a shelter covered by at least fifteen feet of reinforced concrete." As for incendiary bombs, sand would put them out, "but an unconquerable fire would result if water was spread on them."

Prime Minister Chamberlain went on the air and broadcast a last appeal for reason: "How horrible, fantastic, incredible it is that we should be digging trenches and trying on gas masks here because of a quarrel in a faraway country between people of whom we know nothing." He spoke very frankly of his astonishment when Hitler at Godesberg demanded more than he had asked at Berchtesgaden only days earlier. But war? Chamberlain knew that Canada was against it, that the Australians had made it plain they did not wish to be involved, that the South Africans were hostile to the idea.

"However much we may sympathize with a small nation confronted by a big, powerful neighbor we cannot, in all circumstances, undertake to involve the British Empire in war simply on her account. If we have to fight it must be on larger issues than that.

"I am myself a man of peace to the depths of my soul. Armed conflict of nations is a nightmare to me but if I were convinced that any nation had made up its mind to dominate the world by fear of its force, I should feel that it must be resisted. Under such a domination life for people who believe in liberty would not be worth living. But war is a fearful thing. We must be very clear, before we embark on it, that it is really the great issues that are at stake."

In Berlin the little band of conspirators against Hitler believed that the game was up. There would be a war. Then it would be out of the question to attempt to remove the Leader, not while the German army was contesting the field with declared enemies. Ordered to lead his troops in a propaganda march through the heart of the city, General Erwin von Witzleben, hating Hitler and the idea of a war, looked up at the Chancellory, where the Leader was, and felt tempted to make a last-minute coup, to unlimber some guns and lock him up. He continued marching. There was no cheering from the onlookers on the sidewalk, who believed that the passing regiments and batteries were headed for the railroad station to entrain for what would in a day or two be an engaged front line. People turned away or ducked into subway entrances. Only an apathetic and melancholy silence greeted the soldiers.

From a Chancellory window Hitler saw the lack of spectators' enthusiasm and flew into one of his rages, crying out to Goebbels that with such people you could not wage war. But his deadline stood. Roosevelt and the Pope issued appeals for peace. King George prayed for it in the Windsor Castle chapel, and Mrs. Chamberlain with a great throng in Westminster Abbey at the tomb of the Unknown Warrior just twenty years in his grave. Her husband felt he was losing all sense of time, and images of volcanoes and crashing mountains filled his thinking, of going down a thin path with an abyss on either side, that perhaps he was facing a madman who preferred a war without victory to victory without a war. It seemed to the prime minister that history had taken over, inexorable and terrifying.

Sir Harold Nicolson left a meeting at Winston Churchill's flat thinking of how the bombings would produce panics and riots and that those who said, "We must make a stand" would be branded as murderers. The wife of the First Lord of the Admiralty, Lady Diana Manners Cooper, watched men digging bomb shelters in London's parks and likened them in her mind to gravediggers. She saw in imagination death and utter demolishment, frantic crowds stampeding, famine and disease. She looked at the safety measures for her husband's Admiralty House, hoses and sandbags. "We knew that precautions were of no avail.

We took them in the way that one touches wood or crosses fingers."

On the night of September 27 Chamberlain appealed to Mussolini to interecede with Hitler. The next day, even as the deadline ran out, the prime minister addressed Parliament on the lack of progress of the negotiations he had conducted. It came into the minds of many who listened that this would be his last speech as a peacetime chief, that he was to step down from the podium as a war leader.

That morning Benito Mussolini, in response to Chamberlain's request, telephoned his ambassador to Berlin. For a decade and a half the Italian dictator had postured in the role of the intrepid warrior. Now a newcomer had stepped upon the stage to talk about making war, but the newcomer was not an actor playing a part. "This is the Duce speaking," Mussolini said to Ambassador Bernardo Attolico. "Can you hear me?"

"Yes, I hear you."

"Ask immediately for an interview with the Chancellor. Tell him the British government asked me to mediate in the Sudeten question. Tell him I favor accepting the suggestion. You hear me?"

"Yes, I hear you."

"Hurry!"

Attolico rushed to Hitler. "I have an urgent message to you from the Duce!" he shouted when still some distance from the Leader's desk. It was noon.

"Tell the Duce I accept his proposal," Hitler told Attolico. Perhaps he was moved to do so when he saw the people were so unenthusiastic at the sight of von Witzleben's troops. Invitations to the British and French to come to a conference were hastily cabled out.

"Whatever views Honorable Members may have," Chamberlain was saying to the House of Commons, "I believe everyone will . . ." He stopped speaking. A note had been handed to him. A messenger from the Foreign Office had rushed it to Lord Halifax in the Peers' Gallery. He read it and signaled to the prime minister's parliamentary private secretary, Lord Dunglass, to meet him in the lobby. Dunglass rose from his seat behind Chamberlain and went out. Halifax gave him the note. Dunglass went back in, handed the note to Sir John Simon, the chancellor of the exchequer, and indicated he should pass it on to the prime minister.

For an agonizing moment Simon hesitated to interrupt in the middle of Chamberlain's speech. Then he did so. The prime minister read the note to himself. It was from Sir Alexander Cadogan. Chamberlain looked up at the silent Parliament. Years seemed to drop from his face.

"I have something further to say to the House yet. I have now been informed by Herr Hitler that he invites me to meet him at Munich tomorrow morning. He has also invited Signor Mussolini and Monsieur Daladier. Signor Mussolini has accepted and I have no doubt Monsieur Daladier will accept. I need not say what my answer will be."

The House of Commons erupted in a manner never seen before in its long history. People burst into tears of joy. The king's mother, the widowed Queen Mary, cried. Papers were flung up into the air and someone screamed, "Thank God for the prime minister!"

Men and women outside the building who had thought the day might be their last on earth, that German bombers might appear over London at any moment, heard the news and fell upon their knees in the street to offer thanks to God. It was the same in Paris. In Berlin General Franz Halder, who had thought to depose Adolf Hitler, cried, "What can we do? He succeeds in everything he does."

In the morning at Heston Airport just before his plane took off for Germany a third time, Chamberlain said to the reporters that he was reminded of a refrain from childhood days: "If at first you don't succeed, try, try, try again." He said that he hoped that with Shakespeare he might soon say, "Out of this nettle, Danger, we pluck this flower, Safety."

He arrived at Munich and went in an open car past frantically cheering Germans to meet with Hitler and the others. Czechoslovakia was not represented in the talks held at the Königsplatz building named for the Leader. The Czech minister to London, Jan Masaryk, had asked the prime minister and Foreign Secretary Lord Halifax if his country would have a chance to be heard in Munich. They said the answer had to be no, for Hitler would not stand for it.

"If you have sacrificed my nation to preserve the peace of

the world," Masaryk told them, "I will be the first to applaud you. But if not, God help your souls!"

There were never any real negotiations at Munich. The object of the meeting was to give Hitler the Sudetenland and so avoid a war. Details were glossed over. Mussolini, the only participant who spoke all the others' languages, acted as something of a majordomo. Hitler seemed to take his cues from him. But throughout he appeared furious, all too obviously filled, observed Sir Ivone Kirkpatrick, with disgust and irritation, as if he were being "asked to sign away his birthright." His gestures were angry and impatient, his face "black as thunder."

Lord Dunglass, the prime minister's parliamentary private secretary who had handed on the invitation to come to Munich, was astonished and appalled at the lack of courtesy Hitler showed to Chamberlain, at the brusque and peremptory fashion in which he addressed him. It was, Dunglass remembered, the most horrible experience of his career. He had never expected to see a British prime minister treated so.*

Both Kirkpatrick and Dunglass had correctly interpreted Hitler's mood and his attitude toward Chamberlain. "If ever that silly old man comes interfering here again with his umbrella," Hitler told his intimates, "I'll kick him downstairs and jump on his stomach in front of photographers."

The Munich Agreement gave him all he had demanded at Godesberg, gave him the Czech's defensive line, gave him 3.5 million new subjects and their territory, but it deprived him of a triumphant victory march through the capital city of a completely shattered foe. His Germany had lain prostrate only twenty years before and now the world trembled before her, he had won a triumph beyond the dreams of Bismarck or Weimar, the hated Beneš would within days resign and leave mutilated Czechoslovakia. But when Hitler left Munich for the Sudetenland his mood was the same seen by those who studied him at the Führer Haus conference in the Königsplatz.

"It is always the English who are criticizing me," he said to the officers and officials surrounding him. He was at a village eating a luncheon of fruit juice, cereal and some Viennese cream cakes specially brought along by his servants. His voice rose so that people outside the room could hear. "Weak, decadent, led

* He was never to experience anything like similar treatment when years later, as Sir Alec Douglas-Home, he became a successor of Neville Chamberlain as prime minister.

by degenerate aristocrats with no chins, or by old fools like Chamberlain. Yet they dare to stand in my way. I will not allow it! I will attack them and I will destroy them! The French, too! Latin curs and lickspittles! Jew-ridden scum! They will be stamped and squashed if they dare to get in my way!"

It had not entered Neville Chamberlain's thinking at Munich that this would be the Leader's reaction. When the ceremonies were concluded and the agreement signed and Czechoslovakia was slashed apart and left defenseless, the prime minister asked Hitler if he might call upon him the next morning before flying home to London. Hitler assented, and Chamberlain came to the Munich apartment the Leader had maintained for many years, quite modest and furnished in the fashion that might have been expected of a moderately successful merchant of the last years of the previous century. Chamberlain proffered a note. It said that he, the British prime minister, and he, the German Reich chancellor, mutually agreed to settle all future difficulties peacefully, that it was their mutual intention never to permit their two countries to war upon each other.

"Yes, yes, yes," Hitler said, and signed his name.

Back in London Chamberlain waved the letter above his head—like a happy autograph collector, some thought—and cried, "Here is a paper which bears his name."

His car heading from Heston Airport to Buckingham Palace, for the king had asked that he call, could hardly progress through the streets jammed with those who cried with joy and blessed him and the peace he had brought with him. They leaped on the running board of his automobile as it inched along. People swarmed up the lightposts and railings in front of the palace to see him and Mrs. Chamberlain when they came out on the balcony with King George and Queen Elizabeth. They sang and laughed.

He went to Downing Street. An enormous throng gathered outside to sing "For He's a Jolly Good Fellow." The celebration in the streets, where half the city's population turned out, and throughout England and the Empire had been equaled only by that seen on Armistice Day in 1918.

The situation was the same in France, the joy even less restrained. Premier Edouard Daladier had essentially followed Chamberlain's lead but only with considerable misgivings. When his plane approached Le Bourget Airport and he saw masses of people below, his heart sank, for it seemed likely to him that they had come to stone him for what he and the British had done to Czechoslovakia. He ordered his pilot to circle the field twice before finally getting up his nerve to descend.

Instead of stones he found madly happy people, hundreds of thousands of them lining the streets, weeping with joy. Mothers held up children to see Daladier so that they could always remember something of this most supremely happy day. The fervor of the cheering, thought the historian Frederick Schuman, had sounded through the streets of Paris for only one other man before Daladier: Napoleon.

The premier himself believed he had seen in Hitler an "instinctive revulsion" against incorporating into the borders of the Reich any persons of other than German blood, particularly the Czechs, of whom he spoke only with "contempt and disgust." Hitler's sense of nationhood, Daladier reasoned, lay at the base of his detestation of Jews, whom he did not consider Germans, and would constitute a guarantee of his never taking over any other countries. If so, the Munich Agreement would have brought a lasting peace.

At Downing Street the people sang "Rule Britannia," "Land of Hope and Glory," "O God Our Help in Ages Past" and, over and over, "For He's a Jolly Good Fellow." They would not disperse but called unremittingly for Chamberlain. His tall and angular figure appeared at a first-floor window. The last prime minister to say a few words from that spot had been David Lloyd George on Armistice Day, when the guns finally ceased to speak along the Western Front.

"My good friends," Chamberlain said, "this is the second time in our history that there has come back from Germany to Downing Street peace with honor." His allusion was to Disraeli's return from the Congress of Berlin in 1878.

"I believe it is peace for our time."

The next day the *Times* of London said that no conqueror returning from the most glorious battlefield victory had come home adorned with more noble laurels. Lord Beaverbrooks's *Daily Express* printed on its first page that phrase that was to appear there frequently for many months: THERE WILL BE NO WAR THIS YEAR OR NEXT YEAR EITHER.

The first of tens of thousands of letters began to pour in: "I feel with God's help you have given me back my boys. I thank you a thousand times from the depths of my heart, The Mother of Five Sons." President Roosevelt wrote to say that the prime minister had created the best opportunity in years for an international order based on peace and justice. A statue was erected in Portugal, it was proposed that a Paris boulevard be renamed the Avenue September 30, *Paris-Soir* began collecting for a fund to buy Chamberlain a house with a trout stream and *Le Journal* solicited funds for a Neville Chamberlain Peace Bed in a Paris hospital where "anyone even remotely related to anybody English" could be treated free of charge. A quarter of a century had passed since there had been any communication between the former German Kaiser and ex-Queen Mary, who had last seen each other at the Berlin wedding of his daughter, Princess Viktoria Luise. Now from his exile in Holland he wrote to tell her how happy he was that a catastrophe had been averted, that Chamberlain had been inspired by heaven and guided by God.

It was universally believed, said Lady Diana Manners Cooper, that there was never again going to be a war, not then and not ever. "And this miracle had been performed by one man and one man only. The aged prime minister of England had saved the world."

EIGHT

PRIME MINISTER CHAMBERLAIN was viewed as the savior of his generation and those that would follow. His position in England and in the world was such that when, during a House of Commons discussion of Palestine, reference was made to the Prince of Peace, Winston Churchill could whisper loudly, "I never knew before that Neville was born in Bethlehem!"

The mellow Victorian glow that hung over Great Britain and the Empire long after the Queen Empress's passing, the great houses with old silver, fox hunting and grouse shooting and autumnal evenings in England: all now appeared secure. Union Jacks rose to flagstaffs on mornings and sank in evenings on ships and at barracks and coaling stations, outside the Pearl Mosque in the fort at Lahore, on the Chinook Pass in the Yukon and the Grand Harbor with its white ramparts at Malta, where the Imperial Airways flying boats landed on the Nile at Cairo, in air heavy with the smell of flowers and incense and the bells and jammed streets of the East, on reef and tundra, desert and veld. A quarter of the earth's land surface was colored red for Britain on maps, and nearly a quarter of the world's people lived under the rule of that government, which had its headquarters in Whitehall and whose leader resided at Number 10 Downing Street and had latterly returned from Munich to cheers of acclamation and tears of joy.

Not all applauded. On the evening of the great day, when the Cabinet met, Alfred Duff Cooper, First Lord of the Admiralty, submitted his resignation and went before the House of Commons to say that although he now had no post and perhaps no further career, he could at least walk about with his head held high. Having taken away Czechoslovakia's only defensible frontier, Cooper said, the British were now guaranteeing a new frontier that could never be defended. It was as if they had dealt a man a mortal blow and then insured his life.

Churchill said, "We have sustained a great defeat without a war, the consequences of which will travel far with us. We have passed an awful milestone in our history. And do not suppose that this is the end. This is only the beginning."

It could hardly have been pleasant for Chamberlain to hear, and he said something about people who criticized their country being akin to birds who fouled their own nests. Hitler in a speech a few days later replied to Cooper and Churchill: "It would be a good thing if people in Great Britain gradually dropped certain airs. We cannot any longer tolerate the tutelage of governesses. We would like to give these gentlemen the advice that they should keep their noses in their own affairs and leave us alone."

"That damn Winston!" Chamberlain exclaimed when he read Hitler's speech. Everything depended upon keeping things tamped down and quiet in both Germany and Britain.

Peace now hinged on what Germany and England would do. For so long the guarantor of the peace of Europe, an accepted Great Power of the Continent and the world, France had completely abdicated her position. The joyous explosion that followed Munich passed, and Paris felt itself humiliated by what had happened. For a few weeks something of a warlike temper took hold. "Lead and we will follow!" Daladier heard when he entered restaurants. It was said that France had suffered a defeat greater than Waterloo, that France's honor had been interred.

Daladier turned bitter not only against Germany but also Britain, saying to the American ambassador, William Bullitt, that he considered Chamberlain a "dessicated stick, the king a moron and the queen an excessively ambitious woman who would be ready to sacrifice every other country in the world in order that she might remain queen of England." But in a little while the truculence passed and a France empty of initiative and determination resigned itself to following in the British train.

And Britain in effect was Neville Chamberlain. Duff Cooper had opposed him. He was gone from the Cabinet. Anthony Eden was gone. Foreign Secretary Lord Halifax had suppressed in himself by design and with determination the thought that Czechoslovakia had dishonorably been railroaded to a terrible fate. He would no longer oppose his prime minister. There was no one to oppose Chamberlain. His closest adviser, Sir Horace Wilson, habitually addressed him as "Master." (A prime minister, Eden wrote later, ought to learn to hold himself aloof from the easy agreement that meets the expression of his views, for it was dangerous for him to do otherwise.)

But supreme in Britain and the Empire and in the estimation of most of the world, Chamberlain faced a frightful dilemma. He had no sooner proclaimed from Downing Street's balcony that he returned from Munich with peace with honor, with peace for our time, than he regretted what he had said.

"I hope Honorable Members will not be disposed to read into words used in a moment of some emotion after a long and exhausting day, after I had driven through miles of excited, enthusiastic, cheering people—I hope they will not read into those words more than they were intended to convey," he told the House of Commons. "I realize that diplomacy cannot be effective unless the consciousness exists, not here alone, but elsewhere, that behind the diplomacy is the strength to give effect to it."

There was the dilemma. He had said he brought peace. How now was he to ask for the materials of war?

"It is difficult," mused Sir Harold Nicolson, "to say: 'This is the greatest diplomatic achievement in history, therefore we must redouble our armaments in order never again to be exposed to such humiliation.' "

Chamberlain put himself to arming Britain. But it had to be done with the greatest discretion. He was not a fool. He comprehended what he faced, and whom. If he needed proof that Adolf Hitler was explosive, ruthless, brutal, reckless—in short, dangerous—he got it before two months passed. A law was passed in Poland that said all passports must be marked by a special stamp. The stamping must be done in Poland. There was a one-month deadline. To the Germans it seemed the Poles thus wished to denationalize some seventeen thousand Polish Jews residing in Germany. The Germans wanted no more Jews suddenly made stateless and therefore likely to stay on in Germany indefinitely. The seventeen thousand were arrested, jammed into boxcars and sent to the Polish frontier, where they were unloaded and shoved across the border. The Poles made objections about accepting them, and so they sat in the open for nearly two weeks as November's cold weather came on.

Among their number were the parents of one Herschel Grynszpan, a thin seventeen-year-old less than five feet tall who had been sent to live with an uncle in Paris. A tailor and a seamstress respectively, the elder Grynszpans had lived in Hanover for nearly twenty years. "They are going to expel us from Germany and make us go back to Poland," the father wrote Herschel. "What shall we do there, son? And what will they do to us? Thank God you are safe in France." They sat in a field along the Polish-German border.

The boy got a revolver and walked across half of Paris to the Rue de Lille and the German Embassy. He asked to see Ambassador Count Johannes von Welczeck but was instead shown into the office of Third Secretary Ernest vom Rath, who was slitting open the envelopes of the morning mail. No Nazi, and indeed a Prussian aristocrat who disapproved of Germany's persecution of the Jews, vom Rath asked the boy what he wanted. A shot from the revolver took him in the throat.

"Why, why?" he asked, dying.

"I wanted to revenge my co-religionists," Grynszpan told the French police. "I had to make my feelings clear."

The news of the assassination reached a Munich in which thousands of Old Fighters of the Nazi Party, the original supporters of Hitler, prepared to celebrate the anniversary of the failed 1923 attempt to take power. The dispersal by the Bavarian State Police had cost the then-young movement sixteen deaths and given them sixteen martyrs, and their Leader the opportunity in jail to write the bible of National Socialism, *My Struggle*. Hitler was in the beer hall from which fifteen years earlier he had launched the march broken up by the police carbines when he was told of what had happened in Paris.

"The Jewish pig!" he cried. "This is something they will regret!"

Joseph Goebbels told the assemblage what had taken place. "Members of the Old Guard, Ernest vom Rath was a good German, a good servant of the Reich. Do I need to tell you the race of the dirty swine who did this foul deed?"

"Dirty Jews!" came back the answer. "Down with the Jews! Kill the Jews!"

Orders went out to every police station in Germany from

Gestapo headquarters in Berlin: officers were not to interfere with any demonstrations. Through every city and every town mobs raged, burning and killing and smashing the windows, whose shattered bits of glass gave the events the name by which they would be remembered: the Crystal Night. Two hundred synagogues were left in ruins, seventy-five hundred shops and stores destroyed, twenty thousand Jews flung into jail, an unknown number killed.

That Germany under Hitler was a country where arrests took place without charges, that people were released or not released without explanation—the world had learned that years before. This was something different. Saying he could scarcely believe that such things could take place in modern times, President Roosevelt ordered Ambassador Hugh Wilson home. Hitler replied by ordering Ambassador Hans Dieckhoff to Germany.

The information that a bloody and murderous government-sponsored, untrammeled, nationwide riot had raged through that Germany once thought to be the abode of bespectacled pedants and musicians, of window boxes and polite disciplined children, of clock towers and winding cobbled streets and roadways, and cheery *"Guten Morgen!"* reached the British Cabinet as it sat debating the creation of a training range for armored vehicles. (Secretary of State for War Leslie Hore-Belisha wished to buy six thousand acres at Pembrokeshire. Chancellor of the Exchequer Sir John Simon objected: "I have a personal knowledge of this piece of coast, which is one of the most beautiful and unspoilt places in these islands. This piece of country would be ruined.") Lord Halifax sent a protesting Note to Berlin.

Under the chairmanship of Hermann Goering a committee considered what to do about the insurance claims Jews would file. It was decided that any monies paid out would be confiscated by the government, and a one-billion-mark penalty would be levied on the Jewish population of Germany. The committee decided that in addition Jews would henceforth be forbidden to enter theaters, movie houses and circuses. It would be against the law for a Jew to sit in a train compartment with an Aryan. "We'll kick him out and he'll have to sit all alone in the toilet," Goering said.

The committee discussed passing a law forbidding Jews to drive cars. Jewish girls must be prohibited from wearing provocative dresses. Goering stood up to adjourn the meeting. "The pigs won't commit another murder. I will tell you this, gentle-men: From now on, I would not like to be a Jew in Germany!"

His mother had been the longtime mistress of a Jew who fur-nished her and her son with sumptuous living conditions and had been looked upon by the young Goering as almost a father. Joseph Goebbels, by far the most educated of the Nazi leader-ship, had studied for his Ph.D. under two Jewish professors in amicable circumstances. Hitler himself had been warmly grateful to a physician known as the poor people's doctor of Linz who had attended his mother in her last illness for the slightest com-pensation, and had presented him with one of his paintings after his mother died.* All that had been a long time ago, in a differ-ent world. The New Germany was on the march.

Neville Chamberlain exclaimed, "Oh, what tedious people these Germans can be! Just when we were beginning to make a little progress!" Of all men the prime minister was a citizen used to dealing with fellow citizens, the last to understand violence, threats, death. "There is always some common measure of agreement, if only we will look for it," he said—his credo. He dealt with Hitler, thought the member of Parliament Robert Boothby, as if the Leader were "a recalcitrant but well-intentioned town council-lor." All of the prime minister's background had taught him to look for compromise and accommodation, and all of his fear of Armageddon, of the Four Horsemen—"I said the word 'war' and he trembled," Hitler told his intimates—made him see signs of progress and of goodwill; and in bitter Paris it was said that his name should be spelled *J'aime Berlin*.

The description was hardly accurate. Chamberlain knew that Britain must rearm, and at once. He looked at his forces. If the worst came to the worst, he thought, it would be best for Britain to fight only in the blue, in the air and on the water. Let the French conduct the desperate ground operations that in 1914–18 had cost so many millions of dead. But would that be possi-ble? He did not trust France. There had been no army staff con-sultations since the end of the War, and to inaugurate them might well infuriate the violent and unpredictable Adolf Hitler and bring on frightful results.

In addition, to confide details of Britain's military situation

* August Kubizek asked the Nazi authorities that the aged doctor, still living in 1938, not be made to undergo any hardship, for he had been the doctor of Adolf Hitler's mother. He was permitted to live undisturbed.

was to invite the possibility that every secret revealed would be known to German army headquarters in Berlin the next day. For there was hardly a newspaper in Paris that did not have men on the German payroll, and so corrupt was French political life that there were stories that the wife of French Foreign Minister Georges Bonnet had financial arrangements with German agents. And to encourage the French to believe that the British would bail them out of any situation that might arise, what might that not bring—perhaps entangling alliances of the type that had sent the world to hell in the summer of 1914.

"We are like people living at the foot of a volcano," Chamberlain said, "and we remember that it blew up once before."

He looked at Britain's army, at Tommy Atkins and Tommy's officers. It was said that one of those officers at the end of 1914–18 had with vast relief thanked God it was all over: "Now we can get back to real soldiering."

What was that real soldiering? Across the vast Empire with its little scattered detachments of His Majesty's Forces square-bashing about their meticulously kept parade grounds, the Tommies, the Other Ranks, were traditionally esteemed as hardly above the level of the horses and mules that largely furnished the transport. They had always been picked from the ranks of the kind of boy who hung around pubs or ran errands and then got press-ganged into the Regulars. Now he loitered about the Depression-closed shipyards and factories before drifting into a regimental recruiting depot to take the King's Shilling and then a troopship to, say, India, where he was trained in the subtleties of that cavalry drill that in the twenties and thirties gave Britain the finest horse soldiers the world had ever seen, each man an adept at piercing balloons with pointed weapons—*l'arme blanche*—as he put his faultlessly groomed mount over barriers and then drew his edged saber to slash at popping-up dummies. Training manuals dealt with lances and swords, if not with bows and arrows.

Of mechanized and armored power there was very little, for officers bred to the hunting field had not, they said, joined the regiments of their grandfathers and great-grandfathers in order to be garagemen. In any event, they held, it was far more likely for a motor to break down than for a horse to go lame. British officers routinely received several weeks of hunting leave each year in addition to regular furloughs. Work played but a little role in their doings, and their time past noon was their own save

for the two or three months of the annual training season. Cor-
porals at exercises walked across fields carrying boards round
their necks saying THIS REPRESENTS A SECTION or sometimes even
a larger unit; a green flag represented an antitank gun.

Wrapped in scarlet and gold braid and with chain mail on
their shoulders, booted and spurred, officers dined each night at
full-dress and full-course dinners served on the regimental plate.
Smartness in uniform and fashionable tailoring when in mufti
were of the utmost importance, plus sport—polo, pig-sticking,
shooting. It was absolutely *outré* to discuss "shop"—the business
of soldiering—in the mess, and undesirable to be too keen in
anything, for traditionally the British officer was to be seen as a
nonchalant and offhand amateur.

Men spoke in the particular pooh-bah pukka-sahib cavalry
officer's drawl—with plums in their mouths, the Other Ranks
said. It was impossible to hold a commission in a better regiment
without a substantial private income, and very difficult even in
lesser ones, and to rise to the higher ranks of the British army,
thought Lord Chandos, was to rise in an institution as closely
limited as the College of Cardinals in Rome. Chief of the Imperial
General Staff General the Viscount Gort typified the corps of
officers. Very rich, very involved with athletics and fitness despite his lifetime army nickname of "Fatboy," Lord Gort had essentially a subaltern's knowledge of boots and drill and horses.
No one had ever accused him of owning a penetrating intellect
or an advanced worldview.

Behind him and his army was a nation that, briefly milita-
ristic during the Boer War of 1899–1902, had in the years following lost its stomach for large-scale adventures. A column
winding its way into some exotic blazing-sun uplands to disperse
rebellious Fuzzy-Wuzzies or Punjab insurrectionists was one thing,
or a trio of gunboats of the Royal Navy shelling a cluster of riv-
erside native huts. But anything more was anathema to the man
in the street in Surrey or Hampshire. The Great War had for all
time ended Britain's interest in military glory paid for in blood
and gold. When the Oxford Union in 1933 debated that "This
House will in no circumstances fight for its king and country,"
the resolution was passed by 275 to 153.

It was given to Neville Chamberlain to seek to rearm that
Britain that now stood almost defenseless before an Adolf Hitler
whose temperament and manner of doing things were so clearly

revealed by the blood and destruction his Germany had wrought on Crystal Night. All of the Left in England, and the trade unions, opposed the prime minister on the rearmament issue. They stood against Nazism, against German intervention in the civil war in Spain, but they stood also against the demon of war.

Chamberlain tried to walk the tightrope. He set out to rearm, facing opponents speaking of wage scales and Empire requirements, of workers' pay schedules and the need to keep sterling up. Desperate, his voice ever more harsh and his lean, angular figure ever less graceless, he tried to marshal the forces he needed. It was terribly difficult. Lord Dunglass had the task of putting him in touch with younger members of the House of Commons. A thankless job.

"It was absolute murder trying to get him in to the smoking room or to talk out at all," Dunglass remembered years later, ex-prime minister himself then. "He was so shy. He would never expand—never gossip. He made no effort to put himself across and no one could really do it for him." His mind filled with visions of the death of that England that had been so great and so all-embracing and had given not only him but Joseph Chamberlain and Sir Austen Chamberlain before him power and glory, he could not change or undo his remote manner and forbidding way.

"If one went in at the end of the day for a chat or a gossip, he would be inclined to ask, 'What do you want?' "

He had no time for small talk but was entirely nongregarious, reserved, stern. In twenty years of close association, Churchill remembered, he had exactly one single at-ease talk with Neville Chamberlain. He talked then about his experiences as a young man trying to grow hemp in Andros in the Bahamas. "A rare, complex person, half of him hidden from the world," Dunglass said. Yet he was a master of method, Dunglass saw, incapable of an inaccuracy, his precision of thought uncanny, a man utterly nonslipshod, with a great memory wedded to an impulse for action. He was a doer, he wanted action, he hated woolly-mindedness, he was logical, he was direct. What was he not? "It revealed much of Chamberlain," his years-later successor remembered, "that he detested Disraeli for his flamboyance, his appeal to the emotions."

So armed and so handicapped, wishing to make England strong but at the same time fearful of igniting the explosive Hitler,

Chamberlain set out to prepare for the war that he prayed he had averted but that might yet come and soon. He could not completely mobilize his country for the eternally present reasons that Hitler might strike when he was but a half or a quarter prepared and because he could not suddenly suspend the civilian existence England enjoyed. All must be done gradually. There must be no clarion call to bring upon him the protests of his country and the bombs of the German air force alike. But of course there was no clarion call in him. He did not know how to voice one.

Chamberlain believed it was within his and Britain's grasp to make the future bright, but he knew also that there were those who said the race was already over. Charles Lindbergh came to England after the death of his infant son in a botched kidnap attempt. The great flier enjoyed at first his freedom there from the reporters and prying public, which he felt had made life in America impossible. But it came to him after a time that England was nearing the end of a great era, that it was like a dinosaur out of its place in time struggling on in a fatally hostile climate. Stuck in the age of ships, it had never graduated to the age of aircraft. There was but little life left, Lindbergh came to feel, and little virility. The English mind was not attuned to the modern world. It was a gallant place with a great past, but aged.

The flier visited Germany, where he was received with the highest honors, given a medal by Hermann Goering and taken to see the latest developments in German aviation. He flew German warplanes, saw German aircraft factories, and returned to England saying Germany was unbeatable and that her air power exceeded that of Britain, France and Russia put together, not to mention the United States.

Lindbergh gave American ambasssador Joseph Kennedy a letter summarizing his conclusions just before Chamberlain went to Munich. Kennedy passed the letter on to the prime minister. London, Paris and Prague were entirely at the mercy of German bombers, helpless to defend themselves against German air attack, said the greatest figure in world aviation. The virile New Germany was efficient and orderly, Lindbergh thought to himself; it was not just a matter of air power, but of power of the spirit. Criticisms of the Nazis? "It's lies—all lies."

He returned again and again to Germany, five trips in two years. No reporters dogged him there, photographers did not pop up to take his picture. Safe from the freedom of the press he detested, he went perhaps to disliking that freedom of speech in England and America, which was license to him, and finally perhaps to disliking the West's idea of freedom itself.

Instead of combating Germany, Lindbergh said, the Royal Navy should combine with the German air force to "build our White ramparts" against the Asiatics menacing "our common heritage." It was like preparing a suicidal European civil war for England even to think of rearming against Germany. He himself, he said, "did not know real freedom" until he saw Germany. He asked Albert Speer, Hitler's architect, to find him a building lot in Berlin and erect there a suitable home. (Mrs. Lindbergh put her foot down on the plan.)

Lindbergh was no reader or student and did not seem to know men, still less politics and history, but there seemed to be no question of his knowledge of airplanes. Ambassador Kennedy could not conceive that the Lone Eagle was mistaken in his appraisal of German air strength. He began to act upon the flier's ideas. By the time of his appointment to the Court of St. James's in early 1938 Ambassador Kennedy had determined that his son Joseph Jr. was to be the first Catholic President of the United States. Yet he could not help being awed at the diplomatic position he held.

"This is a hell of a way from East Boston, isn't it?" he said to his wife as they dressed for dinner with the king and queen in the suite at Windsor Castle once occupied by Victoria. Early in his term he was intentionally bumptious, receiving the British reporters with his feet on his desk, saying, "You can't expect me to develop into a statesman overnight." Asked if he would wear knee breeches, the prescribed form of Court apparel, he replied, "Not Mrs. Kennedy's little boy." He wore a tailcoat and long trousers.

("Mr. Kennedy's desire to shield himself from the charge of flunkeyism," said the London *Evening Standard,* "achieved the somewhat paradoxical result that the only trousers at last night's Court were those worn by himself and some of the less important waiters.")

Time and the British he met changed him. He associated exclusively with the rich and well born, and perhaps the Irish Catholic flattered by Protestant acceptance came to see things so much their way that Washington grew disturbed. He became particularly close to Chamberlain. Of all the Americans the prime minister ever knew, Kennedy was by far the one he most esteemed. A certain strange pessimism had always characterized Kennedy's approach to many things, and he came to believe that his new friends symbolized an England that was passing away. He was a frequent guest at the country seat of Lord Astor and his Virginia-born wife, Nancy, where the so-called Cliveden Set formed or at least expressed the heart of the appeasement policy, which held that Hitler must be conceded to in the interest of a world whose choice was between Nazism or Communism. At Cliveden Kennedy mixed with those of the upper classes who like Chamberlain saw accommodation as the only barrier to apocalyptic destruction. Kennedy liked to deal with cool, black, emotionless numbers, and the numbers he looked at told him to stop Germany was impossible and to try insane.

"I can't for the life of me understand why anyone should want to go to war to save the Czechs," he said at the time of Munich. Not only the ambassador but the father was giving voice to his thoughts, for he had sons who in a few short years would be of prime military age. If war came he could hardly be sure that America would stay out. It was said of him that he had a hot heart and a cold head—"That's what made the steam in him." The steam poured out over Neville Chamberlain.

•

In October 1938, in the Sudetenland of Czechoslovakia those of non-German ancestry and those of whatever ancestry who did not care to live under the rule of Adolf Hitler left their homes and trudged into what was now called rump Czechoslovakia. German patrols stood along the roads to make sure that the refugees took nothing of value with them. Hitler came and looked at a portion of the thousand miles of fortifications now part of the eastern ranges of the German Reich.

"Let's see what they're made of," he said to one of his generals. "Put some shells into them." A tank and mobile gun were brought up to open fire on a concrete bunker, which took several direct hits before it even began to crumble. Hitler cheered, laughed, slapped the general on the back. "What does it matter how strong the concrete is so long as the will is weak!" He drove past departing Czech refugees and saw some German soldiers handing them food. "Why do they waste good German bread on those pigs?"

By the terms of the Munich Agreement an international commission was to rule on final details of the German takeover. Once the details were worked out, Hitler told a Berlin Sports Palace crowd, no one need be concerned that the truncated country would cause any further European problems. "I shall have no further interest in the Czech state," he said. "I guarantee that. We want no Czechs."

But French and British members of the international commission found that issues about frontier adjustments were not to be decided by mutual give and take. Every settlement and factory area and railway line located anywhere even remotely near the Sudetenland was claimed for Germany. Ambassador Sir Nevile Henderson, the British representative on the commission, pointed to a map showing an industrial area largely inhabited by Czechs and said that really it belonged to rump Czechoslovakia, not Germany. "That's a bit much, surely. Couldn't we possibly spare that?"

"You might possibly spare it for them, Excellency," said the German representative, Colonel Walter Warlimont, "but then, it is not in your power to do so. The German Armed Forces High Command has already decided that the region is part of the Sudetenland, and it will be annexed accordingly." All points were decided in the same fashion: "The High Command has decided . . ." The orders from London and Paris were not to argue.

"Silent, mournful, abandoned, broken, Czechoslovakia recedes into the darkness," Churchill had said when Chamberlain returned from Munich, and now through the darkness came Foreign Minister Joseph Beck of Poland. André François Poncet, French ambassador to Berlin, compared him to a ghoul who in former centuries crawled about the battlefield to kill and then rob the wounded. Beck issued an ultimatum with a twenty-four-hour time limit to Czechoslovakia: he must be given the rich industrial area of Teschen. The Czechs handed it over. Three-quarters of the country's iron and steel was gone, her railway carriage works, her textiles, cement, porcelain and glass works, her electrical power supplies. By Hitler's orders a slice of territory was given to Hungary.

The country changed into a very loose federal state with the Czechs centered in Prague paying most of the bills but having only a slight authority over subjects of different ethnic groups. Berlin remained querulous, showering down complaints and accusations and demands. The borders of rump Czechoslovakia resonated with disorders as the ancient feuds of Central Europe flamed with new brightness.

The German Leader, almost somnolent now, as was his fashion after a period of activity and risk-taking, did not react well to the criticisms of the Munich Agreement, which were beginning to be heard across Germany's western borders, the domain of France and England and, beyond, in America. He had, he felt, made all the concessions, had given up his triumphal march through central Czechoslovakia and its capital. That fellow Chamberlain had spoiled it for him, he said, "cheated me of my entry into Prague." He did not care that Moscow feared that the agreement gave Germany a license to run riot in the East with the blessings of Britain and France. Daladier and Chamberlain had "wriggled like eels," Ivan Maisky reflected, Soviet ambassador to England, to get Hitler to turn against Russia. There had been no Russian representation at Munich, Maiksky thought to himself, and why? Because the point of sacrificing Austria and now Czechoslovakia was to turn the German lightning against Moscow.

Hitler did not care what Maisky believed. He sincerely felt that he had shown great forbearance and consideration. His reward was a West that wondered with the greatest unease what the future held. It was incomprehensible to Hitler that London and Paris feared him. In no way did he threaten the French and British, he said, still less the Americans. He only asked, he told his intimates, for a free hand in places thousands of miles from the West's points of interest. Was he protesting British hegemony in the West Indies half a world from England, or French rule in Indochina, or United States dominance in South America? German influence, economic life, sphere of interest all lay to the east. What was the basis of any Western distress or mistrust?

In his unfocused artistic manner he visited art studios and cafés and restaurants and building sites, and continued what his architect Albert Speer called the "hurling" of "long monologues at associates already amply familiar with the unchanging themes" and who "painfully tried to conceal their boredom." Buildings formed a substantial proportion of his discussions. They above all transmitted a time and a spirit to prosperity, he said. What, after all, remained of the emperors of Rome but their monumental architecture?

So it would be with him. The buildings of his reign would speak for him down the ages. And the New Chancellory must be the most glorious. (The old one built in the previous century was, he said, only "fit for a soap company.") The clearing of a block-long site on Voss Strasse began in early 1938. Albert Speer was told that cost was immaterial in either construction or furnishings: there must be enormous hand-knotted rugs; double doors almost seventeen feet high with immense portals of gilded stone and bronze eagles clutching the swastika in their claws; a gallery 480 feet long, twice as long as the Hall of Mirrors at Versailles; great round rooms with domed ceilings; grand halls and salons; deep window niches to filter the light in the manner of the Salle de Bal at Fontainebleau; lackeys in black-and-gold-braided uniforms and white stockings; polished marble floors.

Forty-five hundred workers, more than had built the Empire State Building in New York, labored in two shifts to erect the New Chancellory. The building was to be ready for the reception celebrating the beginning of the new year 1939. It was a quarter-mile long, with yellow stucco and gray stone frontage. Motionless gray sentries would be trained to melt into the background before snapping to a present arms. The diplomatic reception would be on January 12.

As the old year came to its close Neville Chamberlain sent out Christmas cards bearing the picture of the plane that had borne him to Munich. In the first days of 1939, he prepared to go to Italy for a meeting with Benito Mussolini. It was no secret that the relationship between Mussolini and the Germans to the north was not solidly based. In a few short years Hitler had completely eclipsed his Italian counterpart. Germans, contemptuous of effusive Latins, had come to refer to Il Duce as "the *Gauleiter* of Italy," meaning that they envisioned Rome as a colony of Berlin.

Chamberlain believed he had a special relationship with Mussolini. His late brother, Sir Austen, had scored what was considered the greatest diplomatic triumph of the 1920s, the Locarno Pact meant to assure European peace forever, with the enthusiastic help of the Italian leader. When it was signed Mussolini over and over again fervently kissed the hand of Sir Austen's wife. Now that her husband was gone, Lady Ivy Chamberlain spent much of her time in Rome. Letters to her from her brother-in-law the prime minister were regularly passed on to Mussolini.

Chamberlain knew the Italian had considered Austria to be within his sphere of influence. Now Austria was owned by the German Reich. He had considered Hungary under his protection, but a Hungary lately given a generous slice of Czechoslovakia by Hitler was reckoned a grateful German ally. It would be against human nature for Mussolini not to feel some resentment. Chamberlain wished to work on that resentment and permanently divorce Italy from Germany. With Lord Halifax he took salutes from Italian troops and went to the opera with Mussolini and his son-in-law foreign minister, Count Galeazzo Ciano. The conversations appeared to go well, Chamberlain thought. It seemed to him that he got on well with the Italian leader. He had gotten a favorable impression of Mussolini, Chamberlain told King George when he got back to London. At least he had a sense of humor, "whereas it would take a long surgical operation to get a joke into Hitler's head."

Mussolini's impression of his two British visitors was not as positive. "How far apart we are from these people!" Count Ciano wrote in his diary. "It is another world. We were talking about it after dinner with Il Duce. 'These men are not made of the same stuff,' he said, 'as the Francis Drakes and the other magnificent adventurers who created the Empire. These are the tired sons of a long line of rich men.' "

As the prime minister's train pulled out of the railroad station, the members of the British colony in Rome sang "For He's a Jolly Good Fellow."

"What is this little song?" Mussolini asked.

Two days earlier the reception for the diplomatic corps in Berlin had inaugurated Hitler's New Chancellory. The Leader greeted the visitors one by one, starting at noon. With the others stood the Soviet ambassador, Alexei Merekalov. Alone of all the ambassadors accredited to Berlin he had never been given the honor of hearing a band play Present Arms when he arrived on official business. By Hitler's orders, no German drums had ever rolled for him. No swastika flag had ever dipped. He was the representative of Communism, and anti-Communism, as was often said, was no less the religion of Nazism than anti-Semitism.

Hitler came down the line of diplomats briefly greeting each and shaking hands. He came to Merekalov. They shook hands, and then as cameras popped and people gasped and word of what was happening spread through the astonished gathering, the Leader of the German Reich stood for a long moment affably chatting with the ambassador of the Union of Soviet Socialist Republics.

NINE

WITH A THRUSH singing in the garden, the sun shining and the rooks beginning to discuss among themselves the prospects of the coming nesting season, I feel as though spring were getting near," Chamberlain wrote his sisters in the third week of February. "All the information I get seems to point in the direction of peace."

It had been quite otherwise a month or so earlier. British intelligence sources had reported that Hitler was contemplating attacks on Holland and Switzerland, on the Ukraine, that he was considering a gigantic no-warning knockout air strike against London. (A retired German state secretary told First Secretary of the British Embassy Sir Ivone Kirkpatrick that the allocation of squadrons, selections of airfields, assembly of bombs and selection of targets was well under way.)

Chamberlain's response to Adolf Hitler had been the allocation for the financial year 1938–39 of the greatest annual sum ever acquired out of taxation by Britain for defense; for the specific answer to the rumored air attack, an antiaircraft regiment was brought from Lichfield to park its guns in Wellington Barracks, where they would be clearly in view of the German Embassy.

But there were no hostile moves of any kind by Berlin as the warm weather came closer, and it seemed to Sir Nevile Henderson in Berlin there was reason to hope that Germany would gradually turn to peaceful pursuits. Goering had hinted he would like a British decoration to wear on one of his many and splendid uniforms, and Sir Nevile told Lord Halifax that it was something to keep in mind.

But of course only Hitler really mattered. He must not be treated like a "pariah or mad dog," Henderson said, for to do so might turn him into just that. He must be handled with the greatest care and brought to see how much it was in Germany's interest to keep the peace. Certainly logic indicated he should reach that conclusion, for it was impossible to believe that a war was necessary for Germany, reflected Romanian Foreign Minister Grigore Gafencu. It seemed to him that of all the great Continental states Germany would be the most likely to profit by a long period of peace, for Germany was developing beyond the ability of any neighbor to compete. It would be, Gafencu thought, a lunatic dream, a furious dementia, even to consider a war on European soil.

March came. Chamberlain's feelings about the future continued hopeful. "Very cheerful. Extremely optimistic," remembered Sir Horace Wilson. On March 9 Henderson wrote that the German people longed for peace. As for their Leader: "On every reasonable ground Hitler should be sincere when he says that he is looking forward to a long period of peace. I can find no justification for the theory that he is mad or even verging on madness; I am of the opinion that he is not thinking today in terms of war."

That evening, before leaving on a weekend fishing trip, the prime minister gave a small party for a group of newspaper correspondents, to whom he spoke frankly on a nonattribution, background basis. Europe was settling down to a long period of tranquillity, Chamberlain said. He soon hoped to call a great disarmament conference.

The next day Home Secretary Sir Samuel Hoare addressed a group of his constituents at Chelsea Town Hall. Personally close to Chamberlain, Hoare used to walk with him and both men's wives around the lake in St. James's Park each morning before they went to their offices. He had mentioned his forthcoming speech to the prime minister and had asked what kind of note Chamberlain thought he ought to strike. "Cheerful," was the answer.

Hoare followed his suggestion. He denounced "jitterbugs" who feared for the future of peace. "Confidence," he said, "almost suffocated in the late autumn by defeatism, has returned. Hope has taken the place of fear, moral and physical robustness has overcome hysteria and hesitation."

He spoke of what might be if political confidence returned to all countries. "Suppose that the peoples of Europe will be able to free themselves from the nightmare that haunts them, and from an expenditure on armaments that beggars them. Could we not then devote the inventions and discoveries of our time to the creation of a Golden Age?"

The following day the editors of *Punch* met to plan the next week's issue. A staff artist showed a cartoon he had roughed out. It pictured John Bull, the personification of England, awakening from a nightmare. As he came awake his dream rushed out the window. The Specter of War, read the inscription, had fled. The editors approved the cartoon for the issue of March 15.

•

There was a country that had been the first democracy Central Europe had ever known; and there was its successor, a Czechoslovakia shorn of its Sudetenland and its Teschen and its properties along the border with Hungary, a Czechoslovakia whose eastern provinces of Ruthenia and Slovakia, backward and primitive, grew restive under the rule of the capital city of Prague. In that new and sad Czechoslovakia ruled Edvard Beneš's successors, whose only thought was to avoid antagonizing Adolf Hitler. Everything was agreeable to Prague: German direction of Czechoslovakian foreign policy, reduction of the Czech army, dismissal of editors and government officials not friendly to the Reich, preferential trade agreements, persecution of Jews. England and France were far away. The Czechs had learned that much at Munich.

Even in the days of the Austro-Hungarian Empire Ruthenia and Slovakia had resented the more polished, better educated, more liberal Czechs. To them Czechs were the enemy and Hitler a man who in private conversations indicated he would take at least Slovakia under his wing if it seceded from what was left of Czechoslovakia. On March 9, 1939, the day that in far-off London Prime Minister Chamberlain told reporters that Europe was settling down for a long period of tranquillity, Emil Hacha, the aged and infirm president of Czechoslovakia, was told by his government intelligence experts that reports indicated Slovakia, encouraged by Germany, was about to declare its secession.

Hacha ordered the arrest of the leading officials of his rebellious province. A new set of leaders was appointed in their place. The next day, March 11, the day Home Secretary Sir Samuel Hoare spoke of a coming Golden Age, the Nazi governor of Austria crossed the border into Slovakia and called upon the newly appointed Slovakian leaders. Five German generals accompanied him. He ordered secession from Czechoslovakia. The old Beneš spirit was arising in Prague. Conditions were intolerable. If Slovakia seceded Adolf Hitler would enable the new country to prosper. If not—

The Slovakians stalled briefly. Across the border German divisions gathered. The Slovakians sent a telegram to Berlin saying they were seceding. They asked the Leader to give his blessings to this liberation from Prague. He replied that he would gladly take over their protection.

The deeply disturbed President Hacha asked Berlin if he could call upon an Adolf Hitler the Slovakian officials now openly addressed as My Leader. Permission was granted. His train arrived in Berlin late at night. An SS honor guard was at the station, flowers, the information that a suite at the Adlon Hotel was waiting. With his daughter and foreign minister he went to the rooms. Chocolates from Hitler awaited the daughter.

President Hacha intended to point out to Hitler that his country was being cut apart slice by slice and ask for mercy. At one-fifteen on the morning of March 15, the day *Punch* appeared showing the Specter of War flying away, he was called to the New Chancellory. He went through darkened streets and was shown into a dark-paneled room lit only by a few bronze lamps. A sinister atmosphere, Hitler's interpreter thought to himself. Paul Schmidt did not envy Hacha for what he would go through.

Ill and old, Hacha was not accustomed to conducting business in the small hours of the night. Vaguely he said that he knew that the Leader, who had taken away the Sudetenland, was Czechoslovakia's friend, and that the country would certainly do anything that Leader asked. He himself would keep doing his best to stay in the Leader's good graces. His voice trailed away. "That is all I have to say, really. . . . I'm an old man."

Hitler spoke from the brooding darkness of the half-lit room. He listed ancient instances of Czech hostility to Germans, speaking to Hacha of Czechoslovakia as he had spoken a year earlier to von Schuschnigg of Austria. His harsh voice rose. He stood up, and Hacha and his foreign minister jumped to their feet. Czechoslovakia to Hitler had no history; to say so was "schoolboy nonsense." She did not need an army because an army backs a foreign policy, and she had no such thing. "No foreign policy! No mission, except to face the facts of her situation! No future unless she does so!"

His voice dropped. "And now we face the new situation. I have given the order to the soldiers of the German army. At six o'clock this morning they will march into Czechoslovakia and incorporate it into the German Reich."

The interpreter Schmidt translated what he had said, looking at the Czechs as he did so. They seemed almost turned to stone, Schmidt thought. "Only their eyes showed they were alive." Hitler dismissed them. They were taken into an adjoining room where Goering and Ribbentrop were. A statement requesting Germany to take over Czechoslovakia was handed to Hacha for his signature. Dazedly he said that they wanted him to destroy his nation. He begged for mercy. Goering in reply spoke of the strength of the German air force.

"Sign!" Ribbentrop snarled. Hacha circled the table to avoid the pens the Germans thrust at him.

"Why don't you sign?" Goering asked. "It will save so much trouble. I hate to say it, but Prague—I should be terribly sorry if I were compelled to destroy this beautiful city."

Hacha staggered and fell into a faint. It was three o'clock in the morning. Hitler's doctor was sent for. He gave Hacha a stimulant through a hypodermic needle.

"Think of Prague!" Goering shouted when he came to. Hacha signed.

At their request the Leader today received the Czechoslovak president and foreign minister. The serious situation created in the present Czechoslovak territory was examined with complete frankness.

The conviction was unanimously expressed on both sides that the aim of all efforts must be the safeguarding of calm, order and peace in this part of Central Europe. The Czechoslovak president declared that in order to serve this object, he confidently placed the fate of the Czech people in the hands of the Leader of the German Reich. The Leader accepted this declaration.

At four o'clock in the morning Hacha was driven through the snow falling on Berlin to the Adlon Hotel. Hitler held out his arms to a little group of his secretaries. "Kiss me!" he cried. "Children! This is the greatest day of my life! I shall go down into history as the greatest German!" Two hours later, at six, the German army crossed over into Czechoslovakia, the guns and marching columns plastered with snow.

Hacha took the train back to Prague, his journey slowed by German troop trains given priority. A guard of the Leibstandarte Adolf Hitler detachment of the SS was on guard at the Old City's Hradschin Castle. Hacha was directed to use the servants' entrance. "Don't worry, Father," said his daughter. "Just let us get home." In the banquet hall of the ancient building glowing candles illuminated paintings, suits of armor, sculptures and the just-arrived Leader of the German Reich, which now included the new Protectorate of Bohemia and Moravia as he looked down at the Charles Bridge with its statues of saints over the Moldau. From a buffet table loaded with ham, pâtés, cold meats, game, cheese, fruit and beer, Hitler picked up a small stein of Pilsner and drank. It was the only time anyone ever saw him touch alcohol. He made a face and laughed. "Czechoslovakia has ceased to exist," he had proclaimed before leaving Berlin for Prague.

•

He had rearmed Germany in defiance of the Versailles Treaty; it was difficult to argue with the act. A great nation could not remain helpless forever. He had marched into the Rhineland against treaty restrictions; the move was not unreasonable, for he was after all just walking into his own back garden. He had taken Austria into the German Reich; there was logic to it for Austria on her own was not a functioning state. He had taken the Sudetenland; it was understandable. The German-speaking population there did not wish to remain under Czech rule. For his persecutions and shootings and concentration camps one might feel revulsion, but he was the elected head of the German state and these were internal German matters.

But for the annexation of rump Czechoslovakia there could be no explanations. The world had experienced no shock so great since the outbreak of the War in 1914. To the generation of 1939 the new German assault seemed a parallel to that which had swept over Belgium just a quarter of a century earlier. Hitler throughout his career had portrayed himself as a German seeking to unite Germans, to make his Germany whole. Paintings of him had shown him in armor such as Siegfried must have worn. He was the Kindly Leader, the son of the German race who had risen to be its father. He was against the Jews because they were not real Germans; he stood for Germany alone. He had one faith; Germany, so help me God! he had cried aloud, many times. But now with his soldiers and his tanks he had swooped down upon an entirely alien people and made them his.

On this Ides of March, he lowered the national flag flying from the mast of the German ship of state and hoisted the skull and bones of a pirate vessel. So it seemed to His Majesty's ambassador at Berlin. Hitler now declared himself to live by the law of the jungle, thought Sir Nevile Henderson. He had crossed the Rubicon. Henderson thought of Hungary, Romania, Poland, the Baltic States. None of them could feel safe now. Once in Europe there had been the strength of religion and a shared Christianity, a family of kings and emperors addressing one another as "Sir My Brother." Much had vanished in the Great War, and not least that idea, that view, of the way in which the European world functioned. The old traditions and ways were gone. They would not come again.

Prime Minister Neville Chamberlain was paralyzed by Hitler's latest act. When most aroused, he would become colder, more austere, more convoluted in his fashion of expression; and when he addressed Parliament he was never more himself: "I have so often heard charges of breach of faith bandied about which did not seem to me to be founded upon sufficient premises that I do not wish to associate myself today with any charges of that character. I do not want to make any specific charges of breach of faith, but I am bound to say that I cannot believe that anything of the kind which has now taken place was contemplated by any of the signatories of the Munich Agreement."

Sir John Simon, the chancellor of the exchequer, his close associate, put in that with the secession of Slovakia the Czechoslovakian state had really ceased to exist and with it Britain's guarantee that its borders would be respected. You could not have an obligation toward a nonentity. A lawyer, Simon went on with his case. Perhaps the German occupation of Prague certified the rectitude of the Munich pact. Britain had escaped being put in the position of going to war to protect a state that was not really a valid state. To go to war for the unity of a country doomed to break up by the will of its population was to be more Catholic than the Pope.

"It is natural that I should bitterly regret what has now occurred," Chamberlain said, "but do not let us on that account be deflected from our course. Let us remember that the desire of all the peoples of the world still remains concentrated on the hopes of peace."

It was quite true. No one wanted a war. Yet the British Cabinet was in disarray. Sir Samuel Hoare with his hopes for a Golden Age brought about by appeasement of Germany spoke of retirement. Halifax saw Armageddon ahead. "I can well understand Herr Hitler's taste for bloodless victories," he told German ambassador Herbert von Dirksen, "but one of these days he will find himself up against something that will not be bloodless." Henderson was ordered to London for consultation. He left Berlin feeling he might never return.

Chamberlain had much earlier made a commitment to speak in his home city of Birmingham on March 17, two days after the staggering news came. His talk was to deal with domestic issues and social programs. That would not do now. He went northward by train, writing a new speech as he traveled. Winston Churchill awaited the prime minister's words with "anticipatory contempt," for he expected some sort of self-congratulatory statement about how the prime minister's foresight had detached Britain from the fate of disordered and uncertain Central Europe. What came out was quite different. In that moment Churchill realized that if Chamberlain had failed to understand Hitler, Hitler had underrated the nature of Chamberlain. "He did not realize that Neville Chamberlain had a very hard core, and that he did not like being cheated."

"What has become of this declaration of 'No further territorial ambition'?" Chamberlain asked his Birmingham audience. "What has become of the assurance, 'We don't want any Czechs in the Reich'? Does not the question inevitably arise in our minds, 'If it is so easy to discover good reasons for ignoring assurances so solemnly and repeatedly given, what reliance can be placed upon any other assurances that come from the same source?' Events in complete disregard of the principles laid down by the German government itself must cause us all to be asking ourselves, 'Is this the end of an old adventure, or is it the beginning of a new?

" 'Is this the last attack upon a small State, or is it to be followed by others? Is this, in fact, a step in the direction of an attempt to dominate the world by force?' "

To Hitler the prime minister's new outrage and new position were alike ridiculous. The British Empire for centuries had squeezed people of all races and types and colors into its fold. Why should Germany be called to account for taking over the governing of a few Czechs? That Chamberlain had questioned the validity of his word meant nothing to Hitler. He would never, he told his intimates, tell a lie on behalf of himself, but to lie for one's country, what was that? Had not Count Cavour, revered as the creator of modern Italy, once sighed that if we did the things for ourselves that we do for our countries, what scoundrels we would be! Germany had a destiny to fulfill. She would do so. On the day after the annexation of what had been rump Czechoslovakia, Reich Propaganda Minister Goebbels sent a notification to all German editors that they were not to employ the phrase "Greater Germany" in describing the country as it now was. "This term is reserved for later eventualities." In other words, Germany was not yet set in her boundaries.

Within a week, a part of Goebbels's meaning was made clear. Under threat of immediate bombardment from the sea, Lithuania on the Baltic was ordered to surrender to Germany her port of Memel, taken from Germany under League of Nations auspices after the War. Threatened by Poland years earlier over a border dispute, Lithuania had found herself unable to drum up any diplomatic or military support. She could not hope for any against Germany.

On March 23, deathly ill after his first and only sea voyage, the Leader disembarked from the pocket battleship *Deutschland* to tour his new acquisition. "You have returned to a new Germany which is determined to master and shape its own destinies," he told the people when he got back his land legs.

In Warsaw Foreign Minister Beck faced a suddenly transformed western frontier. He had shared a 1,250-mile-long border with Germany before Germany's annexation of Czechoslovakia; now he shared one made five hundred miles longer by that annexation. Hitler also had an additional seaport in Memel to Poland's north. Beck still believed himself one step in front of everybody else—"There is only one Colonel Beck"—but, shaken by his January meeting with Hitler, he felt pessimistic about Germany for the first time. On the day Hitler toured Memel, he seeded foreign capitals with rumors that the Germans were about to attack Poland, and called up a third of a million reservists. Beck's dreams and fantasies about his country had always been greeted with reserve, as were many of the concepts of romantic New Poland. But this time the possibility existed that what he said was correct.

In the past Neville Chamberlain had failed to follow the traditional British policy of backing smaller European powers against powerful ones; instead, it was said, he had backed powerful Germany against weak neighbors. That was finished now. Perhaps Churchill had only latterly discovered the hard core. Anthony Eden had always known it was there, and had likened the prime minister in ruthlessness to his father, Joseph Chamberlain.

"In the event of any action," the prime minister told Parliament, "Which clearly threatened Polish independence and which the Polish government accordingly considered it vital to resist with their national forces, His Majesty's government would feel themselves bound at once to lend the Polish government all support in their power."

He was days away from his seventieth birthday, gray and grim and old and with the skin above his high cheekbones a parchment yellow. What he was doing was astounding. He had always felt that the defense of Britain came first, the trade routes second, the overseas territories and dominions next, and the defense of the territory of allies last. Now he was putting the destiny of England and the Empire completely in the hands of another country.

"I may add that the French government have authorized me to make it plain that they stand in the same position in this matter as do His Majesty's government." In a little while he would follow his guarantee to Poland with similar undertakings to Romania and Greece. A thrill of horror at what might be coming went around the world.

"Life is a complete nightmare," Permanent Under Secretary of State for Foreign Affairs Sir Alexander Cadogan wrote in his diary. "Shall we ever wake up?"

Joseph Beck of Poland did not see things that way. Still lapsing into talk of a cavalry ride to Berlin, he told people he had decided to accept Chamberlain's guarantee "between two flicks of the ash" of the cigarette he was smoking. But Polish honor decreed that the guarantee must be mutual, he ruled. The two nations were after all on the same level. If Britain were attacked, he said, Poland would come sweeping to her aid. Asked to London for discussions, he inquired after the arrangements and, told that Lord Halifax would be unable to meet him at the station, said he would not come. The foreign secretary of Great Britain must receive the foreign secretary of Poland. There must be a red carpet from the train and a stand from which photographers could get pictures. The British assented. Beck came and, although fluent in English, spoke only Polish throughout his visit.

Hitler's reaction was predictable. The British and Poles had flung down a gauntlet, he said. He was not one to ignore it. Since England took "the view that Germany should be opposed in all circumstances," he told the Reichstag, "and confirms this by the policy of encirclement," he was tearing up the agreement he had with England to limit his naval arrangements. He also renounced the nonaggression pact he had made five years earlier with Marshal Pilsudski of Poland. In London Chamberlain instituted conscription of Britain's twenty-year-olds. Even two years into the Great War there had been no conscription.

Privately Hitler was completely unrestrained in his rage. Admiral Wilhelm Canaris of the German intelligence service called upon the Leader and found him drumming his fingers on a marble table. He seemed to have a strange light in his eyes. "I will make the English swallow a devil's brew!" he said in such fashion that Canaris told close associates, "I've just seen a madman. I can hardly believe it. He is mad, mad. Do you understand? He is mad."

To the Italians Germany now bore the aspect of a neighbor gone berserk. The occupation of Czechoslovakia profoundly shocked them and their leader Mussolini, who regarded himself as the architect of the Munich conference. It would be impossible to present to the Italian people the idea of a formal alliance with Germany, he told his son-in-law and foreign minister, Count Ciano: "Even the stones would cry out against it." Ciano agreed, writing in his diary that Hitler was "unfaithful and treacherous." The Germans were possessed by "insolence and duplicity," King

Victor Emmanuel told Mussolini. They were "rascals and beggars."

But the Germans pressed for an alliance, and Foreign Minister Ribbentrop traveled to Milan to discuss it with Ciano. Some American papers reported that the visitor was given a hostile reception by the citizenry, and thinking his personal prestige was thus questioned, Mussolini telephoned Ciano and told him to agree to an alliance. To Ciano this was a "spiteful reaction to the irresponsible and valueless utterances of foreign journalists," but Il Duce was Il Duce. An alliance was negotiated.

The alliance contained a clause that gave some reassurance to Sir Nevile Henderson, for Germany and Italy contracted to do nothing for at least three or four years that would create a controversy capable of bringing about a war. Each must be informed in advance by the other of any moves that might produce international conflict. Mussolini had thought of terming the agreement the Pact of Blood; he titled it instead the Pact of Steel.

Under any name it was not good news for France and England, and their hopes that Mussolini would be a factor for peace were further diminished when on Good Friday, April 7, the Italians invaded and quickly conquered the mountain kingdom of Albania. Mussolini had perhaps believed his invasion would strengthen his position as a rival to Hitler. Perhaps, jealous, he had wanted an easy victory of his own, but his move instead isolated him and made him seem more a brother to Hitler in his willingness to use force. When on April 15 President Roosevelt sent a public telegram to Berlin, he addressed it also to Rome.

For a long time Roosevelt had wanted to interject his views into the rapidly worsening international scene. He was hampered in his aim by an intensely isolationist America, which, disillusioned by the seeming pointlessness of the Great War, saw a possible second conflict as simply a sign of mad European imperial ambitions and intrigues from which the New World must keep aloof. The 1917 entrance of America into the War was spoken of as a tragic mistake profiting nobody but a small coterie of munitions makers and banking and financial groups. "It would not be fair to say that the House of Morgan took us to war to save their investment in the Allies, but . . . ," said Senator Gerald Nye of North Dakota.

Under Nye's leadership a Senate committee studied the work of the merchants of death and recommended legislation to curb any further activities they might have in mind: a 98 percent tax on all incomes above $10,000 a year if war should come, no loans for governments at war, prohibitions on the sale or exportation of any kind of arms or munitions, no passport issuance for travel to war zones. There might come another world death march, Nye said, but America must not join in.

It was terrible to think of the results of the Great War upon America: battle deaths, the loss of rights, aroused prejudices, the devastating dust storms of the 1930s brought about by the plowing up of prairies for crops for the Allies. Even the Great Depression could be traced to the wild and unrestricted economic expansion the War had brought. The United States, Nye said, could be neither policeman nor doctor to the world. As for those who said America must rearm to preserve the peace, that was truly a monstrous idea. Where was the naval officer who would counsel against more ships? To do so would destroy his reason for being.

To show one's peaceful intentions by building a barbed-wire fence would lead one's neighbor to show his by putting a ferocious dog in his backyard, Nye said; and from there one went to pistols carried at all times. Soon one would say of the neighbor, "The other day I saw him moving supplies of poison gas and hand grenades into his house; now I have a machine gun mounted in the front yard. For the life of me I can't understand why we don't get along better."

By far the majority of Americans agreed with Nye's hatred for and distrust of the monied interests, the international bankers, of the East Coast and of Europe. It was generally agreed that President Wilson had not wanted to go to war in 1917. But disregarding George Washington's warnings about foreign entanglements he had done so, and what had resulted? Graves in France, cynicism, a War-inspired Prohibition, which had spawned a crime wave that had never abated.

Laws aimed at protecting American neutrality were first passed in 1935 and from then on were annually extended, polished and enlarged. In 1938 the Ludlow Amendment calling for a nationwide referendum before any war declaration was defeated only by the narrowest of margins. The President's discretion on such a matter was widely distrusted. If Premier Daladier of France could tell Ambassador Bullitt that the queen of England was ready to plunge the world into war to protect her position, so might many Americans say the same of Franklin Roosevelt. He caused a national uproar on Easter Sunday, April 9, when, on taking his departure from his southern residence at Warm Springs, Georgia, he told the townspeople at the station, "I'll be back in the autumn if we don't have a war." *We?*

In private the President referred to Hitler and Mussolini as "the two madmen" and said that appealing to them about anything might well be as useful as "delivering a sermon to a mad dog," but his telegram to them listed thirty-one countries and asked the German and Italian to give assurances they would not invade them. Hermann Goering was in Rome when Mussolini's copy was delivered. Goering said that perhaps the President was suffering from an incipient mental disease. Mussolini replied that it was possible that Roosevelt's paralysis of the legs was spreading upward into his brain. Hitler at first told his coterie he would refuse to reply to "so contemptible a creature" but changed his mind and gave answer in what the Berlin correspondent William L. Shirer thought the most effective speech of the Leader's career.

It was Poland, Hitler said, that had incomprehensibly mobilized a third of a million men, and England that instituted peacetime conscription for the first time in its history. Yet it was to Germany and Italy that President Roosevelt appealed for peace. No matter. Perhaps Mr. Roosevelt in spite of the labors connected with running his own country was in a position to know best the inner life of the thirty-one countries his telegram listed. He, Hitler, would attempt to allay the fears of one who "felt responsible for the history of the whole world and for the history of all nations."

He told the Reichstag he had asked the leaders of the thirty-one countries to tell him if they felt menaced by Germany. Unfortunately he had been unable to obtain clear insight into the thinking of some on the list. For instance, Mr. Roosevelt desired assurance that Germany would not attack Ireland. "Now, I have just read a speech by De Valera, the Irish prime minister, in which, strangely enough, and contrary to Mr. Roosevelt's opinion, he does not charge Germany with oppressing Ireland but reproaches England for subjecting Ireland to continuous aggression. In the same way, the fact has obviously escaped Mr. Roosevelt's notice that Palestine is at present not occupied by German troops but by the English." And of course Syria was not a free agent; French troops ruled there.

But for the other countries—and one by one he listed them and said he had obtained from such as Iraq and Luxembourg and the others their statements that they did not fear German invasion of their territories. As he slowly read out the long progression of names, the president of the Reichstag, Hermann Goering, sitting behind him, began to giggle. The Reichstag members joined in. With every name, gusts of hilarity came up at the speaker. The climax came when Hitler deadpanned a final guarantee to the American President thousands of miles across the Atlantic: "I here solemnly declare that all the assertions which have been circulated concerning an intended German attack on American territory are rank frauds."

Tears of laughter poured from Goering's eyes. Hitler thanked the American for his "curious telegram" and ended by saying that unlike the situation of the President, his own did not give him the leisure to attend to the entire universe's problems. He was rather occupied with working for the benefit of the German people, a task more precious to him than anything in the world. "Mr. Roosevelt! I believe that this is the way in which I can be of the most service to that for which we are all concerned, the justice, well-being, progress and peace of the whole community."

He had talked for two hours, the longest speech of his career. He had mentioned almost three dozen countries. Russia was not among them.

TEN

HE HAS SOUGHT to strike me a blow," the Polish foreign minister, Colonel Beck, said to the Romanian foreign minister, Grigore Gafencu. There was no need to say who *he* was. "I have parried the blow, as was required. The English are my friends; Danzig is in safekeeping." *He* might take the port of Memel undisturbed. The port of Danzig was a different matter. England's frontier, which was once the Channel and then later the Rhine, now stood on the Vistula. England's guarantee to Poland said so. And at the mouth of the Vistula was Danzig.

The city consisted of four hundred thousand persons, more than 95 percent of them German. They lived in a Baroque metropolis reminiscent of Amsterdam or Brussels, in high gabled houses set on twisting cobbled streets, in an atmosphere established centuries before by the well-off merchants of the Hanseatic League. Danzig had always been rich and powerful, a German trading center. Even under Polish rule in the days of Poland's glory during the sixteenth century Danzig had been virtually an independent city. With the 1793 partition of Poland it became a part of Prussia, capital of the province of West Prussia and under the Kaiser headquarters of the area commander of the German army.

Then came the War and German defeat. Independent but landlocked Poland, said the peacemakers of 1919, needed a port. But it would be unthinkable to give the Poles Danzig, a place made important throughout history by German culture and German ways, and so different from the physical disorder of the Slavic East. Self-determination forbade turning Danzig over to the Poles. The matter was compromised by making the metropolis and its surrounding outlands the Free City of Danzig, to be ruled by a League of Nations high commissioner from what had been the German army headquarters building.

The Free City sat at the mouth of the Vistula to the Baltic, at the top of the fifty- to one-hundred-mile strip cut from Germany so that Poland could have access to the sea. On the west of the strip, the Corridor, was Germany proper; to the east was the German province of East Prussia. Like the inhabitants of the Corridor, those of the old port remained German at heart. German Danzig might become the Free City and Posen might become Poznan and West Prussia Pomorze, but the people did not give up their age-old belief that the Slavdom of the East was morally, socially, intellectually inferior to the Teutons of the West, nor did they forget that for centuries it had been held that Germany's historic mission was to hold back the flood of the East.

No one in the world was comfortable with the Polish Corridor and the Free City. Lloyd George said at Versailles that he could not conceive of a better recipe for a future war than that large numbers of Germans should be made citizens of other lands surrounding or carved out of their former homeland. Sir Austen Chamberlain said privately in 1925 that no British government could or ever would risk the bones of a single British grenadier for the Polish Corridor.

The formerly German lands made Polish never accepted the situation. Nor did their relatives who lived to the west and east and who had to cross the Corridor, by Polish law, in locked trains with blinds drawn. The Vistula flowing through Poland must have an open mouth at the sea for Poland, the Versailles Treaty had said. But, asked Joseph Goebbels, was that logical? Was Switzerland demanding ownership of Marseille or Toulon? By such reasoning Rotterdam should be German. Adolf Hitler asked how the Americans would like a Mexican Corridor cutting off Texas from the rest of the country.

In 1938 Hitler asked Colonel Beck if he would cede sufficient space across the Corridor, a corridor within the Corridor, for Germany to build and maintain a six-lane highway and railroad line from Germany proper to the cut-off East Prussia. Beck refused. In January 1939, when Hitler declined to look at him, when the "I would like" of previous years became "It must be," Beck left the Leader for the first time with a feeling of pessimism. Then came the occupation of Czechoslovakia and the British guarantee of Poland and British conscription, and Beck felt safe. He held the British sword in his hand. The matter was closed. Or so it appeared to him.

But was it so to the Germans? "In reality, it is only an affair of nuances," Romania's ambassador to Poland Franassovici told his German counterpart, Ambassador Count von Moltke. But the German replied, "It is not a matter of nuances, but one of colors. You see this map of Europe? On it Germany is marked in yellow and the Free State of Danzig in blue. Well, the little blue spot must disappear. There must be yellow here. It is absolutely essential. It is a matter of the Leader's prestige."

Gafencu, the foreign minister of Romania, went to Berlin for the parade celebrating the Leader's fiftieth birthday, when the British colonel Mason-Macfarland did not fire. Gafencu heard the clanging metal and the roaring airplanes, and was informed by Joachim von Ribbentrop that the Polish Corridor was "absurd" and the situation of Danzig "impossible." He sat with a Hitler brandishing Danzig newspapers that described Polish indignities against Germans and heard the Leader shout against the Poles in his wild way, no different from his addresses to a crowd of ten thousand or, as in this case, one set of ears.

It was all the fault of England, Hitler cried, an England that in its blindness and selfishness and obduracy aimed to block all Germany spheres of influence, to destroy German economic life, to attack German honor and strength. Hitler told his intimates it was really incomprehensible that an England that had colonized a quarter of the globe, that held alike civilized Irishmen and unlettered tropical savages in bondage, would oppose the right of Germany to seek the return of a city, Danzig, and an area, the Corridor, which had been German for hundreds of years.

"If it is really true that they will plunge into war over this trivial matter, over a mere nothing like Danzig," he told Ribbentrop, "I am convinced that war with England is absolutely inevitable." The British wished to encircle him, he said, and then attack on some excuse. That was their aim.

From Poland, that spring, the spring of 1939, there came a flow of reports that received the same attention in the German newspapers as the reports of a year earlier about Czech acts toward the Sudeten Germans. Mobs of Poles had smashed buildings housing associations of Germans resident on Polish territory, beaten up members of choral societies on their way home from practice, thrown rocks through German store windows. Poles had boycotted German stores, said newspapers in Hamburg and Augsburg and Munich, set fire to them, invaded and destroyed private residences.

"Even five-year-old children sing anti-German songs which frequently contain curses against the Leader," reported the German consul at Lodz on May 8. Two houses belonging to German residents of Poland were set on fire, the consul said, while neighbors cried, "Let the Hitlerites burn!"

Twelve days later members of Danzig's large Brown Shirt contingent broke into the Polish customs post at Kalthof on the East Prussian frontier, roughed up the officials, threw them into a truck and dumped them in a field miles away.

With the customs men out of the picture, a convoy of German arms sped down the road into Danzig. When a Polish official came to investigate, his car was surrounded by Brown Shirts booing and yelling insults. The official's chauffeur drew a revolver and killed one Brown Shirt, a butcher in his off-duty hours.

The German version appeared prominently in every German paper: "A citizen was going through a deserted village in a taxi when he was killed by a Polish chauffeur who had first dazzled the taxi driver with his headlights." Hitler sent a wreath to the butcher's funeral. Soon there were reports that a truck from East Prussia had tried to run a Polish customs post on the Corridor and that the guards fired in the air to halt it. "Fresh attempt at murder by the Poles on Danzig territory," headlined the German papers. WE WANT TO GO HOME TO THE REICH said banners strung across the Free City's streets. WE LOVE OUR LEADER.

The Polish government sent a harshly worded message to local officials of Danzig demanding that interference with Polish customs officials cease. An equally tough response was made. Foreign Minister Beck had England's guarantee and the promise of trailing-along France that if war should break out between Germany and Poland, the French would immediately launch air attacks from the west, that three days after French mobilization a local diversionary offensive would commence, that fifteen days after mobilization a major offensive involving the entire French army would get under way. So armed and without consulting his two Western allies, Beck sent word to Danzig that any attempt for the city to join itself to Germany would be regarded as an act of aggression and would be met as such by Polish force. "You want to negotiate at the point of a bayonet!" said German Ambassador von Moltke. "That is your method," Beck replied.

Streams of reports of German-Polish conflict poured out of the Free City and the Corridor. "It is forbidden to speak Polish here!" German students in a Danzig café shouted to students using that language. A fight broke out. The police came. The café owner let it be known that no Polish customers were desired on the premises, and the German students put up a notice: ENTRANCE IS FORBIDDEN TO DOGS AND POLISH STUDENTS. More brawls followed and university classes were suspended. Arms continually came smuggled into Danzig from East Prussia and Germany proper, as the Free City inhabitants told one another that a Polish attack could be expected at any moment. Rumors in Poland had it that Danzig was preparing to announce its return to the Reich. Dr. Joseph Goebbels came to tell a Free City crowd that political frontiers were of limited duration but that frontiers traced by language, race and blood were unchangeable and eternal. By these standards, he said, the Free City was German:

"We are not gathered here today, citizens of Danzig, to decide whether this great city should return to the Reich, but *when.* Soon, comrades, soon! There is not much time to waste. Just like the Jewish whores who try to sneak into our beds and rob us of our manhood, so do the Poles and British scheme to steal our land and our people. All we ask is what rightfully belongs to us. Danzig is German. It must return to Germany. It is our understandable, clear, definite and sacred wish! But our enemies seek not only to stop us from this, they are arrogantly planning worse than this. Old and ignorant men in London and braggart bullies in Warsaw have made up their minds; they will not only refuse to give what belongs to us, but they will snatch what does not belong to them. Already the Polish wind-and-piss characters in Warsaw talk about claiming East Prussia and German Silesia. And don't fool yourselves, if we let them they will go further than that. They will claim that their frontier should be on the Rhine. It would be convenient for them! They could rub arses with their new friends, the British.

"But will we let them? We will not let them! We will drive them out of Danzig!"

Reich Chancellor and Führer Adolf Hitler *(bottom center)* approaches his Mercedes-Benz sedan through an adoring Berlin crowd on May Day 1934. *(New York Public Library)*

With war gathering over Europe, Britain's rulers arrive on their first visit to the United States. King George and President Roosevelt ride in an open car through the streets of Washington, June 1939. "My mother thinks you should have a cup of tea. She doesn't approve of cocktails," FDR told the king. "Neither does my mother," the king replied. *(New York Public Library)*

The queen and Eleanor Roosevelt follow in procession from Washington's Union Station. Within days parasols became fashionable in America. *(New York Public Library)*

Below: Ambassador to England Joseph Kennedy bids farewell to his family as he boards the S.S. *Manhattan* to assume his position at the Court of St. James *(from the left):* Patricia (14), Kathleen (17), Eunice (16), Robert (12), Jean (9), Edward (7), Rosemary (19) and Joseph Jr. (22). Wife Rose followed later. Upon learning from Prime Minister Chamberlain that war was to be declared, Kennedy told FDR, "It's the end of the world, the end of everything." *(AP/Wide World Photos)*

Marshal Smigly-Rydz of Poland *(center, saluting)* reviews Polish war veterans in Paris. "With the Germans," he said, "we risk the loss of our liberty, but with the Russians, we lose our soul." *(AP/Wide World Photos)*

The Honorable Miss Unity Mitford, whom Hitler said fulfilled his ideal of Aryan womanhood *(left)*. Her relationship with the Leader was the focus of the world's speculation. *(AP/Wide World Photos)*

The head of the British Union of Fascists, Sir Oswald Mosley *(right)*, addressing a crowd of blackshirts: "If Poland whistles, a million Englishmen have got to die." *(New York Public Library)*

A desperate attempt to salvage peace in Europe during yet another meeting, this time at Berchtesgaden *(from left to right):* Chamberlain, Hitler, German Foreign Minister Joachim von Ribbentrop and Sir Nevile Henderson. *(AP/Wide World Photos)*

British Prime Minister Neville Chamberlain departing for Munich to meet with Hitler in 1938: "I believe it is peace for our time." Sir Horace Wilson is to his right. *(AP/Wide World Photos)*

His Majesty's ambassador to Germany, Sir Nevile Henderson, K.C.M.G.: "I do not like war." *(New York Public Library)*

The foreign minister of the German Reich, Joachim von Ribbentrop, a man well traveled through the Allied countries. "Touchy, a bully, arrogant, rude, tactless, impolite, a social climber and *poseur*, petty and spiteful, a great snob—everyone who knew him was in unanimous agreement." *(New York Public Library)*

The ill-fated and much-misunderstood summit at Munich, September 1938 *(from left to right):* Hermann Goering, Hitler, interpreter Paul Schmidt, Italian Foreign Minister Galeazzo Ciano, Mussolini, French Premier Edouard Daladier and Chamberlain. *(AP/Wide World Photos)*

The signing of the Soviet-German nonaggression treaty on August 21, 1939, which triggered World War II *(from right to left):* Russian Foreign Minister Vyacheslav Molotov, Communist Party Chairman Joseph Stalin and Ribbentrop. "A very nice atmosphere," Ribbentrop said to himself. *(AP/Wide World Photos)*

In a tense Warsaw mobilization posters go up ten days after the signing of the Soviet-German pact in preparation for the coming onslaught. *(New York Public Library)*

The Leader announces the invasion of Poland to the Reichstag on September 1, 1939: "I wish nothing other than to be the first soldier of the German Reich." *(New York Public Library)*

Reaction in Great Britain the day after Chamberlain's declaration of war.

ON YOUR FEET
FOR HOURS?
Then Don't Forget That
ZAM-BUK
Removes Pain, Soreness & Cores

Daily Herald

No. 7349   MONDAY, SEPTEMBER 4, 1939   ONE PENNY

WAR DECLARED BY BRITAIN AND FRANCE

We Have Resolved To Finish It—PRIME MINISTER

GREAT BRITAIN DECLARED WAR ON GERMANY AT 11 O'CLOCK YESTERDAY MORNING.

Six hours later, at 5 p.m., France declared war.

Britain's resolution to defend Poland against Nazi aggression was described by the newly-formed Ministry of Information in one of its first announcements, as follows:—

"At 11.15 this morning (Sunday) Mr. R. Dunbar, Head of the Treaty Department of the Foreign Office, went to the German Embassy, where he was received by Dr. Kordt, the Charge d'Affaires.

"Mr. Dunbar handed to Dr. Kordt a notification that a state of war existed between Great Britain and Germany as from 11 o'clock R.S.T. this morning. This notification constituted the formal declaration of war."

WAR
CABINET
OF

Unthinkable We Should Refuse The Challenge

—THE KING

Broadcasting last evening from his study at Buckingham Palace, the King said:—

IN this grave hour, perhaps the most fateful in our history, I send to every household of my people, both at home and overseas, this message, spoken with the same depth of feeling for each one of you as if I were able to cross your threshold and speak to you myself.

For the second time in the lives of most of us we are at war.

Over and over again we

POLES SMASH WAY INTO E. PRUSSIA

OFFICIALS in Warsaw stated late last night that the Polish army has smashed a way across the Northern border into East Prussia, after driving the Germans from several Polish towns in bitter fighting.

London Hears Its First Raid Warning

LONDON was calm yesterday when it heard its first air raid warning.

This is the official statement issued by the Air Ministry:—

At 11.30 a.m. yesterday an aircraft was observed approaching the South Coast.

BLACK-OUT TIME

On the Northern Front the Poles are reported to have defeated the German effort to drive a barrier across the upper part of the Corridor. The Germans fell back behind their frontiers.

The Poles say they have broken through the German fortifications as far as the railway terminus of Deutsch Eylau.

One of the most important towns recaptured is stated to be Tczew.

Dispatches from the front say that German forces fighting is going on at Czestochowa and Katowice. German reports that they have captured Czestochowa are denied.

Warsaw was again raided yesterday by German aircraft.

The most modern and deadly force of its time, the German air force soars over the skies of Poland, September 1939. The Polish army was still mired in the Middle Ages, riding on horseback, armed with lances. *(New York Public Library; AP/Wide World Photos)*

In Warsaw Beck told his Parliament: "We in Poland do not recognize the concept of peace at any price! There is only one thing in the life of men, nations and states which is beyond price, and that is honor." To his countrymen of all levels save perhaps the very lowest their New Poland, Polonia Restituta, represented and embodied romance, gaiety, chivalry, poetry, adventure and knightliness. But to the rest of the world suddenly in 1939's spring seeing Armageddon in the offing it seemed that the pledged word of the West, of democracy, of the future, was in the hands of the unstable and irresponsible leaders of a country freed in the name of liberty and of self-determination that was in fact no less authoritarian, nationalist, totalitarian and racially intolerant than Germany and Italy. Danzig was no longer a place but a principle, wrote retired British army major general Adrian Carton de Wiart from his Polish residence to his old comrade in arms General Hastings Lionel Ismay.

The French journalist Marcel Deat in the first days of May wrote an article whose title expressed all that he and millions felt. That title and what it meant swept over France overnight and leaped the Channel to England, where as in France it was endlessly repeated, with nothing additional needed to explain the implications: *Die for Danzig?*

•

In September 1938, right after Chamberlain's visit to Berchtesgaden and just before his flight to Godesberg on the Rhine, King George VI received a letter from President Roosevelt. It concerned the king's projected trip to Canada, scheduled for June 1939. Would the king, Roosevelt asked, wish to add America to his itinerary? He would be most welcome. "If you bring either or both of the children with you they will also be very welcome, and I shall try to have one or two Roosevelts of approximately the same age to play with them." King George wrote back that he and the queen would be very glad to visit. The two little princesses, however, would not be with them. They were too young for so strenuous a tour.

The visit would be the first ever made to the United States by a reigning British monarch. President and Mrs. Roosevelt applied to the American ambassador to France, William Bullitt, for information on how the French had handled the royal visit of the previous year. Bullitt, personally closer to Roosevelt than any other member of the American foreign service, sent back a detailed report.

"My most onerous diplomatic labor since reaching Paris has been the extraction of these recommendations and I expect you to decorate me at once with the Order of the Royal Bathtub," he began. The king's bed, Bullitt reported, must not be along a wall. He would bring his own cigarettes. His blankets must have a silk cover, there must be a mirror tall enough for him to see himself full-length when standing, there must be four bathroom glasses, one graduated, a bath thermometer, several spoons large and small, matches in the ashtrays. There must be an eiderdown quilt on the king's bed. There must be a reef in the covers at the foot of the bed.

Bullitt's letter, widely distributed to members of his administration by Roosevelt, caused insiders to laugh, particularly at the notion of an eiderdown quilt in a summertime Washington, whose heat was such that British diplomats assigned there received the extra pay given for hardship posts. Secretary of the Interior Harold L. Ickes, who not without reason had long been known as the Old Curmudgeon, did not laugh. He worked himself up into a rage over the British monarchs' needs and those of the courtiers and lackeys and ladies in waiting who would accompany them. If the British thought they were going to go slumming when they arranged to visit the White House, Ickes snarled into his diary, they ought to stay home.

Bullitt's report was of course not known to the vast majority of Americans, but nevertheless a substantial number of them duplicated Ickes's reaction to the proposed visit. It had not been so long, after all, since Big Bill Thompson successfully ran for mayor of Chicago on a platform that included his guarantee that if George V, George VI's father, ever dared to come to the Windy City, he, Big Bill, would personally punch him in the nose. Perfidious Albion, which had dragged the United States into war in 1917, said millions of Americans, could only be sending its king to prepare the way for another rescue of England's chestnuts from the fire.

But what actually was America in a military sense? Her army, including the air corps, consisted of some two hundred thousand men, a number estimated to constitute the thirteenth or fourteenth army of the world. She had nine divisions on paper, none at authorized wartime strength. Germany had ninety ready-to-go divisions, Italy forty-five. Appropriations for the United States military were such that when Brigadier General George C. Marshall got orders to report from Vancouver Barracks near Portland, Oregon, for duty at Washington as deputy chief of staff, it required a flow of letters back and forth between him and Chief of Staff Malin Craig to determine that Craig would be able to scrape up funds enough to transport Marshall and his family east by train instead of forcing them to wait for an army transport to travel by sea through the Panama Canal.

There were no reserves save for an ineffective national guard. Antitank equipment hardly existed. Of modern howitzers and cannons only prototypes were available. There were few antiaircraft guns and less than four hundred tanks, weakly armored. Munitions stocks were small.

Malin Craig had tried to build something approaching a strong force but had been entirely unsuccessful. "They have crucified my husband," his wife said. (The chief of staff discussed the possibilities of a European war with Secretary Ickes at the annual dinner of the White House Correspondents' Association at Washington's Mayflower Hotel in March. Ickes told his diary, "He remarked that such an event would mean the end of civilization as we know it."

It was hardly American strength but the potential that mattered in the spring of 1939. Nine out of ten Americans did not wish that potential to be tapped, and King George and his advisers knew it. For that reason they decided that Foreign Secretary Lord Halifax should not accompany the party, for his presence would be seen as adding to an attempt to involve the Americans in those entangling alliances George Washington had warned against, a warning constantly referred to in 1939 in the American press and on the radio and in private conversations.

The British left Southampton on May 5. They had originally planned to travel on the battle cruiser *Repulse* but decided it would be a mistake to take a valued fighting ship out of European waters. To do so might encourage Hitler to think that Britain did not mean business in offering her guarantee to Poland. A liner, the *Empress of Australia*, was chartered. Princess Elizabeth and Princess Margaret Rose were at the pier to see their parents off. "I have my handkerchief," Margaret said to her older sister.

"To wave, not to cry," Elizabeth replied.

British naval authorities knew that sailing off the Spanish coast was the pocket battleship *Deutschland,* which had taken the sea-sick Leader to Memel two months earlier, and it occurred to them that it might intercept the king's ship to take him prisoner for political ransom. Precautions were accordingly taken.

The royals landed at Quebec and toured Canada and then, on June 9, crossed over the United States border at Niagara Falls, where Secretary of State Cordell Hull boarded their train to escort them to Washington's Union Station. To ward off the blinding sun beating down on the open car headed for the White House, Queen Elizabeth raised a white silk parasol with a dark green lining, and at once, in days, parasols became fashionable in America. (Her parasol, people said, was quite different from the umbrella that characterized for all time Chamberlain's trip to Munich.)

The Roosevelts found the couple "nice young people." (King George was forty-three, Queen Elizabeth thirty-nine to the President's fifty-seven and the First Lady's fifty-five.) The queen particularly charmed those who met or saw her—"The king's tour, the queen's triumph"—and all who heard of her encounter with the eight-year-old motherless daughter of presidential adviser Harry Hopkins were touched by what she did for the little girl. Told of the child's lonely situation and that she wanted to greet the queen of England, Elizabeth suggested that a meeting he held off until she looked the part. The occasion came when she emerged from her White House room to go to a formal dinner party at the British Embassy. By arrangement Diana Hopkins was waiting with Eleanor Roosevelt in the corridor to see Elizabeth come out radiant in sweeping floor-length gown, blazing jewels and diadem. Even those who disliked Diana's abrasive father found it difficult not to be moved when they heard of how she had run to him and cried, "Daddy, oh, Daddy, I have seen the Fairy Queen."

There was a trip to Mount Vernon for the royal couple, an Embassy party for fifteen hundred. Political wives, it was noted, did not curtsy at the party for fear of the voters at home hearing about the spouses of their elected representatives bowing and scraping to the British monarchs. Other women did, holding themselves to be on British soil and so bound by that country's manners. Vice President Garner, with ambitions to succeed to a higher post, was reported to have slapped King George on the back and grabbed him by the forearm at a White House dinner, and President Roosevelt told Secretary Ickes he imagined that this was supposed to show Cactus Jack's home state of Texas how democratic he was. Ickes himself noted how at the after-dinner entertainment Garner failed to applaud the singing of the black Marian Anderson, although he clapped for the white Kate Smith and Lawrence Tibbett. The heat was frightful. Ickes thought to himself that the President ought to install some air conditioning.

King George and Queen Elizabeth left Washington for New York and a tour of the World's Fair. In front of the Polish Pavilion stood a heroic statue of King Jagello, who with his consort, Queen Jadwiga, crushed the Order of the Teutonic Knights at Grunewald in 1410. His arm waved a great sword. Earlier in the year Poland had issued a stamp with Jagello and Jadwiga represented as standing with the downed swords of the German knights at their feet, but even the Poles decided that it might be unnecessarily provocative and so had withdrawn it to substitute a stamp showing the two personages minus the weapons.

George and Elizabeth toured Columbia University, their cavalcade cheered by millions of New Yorkers who gathered to see it pass through the streets of the city. Then they journeyed north to meet again with the Roosevelts at the home of the President's mother in Hyde Park, Dutchess County.

"My mother thinks you should have a cup of tea. She doesn't approve of cocktails," the President said.

"Neither does my mother," George said, gratefully taking one the President mixed himself.

They went to Sunday services at St. James's in Hyde Park. "The service is *exactly* the same as ours down to every word," Elizabeth wrote her husband's mother, Queen Mary, and then spoke on the transatlantic phone to her daughters, who could hardly believe that at the time Margaret was about to go to bed in England their parents in America were preparing to go to lunch.

It was that lunch which above all things characterized the visit of King George and Queen Elizabeth to the United States and made nonsense of the stated opinions of the writer H. G. Wells that the visit of the monarchs to America, what they did, who saw them and what those who saw them thought were entirely meaningless. For the meal took a position in the American imagination that it never lost. The menu at the outdoor picnic on the grounds of the estate of the President's mother included smoked turkey, which Their Majesties had never eaten before, hams cured in different ways from different sections of the country, salads, strawberry shortcake from the nearby place of Secretary of the Treasury Henry Morgenthau, and hot dogs. It was these last that captured the headlines. George VI, the symbol of his country to an America dead-set against war yet concerned with an England loved beyond the suspicions her aims engendered and now in the direst of perils because of a town along the Baltic, Danzig, munched on hot dogs.

When the royal couple took the train from Hyde Park for Canada and the *Empress of Australia,* some five thousand people, the population of Roosevelt's hometown and the surrounding area, turned out to see them off. As the locomotive began to pull away, they waved from the rear of the slowly moving car along the tracks by the Hudson River. A lump came into Eleanor Roosevelt's throat for them and for what might be coming. Her husband, the President, had found something in common with England's king: they had both surmounted disabilities, the king his stammer, the President the disease that had crippled him.

It was eleven at night when they left, the little Hyde Park station illuminated and the people all around singing "Auld Lang Syne," and Roosevelt saw in the eyes of King George and Queen Elizabeth tears.

The king and queen returned to an England made to appear military by the many conscripted men in uniform. Royal Air Force blue particularly stood out. The hot weather had come and with it a feeling expectant, fearful, doubting. The writer-politician Sir Harold Nicolson and his wife, the writer Vita Sackville-West, great gardeners both, together planted seeds on a warm and still day, and would have been happy doing so, as in the past. But they felt a tugging at their hearts and asked each other what would have come to pass in the world by the time these seeds became flowers. To Nicolson it seemed that some very dear person was dying in an upstairs room. At a dinner party he heard H. G. Wells say that just as the dinosaur failed because it concentrated on size to the exclusion of other characteristics, Homo sapiens would fail because he had not developed the right kind of brain. He would destroy himself and then die out as a species. "Just revert to mud and slime."

That summer England's ally, Poland, surrounded by Germany on three sides, listened to a thousand rumors: the Germans were suffering food shortages, unrest, poor morale; their cannons were made of cardboard and their home factories ridden with sabotage while the Skoda armament plants in occupied Czechoslovaia produced nothing of value because sand was thrown into their products by rebellious Czech workers; social conditions in Germany prohibited any thought of war. The skies were brilliantly sunny. There was no rain at all, so that when the wind blew into Warsaw from Siberia it sent up eddies of dust and raised dust storms in the sandy great plain leading west to Germany.

Their cause was just, the Poles told one another, and they had France and England to back them up. They were ready to defend civilization against Hitlerism and would have the courage to call Hitler's bluff, something that had never yet been done.

Major General Sir Edmund Ironside came to Warsaw that summer. He was the ranking British army officer of his rank on the active list. His mission was to look at the military forces of Britain's ally. Six-foot five-inches tall, broad-shouldered and inevitably "Tiny" to his fellow officers, he had been the first of England's soldiers to step ashore in France in 1914. After the War he commanded the British attempt in northern Russia to strangle Bolshevism in its cradle. He spoke seven languages well enough to act as an interpreter in them, and was generally believed to be the commander in chief designate of any future British expeditionary force.

He found a Polish army based upon horse cavalry, the arm that had defeated the Russians in the Miracle of the Vistula in 1920 and was therefore considered in Warsaw to be the unit of choice of those who understood the last word in military strategy. The infantry was equipped with bolt-action rifles and was at least impressive in its physical representatives, who were hardy Polish peasant boys with great faith in their ability to hold a position, as their predecessors had done for other armies during Poland's long Partition. (Napoleon and Hindenburg alike had praised most highly the Polish infantry with its ability to take punishment without flinching.)

General Ironside found the officer corps on the subaltern level to be eager and keen. The higher ranks did not function well together, being as they were a hodgepodge of men inherited from the armies of Austria-Hungary, Germany and Russia, each of which had different methods and aims.

Poland had thirty-two first-line divisions and thirty in the reserve; complete mobilization would produce a force of 1.5 million men. Heavy artillery, antitank guns and antiaircraft guns were all lacking. There was theoretically one armored division; in reality Poland had no tank force. The troops were deployed in the thinnest possible fashion along the more than 1,750 miles forming the border with Germany proper, former Czechoslovakia and East Prussia, with a third of Poland's active-duty soldiers put for prestige purposes in the Corridor, where they stood exposed to double envelopment from front and rear. Poland's soldiery could not conceive of permitting Germany entry into Germany's former territory, and thus maintained a forward concentration that precluded any pulled-in rear grouping in the heart of the country. From such a centered strong point counterblows might be dealt if needed, but Polish pride forbade conceding one inch of the frontier, whatever the circumstances.

Lacking in mobility, dependent upon animal transport, a foot-marching army with hardly any communications beyond those afforded by the primitive civilian telephone and telegraph system, Poland's force had only the slightest capacity for maneuvers. The navy hardly existed. The air force consisted of a handful of obsolete double-wing fighter planes and some cumbersome bombers.

Their temperament was most suitable for attack, said the Poles, possessed as was the national character by dash and élan. The conviction jibed with the inability of a very poor country to afford the construction of any kind of comprehensive defensive fortifications. The topography of Poland was not suited for defense in any case, the land westward from Warsaw being entirely flat and lacking a reasonably sized river or even a single hill upon which a holding effort could be mounted. Asked to survey the Poles' defensive arrangements along their frontier, the British military attaché conducted a tour and then told a diplomatic colleague at the embassy what he had discovered: "I've done my report. It consists of three words: 'There aren't any.' "

Major General Ironside was treated to reviews of cavalrymen carrying pennant-bedecked lances and waving sabers as they charged across fields in their distinctive four-square caps, gallant soldiers to be sure and using live ammunition so recklessly that fatalities were accepted without comment. He returned profoundly depressed to the War Office in London. The journalist Pierre van Paasen looked at the white-gloved Polish officer corps with their jingling medals and thought to himself that the country would be far better off if the soldiers had ten thousand times fewer medals and just one solid, well-paved road.

Off to the west that June, Berlin, like Washington, was entertaining a pair of royal visitors, the Regent of Yugoslavia, Prince Paul, and his wife, Princess Olga. Good-looking, she wore the Romanov jewels of her Russian princess-mother as she captivated her host. Midnight came as Hitler showed Princess Olga through rooms filled with objets d'art. When she remarked that it was perhaps time to retire he said, "Happy people have no clocks."

The military review for the Yugoslavians lasted four hours. Hundreds of planes flew overhead and an endless succession of tanks and big guns clanked past. The sight and sound filled the British ambassador with sadness and horror at such destructive capability. Always anxious to see the good side of things, Sir Nevile Henderson took some slight comfort from noting that the watching crowds, perhaps harking back to the days when armed conflict was thought to be colorful and glorious, applauded most loudly the two or three regiments of horse cavalry, all that was left of the days of pre-War military display. But it was not the applause or lack of it that formed German policy. It was the thoughts of Adolf Hitler. And in the newspapers he read thoroughly there continued stories of the indignities to which Poland subjected its German inhabitants.

Many of the alleged indignities had their origin in Dr. Goebbels's mind, for he was always at his best when on the attack, but some incidents were genuine. There was enough anti-German feeling in Poland for many there to believe that the entire German population, 1.5 million, was one gigantic fifth column whose aim was the overthrow of the Republic of the White Eagle. Every street corner or tavern fracas between people of the two ethnic backgrounds became both in Warsaw and Berlin a clash related to larger issues between the two countries.

In Washington President Roosevelt worked to get a congressional repeal of the neutrality legislation, which embargoed the dispatch of arms to any country engaged in hostilities, saying that the prohibition tied America's hands and made the outbreak of war more likely. On the evening of July 18 he had in the members of the Senate Foreign Relations Committee to ask their aid.

The most dominant member of the committee was the senior

senator from Idaho, William Borah. The dean of the Senate in
years of service, Borah was a farmboy turned small-town lawyer
and then trial advocate who had been in politics since 1906. He
had served as chairman of the committee through the Republi-
can years of 1924 through 1932. Since Roosevelt's election he
had been the ranking minority member. Scholarly, a great reader,
deadly serious, from a remote and little-populated and insular
state. Borah played a tremendous role in the country's life and
thinking. His great interest after foreign affairs was Prohibition,
for which he was an ardent advocate. He held liquor's "natural
haunt" to be a brothel and said imbibing alcohol brought in its
wake "crime, dishonor and death, misery and poverty and re-
morse" to "mark its maledict course."

Borah had never traveled to Europe. His fellow senator, El-
bert Thomas, said it was because a fortuneteller once predicted
he would be drowned at sea. In fact it was known that he disliked water, avoided boats and never swam while on vacation. He
himself explained his reluctance to visit England and the Continent by saying, "I should add little to my knowledge by infre-
quent brief trips. It is often wiser to stand off and obtain a clear
picture. One might become merely confused by firsthand information." Three times he made tentative plans to go, but canceled
them, saying that pressing duties prevented his leaving. Besides,
there was the matter of cost. It was expensive enough for his
wife to go alone, which she did.

Of all the votes he had cast in the Senate, Borah said, the one
he wished most he could change was his vote for war in 1917.
Wilson had been little else but Britain's tool, he said, and had
taken America to fight for selfish European imperialism, for the
Old World's endless quarrels, which had been going on since the
days of the Roman Empire. The United States must stay completely aloof from Europe in the future, he repeated year after
year. In late 1938, after the destruction of the Crystal Night, he
relented somewhat and told William Hutchinson of the International News Service that he would like to visit Germany if he
could be assured of meeting Hitler. "There are so many great
sides to him, I believe I might accomplish something. There's
always the possibility I might get Hitler to relax a bit. I just can't
get that thought out of my mind."

Hutchinson told the Washington representative of the German

News Agency what Senator Borah had said, and the information was passed on to the German ambassador, who sent it to Ribbentrop. An invitation came for the senator to visit Berlin and see the Leader and the foreign minister. But various events intervened. Borah did not go. When the Germans occupied Prague he said: "If Hitler is as wise as I believe him to be, he has no designs whatsoever on France. I know it to be a fact as much as I will ever know anything that Britain is behind Hitler. Britain wants Hitler to be supreme in all Central Europe."

At the meeting in the Oval Office Borah listened while Roosevelt, who always made much of his ability to prepare a good cocktail, wrangled with Vice President Garner about the proper method of making an old-fashioned, and then with the others heard from the President that the arms embargo must be repealed. If Hitler knew that America's productive power was available to Germany's possible future enemies, perhaps the knowledge would act as a brake on him. And brakes were needed, for it was the President's opinion that war could break out "at any time, any day, any week." Roosevelt finished speaking and turned to his secretary of state. "Cordell, what do you think about it?"

Hull echoed his chief's views, saying that failure to repeal the embargo might be a factor in urging the Germans to go to war. Borah announced that he entirely disagreed. "I do not believe there is going to be any war in Europe. I simply want to say it is my opinion, for what it is worth, that we will not have war."

"I wish," Hull said, "the senator from Idaho would come down to the State Department and read the dispatches which come in from all over Europe from day to day and I am sure he would change his mind."

"I don't give a damn about your dispatches," Borah answered. "We all have means of acquiring information. I myself have gone to great effort to secure information from different sources."

Hull grew so angry he felt he was going to explode. Never before and never afterward did he find it so difficult to restrain himself. Another senator began to ask Hull something, but the secretary of state said, "In view of the statement by Senator Borah that the State Department is inefficient I shall not make any replies to any further questions."

The talk went on as he sat silent, several of the men saying it was in their power to make Hitler think twice about unleashing a war. Borah waved his hand dismissively and said, "What's the use of talking like that? Hitler doesn't give a damn what a committee of the United States Senate does. He is moved by deeper impulses than that, whether right or wrong."

They continued to argue, but Borah refused to budge and the majority of the other members took their lead from him. "Well, Captain, we may as well face the facts," Garner said to the President. "You haven't got the votes and that's all there is to it." The White House announced that the meeting had been very friendly and conducted in a very diplomatic way—using "very parliamentary language," Roosevelt told the reporters—but that the President and secretary of state could not bring the committee to their view. Congress adjourned.

"The world is advancing toward a new disaster," the writer Sir Philip Gibbs's Venice hotel waiter had told him as long ago as 1934; "it happens without people wanting it," a market woman in Stuttgart had said. Five years later, in 1939, hardly a person thought otherwise. Of a Paris evening the Polish ambassador to France, Juliusz Lukasiewicz, gave a ball at the embassy. All who attended retained afterward memories of a beautiful summer night and white marble sphinxes gleaming in the gardens as an orchestra played Chopin waltzes and pots of red fire glowed. On the lawn women in elaborate gowns danced with Polish and French officers who had put aside their swagger sticks and canes. The two lovely daughters of the German ambassador, Count von Welczeck, attended. Champagne was sipped and the maiden voyage of the *Louis Pasteur* discussed, but all felt the great and indeed immeasurable weight of what hung over them and of what might lie ahead. In the small hours of the morning Ambassador Lukasiewicz took off his shoes and danced by himself across his lawn. There were those into whose minds came the thought of the ball given by the Duchess of Richmond in Brussels on the eve of the Battle of Waterloo, of the officers leaving her for the field and the fighting. It was, thought *The New Yorker*'s Janet Flanner, a party and a moment desperately brilliant.

That summer the Louvre put on a Ballets Russes de Diaghilev exposition marking the tenth year since the great director's death, and showed curtains and costumes made for his company by such as Picasso, Utrillo, Rouault, Matisse, Modigliani, Braque, Max Ernst and others. More than anything else, Janet Flanner thought, Diaghiliv's ballet seemed to symbolize what a decade after his death was looked back upon as *les beaux jours,* the days of pleasure when the new music and new art of the twenties were thought to have given birth to a happy age after the slaughter of the War. What had replaced those days—it was enough to make the angels weep, she wrote.

With the warmer weather Lady Diana Manners Cooper went to the shore with her son and her husband, Alfred Duff Cooper, who had resigned as first lord of the admiralty to protest the Munich Agreement. Legions of men had loved Diana Manners when she was young. Most had perished in the 1914–18 War. Daughter of the Duke of Rutland and a possible marriage choice for the Prince of Wales, she was in the twenties the world's most beautiful woman, according to the Society figure and dilettante member of Parliament Chips Cannon. Age and the thought of what her England had lost and might lose had sobered her by 1939 and toned down the air of madcap weekend parties and West End escapades that had characterized her for so long, and she sat by the sea and gazed at the water that would no longer serve as a wall, for the attack would come from the air.

She was sure that an apocalypse was shadowed ahead as certainly as the twilight signals the night. "I do not suppose that the people who came to laugh and bathe and drink and picnic at Bognor can have felt quite as despondent, quite so near yielding to despair, as I did, but they too were doubtless in disguise." She was lucky in that her son was still a child and her husband too old for the army, she thought, but she counted herself no happier than her sister or her friends who had sons of military age. "For death I knew was to take the lot of us without discrimination, like the peoples of Sodom and Gomorrah, suddenly by fire and cataclysm, without quarter." Those radiant summer days, by the sea in England, she thought to herself, "all they lit had the poignancy of a child that has to die."

On August 7 Lord Beaverbrook's *Daily Express* printed the slogan THERE WILL BE NO WAR THIS YEAR OR NEXT YEAR EITHER one last time. It never appeared again.

At her family's summer place thirty miles from the German frontier, a young Polish woman who had attended Vassar College in New York State and who worked for the economic research department of the Bank of Poland finished reading *Gone*

With the Wind. Always in the past when warm weather came Rulka Langer went through her winter things and took from them dresses and suits more than two years of age to give to her maid, who would keep some and give others to relatives. Now she thought of Scarlett O'Hara after the Civil War making a dress of green window curtains, and it came into her mind that perhaps the older things might remain her best clothing in days that were to come. She packed them away. All that summer, playing tennis, drinking coffee, riding over roads known since childhood, the thought would come: "Will all this too be gone with the wind next year?"

ELEVEN

IN THE YEARS following the end of the Great War in 1918 there were two pariah countries in Europe. The Austro-Hungarian Empire had made the War and for that it was entirely dismantled, with the countries that had given the Empire its name left as emasculated shadows of their former selves. Few could continue to harbor resentment for two such cripples. It was Germany, however, that had persevered so in the four years of fighting and been the focus of Allied enmity, and Germany that after the Armistice continued as the subject of hatred mixed with fear. Germany had fought and won three wars between 1864 and 1871, and it was Germany that had held the world in thrall from 1914 to 1918. Few could forgive her for that.

The other pariah country was Russia. She had withdrawn from the War, leaving her allies to continue alone while she conducted the bloodiest of revolutions, slaughtering her former rulers, her lawyers, doctors, merchants, professors, anyone who had a claim to be anything other than a worker or a peasant or a leader of those groups. The revolution completed, she burst forward in an attempt to set the Red Flag flying everywhere, to be turned back in the Miracle of the Vistula in 1920.

Then she retired within herself in a xenophobic mood more Asiatic than European. Nothing more was heard from her but the reports of squalor and mindless purges and endless executions. The apostle of a new and to the West repellent manner of living, she had no allies at all in the world, and no friends. Her neighbors, subsidized by the West to form a *cordon sanitaire* that would keep her and her doctrines physically and spiritually in outer darkness, uniformly despised and feared her. They had heard but too clearly, it was said, the screams of Bolshevism's victims across the border. Russia maintained contacts only with the other pariah country.

The association between Russia and Germany during the years after the War, while including some trade, was primarily military. Hamstrung by the provisions of the Versailles Treaty, which forbade German production of any heavy weapons, or the development of new ones, the Weimar Republic's military leaders sought Russian aid in evading the restrictions. In return Germany could offer military instruction for the Red Army's officer corps, instruction normally provided by military intellectuals or senior staff officers but unavailable to the Russians because the men of that capacity in the old tsarist army had long since been shot.

Russia held no brief for the Western peacemakers trying to keep Germany weak. What were the West and its capitalistic aims to her? Using secret funds well concealed from the former Allies, the German army built airfields and factories in blocked-off and secretive Russia. Prototypes were made and tested safe from the eyes of any unfriendly observers. In return delegations of Red Army officers in civilian clothing and described as representatives of workers' organizations came to Germany to study under masters of war. (Mikhail Tukachevsky, the operating chief of the Red Army until his execution, visited Germany five times between 1925 and 1932.)

Hans von Seeckt, the architect of the post-War German army, saw no contradiction in going hand in hand with Russia's military leaders. He would keep his fingers clutched around the throat of German Communism, he said, but he cared nothing for what Russian Communism did or did not do. It was said that it was all the same to him if the Russians chose to be voodoo adherents or sun worshipers. His concerns were limited to perfecting his Versailles-limited army, which he did, brilliantly.

Then Adolf Hitler came to power and German cooperation with Russia ended. Hatred of Communism was as central to that religion of which Hitler was the high priest as was hatred of the Jews. Bolshevism, the Leader had said from the first moments of his political life, was a plague bacillus, a contagious infection, a pestilence. The two decades that passed since the 1919 formation of his views had not seen them alter. "With one country

alone have we scorned to enter into relations," he told the
Reichstag in February 1938. "That state is Soviet Russia. We see
in Bolshevism more now than before the incarnation of human
destructive forces, this gruesome ideology of destruction." Seven
months later at the Party Day celebrations of September: "More
threatening than ever, Bolshevist danger of the destruction of
nations rises above the world!" Russia was composed of Slavic
subhumans. By then the Germans and Italians had been fighting
them for two years in Spain, the Russians supporting the government of the Republic and the Pact of Steel countries backing the
insurgent forces of General Francisco Franco. One hundred and
fifty years of Spanish dispute had culminated in the brutal civil
war whose repercussions sounded now vaguely and now strongly
outside the boundaries of the country. A cry that Spain should
be the graveyard of European Fascism was answered by the shout
that here was represented Bolshevism with all its vile destructiv-
ity. The German and Russian officers who had trained together
on Russian plains in Weimar days sent their forces against one
another, and those of their brave and sad surrogates, the Span-
iards whose war became a training ground for the soldiers of the
dictators Hitler, Stalin and Mussolini. The West looked aside. To
get involved might bring catastrophic results, with the honor and
forces of Britain and France committed. It was better to stay un-
involved—Nonintervention, the phrase had it.

Communist Russia returned the hatred of National Socialist
Germany. Russian doctrine taught that Nazism was the real face
of capitalism, the spearhead of the plutocratic and imperialistic
non-Communist world that was the sworn enemy of the State of
the Workers and Peasants. Here was capitalism with the mask
removed. Soviet children played Fascist-and-Communist, and in
Moscow shooting galleries the targets were figures of Nazis be-
decked with swastikas. Movies portrayed the German government as formed of sadists obsessed with hatred for the Union of
Soviet Socialist Republics. Such was the view of the majority of
men surrounding Joseph Stalin and reflecting his views. The entire point of the West's sacrifice of Austria and Czechoslovakia,
they said, was to strengthen Hitler so that he could wreak capitalism's revenge upon Russia. Reactionary, sinister, ultimately
aiming at the destruction of the Soviet State, the ruling circles of
the West would use Hitler as their weapon.

There was another Soviet viewpoint that held that while capitalism was doomed, Hitler's Germany was not its pure form or its final spasm before a historically determined death. The spokesman for that view was Foreign Minister Maxim Litvinov, the only man of the Russian leadership who really knew the West. He had lived for years in England and had an English wife. With the rise of German power under Hitler, Litvinov became the world's spokesman for collective security. He had for years called for an East and West partnership against the Leader, first in the League of Nations and later, after that body's swift decline following its failure to act on Italy's Ethiopian invasion, in the chanceries of the West.

Little attention was given him. He was suspect first because he was a Jew who could not be expected to have a disinterested view of Hitler and second because he represented a Soviet Russia whose aim might well be a world cataclysm to topple capitalist regimes so that Communism might spring from the ruins. No one in Paris or London could forget that Lenin had welcomed the outbreak of the War in 1914, thinking quite rightly that the slaughter would bring Bolshevism into its own. To believe that Lenin's successor Stalin would fight on someone else's behalf was a laughable concept. The Russian leader had shown himself able to accept the deaths of millions of his own people for what he said was the advancement of Communism, and no one could possibly doubt that he would look with equal equanimity upon the deaths of the foreign millions who would die in a war if the result was the triumph of Communism beyond Russian borders.

In April 1939, days after the British gave their guarantees to Poland and Romania and Greece, Litvinov formally proposed to London and Paris that they join Moscow in a pact against Hitler. To Winston Churchill it seemed impossible that England would do anything but rush to accept the Russian offer, saying, "Yes. Let us three band together and break Hitler's neck." For without Russian aid, how could England make good on its promises? By going overland through Germany at a cost of who knew how much in blood and treasure? By sea? To land where? In King Carol's Romania, the most corrupt monarchy in the world, whose army was led by an officers' corps composed of tailors' dummies wearing corsets and rouge, and whose seaports might well be found occupied by the German army when the Royal Navy arrived?

Prime Minister Chamberlain's government, Churchill told

Parliament, had better "get some brutal truths into their heads."
Without Russia there was no possibility of combating Hitler anywhere but along the same Western Front whose stalemated
slaughter had cost the majority of the million British deaths of
1914–18.

The victorious prime minister of the War, Lloyd George,
echoed Churchill: "Without Russia our guarantees are the most
reckless commitments any country has ever entered into. I say
more—they are demented."

It was not so simple a matter in the prime minister's estimation. Long before, his predecessor Disraeli had spoken of the
two Englands: those who served and the aristocrats who were
served. Disraeli was gone, and the War had changed things, but
not so very much. The geographical conflicts between England
and Russia remained unchanged, as well as the memory of past
disputes from Istanbul to Mukden, in the Balkans, along the
Northwest Frontier. There was nothing in Russia that was likely
to be viewed with approval by a Neville Chamberlain whose interests—bird-watching, poetry, Beethoven, novels—would be regarded there as ludicrous or, even worse, as decadent trivialities
symbolic of the meaningless lolling of the British ruling classes.
The prime minister was not alone in finding little in Russia past
or present that appealed. (When Anthony Eden became in 1935
the first important British statesman to visit Russia after the Revolution of nearly twenty years earlier, King George V had been
far from pleased to hear that "God Save the King" was played in
Eden's honor. He did not at all like it, said His Majesty, that "my
anthem" was played in company with "The Internationale.") But
the prime minister's distaste was more pronounced than most
people's. Chamberlain owned, noted Sir Alexander Cadogan, "an
almost instinctive contempt for the Americans," but for the
Russians he had "what amounted to a hatred." He was capable
of saying to Cadogan that rather than sign an alliance with Moscow
he would resign his position.

But he would not do that. He must have spoken to Cadogan
in haste or anger. For loyal to his memories of the dead Norman
Chamberlain, gone to dust with the other millions, he would do
anything to preserve peace. The cheers of Munich yet rang in
his ears. He considered the Russian offer. What did they have to
put on the table? All wisdom indicated that the Red Army, while
perhaps formidable within its own borders, was not capable of

mounting an offensive outside them. Her officer corps had been decimated in the mindless purges, and her industrial base was primitive. She sat behind her barbed-wire borders adorned with signs braying WORKERS OF THE WORLD UNITE. What service could she perform for an endangered Poland, Hitler's likely next source of trouble? It was all very well for William Bullitt to opine that to drum up support for a stand against Nazism no stone should be left unturned, even "though one might expect to find vermin under it" and for others to say that sometimes it was necessary to sup with the devil; but what fare actually did the devil have to offer?

"I must confess to the most profound distrust of Russia," the prime minister wrote his sisters. "I have no belief whatever in her ability to maintain an effective offensive, even if she wanted to, and I distrust her motives, which seem to me to have little connection with our ideas of liberty, and to be concerned only with getting everyone else by the ears. Moreover, she is both hated and suspected by many of the smaller states."

The hatred and suspicion of which he had written certainly characterized Poland's view of Russia. She was the enemy of Poland for centuries; her Tsar's gendarmerie had always ruled Poland with knout in hand, and the Tsar's successors, the Communists, had come in 1920 to attempt to reclaim by force of arms what the Versailles Treaty had taken away from them. The Miracle of the Vistula was required to turn them back. If they were invited into Poland to assist in a possible stand against Germany, who was to say they would ever leave? Who would evict them? France and England?

It was a frightful dilemma. Any Russian guarantee of Polish independence, the Poles reasoned, could be twisted into a Russian decision to send troops, which, allegedly coming to help, would find reasons to stay forever. President Hacha of Czechoslovakia had found out what the protection of Adolf Hitler amounted to, and now German officials and generals ruled what had been his country. Foreign Minister Beck did not want the Russian version of such protection for Poland. It would be like inviting one invasion in the hope of stopping another. The Polish viewpoint was understandable. "An intelligent rabbit," said Lord Halifax, "would hardly be expected to welcome the protection of an animal ten times its own size, whom it credited with the habits of a boa constrictor."

Even as aligning itself with Russia might give offense to England's ally Poland, so might it give offense to England's possible enemy, Germany. What, Chamberlain asked himself, would Hitler's likely response be if England and France allied themselves with Russia? To be encircled by enemies was the nightmare of every country. The establishment of a new triple *entente* successor to the one against which Germany had fought in the War, the announcement that a circular block was now in place against him, could well fling Hitler into an attempt to repeat the history made when Kaiser Wilhelm unleashed his forces. By joining England to Russia in an attempt to save the peace, Chamberlain reasoned, he might instead bring on a war that could well end with Bolshevism as the ultimate victor, its germs spouting in a ruined world, its doctrines carried forward by Mongol and Cossack hordes no one would have the will or ability to resist.

The prime minister's alternatives were horrible. Hitler was a barbarian, he was the son of that King Death who had been held to reign over the battlefields of 1914–18 and those following, the frightful pocket wars and border incidents and pogroms and massacres. But Joseph Stalin? Was he someone into whose bloody hands England was to entrust her honor and her safety?

Only a year earlier Chamberlain had told his country how appalling a thought it was that England should go to war for Czechoslovakia, "because of a quarrel in a faraway country between people of whom we know nothing." Now he was involved with countries even more distant and remote. He thought of the three Baltic republics, Latvia, Lithuania and Estonia. They had been provinces of tsarist Russia until the Versailles Treaty gave them nationhood. If Britain made common cause with Russia and war came and Germany was conquered, could there be any doubt that the Bear would reclaim its lost Baltic areas as well as Poland? British opposition to Germany was based upon Hitler's seizing territories. Was Britain now to fight a war with Russia as ally and, winning, endorse its ally taking over territories, the very *causus belli* for which Britain would have gone to war?

That thought was in the mind of the Baltic countries when the Finnish Pavilion opened at the New York World's Fair in April. The country's prime minister had said in his dedication speech that the last thing his people wished was an offer of protection from their former rulers the Russians. Estonia and Latvia sent diplomatic Notes to Russia saying they did not feel themselves in any danger from Germany, and then signed nonaggression pacts with that country. If Britain allied itself with Russia, the former Russian possessions, terrified, might well even more definitively fling themselves into Hitler's arms as a refuge from the Soviets.

Chamberlain turned ever more old and gray. His seventy years showed, and that and his strangely out-of-date Edwardian clothing made him seem out of place in the spring and summer of 1939. His parliamentary private secretary, Lord Dunglass, had begun his service to the prime minister feeling admiration for him, then affection. Now it was pity.

Others joined Winston Churchill and David Lloyd George in calling for acceptance of the Russian offer, and a Gallup Poll showed that 92 percent of the British people favored it. Wondering if making a pact might bring chaos and blood, asking himself if he was undertaking something that might lead to a world war on Communism's behalf, untrusting, doubtful, uncertain, Neville Chamberlain decided to instruct his ambassador to Moscow to open talks.

•

"I trust no one, not even myself," Joseph Stalin liked to tell the people around him. Before the Revolution he lived in a conspiratorial world filled with suspicion and betrayal, and for years as Gensek and Vozhd he found new enemies to be executed or sent to Siberia. His entire existence was peopled with the memories of those he believed would have betrayed him, had he been so lax as to give them the chance.

Now the West came to him, that West which had tried to strangle the Revolution in its cradle with armed intervention, that West which had set up and financed a *cordon sanitaire* of anti-Communist nations ringing the Soviet Union. Now it sought to discover if he would join it in an alliance against Adolf Hitler.

The Gensek had long since discarded the Revolution's idealism along with the Revolution's idealists. Power was his concern, and geography, which in the days of the Tsars had made Great Britain Russia's natural enemy and Germany a sometimes ally. Electing to fight Germany in 1914 had brought death to tsarism. What had the West now to offer the regime that succeeded the Tsar? A war concocted at the Munich Conference, from which

Russia had been excluded and at which, perhaps, Germany was given all encouragement to run riot in the East?

"It is not so easy to fool Comrade Stalin," the Gensek liked to say. If the West hoped to push the Germans eastward, he told a Party Congress meeting, "promising them an easy prey and saying, 'Just start a war with the Bolshevists, everything will take care of itself,'" then the West was greatly in error. Russia, he said, would not let itself be drawn into conflict by warmongers who liked to rake the fire with others' hands, to have others pull their chestnuts from the fire.

That was in March. A most interesting speech, thought the German ambassador to Russia, Count Friedrich Werner von der Schulenburg. There followed the submission of the Russian proposal to France and England that they band together against Hitler, delivered by Foreign Minister Maxim Litvinov to British ambassador to Moscow Sir William Seeds. Then came what Winston Churchill described as a long British silence. No response was offered to the Russian proposal.

In Berlin, Russian ambassador Alexei Merekalov visited the principal state secretary in the German Foreign Office, Baron Ernst von Weizsaecker. It was the first time the Russian had called during the nearly one year of his service in the capital. The memory of Hitler's strangely warm attitude at the opening of the New Chancellory was not absent from both men's minds, nor was Stalin's sharp tone against Britain and France in his Party Congress speech.

The two chatted about economic matters, and then Ambassador Merekalov asked what Weizsaecker thought about German-Russian relations. Weizsaecker said they were not helped by reports that Russia might ally herself with Britain and France. Merekalov said that really there was no reason why Germany and Russia might not get on better terms with each other. "And out of normal relations could grow increasingly improved relations."

They parted. Ten days later Hitler delivered his long speech answering Franklin Roosevelt's appeal that he testify to his disinclination to invade the President's lengthy list of countries. Always before the subject of the Leader's vituperation, the Soviet Union went entirely unmentioned. The British silence lengthened.

"This Russian proposal is extremely inconvenient," Sir Alexander Cadogan noted in a memorandum. "We have to balance the advantage of a paper commitment by Russia against the disadvantage of associating ourselves openly with Russia." The Soviet Union, Chamberlain told his intimates, was militarily of little use. The British service attachés in Moscow agreed that both her army and air force were as likely to collapse of their own ineptitude as by enemy pressure in the event of a fight. Russia could perhaps be useful in funneling munitions to Poland should war come. But was an alliance really necessary in order that it so serve? The British and French consulted on what their attitude should be. Litvinov waited for a reply. On May 3, his proposal to the West of April 16 still unanswered, he was told Stalin wished to see him.

When the foreign minister appeared at the Gensek's office he found another close Stalin associate already there. Rigid, highly disciplined, a Party stalwart who would during the purges explain that a man's apparently good service to the People might well have been performed for the sole purpose that he might rise higher to wreak a greater destruction, Vyacheslav Molotov had no experience in foreign affairs. He possessed great determination and was granite-faced and robot-like. He told Litvinov, Russia's foreign minister for nine years past, and a Jew, that Russia must improve relations with Hitler. Litvinov raised objections. Stalin looked on, smoking his inevitable pipe. Molotov and Litvinov argued for one hour. Stalin put down his pipe. "Enough," he said. He thrust a paper at Litvinov. "Sign."

The next day a brief newspaper announcement said that by his own request the people's commissar for foreign affairs had been released from office. When Sir William Seeds came to the Nakromindel, the Foreign Office, he found Molotov in charge. Litvinov had always been found approachable and knowledgeable about the world outside Russia, the British Foreign Office official William Strang remembered. "In personal relations his first instinct would be to be friendly and expansive." Strang had spent three years in the British Embassy in Moscow and took back to London memories of a country where everything was overblown. Litvinov proved an exception. One could cock an eyebrow, Strang found, and bring a grin to his face.

But Molotov: his mind seemed to Ambassador Sir William Seeds to be harsh, unbelieving, vexatious. One had to say exactly what one meant and say it over and over again in the same words. He appeared impervious to any argument contrary to his own views. He knew nothing of the outside world. His favorite word seemed to be "No."

On May 9 Sir William Seeds had to give to this coldly un-emotional figure a negative reply to the Russian proposal for a firm alliance. The time was not yet ripe for the comprehensive scheme the Russians had suggested. Seeds offered an alternative. What Britain desired, he said, was that Russia merely indicate that it would be available to offer help if the British and French found themselves compelled to go to war with Germany.

"He commented unfavorably on our delay in answering," Seeds reported to London. Molotov then pointed out that while Russia was asked to help England and France, there was no British of-fer to help Russia should she become embroiled in a conflict with Germany. The new people's commissar for foreign affairs said the West must join with Russia in guaranteeing it and also all the states adjoining the Soviet Union—Finland, Estonia, Latvia, Lith-uania, Poland and Romania. That was the great sticking point. Each one of the named countries had in the recent past been wholly or partly owned by Russia. They "did not know," as Churchill said, "whether it was German aggression or Russian rescue which they dreaded more." They viewed with "terror" the idea of Russian troops marching on them for any cause. Who was to say the Russians might not one day decide a German at-tack upon their former property was imminent and that the Red Army must therefore come in to take up defensive positions? Who could say that Russia would not manipulate some sort of internal upheaval in a neighbor created against her will and at her expense, declare there was dire danger, and appear in force the next day? And what would follow? The likely treatment by Stalin could make his handling of his own people look mild in comparison.

It came to the British and French that Russia seemed to ask a price for cooperation against Germany: the Baltic republics at least, and perhaps eastern Poland, and perhaps the other coun-tries as well. Those places they could not be given. They were not the West's to give. And should Russia get them, all reason for her to fight Hitler would evaporate. The entire point of op-position to Nazism, of the Polish guarantee, was to protect Poland's western frontiers against Germany. Was the West now to bring

Russia in across Poland's eastern frontiers, and the frontiers of other countries in addition?

In Molotov's office, sitting before his raised desk with pads of paper on their knees like schoolboys, Sir William Seeds and the other Western negotiators writhed under the commissar's coldly brutal words. The Russians were being treated as if they were naive or foolish, like applicants for the position of a hired laborer, Molotov said. "He himself could afford to smile, but he could not guarantee that everyone would take so calm a view."

Articles in the controlled Soviet newspapers pointed out that when the West had decided to conclude a pact with Poland they had in a moment made one, and asked if their dragging manner with Russia did not indicate a conspiracy arranged with Hitler to align the entire world against the Soviets.

At the same time a strangely optimistic British press predicted that a pact was on the point of being reached. "We shall get the alliance," said the London *Daily Express* on May 22. "The marriage will take place. Wedding bells will ring." The *News Chronicle* on May 25: AGREEMENT WITH RUSSIA IN SIGHT. The *Manchester Guardian* on May 27: "It is confidently expected that final agreement with the Soviet Union will have been reached by the end of the week."

It did not seem that way to the Russian ambassador to England, Ivan Maisky. To him the British and French attitude was of "endless new palaver" with every "word or comma" arousing a negative reaction. It was all "sabotage, machinations." He decided to force the issue with the British foreign secretary. "I have come to the conclusion that a great deal depends upon you personally, Lord Halifax. You would meet with the warmest possible reception in Moscow. If, Lord Halifax, you thought it possible to travel to Moscow now I would ask my government to send you an official invitation."

Halifax gazed at the ceiling and stroked the bridge of his nose. "I will have this in mind," he said. It was not the only time he was so approached. "Why don't you go to Moscow, Edward, and lead a delegation?" asked his predecessor, Anthony Eden.

"I should be no good whatsoever," Halifax answered. "They are not my kind of people. Absolutely no rapport with them whatsoever." Eden remarked that Halifax had gone to see Hitler, and so had Chamberlain, three times. Together they had gone to see Mussolini. Were those two their kind of people? But if

Halifax did not wish to go, he, Eden, would be glad to do so. Halifax consulted with Chamberlain on the offer. It was turned down.

The influential Labor Party leader Hugh Dalton held no brief for Molotov. "Yes, you little monkey," he thought to himself when Ambassador Maisky praised the commissar for foreign affairs. But he went to Chamberlain and said that things were dragging along and that a minister of the Crown should go to Moscow to speed negotiations and get an alliance.

"I do not think that this would help matters," Chamberlain replied, and in the second week of June William Strang was sent out. He was a competent professional. He had served in Moscow. He had accompanied Chamberlain on his visits to Hitler. To the Russians he was a clerk. Face-to-face with Strang Molotov referred to him in the third person as "the special delegate from the British government" in a tone of only the most slightly veiled contempt. In black coat, striped trousers and holding his black homburg, Strang sat with Ambassador Seeds and listened as Molotov spoke of how the special delegate brought a rejection from London to the Russian proposals asking that Russia participate in the determinations as to when a threat to Russia's neighbors would require Russian intervention. It was not a rejection, Strang said. It was rather a requirement that there be a clear threat of force by Germany before any action should be taken, and that there be no interference in the internal affairs of any state.

"It was a rejection," Molotov said. Beyond the table at which they might all have sat at equal heights there was an open door. It was never closed, and Strang had the disturbing feeling that beyond it someone always sat listening. He noted that often Molotov at his desk above the others fiddled with something there, and wondered if everything said was being recorded. "A rejection," Molotov said of the British views of his proposals. "I said that I would think about them. I have now thought about them." He raised his voice and then nodded to his translator.

"The people's commissar of foreign affairs," said the translator in French, "says of the British government's new proposals—I will give his exact words: 'If you think that the Soviet government is likely to accept these proposals, then you must think we are nitwits and nincompoops!' " Molotov looked at his translator to ask if his point had been gotten across clearly and the translator switched to English and said: "Simpletons, fools, imbeciles."

Perhaps, thought Ambassador Maisky in London, the French and British did not want to guarantee the Baltic countries because of their hope that the Germans would invade them and from them menace the Soviet Union. That would suit the West, he decided. The fight could then take place between Russia and Germany and the West could happily look on untouched. Russia in the negotiations, Maisky felt, was "bursting through a thick and prickly mass of bushes, in which at every step we were encountering ruts and pitfalls. Our clothes were being torn to rags, our faces, hands and legs were being covered with deep scratches and even bleeding wounds."

The French and British held precisely the same view, but with Russia cast as the impediment to an agreement. At the first sign of trouble from Germany, Molotov said, it would be necessary that the Red Army move into Poland and take charge of the areas around Vilnius in the north and Lvov in the south. From there they could make contact with the German army, he said.

To the French and British such a move constituted a fourth partition of Poland of the type that had divided the country in previous centuries. It was unthinkable that they endorse such an agreement. But, asked the Russians, had not Britain guaranteed Greece and Romania, miles away from England, without even asking their permissions for those guarantees? Yes, they had been very swift to do so! Yet the same Britain questioned the Russian right to guarantee states on its own doorstep. The West's position was found "not entirely favorable," one Soviet communiqué after another reported. "Your statements do not appear to me to be entirely satisfactory," Molotov repeated over and over to Strang and Seeds and French ambassador to Russia Paul-Émile Naggiar.

While all Russian viewpoints were swiftly put forward, the delegates of the West had to refer everything back to London and Paris. That took days. Derisive comments in the Russian press greeted the long waits. "The intolerable delays and endless pretexts for dragging out the negotiations," said *Pravda* on June 29, "give grounds for doubting the sincerity of the true intentions of Britain and France." The paper said, the West seemed to want not an agreement, but *talk* about one in order "to facilitate a deal with" Germany.

The negotiations dragged on. "Molotov does not become any easier to deal with as the weeks pass," Strang wrote to the head of the permanent staff of the Foreign Office, Sir Orme Sargent. The British and French suggested that any move by Russian troops into a menaced country had to be preceded by a plea from that country for aid; that the manner of the League of Nations be followed, with an aggressor nation clearly defined as such before any countermoves be taken. League of Nations procedures? asked Molotov. That would mean that Germany could join with Poland in an attack upon Russia while some faraway meaningless place— Bolivia would serve as an example, he said—held up any remedy by interminable speeches. He was told over and over that the League reference was to the "spirit" and "principles" of the organization, but insisted on denouncing the proposed "procedures."

To him it was entirely clear that the West's muddle, blunder and bungling was to conceal an infamous stall, and he did not hide his feelings. France and Britain suggested that any action on behalf of a menaced Russian neighbor should be contingent on a two-out-of-three affirmative vote between themselves and Russia. The foreign commissar replied that what was needed were concrete guarantees, not endless word-spinning. He demanded that the French and British obtain from the Baltic states an agreement for Russian occupation of their outlying islands and main ports if trouble with Germany seemed imminent. If they would not give it, he wanted assurances of French and British naval action to help get the Russians into those places. But that was impossible for them, they replied. The Baltic republics were sovereign states. One could not simply assault them. It was horrible, the Western negotiators told one another. To agree to Molotov's Baltic proposal meant that a coup d'état or palace revolution or minor disturbance in Latvia could be interpreted by Russia as indirect aggression by Germany calling for intervention, and London and Paris would then be obligated to take such actions against Riga that could plunge them into a war—all on Russia's say-so.

It was an atmosphere of the most poisonous suspicion and distrust. Andrei Zhdanov, an official so high in the government that he was referred to as Stalin's crown prince, wrote in *Pravda* that the West wished to treat the Soviet Union as a "coolie" upon whose shoulders would be placed the weight of all obligations.

Sir Alexander Cadogan told his London diary on June 20 that the Russians were impossible. "We give them all they want, with both hands, and they merely slap them. Molotov is an ignorant and suspicious peasant." On July 3 he noted "the Soviets still being incredibly tiresome" and on July 4 that they were "simply mulish."

The Russians suggested that a simple pact be written: an attack on either Britain, France or Russia would mean that all three would go to war against Germany. Could anything be more straightforward? Certainly not, replied the Westerners, but such an arrangement would leave the French and British guarantees to Poland and Greece and Romania hanging in the air. Yes, said Molotov. But the West would not endorse Russian guarantees to the Baltic republics and Poland.

Yet again they went at it as summer came on, that summer whose end meant the beginning of what had for centuries in Europe been known as the commencement of the military year, when the crops were in and fall rains had not yet arrived to muddy the roads and slow the movement of troops. In London Lord Halifax bitterly said to Ambassador Maisky that obviously the Russians did not want a pact at all, that in negotiations both sides make concessions but that the Soviets had not moved an iota. Maisky replied that the British and French were bringing forth endless amendments, reservations, additions, alterations, artificially thought-up arguments for concessions; they acted, he told Halifax, like two merchants haggling in a bazaar, incredibly inflating their prices before coming down. That was not the Soviet way, he said. His country did not make demands out of measure but simply listed exactly what was desired.

Through the three months of bargaining none of the French or British ever saw the one man in Moscow who really mattered, whose name was the subject of a bitter riddle that asked that the names of the leaders of the major countries be written down,

MUSSOLINI
HITLER
CHAMBERLAIN
DALADIER

along with the question

WHICH
WINS?

and that a line be drawn through the third letter in every name and word. Perhaps he sat silently in his fashion behind the door always open in Molotov's office. There was another matter that called for his invisibility, for as summer deepened he must run with the hare and hunt with the hounds. And he must be very sure the hare should not observe him in the midst of the hounds.

TWELVE

O UR AIR FORCE leads the world!" Adolf Hitler cried to Romanian foreign minister Gafencu. Let there be a war. "No enemy town will be left standing!" Then he lowered his voice and said calmly and gravely, "But, after all, why this unimaginable massacre? In the end, victor and vanquished, we shall all be buried in the same ruins. The only one who will profit is that man in Moscow."

That was in April, but a month later to a dozen of his highest officers he said a war was coming. "Further successes can no longer be attained without the shedding of blood. Danzig is not the subject of the dispute at all. It is a question of expanding our living space in the East, of securing our food supplies. We cannot expect a repetition of the Czech affair. There will be war. Our task is to isolate Poland."

But the West was pledged to Poland, and perhaps soon Russia would be, too, for through May and June the British papers predicted the early signing of a British-French-Soviet pact. "There is no doubt about the eventual success of the negotiations," said *The Observer*; NEARER A PACT WITH RUSSIA, headlined *The Guardian*.

After his talk with Baron von Weizsaecker in Berlin on April 17, the day after Litvinov made his formal offer of a pact to the French and British, Ambassador Merekalov met with Foreign Minister von Ribbentrop and the operating head of the German army, General von Brauchitsch. Then he traveled to Moscow. Meanwhile, Count von der Schulenburg, the German ambassador to Russia, was called to Berchtesgaden for consultations with the Leader. When he returned to his Moscow post he received a request to call on the new people's commissar for foreign affairs, who had been in office for two weeks. Molotov was "most friendly," Schulenburg reported to Berlin. The tone of German newspaper articles about Russia began to undergo a change. Really there was no pressing dispute between Germany and Russia, the papers said, as long as the Russians did not decide to join in the encircling movement against Germany planned by the pluto-democracies, the greedy so-called Christian nations.

Yet Berlin could not clearly understand what Russia had in mind. Molotov in his friendly talk with Ambassador von der Schulenburg had said there was room for increased economic relations between Germany and Russia, but that first the necessary political bases for such relations must be established.

"Political bases?" asked Schulenburg. What exactly did the people's commissar have in mind?

Molotov replied that was something both governments would have to think about.

Schulenburg tried to press him for a more concrete statement but failed in his attempt. "He is known for his somewhat stubborn manner," the ambassador reported to Berlin. The British and French had certainly found that out. "There is a veil, a sort of wall," Chamberlain had told Parliament the day before the unpublicized Schulenburg-Molotov meeting, "which is extremely difficult to penetrate."

What Molotov had hinted at remained in the forefront of German official thinking. Ambassador Merekalov did not return from Moscow to take up his post in Berlin—perhaps the Kremlin wished a lower-ranking man to get his feet wet in negotiations with the Germans; anything he said or did could more easily be disavowed—and so the Soviet chargé in Berlin, Georgi Astakhov, began a series of meetings with a middle-rank German official, Julius Schnurre, who was an expert on Eastern European affairs. The two beat around the bush much as their counterparts from France and Britain were doing in their negotiations with Molotov in Moscow.

But the Germans were more aggressive than the representatives of the West. In response to a summons from von Ribbentrop, Principal State Secretary von Weizsaecker and an assistant journeyed to one of the foreign minister's four residences. "The Leader has decided to establish more tolerable relations between

Germany and the Union of Soviet Socialist Republics," Ribbentrop told his visitors. Although it could not be a certainty that the soil was fertile, it was desirable that some seeds be dropped. Perhaps they would sprout. The two officials prepared a draft statement to be sent to Schulenburg. It offered a German proposal that a more open situation be established.

Ribbentrop took the draft and gave it to Hitler. But he did not like it, Ribbentrop told Weizsaecker. It was too open, it showed the German hand too freely. Schulenburg was ordered to "maintain an attitude of complete reserve." To be too anxious, Weizsaecker wrote the ambassador, might invite a "peal of Tartar laughter." That was on May 26, just about the same moment that Molotov in Moscow was railing at the British and French that he would not be bound by League of Nations procedures, which might see Bolivia speechmaking while Russia was under attack.

Within two days the Soviet chargé in Berlin responded to the German coolness. There was no Russian intention to "bar the door against further Russo-German discussions," he told Weizsaecker. The principal state secretary sent off a message to Schulenburg: "With the approval of the Leader, an approach is now to be made to the Russians. Contrary to the tactics hitherto used we have now after all decided to make a certain degree of contact with the Soviet Union."

From Moscow that day Sir William Seeds was writing home of Molotov: "It is my fate to deal with a man totally ignorant of foreign affairs. He has a rather foolish cunning of the type of the peasant."

On June 15 Seeds and William Strang and French ambassador to Russia Naggiar found the people's commissar unaccustomedly cheerful. "The two ambassadors were surprised to find Molotov so genial in manner," Strang cabled to London. "Though this made the interviews more pleasant, it did not add to their practical results."

They could not know of the talk that he had with Schulenburg that day.

•

William Strang wrote to London that summer that sometimes he wondered if the difficulty in coming to an agreement with the Russians was not due to some "colossal misunderstanding."

Lord Halifax said that no doubt his subordinates were "as bewildered as I am." In Berlin nothing was happening, for the Germans and Russians had again pulled back from each other, the Russians wondering if the German overtures were some elaborate trick that would be revealed when London and Paris joined with Berlin in some new Munich Agreement at Russia's expense, the Germans unable suddenly to throw off the anti-Communist attitude that had fueled Nazism for twenty years.

The two countries took to communicating with each other through third parties, Soviet chargé Astakhov remarking to the Bulgarian minister to Berlin that the Moscow negotiations with the West were going badly and that perhaps Russia really ought to make some arrangement with Germany. But what about Hitler's *My Struggle* and its fervently anti-Communist tone? What about the Anti-Comintern Pact Germany had with Italy and Japan? It called for unceasing enmity toward Russia. Such a statement and such questions, the Bulgarian decided, were not meant for his ears alone. He was meant to act as a messenger.

He passed the sense of the conversation on to the Germans. The Germans in return let the Russians know that Germany had "among our political merchandise a pretty good selection for Russia—normalization or hostility." Which did they want?

On July 18 the Russians gave their answer. A Russian trade representative called upon the German Eastern European affairs expert Julius Schnurre. "I have a message from the commissariat for foreign affairs," he said. "I have been instructed to inform you that the government of the U.S.S.R. is strongly desirous of extending and urgently building up economic relations between the two countries."

That night Weizsaecker cabled Schulenburg in Moscow: "We will act in a markedly forthcoming manner since a conclusion, and this at the earliest possible moment, is desired. Pick up the threads again."

Six days later under orders from Ribbentrop, Schnurre asked Astakhov and a colleague to dinner at Ewest, a small and elegant Berlin restaurant. The three ate and drank. Astakhov remarked that Moscow could not understand why Germany was such a bitter enemy of the Soviet Union. Was it not better to maintain friendly relations? Schnurre said he entirely agreed. And Germany had no intention of menacing the Russians. Certainly a far-reaching agreement on mutual interests was called for. But the

Russian flirtation with the British and French posed a problem. What, Schnurre asked, could Britain offer Russia? "At best, participation in a European war and the hostility of Germany. What could we offer? Neutrality and keeping out of a possible European conflict."

The men commenced their dinner at 9:00 P.M.; they parted after a final brandy and coffee at half-past midnight. Astakhov promised to send a report on the talk to Moscow at once.

In the Russian capital Molotov suddenly and surprisingly told the West's negotiators that it was time to conclude the political discussions. What were now required were military arrangements. Britain and France had no choice but to agree, for soon the harvest would be in and the roads clear for Hitler to march upon Poland if such was his desire. And the German papers were not indicative of peaceful intentions. UNBELIEVABLE AGITATION OF POLISH ARCH-MADNESS. POLAND AGAINST PEACE AND RIGHT IN EUROPE. London and Paris announced that a combined French-British military mission would journey to Moscow, its leader being Admiral the Honorable Sir Reginald Plunkett-Ernle-Erle-Drax, KCMG, DSO, tall, courteous, cold, who, like all Englishmen from good families, thought a French member of the mission, Captain André Beaufre, spoke hesitantly and coughed frequently. To Captain Beaufre he was remindful of the Napoleonic era's Admiral Lord Rodney, minus the wig. Drax was named to head the mission, Beaufre decided, because he was so perfect an English type that he would react to anything instinctively with the same reflexes that had made the Empire great. Associated with him in the British delegation was Air Vice-Marshal Sir Charles Burnett, also a traditional figure in Beaufre's eyes, of the type found in an old hunting print, with high color and bushy eyebrows. A good chap. A monocled major general, T. G. G. Heywood, completed the trio of British military negotiators. But who were they compared to, say, Sir Edmund Ironside, the senior British general on the active list who had led a military mission to Warsaw? They were to Ironside as William Strang was to Lord Halifax: estimable, no doubt—but of the second rank. The Russians would be offended if someone of the highest rank was not sent out to Moscow, Strang had told London; and when he, the slightingly referred-to special delegate of the British government, had to inform Molotov of the impending arrival of an admiral who was practically in retirement and was utterly unknown to anyone outside the most knowledgeable circles of the Royal Navy, of an air marshal who was an aviator and instructor but no strategist, and a general who was purely a combatant, fighting soldier, the look in the eyes of the people's commissar was of such contempt that Strang felt a chill and wanted to avert his gaze. The French were led by General Joseph Edouard Doumenc, of whom it could be said that he had organized the motor transport up the Sacred Way to the defense of Verdun in the War, and that he was the youngest general of that army of great memories that stood between France and the world: he was sixty.

They gathered in London, the West's fighting men. Russia's ambassador there, Ivan Maisky, gave them luncheon. Over coffee he asked Admiral Drax, tall, lean, gray-headed, "tranquil in his movements and unhasty in speech," whether they would be flying to Moscow. "Oh, no, there are about forty of us in the two delegations, if you reckon the technical staff, and we have a lot of baggage. It wouldn't be convenient to go by plane."

A fast cruiser, then, asked the Russian? That would be impressive, military delegations on a warship. A look Maisky interpreted as sour came over the admiral's face. "No, a cruiser wouldn't be suitable either. If we were to go by cruiser it would mean depriving a couple of dozen of its officers of their cabins. Why should we put people to such inconvenience? No, we won't be going by cruiser."

For days they dallied about London and then made for Leningrad on the *City of Exeter,* an old merchant mariner with a top speed of eleven knots, used on the South Africa run and chartered for this occasion. Life on board was very agreeable as they languidly went along through the North Sea and into the Baltic. They played deck tennis. Indian stewards in turbans served curry.

They made Leningrad at eleven at night on August 9, seventeen days after the Russians had been told they would hurry to the rendezvous. They went past the dim, flat coast, melancholy and forbidding, and the old island naval base there. The embankments of the canal jutted far out to sea amid the shoals of the delta and miles of lumberyards and docks at the entrance of the Neva, and then in formal military mess jackets they stood on the deck under the sky, opaline, like mother-of-pearl in the half-twilight of the North, and looked down at Russian soldiers in green caps and at badly dressed bystanders.

They debarked and made for Moscow and a welcoming banquet in what had been the home of a rich merchant before the Revolution. The dining room was huge, mock Gothic, with a monumental high oak roof. Dinner was brilliant, served on tableware that bore the arms of the late Tsar. They went into the music room, white and copied from Versailles with a magnificent inlaid parquet floor. The clothing of the entertainers was amazing: dinner jackets worn with gray slippers and colored shirt, a woman violinist in tennis attire and a singer in a long dress that to Captain Beaufre appeared like something that might have "come from some minor German court in the last century." The clothing was of a piece with everything about Russia: everything was of strange and inferior materials, wretched writing paper and linens, all shoddy and shabby.

Their host at the dinner and leading opposite number in the military negotiations was Marshal Klementy Voroshilov, the people's commissar of defense. He was seconded by the chief of staff of the Red Army and the commanders in chief of the navy and air force. Voroshilov was an effervescent personality, a hunter publicized as Russia's top marksman—this presumably to show that the country's defense was in good hands—and so interested in going to musical events (from which perhaps he derived hints of technique that made him the preeminent singer at the Gensek's late-night get-togethers) that he was known in select official circles as "The Party Boy." Sources had it that he could hardly be taken seriously, for it was said of him that he spent more time at the opera or posing for pictures with his uncounted medals than he did at his job at the Commissariat of Defense. But by any standard he could be expected to be easier to deal with than the glacial Molotov. ("Thank God that fellow will not participate in military negotiations!" said France's Ambassador Naggiar.)

But immediately after the Westerners met with him Voroshilov announced that he had the authority from his government to sign any pact and inquired the exact powers of the two other delegation leaders. General Doumenc showed an authorization to come to an agreement. Admiral Drax had nothing at all. He said he would ask London for some written authority. Voroshilov's obvious displeasure showed that he felt he was facing men with questionable bona fides.

He began to ask the exact Anglo-French plans in case of a war, the figures on the forces available, the means of transport, the number of guns and tanks, the deployment of troops, the disposition of fleets and air forces, how much, how soon, where, the complete order of battle. In short, he wanted to write down every military secret France and Britain had before it was at all certain they would be allied to him. It was more than disconcerting. Admiral Drax and General Doumenc had to ask themselves if the whole point of the meeting was for Voroshilov to know every detail of the most confidential and sensitive military matters.

They equivocated on exact figures as best they might. Voroshilov shifted to the question of whether Russian troops would be permitted to cross the frontiers of their neighbors if those neighbors were threatened by Germany. There was the great sticking point. Poland was in all their minds, that Poland which daily was ranted at by the German press in the most violent tones. "I must insist that from the start we discuss the principle of Soviet troops passing through Poland," Voroshilov said. "This is essential."

It was the last thing Drax and Doumenc wanted to talk about. To give permission was almost to grant Russia the right to take over who knew how many countries. They beat around the bush and said they could not speak of Polish intentions. "I want a clear answer to my very clear question," Voroshilov said. "I want a straight answer. Do the French and British General Staffs think that the Soviet land forces will be admitted to Polish territory in order to make direct contact with the enemy in case Poland is attacked? And further: do you think that our armed forces will be allowed passage across Polish territory to make contact with the enemy? Yet one more thing: is it proposed to allow Soviet troops to cross Romanian territory if the aggressor attacks Romania?"

It was agonizing for the Westerners. They asked leave to confer in private. They returned and Doumenc said they agreed that any concentration of troops "must take place principally in the areas indicated by the marshal."

"I want you to reply to my direct question," Voroshilov said. "I said nothing about Soviet troop concentrations. I asked whether

184 GENE SMITH

the British and French General Staffs envisage passage of our troops."

"I think that Poland and Romania will implore you, Marshal, to come to their assistance," Doumenc said.

"And perhaps they will not. It is not evident so far."

The talks, just begun, appeared stalled. Finally Doumenc and Drax suggested that the Russians direct their questions to the Polish and Romanian governments. They were sovereign states, they could speak for themselves. Or, if preferred, London and Paris could pose the questions. Voroshilov asked for a recess and left for an hour. He returned to say it would be best for the Western countries to apply to Poland and Romania.

Appeals went out to Whitehall and the Quai d'Orsay asking that the vital questions be put to the Poles and Rumanians. No answers were immediately forthcoming, and Voroshilov told Drax and Doumenc that under the circumstances the talks must be halted until an answer was received. Nothing could be more obvious than that he felt the West was merely playing at negotiations when they failed to order—to *order*—Poland to admit the Red Army. London and Paris remained silent.

On August 17 Doumenc cabled home that he had managed to arrange a resumption of the talks for the twenty-first but had done so only to avoid giving the world the impression that all contacts had been broken off. At the same time he ordered Captain Beaufre to Warsaw to see what might be done there about getting an affirmative reply from Poland.

At the French Embassy in the Polish capital the captain heard from Ambassador Léon Noël and the military attaché, General Musse, that the Poles' hatred for Russia was so great that it would be hopeless to get their assent for the entrance of Russia's soldiery onto the soil of Polonia Restituta. It was as if France were to be asked to entrust to the Germans the protection of Alsace-Lorraine. Foreign domination to the Poles, they told Beaufre, was an inexpressible horror. They had endured domination for hundreds of years and it was the lodestar of the nation that they be independent. Nothing in Polish life held so strong a grip on the emotions. Even to pose the question was dangerous, General Musse said; the very image of Russian troops on their soil might drive Poland into Germany's arms as an ally in a war against the West.

Captain Beaufre persevered and finally Musse presented the question to the chief of the Polish General Staff. "I understand your point of view perfectly," General Waclaw Stachiewicz replied, "but I ask you also to understand ours. We know the Russians better than you do. They are a dishonest people whose word is not to be relied upon by us or anyone else, and it is quite useless to ask us even to contemplate a proposition of this nature."

Beaufre asked Ambassador Noël to apply to Foreign Minister Beck, who consulted with the head of the Polish army, Marshal Smigly-Rydz, and brought back their mutual conclusion: impossible. "With the Germans," Smigly-Rydz had said, "we risk the loss of our liberty, but with the Russians we lose our soul."

•

After Julius Schnurre's dinner with the two Russian diplomats in Berlin's Ewest Restaurant in late July, Joachim von Ribbentrop launched appeal after appeal to Moscow for an understanding between Russia and Germany. For years it had been the foreign minister's practice to discover what actions Hitler was contemplating, and then to recommend those very actions. Not personally close to the Leader and therefore not a member of that group whose function it was to form an audience for Hitler's endless late-night monologues, Ribbentrop ascertained what was going on in Hitler's mind from reports given him by Walter Hewel, his Foreign Office link to the Leader. (Like all those who formed the Leader's innermost circle, Hewel was an Old Fighter of the Nazi Party. He had shared Hitler's 1923 imprisonment after the failed beer hall rebellion in Munich.)

In the midsummer of 1939 Hewel reported to Ribbentrop that Hitler was talking more and more about settling accounts with Poland. But first Poland must be cut off from its Western backers. The way to do that was to subtract Russia from the equation, for without Russia, Hitler believed, England and France would be incapable of doing anything for Poland. What after all could they do? A look at the map showed that Poland's situation with a neutral Russia at her back was hopeless.

Yet the Poles were arrogant beyond belief, Hitler said to the people around him. They would not give him Danzig, they would not give him a corridor through the Corridor, they were, he said, his rage rising, a bastard race of a cultural level comparable to a tribe in some African jungle. They deserved a thrashing. They were asking for one.

So Hewel reported to Ribbentrop. There remained the question of Russia. On July 29, as the French and British military missions discussed the best method of getting from London to Moscow, a German courier sped to German ambassador to Russia von der Schulenburg with a Foreign Office dispatch concerning the Ewest Restaurant conversations. "It would be important for us to know whether the remarks made to Astakhov have met with any response in Moscow. If you see an opportunity of arranging a further conversation with Molotov, please sound him out on the same lines."

Should Molotov abandon the restraint he had so far displayed, Schulenburg was told, he was to be given to understand that however Germany arranged matters with Poland, Germany would be willing to safeguard all Soviet interests in that country. Two days later: "Please report by telegram the date and time of your next interview with Molotov. We are anxious for an early interview."

On August 3, Schulenburg was told to inform the Russians that Germany was prepared to speak quite concretely regarding adjustments of German-Soviet interests. Ribbentrop had the previous day talked at great length with Astakhov and had told him that from the Baltic to the Black Sea there was no problem Germany and Russia could not solve to the satisfaction of both countries. "I declared myself ready for conversations if the Soviet government would inform me through Astakhov that they also desired to place German-Russian relations on a new and definitive basis."

In Moscow Schulenburg and Molotov met; in Berlin Schnurre talked with Astakhov. (In England the French and British missions were preparing to board the *City of Exeter*.) Schnurre seemed to be in quite a hurry to come to an arrangement, Astakhov remarked. "We thought it expedient to make use of the next few days in order to establish a basis as quickly as possible," Schnurre replied. Astakhov said that his chief, Molotov, while wishing an improvement in relations, had to know more concretely what the Germans had in mind. Schulenburg was ordered to see him in Moscow. They spoke for an hour and a quarter and, the ambassador reported to Berlin, the foreign minister "appeared unusually open." The British and French were on the way. Unusually open or not, Molotov demanded of Schulenburg to know how the Germans reconciled their new anxiety for good relations with their rigidly anti-Communist attitude of the past. Schulenburg replied that Germany hoped to make amends by more friendly actions in the future.

Meanwhile, the League of Nations high commissioner for the Free City of Danzig, Carl Burckhardt, journeyed to Berchtesgaden to confer with Hitler. He found the Leader looking much older and whiter than he had appeared in 1937, when Burckhardt had last seen him, and strangely "nervous, pathetic, almost shaken at times." It seemed to the high commissioner that there was something womanlike about this Hitler, his "femininity."

But at the same time he was in a murderous rage against Poland: "If the slightest incident happens now I shall crush the Poles without warning in such a way that no trace of Poland can be found afterward. I shall strike like lightning." He yelled and laughed in what Burckhardt thought was a hysterical fashion. "If every time I take a step necessitated by history I find England and France in the way, what can I do?" His voice, Burckhardt remembered, was "fortissimo."

"I have seen idiotic statements in the French press that I had lost my nerve and the Poles had kept theirs," Hitler cried. He was so carried away by his anger that he became unable to speak for some moments. Then: "I shall strike like lightning with the full force of a mechanized army, of which the Poles have no concept. Listen to that."

"I am listening. I know that will mean a general war."

"So be it. If I have to wage war, I would rather do it today than tomorrow." He switched to saying that what he really desired was to live in peace with England. Burckhardt seized on that. "Then would it not be better to have a direct conversation with an Englishman?"

"Language is too big an obstacle," Hitler said. "I realized it last year." His concept seemed strange—statesmen could not be expected to be linguists; that was what interpreters were for. "I understand a little English, I stumble over a few words of French," Hitler was saying. "I had a hard and difficult youth, and was not able to learn languages. An Englishman who could talk German?" He appeared to have forgotten Ambassador Sir Nevile Henderson, who in his youth had gone to live in Dresden and Bonn for the express purpose of learning German, and had mastered it perfectly. "They tell me that General Ironside talks it fluently, the general who went to Warsaw."

"Could I pass on such a wish?"

"Yes."

But Ironside was far away looking to the defenses of an England that was hearing from its ambassador to Poland, Sir Howard Kennard: "Reports are reaching here regarding increased German military activity." Polish intelligence sources were finding evidence of German corps and army headquarters units concentrating along the German-Polish border, of overflights by the German air force. A harsh note from Berlin reached Warsaw: the German government regarded recent Polish representations to Danzig as having the nature of ultimatums, and any repetitions or threats or actions of a decided nature would lead to consequences the responsibility for which would fall exclusively on the Polish government. Foreign Minister Beck as harshly replied that he saw no justification for the German statements and wished to point out that any intervention in the relationship between Poland and the Free City would be viewed as an act of aggression. German newspapers headlined: POLAND, LOOK OUT! The subject of Poland occupied the Leader's mind to the exclusion of almost anything else, and he took to referring to the country's inhabitants as "subhumans."

In his wake Ribbentrop also raved against Warsaw, telling the Italian ambassador to Berlin, Bernardo Attolico, that if the Poles dared to continue in their arrogant course, Germany would crush them in forty-eight hours of unimaginable warfare. Attolico was alarmed. Italy was allied to Germany through the Pact of Steel. Hitler was in a position to drag his ally into war. Attolico filled his dispatches to Rome with fearful predictions of a possible catastrophe, of "the imminence of a new and perhaps fatal crisis."

The warnings seemed for a long time fevered and unrealistic to the ambassador's chief, Italian foreign minister Count Ciano. Attolico appeared "frightened by his own shadow," Ciano wrote in his diary. He had "lost his head" and was "trying to save his country from a nonexistent danger." Then Ciano began to ask himself if perhaps the ambassador was right and that Hitler was thinking of mounting a campaign against Poland, the consequences of which were incalculable. "This insistence of Attolico keeps me wondering," Ciano told his diary on August 2. On August 4: "Attolico's alarmist bombardment continues. The situation seems obscure to me. I am beginning to think of the possibility of a meeting with von Ribbentrop."

The subject of his proposed meeting by then was in full pursuit of Russia. Yet the quarry was elusive. Feeling out the Anglo-French mission through Voroshilov, the only man who mattered in Russia continued to sound out Germany through Molotov and Astakhov. It was an auction. But while the West dallied about, weakly attempting to secure Poland's permission for the entrance of Russian troops in case of a war, Ribbentrop kept raising his bids. Germany would establish a basis for good relations with the Soviets, which would endure for generations, Germany had a basic, inborn sympathy for Russians, the two countries must speedily clarify their situations vis-à-vis one another and arrange things in Eastern Europe to their mutual satisfaction. Molotov told Astakhov to inform Julius Schnurre that Russia was ready to talk more openly to Germany, but in slow stages. "The discussion could be undertaken only by degrees."

But Hitler could not wait to discuss things by degrees. Under a brilliant August sun the Polish roads were dry and hard; but in the middle days of September the rains would come and troops and tanks would be mired in depthless mud. On August 14 Schulenburg was sent a telegram by Ribbentrop that he was instructed to read out to Molotov word for word.

German-Soviet relations, the ambassador read out, had "come to an historic turning point. There exist no real conflicts of interest between Germany and Russia. It has gone well with both countries previously when they were friends and badly when they were enemies." Years of hostility must be cleared away. The Western democracies were trying to drive Russia and Germany against each other.

At the end Ribbentrop's daring last bid was offered: "I am prepared to make a short visit to Moscow in order, in the name of the Leader, to set forth the Leader's views to M. Stalin." He alluded to what the Leader's views might mean to M. Stalin: they concerned the Baltic states and Poland, areas for which Russians of past generations had fought and died but which the Russians of the present had lost because of the West and its Versailles Treaty.

In Rome the frenzied telegrams from Attolico, who had picked up rumors of the secret German appeals to Russia, moved Count Ciano to see Ribbentrop. He went north into Austria and to the German foreign minister's estate at Fuschl confiscated from an aristocrat sent to Dachau. Attolico had begun to say that his sources indicated Hitler was definitely going to make war on Poland.

"But is it possible," Ciano asked himself, "that all this should take place without our knowing it, after so many protestations of peace made by our Axis comrades?" Such a war could never be localized but must spread into a cataclysm disastrous for all, Mussolini had told his foreign minister, and Ciano agreed completely and was determined to make the Italian viewpoint entirely clear to the German foreign minister. In the garden before dinner he walked with Ribbentrop. Neither man spoke the other's language, but both spoke English.

"Well, Ribbentrop," Ciano asked, "what do you want? The Corridor or Danzig?"

"Not that anymore," Ribbentrop replied. He spoke in an entirely emotionless fashion, as if, Ciano thought, he were referring to some inconsequential administrative detail. His eyes were cold, circular, moonlike, metallic. "We want war!"

Ciano was shocked and horrified. He suggested solutions that might offer satisfaction to Germany and avoid a resort to arms. Ribbentrop rejected them. They are possessed by the demon of destruction, Ciano said to himself. The men went into dinner and the atmosphere between them was so cold that not a word was exchanged throughout the meal.

In the morning the Italian tried again. Nothing registered upon his host. He left Fuschl and made the half-hour trip across the former German-Austrian border to the Leader's Berchtesgaden. Hitler was cordial but unmoved by any advocacy of a peaceful solution. "I realize there is no longer anything that can be done," Ciano wrote in his diary. "He has decided to strike, and strike he will. All arguments will not in the least avail to stop him. He continues to repeat that he will localize the conflict."

Even Hitler's physical gestures revealed a will to action. He would attack Poland, Ciano felt, no matter what Poland did or did not do. Ciano returned to Rome disgusted with the Germans and frightened of what might be coming, and told Mussolini that whatever happened Italy must not follow the Germans into a war. Il Duce at first appeared to agree, but then took to saying that his honor demanded that he fight if Germany did. Ciano was distraught. An Italian diplomat in Warsaw sent him a description of filled churches, and the people singing a hymn: "O God, Help Us to Save Our Country." Ciano wrote in his diary, "These people will be massacred by German steel. They are innocent. My heart is with them."

He got Mussolini to change his mind yet again and say he would not blindly march with Germany. Yet perhaps the West would give in, Mussolini mused, and then perhaps there could be booty for Italy to be found in Yugoslavia. Ciano spoke with him for six hours straight, but two days later Mussolini declared he must go with Germany. Ambassador Attolico came from Berlin to join his voice to Ciano's in a plea that they stay aloof, but Mussolini, always really an actor impersonating a statesman, and a melodramatic actor at that, said that if he told Hitler he was renouncing the Pact of Steel, it was possible the Leader would forget about Poland and turn on Italy.

Mussolini finally said he would support Germany at all costs. Attolico was overwhelmed with grief at the news. The next day Ciano made yet another plea. The Germans had betrayed their partners, he said, and acted as if Italians were servants. "Tear up the pact," he told Mussolini. "Throw it in Hitler's face." He himself would be happy to carry out the mission. "I shall go and speak to the Germans as they should be spoken to. Hitler will not have me put out my cigarette as he did with Schuschnigg!"

His words were brave and he meant them, but he said them in Rome, not in Berchtesgaden. There he had quailed before Hitler, as others had and would again, and said that perhaps the Leader was right, that perhaps England and France would never fight: "You have been proved right so often before when we others held the opposite view, that I think it very possible that this time you see things more clearly than we do." By then he was convinced that nothing could stop the war that was coming, thinking of the Germans that the madness of the chief had become the religion of the followers.

•

Poland would not budge under the bombardment of appeals from the French and British. "In no case would the admission of Soviet troops into Poland be agreed to," Foreign Minister Beck told the British military attaché. "I do not admit," he told the French ambassador, "that there can be any kind of discussion whatsoever concerning the use of our territory by foreign troops." Finally, under extreme pressure the Poles said they did not wish to be consulted about the Anglo-French negotiations with the Russians, but that when an arrangement was reached, it could be laid before the Polish government.

The French took the grudging and high-handed response, highly amplified it, and presented to Marshal Voroshilov an assurance of Polish permission for the entrance into that country of Russian troops. Voroshilov received the information skeptically. Why was only France presenting this alleged permission, he inquired? What about England? For that matter, if the Poles were now amenable to Soviet desires, why did they not send a delegation to discuss matters?

"The Soviet military mission cannot picture to itself how—" he said. He announced he was off for a day's duck hunting. Indeed there was nothing better for him to do, for Russian interest was concentrated elsewhere. In response to Ribbentrop's August 14 offer to come to Moscow Molotov had replied that such a visit would require preparations. His foot-dragging infuriated Berlin, but he did offer one concrete suggestion: would Germany be interested in signing a nonaggression pact with Russia? The German answer instantly came back: they would sign a nonaggression pact, arrange things with the Baltic states, use their influence with Tokyo to end the sporadic fighting of Japanese troops with Russian units along the Chinese border, anything and everything. But it must all be done speedily. "Germany is determined not to endure Polish provocation indefinitely." They wished Moscow to know that Ribbentrop was prepared to leave for the Russian capital at a moment's notice.

A day passed. Berlin demanded of Ambassador Schulenburg that he obtain an immediate affirmative reply from Molotov. Schulenburg reported back that he was doing his best. The sun shone from a cloudless sky upon a Poland that never before had known so dry a summer. There were no foreign tourists on the sandy Baltic beaches of the northern end of the Corridor—"The Polish Riviera"—for each day the German newspapers grew more threatening. The Poles were butchering their citizens of German blood, they were castrating men, the papers said. But Poland's day of reckoning was on the way.

On the beaches near Danzig Dr. Haskell Nordon of Warsaw swam and walked the dunes and looked out at the shiny metallic green of the sea where now and then a ship of the tiny Polish navy went by, symbol of the situation upon which was focused the eyes of the world. The doctor met a girl on the shore. They took lunch together. He snapped pictures of her and was approached by two men who identified themselves as members of the Polish military intelligence and pointed out that behind the girl posing for the camera were port installations. Nordon was able to show he was not a spy, and he and the girl went away impressed with the alertness of the military authorities.

In England a wet July became the wettest first half of August in memory. The rain turned springs into rivulets. The Michaelmas daisies came to blossom prematurely. Government public information leaflets dealt with the use of gas masks, the technique of putting tape on windows so that they would not shatter into a thousand dangerous shards if bombs fell nearby, the procedures to be used for the evacuation of children from threatened areas. Parliament stood adjourned—"Go off and play, but take your gas masks with you," Chamberlain seemed to say, Winston Churchill thought. On August 16, the prime minister himself went to the Highlands of Scotland for some fishing.

Back from his American tour, the king, with his wife and daughters and Lord Louis Mountbatten, visited Dartmouth Naval College, where a quarter century before he had been a cadet. There was a mumps and chicken pox epidemic at the school and so the two young princesses were kept away from most of the students but permitted to play croquet with a group of those who were free of the diseases, among whose number was Cadet Captain Prince Philip of Greece, Mountbatten's nephew. Princess Elizabeth, thirteen, had perhaps seen Prince Philip, eighteen, at a wedding years before, but did not remember.

In the first days of August the Duke of York's Camp set up by the king just twenty years earlier opened for a week. In the past both as Duke of York and then king, the monarch had usually appeared for a day, but for this session he appointed himself camp chief and was with the four hundred boys for the entire period, eating with them and participating in their activities. He led them in camp songs with special gestures and waves. The queen and two princesses came for evening meals. On the last evening he lit a great bonfire and with the boys sang "Auld Lang Syne" and then stood silently while everybody else sang "God Save the King." The mood of the camp had been more solemn and with less ragging than any of the nineteen preceding sessions. The king led the boys to motor coaches that would take them home and then, standing by himself, waved good-bye to those who would man his army, the Royal Navy and the Royal Air Force if events in Moscow, in Warsaw, at Berchtesgaden and Paris and London brought a war.

•

On the evening of August 19 Ambassador von der Schulenburg in a telegram marked *Secret, Most Urgent* was able to tell Hitler and Ribbentrop what they wanted to hear. Molotov had agreed that Germany's foreign minister could come to Moscow for the signing of a nonaggression pact. He was to arrive on August 26 or 27. An attempt to arrange an earlier meeting, Schulenburg cabled, "was, unfortunately, unsucessful."

But it had to be made successful. German army units were maneuvering toward the Polish border, their commanders unanimous in feeling it was all a bluff and that the Leader would get Danzig and the Corridor in the same fashion as he had gotten rearmament and the Rhineland and Austria and the Sudetenland and the rest of Czechoslovakia. But for the bluff to be effective there had to be the threat of an advance into Poland. That threat had a time limit, for once the autumn rains began, the threat evaporated. Adolf Hitler had spent twenty years saying Communism was an invention of the Jews and Russia a criminal state, but hours after Schulenburg's telegram came in, he reached beyond pride and above Molotov and did what neither Chamberlain and Daladier, nor anyone else, had ever done.

M. STALIN, MOSCOW:

   THE TENSION BETWEEN GERMANY AND POLAND HAS BECOME INTOLERABLE. IN MY OPINION IT IS DESIRABLE NOT TO LOSE ANY TIME. I THEREFORE PROPOSE THAT YOU RECEIVE MY FOREIGN MINISTER ON TUESDAY, AUGUST 22, BUT AT THE LATEST ON WEDNESDAY, AUGUST 23. I SHOULD BE GLAD TO RECEIVE YOUR EARLY ANSWER.

ADOLF HITLER

That night he could not sleep, and seemed in a state approaching a nervous breakdown. He paced up and down his study at Berchtesgaden, eating apples. The house was deathly silent. The servants avoided him. Eva Braun brought him milk soup. He sipped it, belched, put it down. In the middle of the night he telephoned Goering. Dawn came. The day passed. Twenty-four hours had gone by, the longest day of his life, he said later. Sleepless for that period, he saw the sun descend and another night wear on until at 10:50 P.M., August 21, the teletype rattled. He ran to it.

TO THE CHANCELLOR OF THE GERMAN REICH, MR. A. HITLER:
I THANK YOU FOR THE LETTER. I HOPE THAT A GERMAN-SOVIET NON-AGGRESSION PACT WILL BRING ABOUT A DECIDED TURN FOR THE BETTER IN THE POLITICAL RELATIONS BETWEEN OUR COUNTRIES. THE SOVIET GOVERNMENT HAS INSTRUCTED ME TO INFORM YOU THAT THEY AGREE TO MR. VON RIBBENTROP'S ARRIVING IN MOSCOW ON AUGUST 23.

J. STALIN

He flung his hands into the air. "It's done! We've done it! Now we can spit in everybody's face!" He beat his fists against the wall. "Now I have the whole world in my pocket!"

The next day Ribbentrop went from Berchtesgaden to Berlin and with a party of thirty, including diplomatic aides, photographers, interpreters and press representatives, flew to Königsberg in East Prussia. That night in the Nearby Villa outside Moscow Joseph Stalin remarked to Nikita Khrushchev that the German foreign minister would be arriving the next day. A joke, of course, Khrushchev thought. But the Gensek indicated he was serious. Khrushchev gaped at him. "Why should Ribbentrop want to see us?" he asked. "Is he defecting to our side, or what?"

"No, Hitler has sent us a message saying, 'I ask you, Herr Stalin, to receive my minister, Ribbentrop, who brings with him some concrete proposals.' "

Dazed, Khrushchev said he was planning to go hunting at Marshal Voroshilov's preserve the following day. Stalin told him to go ahead. In the morning Ribbentrop's two Condors crossed into Russian territory, the travelers looking down and noting how different the dark, thatched roofs were from the red tiles of Germany. They landed in Moscow around noon. The first thing that caught the eye of the interpreter Paul Schmidt was a swastika flag floating in the breeze. When he had learned that Ribbentrop was going to Moscow to sign a pact, Schmidt's first reaction was to say to himself that by the nature of his profession he was unlikely to find himself speechless, but that if asked to express his amazement he would have found himself at an utter loss for words.

The Germans emerged from the planes and were greeted by Molotov's aide Vladimir Potemkin. Their welcomer's name was reminiscent of the long-ago Russian statesman remembered for constructing miles of bogus false-front villages for the empress Catherine. A Russian named Potemkin was symbolic of the unreality of this entire affair, Schmidt thought. They stood at attention as a band played "The Internationale" with its call for the masses to rise in Revolution, and then the hastily learned and practiced "Horst Wessel" with its gory demand for the slaughter of all Communists.

Ribbentrop passed through the ranks of a Red air force honor guard drawn up for inspection. The troops were very smart. Then the Germans went under massed hammer-and-sickle Soviet flags side by side with swastikas that they could not know were the only ones available in the Russian capital and had been borrowed from movie companies engaged in turning out anti-Nazi movies. (The film *Professor Mamlock* had been hastily withdrawn from Russian theaters. It portrayed a German government plotting the ruin of the Soviet Union.)

They got into cars that appeared to be modeled on American Buicks and drove to the former Austrian Embassy, which would be the headquarters for their stay. At about three-thirty in the afternoon Ribbentrop went to the Kremlin accompanied by Ambassador von der Schulenburg and Embassy Counsel Gustav Hilger. A Russian colonel led them to a small door, from which a short flight of stairs led to a tower. An official took them into a long room. Schulenburg could not suppress a cry of surprise when he saw who was waiting for them: with Molotov was Joseph Stalin. Never before had Schulenburg, or any ambassador, actually met the Gensek and shaken hands with him.

Through an interpreter Ribbentrop said he wanted to make a settlement with Russia that would be valid for the longest possible time. Stalin asked Molotov if he wanted to reply. The foreign minister asked Stalin himself to do so. Briefly and precisely, in what Ribbentrop thought was a clear and unambiguous fashion, Stalin listed his desires and outlined them on a map using a red pencil. He wanted the Baltic states, the eastern sections of Poland and parts of Romania to be understood to be in the Russian sphere of interest. Germany and Russia must agree not to attack each other. Each would remain neutral should the other become the object of belligerent action by a third Power. Russia would deliver certain amounts of wheat and oil and other raw materials to Germany. Germany would give Russia a battle cruiser

and experts to outfit it plus machine tools and industrial installations.

Ribbentrop agreed to everything, but when Stalin expressed
interest in the Latvian warm-water ports of Libau and Windau,
he said he would have to consult the Leader. The Germans adjourned to their headquarters, where Ribbentrop announced to
those waiting there, "Things are going splendidly, we shall certainly arrive at an agreement before the evening is out." He
seemed to Paul Schmidt to be positively bubbling over with enthusiasm about Molotov and Stalin. He put in a call to Hitler and
told him of the Russian request that the Latvian ports be assigned to their sphere of interest. Hitler sent an orderly for an
atlas, looked at the map of the Baltic coastline, noted that the
ports were a stone's throw from East Prussia, but told Ribbentrop to tell Stalin he was welcome to them.

With Schulenburg and Hilger the German foreign minister
returned to the Kremlin to say the Latvian question was settled
and that the pact could now be signed. He handed Stalin a draft
of a proposed communiqué containing a flowery description of
the eternal friendship that had ever existed between the German
and Russian peoples. Ribbentrop himself had composed it. Stalin
read, smiled, and in his mild way asked, "Don't you think that
we have to pay a little more attention to public opinion in our
countries? For years now we have been pouring buckets of manure over each other's heads, and now all of a sudden are we to
make our peoples believe that all is forgotten and forgiven? Things
don't work so fast." The passage was removed.

As flashbulbs popped, the Russo-German Pact was signed, the
Nazi-Soviet Agreement immediately to be released to an astonished world: "The government of the German Reich and the
government of the Union of Soviet Socialist Republics, desirous
of strengthening the cause of peace . . ." and going on to arrangements of which the world must never know: in the event
of a territorial and political transformation the Baltic states, for
which Tsar Peter the Great had made war for twenty years, would
bloodlessly revert into Russia's lap along with eastern Poland and
part of Romania. "This protocol will be treated by both parties
as strictly secret."

It was getting on to midnight. Supper and drinks were served.
"I know how much the German nation loves its Leader," Stalin

said. "I should therefore like to drink to his health." Hitler was, Stalin said, using Russian slang, "a good guy." Molotov proposed the health of the German foreign minister. They drank to the pact, to the new era of German-Soviet relations, to the German nation, to Stalin, to the Soviet government, to favorable future relations between Germany and Russia.

The conversation became informal, Stalin remarking as he had before and would again in other company that he was an Asiatic, and then going on to speak of his contempt for Great Britain. Ribbentrop said that it was England's aim to disrupt good relations between Germany and Russia, and Stalin agreed. "If England dominates the world," he said, "this was due to the stupidity of other countries that always let themselves be bluffed."

It was ridiculous, for example, he went on, that "a few hundred British" should dominate India. Ribbentrop talked about "typically stupid English" diplomatic maneuvers and said he had told the Leader that every hostile British act in case of a German-Polish conflict should be answered by German bombers appearing over London. They turned to a discussion of British influence in Turkey. The English spent five million pounds there buying up politicians, Ribbentrop said. Far more, said Stalin.

Joachim von Ribbentrop was vain, "such an imbecile," said one of his subordinates, "that he is a freak of nature." He was a fit subject not for the attentions of such a diplomat as Baron von Weizsaecker, thought that official, but for the baron's brother, who was a professor specializing in the study of mental diseases; he was touchy, a bully, arrogant, rude, tactless, impolite, a social climber and poseur, petty and spiteful, a great snob—everyone who knew him was in unanimous agreement—but he had now negotiated a pact so enormous, so world-shaking, that his chief, the Leader of the German Reich, would in days anoint him another Bismarck, or greater still.

When he went to Paris in the wake of the 1938 visit of the king of England, Ribbentrop had seemed positively "pathological" in his demands that the French treat him to the same displays and offer the same honors as they had given King George, thought the German ambassador to Paris Count von Welczeck, and all who met him at the station saw that he held his nose so high in the air that he tripped over the rails. But now half-drunk on sparkling Crimean wine he contested on equal terms with Joseph Stalin, the absolute ruler of a sixth of the world's surface, in expositions of goodwill. It was a joke in Berlin, he told the Gensek, that those who understood things said that the Gensek himself would yet join the Anti-Comintern Pact. Stalin with his mild manner, smoking his pipe, remarked that the Germans had apparently understood the reference in his speech of six months earlier when, referring to the West, he had said Russia did not intend to pull others' chestnuts out of the fire.

They laughed and drank. Ribbentrop asked if a German photographer could take pictures of just the two of them. Stalin assented. It must certainly have been the first time a foreigner took a picture in the recesses of the Kremlin, Ribbentrop thought to himself. But the man went too far, getting a shot of the two drinking together. Stalin waved the photographer away and Ribbentrop told him to give over the spool from the camera. He handed it to Stalin but the Gensek said that was not necessary. He only trusted that the picture would not be published. A very nice atmosphere, Ribbentrop said to himself. In the small hours of the morning just before the visitors left the Kremlin Stalin took him aside and in the most serious fashion told him that Russia would never break the word she had given in the Nazi-Soviet Pact. They parted.

When Ribbentrop awoke in the former Austrian Embassy, he looked out the window and saw a group of men looking at him from the windows of a building opposite. They were members, he was told, of the British and French military missions. Ribbentrop and his people boarded their Condors and flew out of Moscow. They had been in Russia for twenty-four hours.

The French and British met with Marshal Voroshilov for a final time to conclude the negotiations between their countries and Russia begun more than four months before. He was sorry, Voroshilov said, that he had been unavailable for a couple of days, but he had been out duck shooting. He did not go into the particulars of the hunting, which had seen him bring down one less bird than did Nikita Khrushchev. The days' bag was taken to the Nearby Villa, where it was prepared for Joseph Stalin's table, the Gensek cheery and joking and in high spirits about the signing of the pact. (It was a sign of his good mood, Khruschev noted, that he took a favorable view of his subordinates' hunting expedition. When in a less pleasant mood he, like Hitler, condemned the chasing of animals and birds as a waste of time.)

The British and French would now depart, Stalin said to

Khrushchev as the ducks were being cooked. It was well that they do so. They had never meant to sign with Russia, they just wanted to incite the Germans against the State of the Workers and Peasants. Marshal Voroshilov echoed his chief's words, saying to Admiral Drax and General Doumenc and the others that to continue discussions would be pointless. And really, he asked, had there ever been a point to the talks? What had the West offered Russia? "Do we have to conquer Poland in order to offer help to the Polish people?"

The military missions took their leave. Two Russian generals saw them off on a train for Finland. They related the departure to comrades later: "The locomotive whistle blew. The train began to move slowly. We turned to each other and without saying a word burst into laughter."

The military missions crossed the border. At the first station out of Russia the train stopped and everyone heaved a sigh of relief. Captain Beaufre remembered how Admiral Drax did a little dance on the platform.

THIRTEEN

IHAVE SUMMONED YOU," Hitler said, "to strengthen your confidence and to explain to you the reasons that moved me to make a certain number of decisions." The audience was already bored. It consisted of nearly one hundred of Germany's top officers, brought from their posts to Berchtesgaden in plain clothes. General Erich von Manstein noted that Goering's idea of plain clothes consisted of a green jerkin with big buttons of yellow leather, gray shorts and gray silk stockings "that displayed his impressive calves to considerable effect." His "dainty hosiery was offset by a pair of massive laced boots. His paunch was girdled by a sword belt of red leather richly inlaid with gold, from which dangled an ornamental dagger." Hitler began discussing the leadership of other countries. Von Manstein studied Goering's attire. "I suppose Fatboy's here as a strong-arm man," he whispered to his neighbor.

Hitler was talking about Turkey. It was governed by "cretins and half-idiots." King Carol of Romania? "The corrupt slave of his sexual instincts." The king of the Belgians and the Nordic kings? "Soft jumping jacks." Mussolini, of course, was a great man but hampered by the Italian royal family, "that nitwit of a king and treacherous scoundrel of a crown prince." One of the listening generals fell asleep in his chair.

"I decided to go with Stalin," Hitler told his officers. "Stalin and I are the only ones who visualize the future." He turned to his favorite subject: himself. "I possess an authority that no person in Germany has ever possessed before me. My very existence is therefore most vital." He went on about his importance. This entire meeting, General von Manstein told himself, was, of course, a big bluff aimed at scaring Poland. The gathering, hardly to go unnoticed by the intelligence services of every European nation, constituted a political squeeze to Poland. In response that country would likely give up the Corridor and Danzig.

"Warsaw is now isolated," Hitler was saying. "Any danger of Germany being encircled is removed. I have got Poland where I wanted her. The Russo-German nonaggression pact knocks the cards out of the hands of the Western powers."

They broke for lunch, a buffet served outside on the terrace and including caviar, a delicacy the Leader liked very much but rarely served or ate because of its expense. At the conclusion of the meal so different from the dreary fare usually served at what Hitler liked to term "the merry Chancellor's restaurant," the group returned to Berchtesgaden's great hall, where everybody took seats save for the host, who stood by a grand piano.

"For us it is easy to make decisions," he said. "We have nothing to lose. We can only gain. Our economic situation is such that we have no other choice: we must act. We are facing the alternative to strike or be destroyed with certainty sooner or later."

They had heard it all before. He went on to Germany's destiny to do what it would with Poland and turned to Poland's champions in the West. "They did not count on my great powers of resolution. I experienced those poor worms Daladier and Chamberlain at Munich. They will be too cowardly to attack. Our enemies are men who are small, below average. No personalities! No masters! No men of action!"

But no one could say how long he, Hitler, the Leader, might live. "Therefore it is better that we should start the conflict now!"

There was a stir in the hall. He was actually speaking of a real war, an actual commencement of hostilities, and in between his interminable talk of things he had said before a thousand times, something new was coming to the surface. "Our strength lies in our quickness and our brutality. Genghis Khan sent millions of women and children into death knowingly and with a light heart. History sees in him only the great founder of states. As to what the weak Western European civilization asserts about me, that is of no account. I have given the command and I shall shoot everyone who utters one word of criticism."

He went on and on and on as always he did, the slaughter of the Armenians by the Turks in 1915, the successes of Frederick the Great, but also: "A long period of peace would not do us any good." As always one had to wade through his endless monologues filled with imprecisions and hazy generalities, through the interminable flow of words of how eighty million Germans must get what was their right:

"I will find a reason for starting this war. It matters little whether this reason is plausible or not. The victor does not have to account to the vanquished. In time of war, at its beginning and during the course of operations, it is not law that matters, but victory.

"Poland will be depopulated and settled with Germans," he said, the dreaming orator on the stump who looked back upon his days of haranguing crowds in the streets during the days of *My Struggle* as the happiest in his life. The "vons" before him waited. Eventually he had to stop talking. Russia would in time share Poland's fate, he said. "Then there will begin the dawn of the German rule of the earth."

He droned on, suddenly now and then coming back through discussions of his mission given him by Providence to things more concrete: "I have but one worry, namely that Chamberlain or some other such pig of a fellow will come at the last moment with proposals. He will fly down the stairs."

He returned again to something approaching a concrete statement of policy: he would, he said, invent a reason for starting the war. "Whether the world believes the reason amounts to a pile of shit.* The world believes only in success. For you, gentlemen, fame and honor will come as they have not since centuries past. Be hard, be without mercy. The citizens of Western Europe must tremble with horror. And now, on to the enemy. We will meet again in Warsaw."

He had talked, with an hour's break for lunch, for more than six hours. Ribbentrop had not even gotten back from Moscow. "I will probably order the start of operations on Saturday morning," he said. He stared at his audience unblinkingly and strode from the room. He had actually said he was going to launch a war in four days, on August 26. General von Manstein didn't believe it. A bluff. Noise. Hitler. Von Manstein went off to spend a day with his family.

•

* *Scheissegal.*

The reaction of the rest of the world to the Russo-German pact was quite different. President Roosevelt had been off on a summer excursion along the New England coast aboard the cruiser *Tuscaloosa* when word reached him. He immediately ordered the ship to put in for Sandy Hook, New Jersey, and a special train for Washington. Secretary of State Hull rushed north from his vacation at White Sulphur Springs, West Virginia, to meet his chief at Washington's Union Station. "It seems unbelievable," Roosevelt said of what the respected political commentator Raymond Gram Swing termed "the most outstanding political miracle for hundreds of years."

It was all of that to Russia's ambassador to England, Ivan Maisky. When British newspapermen came to ask his reaction to the first reports of what was instantly called a bombshell, stunning, stupefying, paralyzing, he said it was impossible. The very idea was capitalist propaganda. Then came official confirmation from Moscow, and the world's Communists took a deep breath and declared that here was new proof of Comrade Stalin's idealism. Had not England and Germany agreed not to go to war at Munich? What was different about the agreement between Russia and Hitler?

It was a good Communist's first duty to accept what the Moscow leadership decreed. The young Communist journalist Richard Rovere found only one colleague on New York's *New Masses* willing to wonder with him what it all meant. "It may be the greatest thing since Grant took Richmond," said the other man, "but the dictionary I use doesn't have the words for it." All the other staff members disagreed. Stalin had done it. It was therefore correct. There could be no other viewpoint. A numb Rovere took his doubts to the young woman with whom he was in love, a Party firebrand. "Sylvia, how the hell can any of us defend a pact with *Hitler?*"

"Renegade! Traitor! You're a baby—a spoiled baby! We're better off without you."

"But doesn't it make you sick?"

"You think you know better?"

"We were talking about a united front against Hitler. Now a united front *with* Hitler."

"Oh, shut up!"

They visited some comrades, who told Rovere he was a political dilettante. He sputtered and stalked out. He never saw Sylvia again.

For them it was but a matter for passionate discussion. Everything was thousands of miles away across an ocean and half of Europe. The Communist press, which that Rovere deserted but which Sylvia and the others continued to read, explained that any potential war was a conflict between the Polish landlords and French and British imperialists, supported by American big business out for profits, on one side, and Germany on the other side, and therefore of no interest whatsoever to the State of the Workers and Peasants. All criticisms of Germany and Nazism vanished from the Soviet press, stage and screen, to be replaced by articles on German-Russian friendship, publications of Bismarck's memoirs, productions of Wagner's operas. The matter was settled for Russia.

It was different for England. Secretary of the Committee on Imperial Defense General Hastings Ismay came rushing down to London from Scotland, where he had been shooting grouse and playing cricket with young relatives, certain that the pact meant Hitler would attack Poland. After Munich, Ismay had felt peace might be preserved. Now he prayed that England would go to war the instant Hitler laid hands on Poland. "If we did so, we might or might not be destroyed. But if we failed to do so, we would be dishonored forever." He felt himself neither frightened nor even excited. Instead, rage mixed with guilt possessed him. The Cenotaph, the empty tomb erected in honor of those whose bodies lay elsewhere, the dead of 1914–18, was almost on the doorstep of his Whitehall office. Each time he looked at it, he saw men raise their hats as they passed. He told himself that he and his entire generation had failed those who had died in the War to End War. "How had we been so craven or so careless as to allow this to happen?"

He thought of the poet John McCrae: "If ye break faith with us who die, we shall not sleep, though poppies grow in Flanders field." Ration books had been printed up some months earlier, and proclamations of emergency regulations, and storage of food and oil had been arranged, and evacuation schedules made, and the Royal Navy and Air Force alerted, but Ismay told the prime minister that Institute Precautionary Stage telegrams should be dispatched to every part of the Empire.

Chamberlain replied that he had not given up hope yet, and that to take the step might give the impression that war was inevitable. To a hastily summoned Parliament of sunburned members returning from an abbreviated recess—Parliament had risen on August 4, the twenty-fifth anniversary of the outbreak of the Great War—he said he would not attempt to conceal that the pact came to his government as a surprise, "and a surprise of a very unpleasant character." But there could be no question of France and Britain considering themselves relieved of their obligations to Poland. "We felt it our first duty to remove any such dangerous illusions." The method he chose to accomplish this was to direct his ambassador to Berlin to deliver a personal note from himself to Adolf Hitler.

The assignment was not one to be relished by Sir Nevile Henderson. Slim, bright-eyed, dapper, always with his red carnation in his buttonhole—"The man with the flower," Hitler called him—good with languages, involved with shooting, tennis, golf and cricket, very aware of the social superiority or inferiority of everyone with whom he came into contact, he had all the outward points of the British diplomat born into that kind of family whose sons were eligible for service with the Foreign Office.

No less appropriate person could have been called upon to deal with Adolf Hitler. He had never regarded the German leader as representing dark forces, but more as a bewildering individual whose rise and reign were alike inexplicable. It seemed to Henderson that the waters flowing under the bridges of his youth had been stagnant. Then as the world changed, the waters began to flow faster and faster in a social transformation of all about him, a flood seething and boiling in a new world replacing the one to whose values and ways he still clung, and in the end throwing up an Adolf Hitler. A bachelor, his father and much-beloved mother gone, Henderson had no family. His work and position were everything to him. His England was disappearing in the raging waters and with it, perhaps, his identity; and he sought to rescue and give meaning to his life by an attempt to do something great in Berlin. It was the mission given him by the Providence that saved him when he was drowning as a boy back at Eton in that Edwardian high summer of the days of England's greatness, when the waters were still. He was as one in his response to a declining ruling class and disappearing order with his counterpart in Warsaw, Sir Howard Kennard. This was no time to be an ambassador, Kennard said to the Polish princess Virginia Sapieha. It used to be a gentleman's work. "Now it's a question of fighting with gangsters. Why, we don't know how to talk to these Germans. We don't belong in this era. What I want is a lace ruff around my neck and a date to dance the minuet, of an evening, with the queen."

Ambassador Henderson saw a war on behalf of Poland as insanity. A year earlier Chamberlain had remarked privately that the Czechs as a people were "not out of the top drawer" and to Henderson the Poles were far below even that. Had Providence, he asked himself, given England an island in order that she might send millions from it to fight on the Continent, and for such a country as Poland? He thought back longingly to the limited British expeditionary forces of the past, those of Marlborough and Wellington, composed of a handful of slum or farm boys born hungry and raised skinny whose civilian function it was to stand before taverns in order to get a penny for holding a gentleman's horse and who would not be missed if they fell in some remote one-day affair. To the Leader Henderson was a high-toned fool speaking German in his English plums-in-the-mouth fashion, which sometimes Hitler mimicked, sending his coterie into the same gales of laughter that possessed them when he imitated Mussolini's Italian-accented rendition of their language.

Aflame with the aftermath of the speech he had just delivered to the one hundred officers, and involved with the planning for the Polish war scheduled to start in days, Hitler did not wish to deal with Henderson and a letter. But Ribbentrop was still en route from Moscow, and protocol said an ambassador with a Note had a right to be received by the head of state when the foreign minister was not available. A German plane was put at Henderson's disposal and he flew from Berlin to Berchtesgaden.

"Apparently the announcement of a German-Soviet agreement is taken in some quarters in Berlin to indicate that intervention by Great Britain is no longer a contingency that need be reckoned with," Chamberlain's letter said. "No greater mistake could be made. Whatever may prove to be the nature of the German-Soviet Agreement, it cannot alter Great Britain's obligation to Poland, which His Majesty's government have stated in public repeatedly and plainly, and which they are determined to fulfill.

"It has been alleged that if His Majesty's government had made their position more clear in 1914, the great catastrophe would have been avoided. Whether or not there is any force in that allegation, His Majesty's government are resolved that on this occasion there shall be no such tragic misunderstanding. If the need should arise, they are resolved and prepared to employ without delay all the forces at their command, and it is impossible to foresee the end of hostilities once engaged. It would be a dangerous delusion to think that, if war once starts, it will come to an early end, even if a success on any one of the several fronts on which it will be engaged should have been secured.

"I trust that Your Excellency will weigh with the utmost deliberation the considerations which I have put before you."

Hitler listened and erupted. Everything was England's fault, he shouted at Sir Nevile Henderson. Germany was trying to end the chaotic situation on her Polish border, where conditions resembled some Balkan nightmare characterized by murder, arson, atrocities, frontier incidents, and England madly stood in her way. What did England want? Germany must solve the Danzig and Corridor problem. His voice rose to a scream. The Poles were raping German women. They were emasculating German men. They had castrated six Germans! Surely not six, Henderson said. Perhaps one.

"Six!"

The German communiqué summed up their meeting: "The Leader left the British ambassador in no doubt that obligations undertaken by the British government could not cause Germany to renounce the pursuance of her vital national interests."

It did not mention what made tears come into Henderson's eyes. "I am fifty years old," Hitler said. "It is better to make war now than when I am fifty-five or sixty. The Danzig question will be settled now, one way or another!" In his voice the German language was indescribably harsh. "Tell them that!"

Henderson withdrew to fly to London. Hitler went to luncheon with the woman the world regarded as his love. (In common with Unity Mitford the world was largely unaware of the existence of Eva Braun.) Unity Mitford looked forward to the annual Party Day celebrations at Nuremberg, a week-long event she had always enjoyed enormously, the pounding drums, the martial music and the marching thousands in uniform and the Leader's hypnotic oratory and she, the golden, blonde, beautiful princess of the rally, standing with her swastika badge by Nazism's dignitaries. She had never missed a rally since 1933. She had turned twenty-five earlier that August. She could not know, for it was the most carefully kept secret, that the Party rally scheduled to begin on September 2 had been canceled. The German train system was intended to be involved in other duties, transporting troops and supplies to Poland.

To Unity Mitford her country's ambassador to Berlin was "this idiot Henderson," for even his markedly restrained questioning of some of the Leader's acts was to her outrageous. Her family had at first thought her infatuation with Hitler and the Nazis to be little short of lunacy, and also her letters home adorned with childishly drawn swastikas: "Well, it's wonderful to be in the Deutsches Reich once more, what do you think, I saw the Führer the *very day* I arrived, if that isn't being the Luckiest Person in the World I'd like to know what is. Heil Hitler! Love, Bobo."

Her sister Nancy's return letters addressed Unity as "Darling Head of Bone and Heart of Stone." But the family had learned to accept her views and those of her sister Diana, the wife of Sir Oswald Mosley.

As head of the British Union of Fascists, dressed in black uniform, peaked cap and breeches, the ensemble very remindful of that worn by Heinrich Himmler's SS troops, Mosley cried that war for Poland was always a crime but that with the signing of the German-Soviet Pact it was madness. The British government by its guarantee, he said, put the lives of a million Britons in the pocket of any drunken Polish corporal who might in the idiotically vainglorious Polish fashion precipitate a border incident that could lead to war. "If Poland whistles, a million Englishmen have got to die." The placards held by his listening followers read WHO THE HECK CARES FOR BECK? NO WAR FOR WARSAW.

Mosley and his tiny group of adherents were almost alone in saying there must be no war no matter what happened between Germany and Poland. By far the majority of the British seemed to feel with General Hastings Ismay that their guarantee must be honored. But that it would be horrible no one doubted. Harold Nicolson was called from luncheon on August 24 to be asked by a representative of the Air Raid Protection Service if his Buick could carry an eight-foot stretcher or "only sitting-cases and corpses." Britain prepared to arm her merchant ships. Censorship of cable messages was instituted.

The previous day, across the Channel, the lawyer and reserve officer René de Chambrun was awakened early by two gendarmes who handed him orders to join his unit at once. It was his birthday. He packed, got into his uniform smelling of camphor, said good-bye to his wife, the daughter of the prominent politician Pierre Laval, and took a taxi to the Gare de l'Est. He assumed he was one of a small number of men called up, for there had been no official proclamation of any mobilization, but when he arrived at the station he found it jammed with reservists carrying parcels, bundles, weapons. He had always automatically thought of the Gare de l'Est when he heard the word "war," for it was from that station he saw his father off to the Great War in a swarm of soldiers.

Chambrun went with others of the 162nd Régiment d'Infanterie de Forteresse toward Metz. At the assembly point enlisted men came pouring in by foot or on bicycle, for most of them were local to the area and so quickly available to bring the unit up to strength in a hurry. The following day at dawn they marched toward the entrances of the Maginot Line. The people along the route handed them brandy and coffee. There was no official announcement of the calling to the colors of half a million fortress and specialist troops for fear of inciting the Germans. But in front of American ambassador William Bullitt, Premier Daladier had ordered the mobilization by telling his army and navy commanders that they must prepare for an immediate conflict.

On the day that Chambrun went to the Gare de l'Est Bullitt learned from Foreign Minister Georges Bonnet that the highest circles in France did not think there was the "slightest chance" of maintaining the peace. Bullitt sent the information to Washington, adding that he himself had only one suggestion to offer: perhaps it would be beneficial if President Roosevelt publicly pointed out that nothing "could conceivably justify the devastation of Europe and the sacrifice of thirty million men."

Roosevelt acted on Bullitt's thought and sent appeals for peace to President Moscicki of Poland, Hitler and the king of Italy: "The unheard voices of countless millions ask that they shall not be vainly sacrificed again." The message was drafted by Under Secretary of State Sumner Welles and the President's longtime confidant A. A. Berle, who thought to himself that it would have "about the same effect as a Valentine sent to somebody's mother-in-law out of season and all that quality of naivete which is the prerogative alone of the United States."

The Polish president cabled back that Poland would do everything possible to keep the peace. Roosevelt had appealed personally to Italy's King Victor Emmanuel III rather than Mussolini in the hope that it might influence the monarch not to sign a mobilization order, and so Ambassador William Phillips tracked the king to his fishing camp in the mountains near Turin. A heavy rain was falling. Victor Emmanuel studied the message and said he would refer it to his government. He went back to his fishing. No acknowledgment of any kind was received from Hitler, and Roosevelt appealed to him again, saying Poland had accepted the concept of a peaceful settlement of any difficulties. "All the world prays that Germany, too, will accept." Again no answer was received. "I have the horrible feeling," Berle wrote in his diary on August 25, "of seeing a civilization breaking, of seeing it dying before its actual death."

That same thought came to Lady Diana Manners Cooper at her summer home by the sea at Bognor. At a picnic on Ha'nacker Hill on the green Sussex Down she looked at an old mill, its sweepers gone, its clapper still. Her friend Hilaire Belloc had written a poem about it:

> Spirits that call and no one answers;
> Ha'nacker's down and England's done.
> Wind and thistle for pipe and dancers
> And never a ploughman under the sun.
> Never a ploughman. Never a one.

It had come true, Lady Cooper said to herself. They were all doomed. Others feverishly fought down their fears. The literary figure Gertrude Stein assured her friends that there was nothing to worry about. "A great general and a great optimist," remarked the photographer Cecil Beaton, a guest in the house in the French countryside Miss Stein shared with her friend Alice Toklas.

Beaton had come over from London after photographing the queen in Buckingham Palace, led to Her Majesty by a scarlet-liveried page through dark red-carpeted corridors hung with petunia-crimson velvet. Bowers of flowers filled the room in which he began to work with her, hydrangeas, sweet peas and carnations forming almost a haze as she stood before walls of French silk embroidered in bouquets of silver. She was in a ruby-encrusted gown of gold and silver. She spoke in gentle, staccato expressions. He followed her to other rooms to get her in different attire, passing rows of family portraits, busts on columns, gilt chairs and bemedaled servants. The furniture was a combination of Regency and Edwardian. They went through drawing rooms with double doors and she posed in spangled tulle with a tiara, then diamonds, then pearls. He took shots of her against pillars, in doorways, on sofas, against a precious Louis XV desk, then of her in a champagne-colored lace dress and hat, with a parasol, on a terrace and in a garden. Through an open window he could hear the hum of a distant buzz of traffic and see the curious crowd beyond the railings. He took away an evocative memory: the Changing of the Guards heard from inside, the pounding about of troops, the shouting of the officers, which to his ears resembled the sound made by somebody retching.

"Oh, no, no," Gertrude Stein said to him, "war isn't logical, no one wants a war." It was almost a breach of etiquette, Beaton thought, to mention to the newly titled general that events looked black and the prospect horrifying. "Yes, of course Hitler is making a speech," Miss Stein said. "He's always making a speech. Of course, Roosevelt's going to talk. He's always talking. No, no, things, things aren't serious." Yet in the village men were reporting to their units. "Almost in defiance of the general" her guests read newspaper stories headed SITUATION PLUS GRAVE.

Gertrude Stein faced reality when the local butcher telephoned that he could not supply meat on order because the army had requisitioned everything for the soldiers called to active service. Panic seized her and Alice Toklas and the Chinese serving boy and the cook.

"There is an unwelcome taste in my mouth at the thought of the future," Beaton said. He decided to get back to England and took a train that traveled hours behind schedule, the compartments filled with more and more people, who bundled into the little available space.

On the twenty-fifth of August, under relentlessly clear, sunny skies, Polish peasants along the German border took their horses to central points, where army officers waited to make purchases. Orderlies stood by with military trappings to throw over the remounts needed to pull the artillery and carry the reservists.

Rulka Langer, who had saved her dresses with Scarlett O'Hara in mind, looked on at one such sale near Lemberg. Days earlier she had been talking with some relatives about the magnificent wheat and rye crops. No one had ever seen anything similar. "Exceptionally good crops," someone said, "mean war." "So they say," another replied. They were thirty miles from the German frontier. In the evening they listened to the battery-powered radio receiving set and learned of what had taken place between Ribbentrop and Stalin in Moscow. "Unbelievable," she heard the others say, "absurd . . . monstrous. Two age-old enemies of Poland uniting again. . . . Why, this meant . . . this meant . . ." But no one permitted himself to say what it meant. They sat silent. "Even in thoughts they dared not formulate the full implications."

The American-born princess Virginia Sapieha was visiting friends in Poznan, twenty miles from the German frontier. The night before the announcement she said it was unthinkable a war would take place. "I still think it's against human nature to go out and fight."

"You're so American," said her hostess.

That night the host proposed a toast: "Ladies, gentlemen, and Germans." Everybody laughed.

In the morning under the inevitable cloudless sky and burning sun Princess Sapieha and her hostess drove a horse carriage to a lake and watched their little daughters splash each other. They sang Polish songs on the way back. Then they played billiards. The doors were open to a quiet stretch of lawn. There was no sound but the click of the balls. The telephone rang. It was for Princess Sapieha's host. He came in and said he had gotten a call from army headquarters in Warsaw. It gave him the news of the pact. The ladies hung the cues on the rack and put the billiard balls into the table pockets. "This is the end," the host said.

Rulka Langer looked at the peasants selling their horses. At the railroad station, as at all Polish railroad stations, freshly called reservists waited for trains, summoned, it was said, for a month of practice maneuvers while their womenfolk in red kerchiefs bound around their heads worked the fields. Dust rose into the dry air. "God's blessing," people called to the reapers of the brilliant crop. "May the Lord give it," they replied. For a thousand years that had been the harvest-time greeting.

The cottages of single-file villages stretched for a mile or more along the road. Traditionally they were painted before each springtime Whitsun with a mixture of whitewash and bluing. It had not yet faded as it did each year when the days shortened. The fronts were adorned with nasturtiums, roses, sunflowers and tall honeysuckles reaching to the thatched and moss-covered roofs. The white- and gray-saddled geese were fat. Mrs. Langer heard a mobilized boy promise to bring his girlfriend a new carpet from the loot he said he would collect in Berlin.

"Of course," she heard people say, "the best solution would be to have the last German soldier choke to death on the last Russian"—but failing that, Poland would dispose of matters to its own satisfaction. To refer to the Germans who were filling their newspapers with screaming headlines of German citizens of Poland being whipped and murdered, of innocent families beaten to pulp—HORRIBLE POLISH MURDER, GERMAN ENGINEER MURDERED; NEW AND TRAGIC VIOLATION OF THE FRONTIER NEAR DANZIG, ENGLAND IS RE-SPONSIBLE—one had only to refer to Them, to say that They would soon be coming.

A government pamphlet instructed those in the line of Their likely path of attack to burn crops, take away as many cattle as possible, then slaughter and fling dirt on the bodies of the rest. The rich began burying silver, guns and wine in outdoor pits or in ancient hiding places under the floorboards of their homes. People spoke of wandering bands of thieves, as had come through in the last war, and many peasants ceased coming to work, preferring to stay home and talk things over while they waited to be mobilized. At night they stole out to dig up their overlords' potatoes. The army halted the sale of all oil, and no more than a barrel of gasoline or naphtha could be purchased. There were no candles to be had at the stores and no sugar.

But they were like children playing Indians, thought Princess Sapieha. How sheepish they would feel when the excitement blew over. The radio reported strikes in German steel factories, food shortages, unrest of all kinds; and kitchen girls unable to read or write assured her that the Germans were weak and starving and that Mussolini would keep the peace.

Rulka Langer decided she had to get back to Warsaw, where she and her children were living with her mother while her husband was away on a commercial trip to America. She went on trains jammed with people rushing home from interrupted vacations. They gained entrance by climbing through the window or riding on the buffers between the cars.

The lobbies and restaurants of Warsaw's Bristol and Europejski hotels, wrote the London *Daily Telegraph*'s Clare Hollingworth, were jammed until five in the morning with a mass of diplomats, officers, gigolos, courtesans, spies, all jostling and hugging and whispering and laughing, mixed and tumbled like a dream. They kept telling one another, "The German motor units will be useless in our fields"; "We shall be in Breslau in a month, Berlin in three." "You will see," a high official said to her. "We shall march to Berlin in three weeks."

Rulka Langer arrived at her family's Warsaw apartment. She said to her long-widowed mother that she thought it best that the older woman take the children and go to a friend living a few miles outside Warsaw. The mother said she would do whatever her daughter said. "I'm old now, I've had enough responsibility all my life. It's your turn to take the command, and the responsibility, too. Only don't make us go till war actually breaks out, will you?" Her daughter was touched and scared at having her mother hand over the command. She had always been a wonderful leader.

Princess Sapieha returned to Warsaw, to find that all her friends had taken to staying up as late as they could, eating in jammed restaurants, where they listened to scraps of supposed information about what the German ambassador von Moltke was alleged to have said to Foreign Minister Beck, or that Poland's ambassador to Berlin was flying home with new proposals. Afterward they went to nightclubs rather than returning home. Perhaps they felt there was something unmanly about sleep at such a time, she said to herself. Or perhaps it was the feeling of warm safety given by being in a herd, by being in public, those August nights. People were laying in stores of antiseptics, bandages, fluids for fire extinguishers, sugar, soap, candles, gas masks. The Great War had taught that flour became wormy if kept too long. Preserves and jam were better.

The Free City of Danzig filled up with more and more young, fit Germans calling themselves tourists or members of sports teams coming to play against Danzig counterparts. German ships alleging mechanical troubles that forced interruption of journeys elsewhere were continually docking to unload boxes that all too obviously contained ammunition and guns; there were fortifications going up on the outskirts of the town protected by barbed wire with VERBOTEN showing to the outside and COMRADES, KEEP YOUR MOUTHS SHUT LEST YOU REGRET THE CONSEQUENCES facing inward to the Danzigers. Field kitchens and barely camouflaged antiaircraft guns could be seen.

There was no official publicized Polish call-up of reserves, but before even Ribbentrop got back to Berlin from Moscow, policemen in every corner of Poland began knocking on doors. In the early-morning hours of August 24, they came to the Warsaw home of reservist Jan Karski, an artillery second lieutenant. That night Karski had been to a party at the legation of the Portuguese minister. He had ended his university studies four years earlier, spent his obligatory year of army training, studied abroad for a year. He was interested in the Portuguese minister's daughter. Her father's legation had blue wallpaper and Italianate furniture and vases of long-stemmed flowers. There had been a discussion of Warsaw's botanical garden compared with those of other European cities, talk of the theater, and many witty remarks made at the expense of a friend of Karski's and a young woman when they vanished from the room. Of politics there was very little talk. A second daughter of the minister and a son demonstrated the Portuguese tango. Before leaving, Karski made dates for lunch, dinner, for riding. The hammering on the door awakened him. He came down the steps half-asleep and then broke into an angry run. He yanked open the door.

A policeman handed him a red slip of paper. It was his secret mobilization order giving him four hours to leave his residence and be en route to his unit at Oswiecim—later to be more widely known under its infamous German name, Auschwitz—on the German border. He woke his brother and sister-in-law, and all three agreed this was a very limited mobilization. His sister-in-law told him not to bother to take winter underwear: "You aren't going to Siberia. We'll have you on our hands again within a month."

Karski decided the whole thing might be fun. The area around Oswiecim was largely open country, good riding country. He told his brother it was too bad they didn't need any old men at the moment. He was twenty years older. "My brother threatened to take some of the cockiness out of my hide." The sister-in-law had to tell them to stop behaving like children.

Karski went to the railroad station and saw what appeared to be the entire male population of Warsaw gathered there carrying military lockers. He got into his train. It was packed with called-up reservists; even the corridors and lavatories were filled. They cheered as they cleared the station. At each stop more men jammed in, no longer city boys but peasants, more serious and businesslike. Their mothers clung to them, weeping. "Let me go," Karski heard one boy say. "Soon you can come and visit me in Berlin."

A fellow second lieutenant told of his adventures at a ball the previous night. His success with the ladies had been remarkable, according to him. He was besieged by "importunate belles." When he made his way home, he saw a police officer going up the steps. He shrank back, wondering "which event in his reckless existence had attracted the notice of the law," and then crept into the house to discover to his relief that his presence was desired merely in an army camp and not a courtroom. Everybody laughed.

It was the twenty-fourth of August. Hitler had already issued the order to march.

FOURTEEN

HE WAS something like a child who must have his way and whose response to contrary opinions is a tantrum followed by a thousand explanations of why his wishes must be followed. Sir Nevile Henderson, back from London, went to the New Chancellory where the Leader interrupted lunch at the sound of a roll of drums below announcing the ambassador's arrival. He heard from Henderson that there must be a peaceful settlement of the Polish problem, and replied by offering inducements for England to stand aside. He "accepted" the British Empire, he said; let him have his way with Poland and he would do everything for that Empire. He would send his German army to defend the British against any enemy, he would disarm, he would guarantee no German expansion into France. Let him settle the Polish issue and he would retire from public life. He never wanted to be a politician in the first place, he said. It was not his nature to be one, for he was at heart an artist.* Let Henderson go back to London with the word. He would give him his personal plane for the flight. Henderson departed.

To Ribbentrop, who had just returned from Moscow, it did not matter what the ambassador said or did not say when he arrived in London. England wouldn't fight. Neither would France. They wouldn't dare. He convened his Foreign Office staff and cried, "If I hear that any official expresses a different view I will

---

*Told by the British of the Leader's statement, American ambassador to London Joseph Kennedy passed the information on to Secretary of State Hull, adding that Hitler already was an artist. "But I would not care to say what kind."

shoot him myself in his office and be responsible to the Führer for my action."

At the New Chancellory the drums rolled again for the French ambassador. Robert Coulondre had filled his dispatches to Paris with information that the German aircraft factories were working on planes that would soon be out-of-date rather than halting production in order to adapt for construction of newer models; that owners of horses and motorcycles had been told to be ready to hand them over to the army; that doctors had been ordered to keep themselves at the disposal of the military. Hitler said to Coulondre that he had no wish to fight France but that Poland's provocations against its citizens of German blood were intolerable.

"Are you aware that there have been cases of castration? That already there are more than seventy thousand refugees in our camps? Yesterday seven Germans were killed by the police in Bielitz. Our airplanes can no longer fly between Germany proper and East Prussia without being shot at." He raised his voice. "No nation worthy of the name can put up with such unbearable insults. France would not tolerate it. These things have gone on long enough. I want to state again: I wish to avoid war with your country. I will not attack France but if she joins in the conflict I will see it through to the bitter end."

He rose as if to end the interview.

Ambassador Coulondre knew he had only a minute. "In a situation as critical as this, Herr Reich Chancellor," he said, "misunderstandings are the most dangerous things of all."

Hitler sat. "Therefore, to make the matter quite clear, I give you my word of honor as a French officer that the French army will fight by the side of Poland if that country should be attacked."

The ambassador's voice rose. France was prepared to do everything for peace. But there was a point beyond which it could not go.

"Why then did you give Poland a blank check to act as she pleased?" Hitler shouted. Coulondre began to reply but Hitler jumped up and held out his hand to terminate the discussion.

By then the provisional orders for an invasion of Poland at four-thirty on the morning of the following day, August 26, had gone out. For all of the twenty-fifth, Hitler had debated giving the final word. At 3:02 P.M., after speaking with Henderson, he opened the door to the Chancellory's music room and stood on the threshold, pale but calm, noted a waiting officer, and said in what the officer thought was a rather forced and even slightly theatrical manner: "Case White." It was the code name for the invasion.

The officer ran to a telephone and passed the two words on to the Operations Department of the Supreme Command of the army, and twenty-three minutes later a message in cipher was received by the units along the Polish border: Operation Case White: D-Day = 26.8. H-Hour = 0430. Colonel-General Gerd von Rundstedt, commanding Army Group South, ordered an approach march to commence at 8:30 P.M.

Ammunition boxes were broken open and engines tested. Von Rundstedt sat down for a meal with his chief of staff, Erich von Manstein. Their front was 275 miles. They had been quartered in the Monastery of the Holy Cross in Neisse for some weeks. The stew they had for lunch each day was quite good but the army bread and hard-pressed sausage served each evening was pretty bad.

Neither officer had in the past thought there would be a war. Hitler after all, they reasoned, had gotten everything he wanted before without fighting and had often said he would never be idiotic enough to get into a war for Danzig and the Corridor, let alone an insane two-front war such as that begun in 1914. In addition, to von Manstein's professional eye the Poles' situation was so palpably hopeless that he could not conceive that Warsaw would actually fight.

The Poles, reasoned von Manstein, faced the Germans on an arc of 1,750 miles along the German border combined with that of former Czechoslovakia, and in East Prussia. They were surrounded on three sides, and in the Corridor were covered from the front and rear. The land from Germany proper east to Warsaw was entirely flat with hardly a hill or river or forest, and therefore extremely difficult to defend, even if they had decent artillery and tank defenses, which they did not. By the standards established along the Western Front of 1914–18, some four hundred divisions would have been needed to hold an attacking enemy. Poland had thirty active and thirty reserve divisions.

And what divisions. None was motorized. They were eighty years behind the times with their horse cavalry ideas, the British military expert B. H. Liddell Hart had written, for even the

American Civil War had shown horse charges were futile. The Poles ignored that fact. If they had any hope at all, it would be to pull back behind the river lines in front of Warsaw and concentrate there, while keeping ready a strategic reserve. From such an inner defense they would be able to judge the direction of any German thrust and try to deal out counterblows.

Instead, the Poles manned every inch of their long frontier, regarding each point of their thin-as-a-crust line as a sally port from which they could mount an invasion of Germany. Poland was like a balloon. One had only to pierce those flung-out lines and the entire structure would collapse. Their transport and communications were defective. They had no trucks and depended upon a primitive civil telephone and telegraph network, decades behind anything in the West. They could never form a concentration of massed forces, forwardly deployed as they were.

Yet the Poles were filled with confidence. Germany was weak and Hitler a bluffer, the called-up reservists told one another. Poland was strong, united, prepared. "England and France are not needed, we can finish this alone," a superior officer told Lieutenant Karski, the reservist fresh from the Portuguese minister's party. Poland was preparing for war, thought the reporter Edward W. Beattie, like a knight donning his white-plumed helmet to go out and smite the heathen. The Battle of Grunwald, when the Poles and Lithuanians crushed the Teutonic Order, was much discussed. That was in 1410. Cabdrivers talked to Beattie about the coming Battle of Berlin. In Krakow he met a group of young reserve officers off to join their regiments. Their names formed a list of Polish nobility. They were cavalrymen, they told him. He asked whether the cavalry was motorized. The question made them indignant. "Certainly not. A gentleman's place is in the horse cavalry."

In Berlin, Colonel Erwin Rommel was ordered to report to Hitler. It was 3:45 P.M., less than an hour after the attack order had been sent out. Rommel was informed that he was now a general. He had impressed Hitler at Nuremberg's Party Day celebration in 1936 when Hitler told him that he was going to go for a drive and wanted no more than six cars accompanying his own. When the six had passed, Rommel stepped into the road and put his body in the line of the many other cars whose occupants wanted to go along. Rommel was energetic, physically tough despite his small and stocky stature, blunt in his speech. A man who in civilian clothing seemed to some a figure reminiscent of a small-time hoodlum, he was uninterested in art, architecture, scenery, in anything but soldiering. Rommel was one of the few officers of the German army known for his regular use of the stretched-out Nazi hand and arm greeting and accompanying *"Heil Hitler!,"* for most professional soldiers kept to a military salute. He was told he was to be the commander of the Leader's mobile headquarters during the attack on Poland. He was given an escort battalion of twelve officers, ninety-three noncoms and 274 men. An hour after his appointment, Rommel entrained with them for Bad Polzin, a little railroad town in Pomerania near the Corridor.

Another visitor was announced in the New Chancellory, Italian ambassador Bernardo Attolico, who for a month and more had filled the cables to Rome with warnings that Hitler seemed to be heading for war. No idea was more repugnant to Attolico, who in appearance was more representative of a scholar, or most people's idea of a professor, than a diplomat. Slightly bent, he looked out at the world through thick glasses. He spoke little or no German. His wife, a classic Roman beauty who acted as his interpreter, was equally against war. Italy's foreign minister Count Ciano had for a long time believed the devotion of the couple to peace was a result of Attolico's position as a very rich man. He had considered him a hysteric. Then Ciano talked with Ribbentrop and learned to his horror that the Germans actually wanted a war against Poland. He joined Attolico in appealing to Mussolini to stay out at all costs.

The situation was very difficult for Mussolini. For fifteen years he had filled the European air with bombast about eight million Italian bayonets arising from the stout forest of people who formed the nation, about how war was for a man what maternity was for a woman. Then, on August 25, the day the British and French ambassadors were received, when Colonel Rommel became General Rommel, when von Manstein and von Rundstedt learned they were to march, Hitler suddenly informed Mussolini that war might break out at any moment.

The actor posing in the raiments of the warrior shrank into his ill-fitting garments. Hitler had developed, Mussolini said, the habit of writing him a letter every time the Germans took over another country. Yet he did not wish to be like a dance partner going from swain to swain at a waltz, turning toward Chamberlain and Daladier now and Hitler later.

Ciano worked on him, and the king, and finally Il Duce got off a cable to Attolico in Berlin for his ambassador to tell Hitler it would be impossible for Italy to move unless vital war materials were granted her. Baron Ernst von Weizsaecker, state secretary of the Foreign Office, was not surprised. Of course, the Italians would leave Germany in the lurch, he said to Ribbentrop, who shouted, "I disagree with you one hundred percent. Mussolini is far too great a man to do that." The Italian leader was asked to outline his needs. Count Ciano took care of the task for him, with relish. Italy needed coal, steel, lumber, copper, potassium, salts, rosin, rubber, nickel, tungsten, guns, machinery parts in gigantic amounts. The figure Ciano named came to seventeen million tons, requiring seventeen thousand railroad cars for delivery. "It is enough to kill a bull if a bull could read," he wrote in his diary.

To von Weizsaecker Rome's defection was of little account, for he had come to the conclusion that Hitler would make war no matter what anyone did. The Day of Judgment was at hand, the state secretary told himself. "Hitler was now the prisoner of his own methods. He could no longer pull the horses to one side without being thrown out of the chariot. And riding on the lead horse was the Devil." The decision to move into Poland horrified von Weizsaecker. "This afternoon has been the most depressing one of my life. It is an appalling idea that my name should be associated with this event."

Yet Hitler was severely shaken by Mussolini's reluctance to fight. His sole ally had deserted him. He roamed the Chancellory, assuring his people that England and France would do nothing, that Germany would conduct a Silesian war limited to Polish territory of the types that Frederick the Great had waged there. More bad news came. The British-Polish arrangement, whereby each guaranteed the other's independence, was formalized in London that day, the Polish ambassador to the Court of St. James's affixing his signature along with that of Lord Halifax. The pact had been agreed upon but never formally signed.

It was really just a formality of no great importance, but news of it rocked Hitler. Perhaps, he reasoned, this was London's answer to his offer to defend the Empire with the German army.

Perhaps the British had learned of Mussolini's defection and this was their quick response. (It was not. The Italian decision to decline to fight was not yet known in London.) He sat at his desk reading the terms of the published treaty between Poland and England, looking for a loophole. There was none. For a long time he sat silently brooding. He sent an officer to tell his military aide General Keitel to come at once.

Keitel arrived. "I need time," Hitler told him. "Can the troops be stopped?"

"I would have to look at the timetable."

"Then send for it, man!"

The pages of troop dispositions and movement schedules were brought. Keitel pored over them. "Yes, my Führer," Keitel said. "I think it can be done. There is just time."

"Then give the order. Cancel the attack! I must see if I can prevent British intervention."

Teletypes started clattering and telephones rang along the Polish border, where more than sixty infantry and eight fully motorized divisions were making their approach march in the gathering darkness. The fully fueled planes of the German air force stood ready in takeoff positions on the tarmacs.

DO NOT—REPEAT NOT—COMMENCE HOSTILITIES. HALT ALL TROOP MOVEMENTS.

The field commanders were flabbergasted. March orders on such a scale, involving a million men, detailed, intricate, mathematically worked out, were considered irreversible. When in the first moments of the Great War the Kaiser had asked if the orders could be changed so that troops heading for the Eastern Front could be turned to go to the West, the general commanding his armies had been so shocked that something broke in him, never to be whole again. Generals von Manstein and von Rundstedt could not understand how a German Chancellor could issue so momentous a decision as to invade a neighboring country and then cancel it within a space of mere hours, and this at the eleventh hour, when along the moonlit roads long columns of men and machines were on their way.

Staff officers rushed to halt the lead elements of the three German army groups, for there was a strict security ban on wireless traffic. Scouting planes took to the air to land in dark fields and disgorge officers ordering even the most advanced reconnaissance units to turn back. Some patrols had actually penetrated Polish space. They were caught and stopped, save for one fourteen-man squad, which went on and at dawn charged forward and attacked Poland by itself.

But what madness! cried those in the Wilhelmstrasse Foreign Office and the Bendlerstrasse military headquarters who had come to regard Adolf Hitler as a disaster for their Germany. Such irresponsibility was of an order of which no one had ever dreamed. Hitler acted, thought General von Manstein, as if taking the Fatherland into war was an "ill-considered frivolity." The madman would never recover from this impulsive change of heart, said Admiral Wilhelm Canaris, the head of the German intelligence service.

"Peace is safe for twenty years," Canaris said. His associates of the group that had spoken of the need to do away with Hitler were in complete agreement. It was the happiest moment they had known in years, for despite their hatred for a head of state who was irrational, without manners, dangerous, violent, and ultimately vulgar, they could not find it in themselves to do away with him.

"These generals who plot Hitler's downfall seem to wait for orders from the Führer himself before they will act," Ulrich von Hassel, the former German ambassador to Italy, had remarked when told that Chief of Staff Franz Halder, who habitually wore a revolver when meeting with Hitler, could not force himself to use it. But Halder was the last of a line that for three hundred years had produced officers from father to son, and the word "treason" and the words "conspiracy against the State" were not in his vocabulary. The politicians should get rid of Hitler, he said. It was they who had brought him to power. Now the problem was solved. Hitler had dealt himself a blow from which he could not recover. It was only a question of time and the manner employed to remove him from the political scene, said Admiral Canaris's chief assistant, Colonel Hans Oster. It must be accomplished "with the least trouble and the most elegance."

The rest of the world did not know of the conflict just barely avoided, and did not share the would-be conspirators' confidence of a peaceful future. (The attack of the German patrol that had invaded Poland on its own and exchanged fire with Poles and sustained casualties was explained away in Berlin by saying it was the work of an irresponsible Slovakian gang.) The American Embassy in Paris prepared to ship dependents to Madeira aboard a waiting cruiser. Gasoline was in such short supply that people filled tea kettles and champagne bottles with it. Two and a half million Frenchmen were with their units; tens of thousands of civilian cars had been requisitioned to take children from an endangered Paris. The British fleet was at sea, and by government order all German merchant ships were at their home bases or making for neutral ports. Work on the new Munich subway system was halted as laborers and their machines were sent off to work on the West Wall defenses facing France. Soap, coffee, tinned goods vanished from store shelves. Cranes hoisted anti-aircraft guns to the tops of city buildings and practice blackouts were held.

In Holland the Dutch army practiced a new technique of wrapping roadside trees with girdles of dynamite to be exploded if an enemy came. Charges were placed in canal bridges whose demolition would flood the countryside and make it impassable. The State Department in Washington advised Americans not to go to Europe, and safety regulations on the number of persons permitted to board ships sailing for home from European ports were temporarily relaxed. Mrs. Sara Delano Roosevelt left France, where she had been staying with her sister Mrs. Dora Delano Forbes in the latter's Paris home, saying she wanted to remove herself from a threatened area "so as not to add unnecessarily to my son's worries."

War hung in the air, the unwanted child awaiting its dreaded birth, the buried evil spirit emerging from its temporary grave. War invaded the dreams of the French writer Albert Camus. In 1914, when he was less than one year old, war took his father at the First Battle of the Marne. Now it came back to him. He dreamed that the French entered Rome as triumphant conquerors. He thought of the entry of the Barbarians into the Eternal City. But in the dream he was in their ranks. Images of a guilty love, death, madness and decay filled his mind. One used to wonder where the Beast lived, he wrote. "Now we know where it lives, that it is inside ourselves."

Camus looked at the soldiers at the station going to join their regiments. A woman was crying. "But I never thought it would be like this, that it would hurt so much," she said. "It's funny, people rushing off to get killed," another woman said. Yet everything was the same, Camus saw, the same sky, the sun, the light in the streets, even the grasshoppers. "We have lived hating this beast. Now it stands before us and we can't recognize it."

In a small town where he lived outside Paris the Dutch journalist Pierre van Paasen spoke with the old *cantonnier* whose job it was to mend the roads. "*Alors!*" the workman said. He was old and gnarled and weather-beaten. "It's for Poland this time, *hein?*" That was not what the posters said, van Paasen replied. The posters said that freedom was menaced and that France must defend freedom. The *cantonnier* spat yellow juice into his road. That was what they were told last time, he said. And what did it get them? Were they better off? "Isn't it idiotic to try again a remedy that turned out to be poison?"

He scraped the road in quick, angry blows, spat again. "Monsieur knows my son?" Van Paasen nodded. He had worked all his life to give the boy a good future, the old man said. Now the son was a teacher in Dijon. His voice began to tremble. "He leaves tomorrow, monsieur. I have not slept. I have not eaten. I cannot swallow the smallest crust of bread. It sticks here. Here!" He pointed to his throat.

"Tomorrow," he muttered. "For Poland. Or, as you say, for freedom. My boy, for Poland! In the name of God! Why do we have children? To see them slaughtered? What freedom is that? What a horror!"

Van Paasen left him. The horses of the village were being mobilized. Even the old horse who pulled the garbage cart was requisitioned. "In the long, tail-switching procession I recognized that old acquaintance by his soft, melancholy eyes. Fifteen years I had known him, and I had sometimes dreamed for him of a grassy meadow by the side of a still pond at the end of the trail. Now he ambled off to the battlefield with his tired and sagging knees."

On the walls of the *mairie,* posters told which military classes were called to the colors, what articles and personal effects were to be taken along, what houses were to be requisitioned. There were warnings that sand was to be kept in readiness to sprinkle on incendiary bombs. If water from a faucet was red, it meant the source had been contaminated by poison gas or disease germs.

Van Paasen went to his home. The government had ordered the destruction of all domestic pets of foreign nationals. France did not have the food supply to feed them. Van Paasen had waited until the last hour of the last day to kill his friend of twelve years. He told the maid to open a can of *pâté de foie gras,* for Michel's last meal.

"Monsieur is not thinking of feeding that dog *pâte,*" she said. "Not while our brave French soldiers are eating dry bread in the Maginot Line."

The veterinarian came. Van Paasen held his hand over Michel's brown, trusting eyes while the injection was given, and then walked the streets of the village. He met the curé and told him.

"Monsieur, he will be waiting for you at the gate of heaven," the curé said. "He won't go in till you have come."

"Monsieur, heaven would be misery without him," Van Paasen said.

At the station he saw a man agitatedly speaking with an army colonel. "Look, look at this, my four kids," the man cried. "They have no mother. I am leaving. I have been called, Colonel! I am going! For Poland! For Poland!" He screamed the word.

"Be quiet, my friend," the colonel said. "What is the good of shouting? *Voilà,* there is the train."

"For Poland!" the man cried at the top of his voice. "Ah, shit! Shit! My four kids! For Poland!"

To the south, on the Riviera, the silent-movie star Pola Negri went to a ball at the Palm Beach Casino in Cannes. The summer season had never been so brilliant, the flower festivals never so gorgeously imaginative. She had never before seen the clothing and jewels of the women so magnificent nor such vast sums as gambled by the men at the gaming tables, but there was a quality of desperation, it seemed to her that summer, in the search for pleasure. The ball began. There were papier-mâché sculptures festooned with ribbons and blossoms. There were fireworks and rockets. A summer storm came. "We scurried for shelter, catching muddied silver heels in spattered silken hems, trampling bruised and battered flowers. Trellised walls crumbled around us."

Across Europe, in Pola Negri's homeland, Poland, Rulka Langer, whose mother had handed over the command of the family to her, learned from the cook that flour could not be had for love or money; neither could rice, oatmeal, cream of wheat or macaroni. The vacationers rushing back to Warsaw had cleaned out the stores. Mrs. Langer phoned a friend at the American Embassy to ask if he would lend her a car and chauffeur to get her mother and children out of the city. He said he would. "Anytime?" "Anytime." On the first day of the war, then. And how far off, she asked herself, was that day?

She went to dig air-raid shelters with fellow employees of the Bank of Poland. She felt a bit foolish carrying a spade in high heels and with a pert hat cocked over her eyes while she wondered how to handle her red handbag and gloves. In the streets she saw equally incongruous spade-carrying clerks with briefcases, girls in fluffy silks, businessmen. She looked at a poster representing a gas victim with horribly purple face and bulging eyes, and worked to help dig zigzag trenches seven feet deep. The ground was soft yellow clay at first, but then the diggers ran into tree roots and stones. It was hot. The people looked up at the sky as if expecting the German planes at any moment. They threw dirt on one another's shoes and prodded the ribs of their neighbors with the spade handles. It was the first time she had touched a shovel or pickax. At the end of three hours she was stiff, sore, exhausted. The sky was completely blue with not a cloud hinting of the rain that could halt the motorized German columns. She went to dinner at an eighteenth-century French château-like restaurant with a wide lawn sloping down from the terrace to the Vistula. There was a park with old trees. She and her escort dined on a little table on the lawn and strolled by the river. She saw a boat in the darkness and whispered, "It's coming."

"What's coming?" asked her escort in a low voice, but she did not answer, for she did not know if she meant the boat or the war.

FIFTEEN

ALL THROUGH THE 1930s the world had wondered who had what power in the New Germany. A body of thinking grew up that held that there were radical and conservative wings in the Nazi Party and that they combated for influence with Adolf Hitler. There were no such divisions and no combat. The leading men of the German government held power over their subordinates, but never over their superior, who was the only man who mattered.

Joseph Goebbels, minister of propaganda, was brilliant, lettered, an exciting writer and dynamic orator. He made no real decisions, but was essentially an inspired technician who did as the Leader desired. Heinrich Himmler, the head of the secret police, was a capable bureaucrat whose efficiency was compromised by concepts his colleagues found bizarre. A former chicken farmer concerned with better egg production and body weight for fowls, he aspired to create a higher race of humans by following methods that appeared to work with poultry. Always mild, quiet, shy, he mixed scientific research projects with crackpot ventures into astrology, and sponsored racial and archaeological and anthropological studies with predetermined results. It was difficult to take him seriously.

Alfred Rosenberg, the official Party philosopher, was a foggy man whose writings were incomprehensible to anyone save himself. Rudolph Hess, the deputy Führer and Hitler's designated successor, was sincere but befuddled, very awkward, very confused. Foreign Minister Ribbentrop was unanimously esteemed to be a conceited nincompoop whose only talent lay in divining what thoughts were in the Leader's mind.

That left the chief of the air force and economic administrator. Hermann Goering had been a great hero in the War. Germany had awarded less than one thousand Pour le Mérite decorations in the four years of fighting and one of them adorned the neck of the dashing captain. Uneasy in the Weimar Germany that followed the War, Goering had migrated to Sweden. Handsome and slim in those days and a gentleman by birth, for his father had been a high official of the overseas German Empire, he attracted the attention of a Swedish baroness, Karin Kantzow. She left her husband. The couple married. Goering attached himself to Hitler's movement, or, considering the gap between himself and an Austrian-born corporal, bestowed himself upon it, and rose with it to power. By then his baroness was dead. He married again but she remained ever foremost in his mind. His magnificent country estate was named for her: Karinhall.

Goering made a good thing of Nazi Germany. He lived in a style approached by not half a dozen nobles of the late Empire, perhaps not even the Kaiser. Hitler might quail at the price of caviar, but no luxury was beyond Goering. Yet the German people, starved for consumer goods so that the air force could have planes and the army, tanks, never resented him. Our Hermann. Jolly in a good-natured fat man's way, quick with a joke and a laugh, he was personally the most popular man in the country, for Hitler was not popular as the word is generally understood, but revered. (The Leader had never said he was a god as such, only a man sent by and inspired by Providence, but the people did not see the distinction.)

War did not fit into Goering's plans. He had opposed it during the Czech crisis in 1938. He opposed it in August 1939. He had seen enough of war in 1914–18, and found living like a later Roman emperor a far more pleasant way of life. In early August he got in touch with a Swedish friend, Birger Dahlerus, a prominent civil engineer who was the employer of the dead Baroness Karin's son, Tomas Kantzow. He asked his friend, who was well connected in England, whether he would act as a go-between with some prominent Britishers and thus through unofficial channels smooth over the differences between England and Germany. Dahlerus was willing. He spoke with the Swedish prime minister, who discussed the matter with their country's foreign minister, and said such a matter must be conducted on a strictly private basis, and not on Swedish soil. To do so might compromise Swedish neutrality.

Dahlerus arranged a meeting with Goering and seven prominent British businessmen at the home of his German wife near the Danish border. He ran up a Swedish flag to indicate the disinterested attitude of the host. Goering was very pleasant to the Britons, telling them to ask whatever questions came to mind. They said it was difficult to trust Germany. Any German complaints always seemed to end up with the territory complained about getting incorporated into the Reich.

Goering replied that England was too critical and suspicious. He assured his listeners that Germany desired nothing from Poland but the Corridor and Danzig. Toasts were drunk to peace. That was on August 7.

On the twenty-third, the Soviet-German Pact signed, Dahlerus got a worried call from Goering. The situation had become very serious. Could Dahlerus come to Karinhall the following day? The two men met and Goering said the pact made a German arrangement with England even more logical than before. But Poland must give up Danzig and the Corridor. He was meeting with the Polish ambasssador to Germany, Josef Lipski, that afternoon in Berlin. Perhaps he could make Lipski understand.

In Goering's little two-seater, Dahlerus drove with him thirty miles south to Berlin. When the car halted for red lights, it was notable how people cheered Goering. There was no need for a bodyguard, Dahlerus saw. Urged by Goering to go to London to explain the situation, Dahlerus met there with the businessmen who had come to the conference at his wife's home. They seemed hopeful of some accommodation.

Goering meanwhile had held his talk with Ambassador Lipski. The Pole was down to finding hope for peace in an invitation sent him on August 11 by an assistant to Goering in his capacity as chief huntsman of the Reich: "I take the liberty of inviting Your Excellency for hunting in the state forest. As I perceive from my list, Your Excellency has already taken red deer, elk and chamois in the German preserves, but no muffle-ram. I would like to suggest October or November."

But face-to-face with Goering, Lipski learned that Germany must have the Corridor and Danzig. Hitler had always said the opposite, Lipski said. Goering told him not to have illusions. They parted with Goering saying he would regret having to launch his air force upon Poland and Lipski replying he would join his country's forces to shoot at the planes.

That night Dahlerus tried to call Goering from London but found all telephone communication with Berlin had been broken off. By then his friends had put him in touch with Foreign Secretary Lord Halifax, and with the aid of the Foreign Office he was finally able to get through to Goering, who said the situation was deadly serious. Hitler had taken the official signing of the British-Polish guarantee as a direct announcement that Britain did not want a peaceful settlement.

The next day, Saturday, the twenty-sixth, the mood of Dahlerus's friends had entirely changed in the wake of the reports from Ambassadors Henderson and Coulondre of their interviews with Hitler. The friends were sending their families out of London. Dahlerus went to see Halifax and asked if he could deliver a letter to Goering. Perhaps it would lighten the tension. Halifax excused himself to talk with a Chamberlain who, he told his sisters, felt like a coachman negotiating a carriage down a difficult path on the edge of a steep cliff.

Chamberlain was almost more concerned with Poland than with Germany, for he had come to fear that Polish intransigence might well drag the world into war. He was even afraid to make any significant loan to Warsaw for fear that possession of the money would make the Poles even more bellicose. At the same time Chamberlain was negotiating his way through hidden channels to discover if an enormous British loan to Berlin, one billion pounds, the largest financial transaction in history, might make Hitler more peaceable. Birger Dahlerus, an entirely unofficial person with no diplomatic experience, seemed a slender crutch upon which to lean in determining whether there would be war or peace, but Chamberlain was willing to grasp at anything. He had perhaps begun to believe that Sir Nevile Henderson was not the right man for the job of speaking up to Hitler, that his ambassador in Berlin would never find it in himself to rise above diplomatic procedures and thunder and shout.

It was known in London that Hitler had indicated to High Commissioner Carl Burckhardt that he might meet with Edmund Ironside, the soldier who had gone to Warsaw to estimate Polish capabilities. There had been talk in London that Ironside, all six feet five inches of him, should go pound on Hitler's desk and

roar in parade-ground tones that Britain would fight. Nothing
came of the discussions.

Chamberlain told Halifax to give Dahlerus a letter to Goering.
The Swede flew with it to Berlin. The regular air service was
disconnected, so in the plane that had borne Henderson home
for consultations Dahlerus went to Amsterdam and from there
to Berlin and from there to Karinhall. Goering was not at his
estate but in his private train heading toward Berlin. Dahlerus
was delivered to the train, where he handed over the Halifax
letter. It said essentially that the British wanted peace but that
Germany must understand that they would support Poland.

Able to read, but not speak, English, Goering laboriously
studied the letter. Impatient with his slowness, he jumped out of
his chair and told Dahlerus to translate the words. The train got
to Berlin. Goering dropped Dahlerus at the Esplanade Hotel,
saying he was going to Hitler. It was midnight. After a time two
German colonels came to the Esplanade and told Dahlerus that
Hitler wished to see him. He went with them in a large open car.
Lights were burning everywhere in the New Chancellory. The
great carpeted halls were crowded with officers and officials. The
two escorts led Dahlerus past walls covered with old paintings.
Orchids were the exclusive floral decorations. They went into an
anteroom and then into Hitler's study. The Leader was standing
with Goering. He looked fixedly at his visitor.

"Good evening, Excellency," Dahlerus said.

"Please," Hitler said, indicating a chair. Dahlerus sat.

Hitler had always said that his nerves were equal to anything.
The day just passed had tested that concept. He had ordered
and then called off an invasion of Poland. He had met with the
French ambassador, Robert Coulondre, who brought him a letter from Premier Edouard Daladier. The son of a baker, a physically powerful man known as "the Bull," Daladier had taken over
the job of premier on the last day of January 1933, one day after
Hitler became Reich Chancellor. Voted out, he had then come
back. He was an ex-enlisted man of the War and it was in that
capacity that he addressed his opposite number in Germany.
Coulondre read the letter aloud:

" 'Like myself, you were a soldier in the last war. You realize,
as I do, how a people's memory retains a horror for war and its
disasters. If the blood of France and that of Germany flow again,
as they did, each of the two peoples will fight with confidence in

its own victory. But the most certain victors will be the forces of destruction and barbarism.' "

When he had finished reading, Coulondre added his own thoughts. For once Hitler kept quiet. "I adjured him," Coulondre remembered, "in the name of history and for the sake of humanity. For the sake of his conscience, I begged him who had built an empire without shedding blood not to shed it now, not to shed the blood of soldiers nor that of women and children. I confronted him with the terrible responsibilities he would assume toward Western civilization. I told him that men who feared him would perhaps be astonished, but would admire him. Mothers would bless him. Perhaps I moved him."

But when Hitler replied he spoke of Poland's "morbid" attitude, that Poland knew she was committing suicide but thought that with British and French support she would rise again. German honor was involved and things had gone too far. "I did not prevail; his mind was made up," Coulondre remembered.

After such a day, Hitler looked at Goering's Swedish friend fresh from London. His impulse as always was to talk. He began to lecture Dahlerus, describing his rise to power, of surviving innumerable difficulties, how England would not cooperate with him, his doubts as to English sincerity. Goering was entirely silent. The monologue went on for twenty minutes. Dahlerus began to fear Hitler would go on and on and that he would never get to say a word. When for a moment Hitler paused, Dahlerus put in that he could not share the Leader's view of the British. "I have lived as a workingman in England for some time and I know all classes of Englishmen," Dahlerus said. As a youth he had been a laborer in a Sheffield factory.

"You have worked as a common laborer in England?" Hitler asked. "Tell me about it."

They began to exchange questions and answers as though, Dahlerus felt, they were ordinary people enjoying a normal conversation. He spoke of his respect for the British people, their ways and their qualities. It came into his mind that he was the first person to tell Adolf Hitler anything real about England, for he seemed a man whose knowledge of the British was nil. For half an hour they chatted away, but then the interested listener and inquirer gave way to the Leader of the German Reich, whose path marked out by his destiny was being incomprehensibly blocked by England.

Hitler's face stiffened and his movements became peculiar. The German air force was unconquerable, the British air defenses pitiful, he told Dahlerus. A German infantry company bore no resemblance to any unit of its size ever seen before. It had antitank equipment, small quick-firing guns, machine guns. It was brilliantly drilled. His armor was invulnerable to the antitank guns of any enemy, his own guns of that type would destroy the armor of any who stood in his way.

Dahlerus saw he must not excite the Leader. Slowly and quietly he spoke of British toughness and endurance. Hitler listened and seemed to be lost in thought. Then he got up and began to walk up and down, saying that Germany was irresistible. He stopped his pacing and stood in the center of the room, staring. Something had snapped. "If there should be war, then I will build U-boats, build U-boats, U-boats, U-boats, U-boats!" His voice blurred and became more and more indistinct and Dahlerus could not make out what he was saying. "Then he pulled himself together," Dahlerus remembered, "raised his voice as though addressing a large audience and shrieked: 'I will build airplanes, build airplanes, airplanes, airplanes, and I will destroy my enemies!' He seemed more like a phantom from a story book than a real person."

The Swede looked over at Goering. "But he did not turn a hair."

Hitler seemed like a man in a trance. "War doesn't frighten me, encirclement of Germany is an impossibility, my people admire and follow me faithfully. If privations lie ahead for the German people, I shall be the first to starve and set my people a good example. It will spur them to superhuman efforts." His eyes were glassy. "If there should be no butter, I shall be the first to stop eating butter, eating butter. If the enemy can hold out for years, I can hold out for one year longer. I know that I am superior to all the others!"

He returned to himself. Let his visitor go to England again and tell them that. The shaken Dahlerus said that he needed something concrete to tell the British. Goering took an atlas and marked in red pencil the Corridor and Danzig. Dahlerus went back to the Esplanade Hotel. It was four-thirty in the morning, August 27. He had been talking with a madman, Dahlerus told himself. The twisted mouth and staring eyes, the raving. At eight he flew to London in a plane provided by Goering. Croydon

Airport was free of all traffic from the blockcd-off Continent, and the arrival of a German plane created a sensation. He was asked who he was.

"I do not know who I am," he answered.

He went to Number 10 Downing Street, where Chamberlain, Halifax and Sir Alexander Cadogan received him at once. The prime minister asked what impression Hitler had made upon Dahlerus.

"I shouldn't like to have him as a partner in my business."

•

On the evening of the twenty-eighth Sir Nevile Henderson took a bath, put on evening dress, drank half a bottle of champagne to fortify himself, and reported to Hitler that the British did not accept the Leader's offer to defend and guarantee the Empire. Perhaps Hitler's ability to make a deal with Russia made him believe he could do the same with England, Chamberlain had reasoned. That was wrong. "His Majesty's government could not, for any advantage offered to Great Britain, acquiesce in a settlement which would put in jeopardy the independcnce of a state to whom they have given a guarantee." There must be a just arrangement between Poland and Germany; if Hitler did not understand that he risked a war with Britain. "Such an outcome would be a calamity without parallel in history."

Hitler accepted Chamberlain's view quite calmly, and began to speak of the need for a British-German alliance. Henderson felt relief at his attitude. He had never understood Hitler's appeal to the German people, could not see what appeal the Leader had for anybody. But at least he was being reasonable. That was more than Henderson believed could be said for the Poles. Henderson had always thought them crazed in their megalomania and medieval knight-errantry romanticism. Their general irresponsibility, Baron von Weizsaecker of the German Foreign Office had told Henderson, released England and France from any obligation to follow in their lead, "to follow blindly every eccentric step on the part of a lunatic." Henderson could not but agree. He had served in the British Embassy in Moscow during tsarist days and had come away with a profound distaste for Slavic ways. He went away from Hitler hopeful that all would yet be well.

But in the morning the German papers screamed that Poland

was in a frenzy of war fever, that the Poles were mobilizing, slaying their German citizens, firing across the border, preparing to invade. In England all public services slowed down. The mail and delivery of newspapers were late, telegrams were held up, people were asked not to use the telephone save for urgent matters. One saw buses and commercial vans filled with troops, motor dispatch riders wearing steel helmets. Blood donations were requested. Letters to the editors of papers asked that the cruelty shown dachshunds in 1914 not be repeated, for they had been stoned in the streets then. Workmen painted white lines down streets in preparation for expected blackouts.

In Munich the London *Daily Express* reporter Ernest Pope dropped in on British consul general Frank Fulham and found him burning documents. Smoke was coming from the chimney and spreading across the Pranner Strasse. The reporter asked if Fulham had been given instructions to evacuate British civilians. "No, damn it," Fulham said. Even as they talked a Reichspost messenger brought a telegram from the British Embassy instructing Fulham to do so.

Two weeks earlier, along with all the *Daily Express* reporters on the Continent, Pope had been asked to indicate if he expected a war in 1939. Ten of the twelve had said they did not think so; two were doubtful. Pope had been with the majority, saying however, that he would not bet more than two weeks' salary on his prediction. His observations at the annual July celebrations of the Day of German Art in Munich had made him uneasy. The usual hours-long parade featured floats symbolizing "Valhalla," "The World of Richard Wagner," "Blood and Soil," "Day," "Night," "Heroic German Song," "The Sacrifice," "Faith and Faithfulness." There was also the "Night of the Amazons" spectacle, in which one hundred practically naked girls in tights or covered only by silver paint fought sham battles. None of these exhibitions made more of an impression upon Ernest Pope than similar displays in previous years, although he wrote of the Amazons that they had given him an idea of what the war of the sexes must have been like prior to the invention of clothing. What disturbed him was a float entitled "The Gates to the East." The previous year a similar float had shown Austria and the Sudetenland. This one showed Poland. It was followed by the "Sovereign German Eagle," gigantic, and then army troops and finally the grim Deutschland Regiment of the SS.

In the evening Consul General Fulham, in accordance with the Reichspost message from the British Embassy, officially warned all British subjects in Bavaria to leave Germany at once. A particular British subject called upon him and after offering a *"Heil Hitler!"* said she did not intend to leave. "Then you no longer have the protection of Great Britain," Fulham told Unity Mitford.

"I have the much better protection of the Führer," she replied and went to spend the next day, the twenty-ninth, sunbathing on the balcony of her apartment while she listened to the radio. Her bedroom had two swastika flags with their ends folded down over the pillows like drapes. Hitler's photo sat on the bed table with lips and eyes painted in. "I did that because it looks so nice," she told people.

In the evening Henderson went again to Hitler. He drove the three or four hundred yards from the Embassy to the Reich Chancellory in the complete darkness of a test blackout of Berlin. There was a large crowd in the square opposite the courtyard where he left his car. A guard of honor was drawn up to receive him. The drums rolled. State Secretary Meissner remarked he was glad to see the ambassador still wearing the red carnation he had worn every day of his service in Germany save for the three days preceding the Munich Conference, when it had seemed to him that war was moments away. That Meissner noticed his flower and seemed pleased was significant, Henderson told himself.

The British ambassador went to Hitler. The previous night he had left the Leader with some hope for the future, so all the less was he prepared to be met with a distinctly more uncompromising attitude. Edition after edition of the Berlin papers had all day screamed in inch-high headlines of the murders of Germans in Poland. Poland was guilty of "barbaric actions which cry to heaven," Hitler yelled at Henderson. They must cease. And the Poles must give up Danzig and the Corridor. They must send an emissary to arrange it. The emissary must arrive the following day, Wednesday, the thirtieth. Otherwise, "My soldiers are asking me yes or no." It was not for Henderson to know that the soldiers were asking nothing, that the operating head of the army, von Brauchitsch, had never in his life asked for anything but orders, that von Manstein and von Rundstedt along the Polish border were telling each other there would be no war, that Rommel was writing his wife, "There are some snags, and they'll take some time to straighten out. The Führer will obviously reach whatever decision is proper." The demand for a Polish emissary and the implied threat sounded like an ultimatum, Henderson said.

Not an ultimatum at all, Hitler replied. Merely a statement that emphasized the urgency of the matter. Sir Nevile did not care how many Germans were being slaughtered in Poland, Hitler said, but he, the Leader, cared. Henderson denied the charge that he was inhumane. The rest of the interview was conducted in the coldest possible manner. Filled with gloom, Henderson left. On his way out he passed an anteroom crowded with officers. Their presence did not dispel his apprehensions. He returned to the embassy to fill the cables to London with pleas that the Poles be forced to send an emissary at once.

At two in the morning he received a reply from Halifax. It was unreasonable of the Germans to expect that the British could produce a Polish representative that very day, the thirtieth. They must not permit themselves to expect it. Word of Halifax's reply flung Hermann Goering into a rage. He asked Birger Dahlerus to his Berlin residence and bombarded him with denunciations of Warsaw. "We know the Poles," he raged at the Swede. They were inferior, shameless. Germany could not tolerate their insolence. They were inhuman. A German officer on the frontier had seen Polish soldiers shoot down five German-blood refugees trying to swim a river on their way to safety in the Fatherland. "The Poles are mad."

But madder still would it be for France and England to fight on behalf of such a people. Goering urged Dahlerus to go again to London and explain that view to the British. Dahlerus left at five in the morning and before noon was with Chamberlain, Sir Horace Wilson, Cadogan and Halifax. They were doubtful about getting a Polish delegate to go to Berlin for conferences with Hitler, for in the forefront of their thinking were the examples of von Schusschnigg, who lost Austria by such a meeting, and of Hacha, who lost Czechoslovakia.

Colonel Beck held the same opinion. He would never go to Hitler. He told the British and French ambassadors in Warsaw he was going to declare a full mobilization of Poland's forces in their entirety. The posters were already printed. But full mobilization, the Westerners pointed out, was the final warning, and a threat in itself. It was the orders calling for full mobilization on the part of potential enemies that in a chain reaction had flung the world into war in 1914. They urged Beck to hold off. He said he would. For one day. The lettering on the posters calling for full mobilization on the thirtieth was done over with the number "31" stamped on in purple.

"Let's drop the all-or-nothing game," Hermann Goering said to Adolf Hitler. He had begged for a peaceful solution at least three times and had been shouted at in return. "All my life I have played for all or nothing!" Hitler said. A thousand rumors consumed Europe. Germany was going to spread deadly diseases into Poland through lavatory paper and bandages; electric forces would incapacitate defending planes; the Germans had a ray gun powered by the sun; super-cannons from the Hartz Mountains would fling shells of one hundred tons into the British capital ("It would need only twelve such shells to destroy London completely"); Germany had death-ray equipment that would liquidate all life.

The American reporter Edward Beattie saw a sign bearing a large black arrow in the London Zoo that, he thought, constituted a commentary on the Europe of the late summer of 1939: AIR RAID SHELTER IN MONKEY HOUSE. Of the first fourteen items on the evening news radio program in Germany nine dealt with Polish atrocities. Warsaw forbade the sale of alcoholic beverages throughout Poland: for reservists to be called by full mobilization the following day, every able-bodied man up to the age of forty had to arrive sober at his destination.

France's ambassador to Berlin, Robert Coulondre, sent by special messenger a note to Premier Daladier, who read it aloud to his Cabinet. An attack against Poland had been planned for the twenty-fifth, Coulondre reported, but had been called off. "We have only," he concluded his note, "to hold fast"—and when he read it aloud, Daladier banged his fist on the table—"hold fast"—another bang on the table—"hold fast."

Midnight of August 30 approached. Sir Nevile Henderson had waited until the last moment of the German deadline for the dispatch of a Polish emissary. He drove to what had long ago been Bismarck's office. "Where's the Pole your government was to provide?" asked Foreign Minister Ribbentrop. To the watching interpreter Paul Schmidt he appeared to be in a "state of almost shivering excitement," with a pale face, set lips, shining eyes. He had addressed Henderson in German and then waited for Schmidt's translation.

Speaking half in English and half in German, Henderson replied that it was unreasonable to expect the British to produce an emissary. London after all could not order the Poles around like children. He handed over a statement showing that the British had asked the Poles to prevent any displays of bellicosity along the frontier, to practice the utmost restraint. Germany should do the same.

"The Poles are the aggressors, not we!" Ribbentrop cried. "You have come to the wrong address."

Henderson returned to the subject of a Polish emissary, saying the normal diplomatic practice was to transmit proposals through a country's ambassador before asking that a representative with plenipotentiary powers be sent.

"That's out of the question," Ribbentrop shouted. His entire attitude, Henderson saw, conveyed the utmost hostility. "We demand that a negotiator empowered by his government with full authority should come here to Berlin!"

Henderson's face turned red. His hands were trembling. He began to read out an additional statement calling for restraint, but Ribbentrop jumped up to ask, with his arms folded across his chest, if the ambassador had anything more to add. Henderson said that he had. He said there were reports that German infiltrators were committing acts of sabotage in Poland.

"Have you anything more to say?" Ribbentrop cried, and roared, "That's a damned lie of the Polish government. I can only tell you, Herr Henderson, that the position is damned serious!"

Henderson lifted an admonitory finger. There was no Herr Henderson and had not been since he got his KCMG seven years earlier. Touched on the shoulder by the sword of his sovereign as he knelt before him, he had arisen as Sir Nevile. "You have just said 'damned,'" Henderson shouted. "That's no word for a statesman to use in so grave a situation."

Ribbentrop's breath was taken away. He had been reprimanded like a schoolboy. "What did you say?" he roared, jumping out of his chair. Henderson also jumped up. They glared at each other. According to diplomatic convention, the interpreter Schmidt should have arisen also, but he did not know how to act should diplomats turn from words to deeds. He remained seated and pretended to write in his notebook as he listened to the two men breathing heavily above him. At any moment they will come to blows, he thought to himself, and the least that will happen is that the foreign minister of the German Reich will throw His Britannic Majesty's ambassador out of the door. He kept aimlessly scribbling. Finally Ribbentrop sat. Henderson followed.

Ribbentrop took out a piece of paper and began to read from it very swiftly and in a tone of the utmost scorn and annoyance. He almost gabbled through sixteen points that he said the Germans had been prepared to offer the Poles, had they sent an emissary. When he finished he contemptuously threw the paper on his desk, saying it was now a dead number due to the Polish failure to send a representative. Henderson had picked up some six or seven of the points from the high-speed recital, the "jabber of words" Ribbentrop threw at him. They had seemed very reasonable, calling for plebiscites in the areas disputed between Germany and Poland. He asked for a copy of the text, as was normal in diplomatic usage.

Schmidt could hardly believe his ears when Ribbentrop replied, "No, I cannot hand you these proposals." Henderson thought he must have misunderstood. He repeated his request. Ribbentrop again said Henderson could not have the paper. "It is out-of-date, as the Polish envoy has not appeared."

So the proposals were just for show, like certain proposals of League of Nations days, Schmidt thought, and never meant to be put into effect. Henderson left. The last chance for peace was gone, he said to himself. They had been looking into the mirror of the past, France and Britain, Henderson told himself. Now the mirror had cracked before their eyes.

He went to the British Embassy and called Ambassador Lipski of Poland to tell him the only suggestion he had was that Marshal Smigly-Rydz, head of the Polish army, should meet with Goering. Maybe they could work something out.

It was two in the morning. He slept. At eight he called Lipski and asked him to come over from the Polish Embassy. The ambassador was on the line to Warsaw and could not leave, so First Secretary Henryk Malhomme came in his stead. He and Henderson had become friends when both served in their respective embassies in Belgrade years before. Malhomme found Henderson looking ten years older than he had days earlier.

"Malhomme," he said, "I do not like war. I do not like war." There was a long silence. Henderson repeated again what he had said, several times. Then he told Malhomme that he considered his mission in Berlin to have failed. There was going to be a war. But when Britain after long years won through, he would like Malhomme, as an old friend, to let it be known that he had never been against Poland, but only in favor of peace. It was understood between them that Henderson would not see the day of Poland's eventual liberation, for it was an open secret in diplomatic circles that he was fatally ill with cancer. They shook hands.

The veteran diplomat Ulrich von Hassel was announced. He was a member of that loose group of Germans who believed Hitler to be inspired by Satan. He had talked with State Secretary von Weizsaecker about Ribbentrop's meeting with Henderson, and von Weizsaecker had urged him to go to Henderson and urge the immediate dispatch of a Polish emissary with plenipotentiary powers to Berlin. Von Hassel told Henderson von Weizsaecker's view, and Henderson said he agreed, but what could he do? Could the English be expected to order the Poles around like stupid little boys?

Von Hassel said this Polish silence was dangerous, this Slavic behavior he and Henderson had known when they both served in the Leningrad that had in their time, before the War, been St. Petersburg. How he wished, Henderson said, those older times would come back. Von Hessel reminded him of the time when Henderson saw a shadowy figure sneaking through the British Embassy, threw himself forward and began to pummel and choke it. The shadowy figure turned out to be Henderson's chief, the British ambassador, not a burglar. They smiled together at the memory.

That morning Sir Harold Nicolson, the son of that ambassador, learned that the British government, in view of the latest developments, was ordering the evacuation of three million young children from London and other major cities. Ordinary transport services would be drastically reduced so that buses and trains could bear the children away. Roads out of London would be one-way. The children were to assemble at their school. Their teachers, still on summer vacation, were being called back to superintend them. Parents were told to send along a change of underclothing, night clothes, spare stockings or socks, a toothbrush, a towel, soap, face cloth, a handkerchief and if possible a warm coat or mackintosh. Transport would be paid for by the government. Children below school age were to be accompanied by their mothers or some responsible person. Those of school age were to have their names written on a strong piece of paper sewn to their clothing. No destinations could be indicated, but parents would be informed of their child's whereabouts as soon as the child was placed in a country location, be it a laborer's cottage or the country seat of a duke. The evacuation would commence at five-thirty in the morning of the following day, the first of September.

Sir Harold Nicolson had found his place in life in the highest circles of political and social and literary England. Churchill was "Winston" to him in private conversation and Chamberlain "Neville." Lady Nicolson was the writer Vita Sackville-West, the model for Virginia Woolf's *Orlando*. Together they maintained Sissinghurst, one of the great gardens of England. That the children were being sent away meant to Nicolson that all was over.

"It is odd to feel that the world as I knew it has only a few hours more to run," he wrote in his diary.

Hitler that day, Thursday the thirty-first, was very calm and self-assured, a sign to those who knew him that he had made up his mind. The sound of airplanes heading east was heard in the Berlin streets. The streets of Warsaw owned a new aspect, for with full mobilization declared, people did not so much stroll in the summer heat as walk briskly. Volunteer nurses hurried along smiling brightly, a little self-conscious in their new, very white, starched uniforms. People wore Red Cross badges or the green-and-yellow badges of the LOPP, the air and antigas defense equivalent of London's ARP, the air-raid protection. Every window in the Polish capital was covered with a checked pattern of white paper and stickers that would protect against the air vibrations of nearby explosions. Inside, the windows were covered with black so that no light would shine through to guide German bombers, and each home had a room whose windows were made airtight with cotton, glue and petroleum jelly so that no gas might come in. Felt and nails were recommended to prevent seepage under or above the door. The world was down to being thankful that no ultimatums had been issued, and united in urging Polish overtures to Germany. They would have to do something, thought Poland's ambassador to Britain, Count Edward Raczynski, or they would find themselves in a situation where the British govern-

ment would be able to say, "Look at those Poles. How unreasonable they are!" Then the stage would be set for Poland to be left
in the lurch.

Ambassador Lipski was told to go to Ribbentrop and tell him
the Poles were willing to open discussions on the basis of the
sixteen points that Ribbentrop had so speedily read out to Sir
Nevile Henderson. Lipski had gotten the text of the points from
the indefatigable Birger Dahlerus after a British embassy official,
Sir George Ogilvie-Forbes, told the Swede that Ribbentrop had
been rude, negative and unpleasant and that his high-speed
reading of the sixteen points enabled Henderson to understand
"only three words." Dahlerus told Goering in the field marshal's
train and Goering said, "I'll do it, I'll take the responsibility."

Goering handed the text to Dahlerus and over the telephone
Dahlerus read it out to Forbes, to the requests of his listener that
he slow down and demands from Goering that he hurry up. Then
Dahlerus went to the British Embassy, where Henderson said he
should go with Forbes to Lipski. The two drove to the Polish
Embassy and found the hall crowded with packing cases and the
staff and servants preparing for departure. Lipski received them
in an office cleared of most of its furnishings. He was pale, his
fingers trembled and he appeared almost on the verge of a
breakdown. He asked Dahlerus to read him the sixteen points,
but appeared too nervous to understand the words.

Forbes wrote down a summary, but Lipski said he was incapable of reading it. Dahlerus said he would dictate the summary
to a secretary, and while he did so Lipski wildly said to Forbes
that really he had no interest in the summary or anything else,
for on the basis of his knowledge gained from five and a half
years as Polish ambassador to Germany, he knew that if there
was a war, there would be immediate uprisings all through the
Reich and that "the Polish army would march in triumph to
Berlin."

They left him as he pulled himself together to ask Ribbentrop for an interview. Forbes went back to the British Embassy
while Dahlerus went to Goering's Berlin house, a mansion set in
a large park and the former residence of the president of the
Prussian Diet. He pointed out to the field marshal how the British were trying to get negotiations going, and asked him to lunch
at the Esplanade Hotel.

There Dahlerus told the chef to do his very best. Perhaps it would put Goering in a good mood. They began with lobster and went on to other delicacies and ended with coffee and excellent old brandy. Goering expressed himself as pleased with everything but the after-dinner cigars, and smoked one of his own long Austrian ones. (Dahlerus took note of the field marshal's attitude toward goods purchased with someone else's money: after sipping the brandy Goering ordered two bottles sent out to his car to take home.)

When the two men rose, they decided to ask Henderson to join them at Goering's, and the ambassador sat with them around a low, round table in a drawing room. They talked very pleasantly, but it came into Henderson's mind that if the commander of the German air force had time for a leisurely meal and long afternoon chat, everything must be set, all details of an attack taken care of.

As they talked, Lipski arrived at the German Foreign Office to see Ribbentrop. It was the ambassador's first meeting with him since March, almost half a year previous. The interview did not take long. Did Lipski, asked Ribbentrop, have full plenipotentiary authority to conduct negotiations on the Polish-German differences? Lipski said he did not, he was only present to say his government was considering talks. "There is no point in our continuing this conversation," Ribbentrop said.

In the little Pomeranian town of Bad Polzin, where he had been ordered to set up the Leader's field headquarters for the proposed and then canceled August 26 invasion, Erwin Rommel wrote his wife from the railroad station waiting room, where he had established his office: "I'm inclined to believe it will all blow over and we'll end up getting back the Corridor just as we did the Sudetenland last year." With no pressing duties for them to perform, he had put his men to helping the local farmers with the harvest. "Waiting is a bore," he told his wife, "but it can't be helped. The Führer knows what's right for us." His telephone rang. He was ordered to stand by and not leave his means of communication.

To the south at the Monastery of the Holy Cross in Neisse, Generals von Manstein and von Rundstedt received at five o'clock: D = 1.9: H = 0445. Again as they had on the twenty-sixth, they sent their troops out on the roads to the Polish frontier in an approach march, telling each other that, as five days before, it was all a bluff and there would soon be a counterorder. They sat up together as the sunset and evening and then night came upon them as earlier it had upon a Warsaw so completely blacked out that the darkness seemed velvety. People strangely whispered when one passed them in the streets, whispers everywhere, thought Rulka Langer, but you could see no one. Trains, horses, the few trucks the Polish army had, moved between the capital and the German border, carrying men and arms to the frontier positions.

Along that border, at the little German town of Gleiwitz, the SS officer Alfred Helmut Naujocks led a small detachment into action. For three weeks Naujocks had been with his men at a military training school that had been cleared of all the students. His men were dressed in Polish uniforms and carried Polish carbines given them by the German military intelligence service. They carried Polish military identifications and paybooks. That afternoon Naujocks had received from Reinhard Heydrich, Heinrich Himmler's right-hand man, a two-word telegram: GRANDMOTHER'S DEAD. It was the code order to carry out his mission. With his men he went through the darkness toward the forestry station at Pitschen on the frontier and the Hochlinden customs post between Gleiwitz and Ratibor. With the Germans dressed in Polish uniforms were a dozen concentration camp prisoners, also dressed in Polish uniforms. The prisoners were unconscious, but alive. They had been given lethal injections by an SS doctor.

It was nine-thirty. The German radio released the text of the sixteen reasonable points, along with the information that the Poles had rejected them. "It's all very unimportant," said Beck in Warsaw when he heard of the broadcast. "The Germans will agree to talk, and they will talk. But of course I won't consent to go to Berlin. The meeting will have to take place in one of the neutral countries or perhaps on the border."

A section of Naujocks's command charged the German customs post from the Polish side and destroyed it. Another section attacked the forestry station. Naujocks led a third group to the Gleiwitz radio station, burst in, took it over and seized the microphone. A Polish-speaking SS man delivered a brief speech. The time had come for war with Germany, the SS man cried. Let the Poles strike down Germans. As he spoke, unconscious concentration camp prisoners in their Polish uniforms were brought in and laid down in the station and in the entryway. Naujocks bent over one and pried open the eyes. They were without pupil reaction, but Naujocks could tell by the breathing that the man was still alive. Shots were fired into the prisoners and sprayed around the radio station. Naujocks and his men left.

A group of German reporters were brought to the station a short while later. They were shown what appeared to be members of the Polish army shot down by German forces who had retaken the station. By ten-thirty Germany broadcast to the world that Polish troops had seized a German station and had had time to send an appeal for a Polish crusade against Germany before German defenders rushed to the scene and killed the invaders.

"I shall find a reason for starting this war," Hitler had told his officers at Berchtesgaden eight days before. "Whether the world believes the reason amounts to a pile of shit."

SIXTEEN

KRAKOW was the Polish city of importance closest to German-controlled territory. It lay less than one hundred miles from former Czechoslovakia. Its university of quiet, arched courtyards dated from the fourteenth century. In the early morning hours of Friday, the first day of September, all of the schools of the city were being utilized as staging points and barracks for the reservists massing to move to the frontiers. The city hummed with activity. One heard recruits arriving from trains sent from interior Poland, and regiments moving out.

The city had cobbled streets, old fortification walls, Gothic churches, the Royal Castle on the hill overlooking the Vistula. Tuesdays and Fridays were market day, when Krakow changed into a vast village filled with the clanking and creaking carts of the peasants from outlying villages bringing their products to sell, as they had for ages into the dim past. Above them, from the tall tower of St. Mary's Church on Market Square, a trumpeter sounded a call ending on a broken note as a trumpeter had for the previous five hundred years to commemorate one who had ended when an enemy archer sent an arrow into his throat.

Thousands of pigeons lived in belfries of the churches of Krakow and in the recesses of the old city walls. At a few moments before five in the morning of that Friday market day, the pigeons soared up and began to fly in great circles, a great swarm. No one understood why they did so. The birds had heard or sensed something coming through the air. After a little while there appeared in the early morning light waves of German bombers, which had flown over the source of the Vistula in the Carpathian mountains, and the forests and fields. They came spitting fire and bombs and death. Krakow now understood the pigeons.

In the north the German warship *Schleswig-Holstein,* supposedly docked in Danzig for ceremonies honoring the German war dead of 1914–18, swung her gun toward the Polish marine bunkers on the Westerplatte, a little spit of fortified land reaching into the Baltic, and opened up. All across the long frontier, the German tanks and infantry roared into Poland, machine-gunning the police huts and customs offices behind the red-and-white border gates as they came.

The U.S. ambassador to Poland, Anthony J. Drexel Biddle, came awake in the house at Konstancin on the Vistula twelve miles south of Warsaw, which he had rented for his family and staff because it seemed a safer location than a Warsaw that would be in danger in the first moments of a war. Biddle lay still. Everything seemed tranquil. He wondered why he had awakened. It was five-thirty in the morning. He heard the crash of bombs and jumped out of bed. He telephoned the British Embassy in Warsaw and got counselor Clifford Norton.

"They're attacking!" Biddle cried.

A German plane came over and dropped several bombs. One hit a villa nearby. Another came down to explode in Biddle's garden. The plane was five hundred feet over his head. He could distinctly see the pilot's face.

"They're attacking *me!*" he shouted into the phone at Norton. He decided not to use the cable to Washington, which would take time to code, and so tried to get through on the phone. He was told the lines to America through Berlin were out and put through a call to the American ambassador to Paris. The line there went through Copenhagen. He reached Bullitt, who called Washington. It was a little before three in the morning, Washington time. The White House operator woke Marguerite Le-Hand, the President's longtime secretary, and said Ambassador Bullitt was on the line with a most urgent call for his chief. "Put him through," Miss LeHand said. The phone by Roosevelt's bedside rang.

"This is Bill Bullitt, Mr. President."

"Yes, Bill."

"Tony Biddle has just got through from Warsaw, Mr. President." He told the President of Biddle's report.

"It's come at last," Roosevelt said. "God help us all."

A strange and startling feeling of familiarity came upon Roosevelt, as though he had been through this scene before. It must be the memory of his days as assistant secretary of the navy during the War, he decided, when he had a direct line to the Navy Department, which often rang at night. Perhaps, he thought, his feeling was not so strange; this call was like picking up again an interrupted routine. "Thank you, Bill, I've got to call Cordell and the others now."

He propped himself up on a pillow, lit a cigarette and started putting in calls. The secretary of state turned on the light by his bed when the phone rang. "Cordell," Roosevelt said, "Bullitt has just been on the phone."

As soon as he recognized the President's voice, Hull knew what he was going to say. "There flashed through my mind," he remembered, "that here perhaps was the end of civilization as we knew it."

The President got through to the army's George C. Marshall. It was the day he was scheduled to be sworn in as a permanent major general and a temporary four-star general holding the post of chief of staff. Marshall did not know the President well, and what little he knew about him he did not like. A year earlier Roosevelt held forth about air defenses to a group and turned to the then deputy chief of staff to ask if he did not agree. "Don't you think so, George?" Roosevelt asked in his immediate first-name fashion. Marshall gave him a glare from blue eyes normally cold, but on this occasion freezing. He did not appreciate the "misrepresentation of our intimacy."

"I don't agree at all," Marshall said. Roosevelt gave him a startled look, and several men told Marshall at the meeting's end that his tour in Washington was concluded. But Roosevelt got over the slight—although never in his life did he again call the general "George"—and after speaking with the President, Marshall went to the adjutant general to take his two oaths of office. Roosevelt announced that he would hold a press conference, and then as Washington's temperature rose to 86 degrees, said in response to a question that he hoped and believed America could stay out of the war. A poll showed that one-tenth of one percent of the American people wished to fight on Germany's side. Three percent wished to stand with the Western powers and Poland. The remaining more than 96 percent wished to stay neutral.

In England the children of the cities, summoned by government order the previous day, gathered in their schools and prepared to march to the trains and buses that would carry them from the expected drop points of the German air force bombs. It was the greatest evacuation in history, three million children. *New York Times* reporter Frederick T. Birchall went to a Whitechapel school. The children were all neat and clean, each wearing a haversack, most homemade. Those worn by the poorest children were made of old pillow slips. Inside were clothes, toilet articles and a bite to eat. Around each neck hung a cased government-issued gas mask. It was formed into the face of, and decorated with the features of, Mickey Mouse.

Birchall had more than forty years of newspaper experience, most of that time spent with the dispassionate *Times,* but when he saw gas masks hanging around the necks of children, he broke down and a flood of profanity coursed out of him. It was directed at Adolf Hitler. He was not ashamed for his words.

The schoolmistress addressed the children in the assembly hall. They were all going on a holiday and it would be nice to begin it with a little prayer. In their treble voices they chanted: "May God take us all in His keeping and bring us safe back to our mummies." They sang "Tipperary" and a song Birchall took to be about a choo-choo train. They formed into a straggling line, the smallest ones hand in hand with older children, and moved off to the nearest railroad station. Mothers went along the line until shooed off for fear they would upset the children. The mothers ran ahead to the station. All along the line of march windows opened and people leaned out calling, "Keep smiling" and "Don't get your feet wet."

At Victoria Station a school came in singing "The Chestnut Tree." Their parents watched from behind a barrier. The young voices filled all that part of the station, and people passing by smiled and then, understanding, began to weep. The train filled and left. Parents from another school took the place of those gone back to homes with little beds that would be empty that night, and as their children arrived, there were cries of "Here they are! Oh, here they are!" The children were smiling as they passed by the barrier, looking round for parents calling, "Ta-ta" and "Good-bye, dear." The children did not stop, but kept walking. "Cheerio, Mum." "Bye-bye." The parents standing close to the barrier railings gave a last wave. "Well, we can't do any more," said one woman. "Thank God they've gone."

•

When the Poles had given consideration to a possible German attack—and they had given the subject very little thought, preferring to dwell instead upon their own great cavalry drive concluding with a victory parade in Berlin—they had imagined a prolonged, heavy artillery barrage followed by a German infantry forward push. Troops would move in a line and advance from one point to another—positional warfare. Such was the method that had finally ended the stalemate on the Western Front in the Great War. Such was the military doctrine of the victorious Allies of 1918 as concerned any possible European war. Air power, it was universally believed, was for long-range missions against enemy cities and factories. Tanks were to accompany and serve infantry and to perform scouting and reconnaissance missions. But such tactics demanded masses of troops. Limited by the Treaty of Versailles to an army of only one hundred thousand men, the German military thinkers of the Weimar period had evolved far more economical, completely new concepts. When Hitler came to power, he had endorsed their thinking. The resulting product was demonstrated on the morning of September 1, 1939.

Flying against their targets with no war declaration to signal their coming, the German air force concentrated its surprise attack on Poland's airdromes. (The bombing of Ambassador Biddle's garden was unintentional and atypical.) In hours what there was of Poland's air force was destroyed on the ground. Unopposed in the air, not a long-range force but an air arm to support the German ground forces, the planes then attacked military bases, railway tracks and junctions. All along the long and thinly held frontier the barracks of the Polish army erupted into flame. Asked by German ambassador von der Schulenburg to give navigational aid to planes hitting targets in eastern Poland, the Soviet Telecommunications Ministry did so through its radio station at Minsk, a few miles from the Polish border.

Then the tanks came in. Very light, the largest weighing only twenty tons, they moved swiftly in columns three to ten miles across over flat, sandy soil baked hard by the unremittingly brilliant sunshine and rainless days of the summer. When one detachment arrived at the Oswiecim post of the artillery lieutenant Jan Karski, the barracks were almost in ruins from the incendiary bombs dropped by the Stukas and Heinkels. The tanks completed the job. Karski's battery ceased to exist as a functioning military unit, but the survivors were told to take guns, supplies and ammunition, and make for Krakow.

The railway station was burning and the tracks in ruins, but repairs were hastily made. Karski and the others got on a train that but a few hours before had been bringing in men called up by the full mobilization order of the previous day. As they left, Poles of German background fired at them from their homes. The train did not go far when from out of the blazing sun came half a dozen German planes, dropping bombs and strafing with their machine guns. More than half the cars were hit and most of their occupants killed or wounded.

Those men able to travel trailed east, no longer an army, a detachment, a battery, but a group of individuals on a highway jammed with thousands of others mixed in with civilian refugees. They passed smoking and abandoned ruins. The railroads were completely torn up. Karski hoped they could find a base of resistance where they could stand and fight, but there was no suitable place in the flat, featureless landscape. Planes and tank detachments harried them. They were almost a mob now, he said to himself. Motorized German infantry with attached tank units came after them. It was not yet afternoon.

In the Corridor, where the Poles had stationed a third of their forces, tank columns came roaring in from East Prussia and Germany proper. They came from two sides at massed horse cavalry, machine-gunning and shelling. Swinging sabers and leveling lances at the tanks, the horsemen found gaps in the formations and fled. The screaming of horses left wounded on the field was like that of women in agony. The German tank officers ordered their men to get out and with their sidearms dispatch the animals, thousands of them, their hooves sticking into the air.

Rulka Langer, who had not given away her winter clothing after reading *Gone With the Wind*, arrived late at her job at the Bank of Poland in Warsaw. The bus she usually took never showed up and she had taken a streetcar. She called the American friend who had promised to send a car for her mother and children on the day the war broke out. Her questions were curt, as were his answers.

"Yes, Dan would send me his car and chauffeur exactly at twelve. Thanks. I rang off. We did not mention the war, we did not discuss anything, every moment seemed strangely precious and could not be wasted on idle talk. Same with Mother. The war has broken out. Could she and the children be ready at noon? Yes. I would come home and see them off. Mother, be sure the children don't take too many toys. Have to travel light. All right. That was all."

She hung up. Sirens outside began to wail and the air raid loudspeaker came on: "I announce an air raid alarm for the city of Warsaw."

She and her co-workers closed the windows and put on gas masks and flocked onto the staircase of the building.

The loudspeaker kept monotonously repeating the same words. "The alarm is on. The alarm is on. The alarm is on."

After a time the all clear sounded. She went upstairs to her office.

"I announce an alarm for the city of Warsaw. I announce . . ."

They went to the staircase again. She found her curls a nuisance, for they got into her eyes under the mask and almost blinded her. One wisp kept bothering her nose. There were three alarms but no bombs dropped. She went to her home. Her mother had lived there for the forty years of her married life. The building had a marble staircase with enormous mirrors on each landing. In one room of the apartment hung a picture that had been in the family for two hundred years. It showed against a background of gold a dark-faced Madonna holding a tiny upright Holy Child. They knelt before it. Out of the corner of her eye she saw her daughter trying to bend the knees of her doll, Stas, so that Stas could kneel also. The knees would not bend. Mrs. Langer's mother arose and with a wide, sweeping gesture traced a cross as if blessing the whole apartment. She went out the door. "Don't forget to wind the clock on Monday."

Mrs. Langer went to her hairdresser to get her curls clipped off. Business was very busy, the hairdresser told her. Everybody wanted shampoos, marcels, permanents, everybody wanted her hair set for the war.

•

In Berlin, Birger Dahlerus sat with Sir Nevile Henderson in the study of the British Embassy. Outside they saw Hitler pass in a procession of cars. He was headed for the Kroll Opera House for a session of the Reichstag.

It was fiercely warm inside the building. Perspiration dripped from Hermann Goering's round face as he sat in the Reichstag president's chair on a raised dais behind Hitler. He almost appeared to have emerged from a steam bath. The room had dark red walls, maroon carpets, and a great, brightly lit red eagle on the wall.

Wearing an army uniform, Hitler began the same speech he had given a thousand times before, the same denunciations of the Versailles Treaty in the same words. He turned to Danzig and the Corridor. He had made proposals. The Poles rejected them. He had warned them. They defied him. Then they attacked Germans on their territory, and then the Reich itself at the radio station and customs outpost and forestry station near Gleiwitz. "I am wrongly judged if my love for peace and my patience are mistaken for weakness or even cowardice," he said. "I therefore determined to speak to the Poles in the same language as that in which they had been speaking to us for months." Hitler did not ask for a war declaration, for he simply referred to a "special engagement" for the armed forces. The members of the Reichstag roared. They were not parliamentarians in any Western sense. Their function was to offer approval. They had never held a vote recognizable in London, Paris or Washington. In Berlin's streets and in the streets of every German city and town, loudspeakers blared out the sound.

"My whole life belongs to my people from now on in a new sense," Hitler cried. "I wish nothing other than to be the first soldier of the German Reich. I have therefore put on that tunic which once before was the dearest and most sacred to me, and I shall take it off only after victory has been won. Or I shall not live to experience the end."

Now, thought the American reporter Wallace R. Deuel, looking down upon Hitler, the world of 1939 is gone as the world of 1914 went. The roar of the listeners came through the loudspeakers outside.

"One word I have never known: capitulation. In the same

measure in which I myself am prepared to sacrifice my life for my people and for Germany, I demand the same of every other person.

"Germany—Hail Victory!"

Hitler spoke for thirty-four minutes. Then his car took him back to the Chancellory through a somber Berlin, whose citizens had not applauded, nor even stood at attention as the national anthem came through the loudspeakers, but had scurried away. It was getting on toward noon. The phone rang in the British Embassy. It was Goering, asking Dahlerus to come to him. The Swede went to a packed Wilhelmstrasse blocked by cordons of police and was led by two officers past Hess and Himmler and others to the field marshal. Goering proudly told him that Hitler had decreed that he was now second in line of command. It would strengthen his power to work for a peaceful solution with the West. He asked time and time again if England really desired a peaceful settlement. Would it be possible? Dahlerus replied that the German onslaught upon Poland was hardly a basis upon which to build a happy solution. But perhaps Goering could meet with the English and arrange something. It was conceivable there was yet a tiny chance.

Goering took Dahlerus to Hitler, whose bearing and manner at once struck the visitor as being of an abnormal nature. "He came close up to me and with fixed, staring gaze began to speak. His breath was so foul that it was all I could do not to step back." Everything was England's fault, Hitler told Dahlerus. She was selfish. She had thwarted Dahlerus's efforts to bring about a peaceful solution. Yet Germany would still meet England halfway. "But if the British do not understand that it is in their own interests to keep out of a fight with me, they will live to repent their folly. If England wants to fight for a year I shall fight for a year, if England wants to fight two years I shall fight two years."

He waved his arms and shouted in Dahlerus's face. His voice rose to a shrill scream. His arms milled wildly in the air. "If England wants to fight for three years I shall fight for three years." His body jerked about. "And if it is necessary I will fight for ten years!" He waved his fist and bent over so that it almost touched the floor.

A man not in full possession of his faculties, Dahlerus thought to himself, or worse, a fiend. He fled the Leader and from the British Embassy telephoned Sir Alexander Cadogan in London.

Cadogan said that for there to be a hope for peace the Germans must cease hostilities and withdraw their troops to the German-Polish boundary. Dahlerus went to Goering and found that the field marshal seemed unable to understand the consequences of the German attack. Perhaps it was because he was now given the opportunity to see what his air force could do. In front of Dahlerus Goering called in two aides, made them a long speech and presented each with a sword of honor to carry gloriously through a war.

All these people are in some crazy state of intoxication, Dahlerus said to himself. He went to his hotel, where a skinny waiter stopped him, described how he had fought through the last War—already they were calling it that—and now had a wife and child and wondered if Dahlerus could do something to get him exempted from further service. The waiter and the others in the hotel, Dahlerus thought, behaved like timid animals facing an approaching danger.

Lady Diana Manners Cooper was in High Street of Bognor, near her seaside home, near the Ha'nacker Hill mill whose doom Hilaire Belloc had compared to the doom coming for their England, when she saw a group of people clustered about a car whose radio was on. She had come into town with her little son, John Julius, to buy fresh prawns for lunch. Her husband, Alfred Duff Cooper, formerly first lord of the admiralty, was playing golf. With her laughing boy talking of the Fun Fair he wanted to visit, she went to the car and listened to its radio for a moment. Nineteen fourteen had found her excited and exhilarated, irritated perhaps over the disruption of her social life but never dreaming of the catastrophic consequences that would ensue. The news this time made her see in imagination a London destroyed, its population choked by gas, and with famine and disease running wild. She saw her seven military-age nephews dying obscure and muddy deaths while those at home, frantic with terror, were bombed to extinction beneath razed towns.

"Nothing will ever be the same again," she said to John Julius. He was a child. He paid her little attention. Her husband finished his golf round—he had never played more poorly—and went to the clubhouse for a drink. Two men sat at the bar talking about horse racing. "Hitler started on Poland this morning," one of the men remarked to Cooper. He asked what the man meant, and was told. The two men at the bar went back to talk about the coming St. Leger Stakes. Cooper got his car and drove home. "My heart felt lighter than it had felt for a year." The waiting, he felt, was over at last. When his wife told him she was thinking of killing herself so as not to see what was coming, he laughed. So she banged the door, she remembered, against Death, his scythe and his hourglass.

A telegram was delivered. Parliament would be meeting at six that evening. They drove to London and Cooper took his seat. Gigantic balloons to protect against low-flying enemy planes hung like black spots in the air. The metal cables holding them to the ground would shear off a wing. The Distinguished Strangers Gallery filled. Ambassador Maisky of the Soviet Union found himself seated at the side of Ambassador Raczynski of Poland. The Speaker arrived. The House arose and bowed to him. The chaplain offered a prayer. "Let us this day pray for wisdom and courage to defend the right."

Chamberlain spoke. "The responsibility for this terrible catastrophe rests on the shoulders of one man, the German Chancellor," he said. He hit the podium in front of him with his clenched fist. He told how the sixteen reasonable points had never been presented to the Poles, that it was all a fraud. "Well, I never!" exclaimed Lady Astor from her seat.

The prime minister told Parliament that Sir Nevile Henderson would be instructed to hand a statement to the German foreign minister. He took off and then put on his pince-nez and fumbled with his papers and read the statement aloud. The House adjourned and members went out into the still-light streets to dine. Sir Harold Nicolson had come to London from the country past schoolboys filling sandbags at Maidstone. He went to his club, the Beefsteak, and saw there the Duke of Devonshire, sane and amusing. One had to admire a man of such position for showing no gloom or apprehension, Nicolson thought to himself, for Devonshire must know that this day's doings would take away his grandeur forever. The Coopers went to the Savoy Hotel Grill, where they dined with Churchill.

When Nicolson left the Beefsteak the sun had set. He was startled to find a perfectly black city. "Nothing could be more dramatic or give more of a shock than to find outside not the glitter of all the sky-signs, but a pallor of black velvet." It was like a contradiction of civilization to find a great world capital turned dark as a remote country village at midnight.

The Coopers came from the Savoy and blundered along in the blackness until a car belonging to the Duke of Westminster, its headlights covered and revealing only blue slits of light, came along and gave them a lift. Immensely rich, "Bendor" to Lady Diana when she had loved him long ago, Westminster began denouncing the Jews. The Savoy was filled with them, he complained. He went on to say that he rejoiced that England was not yet at war and that Hitler knew, after all, that the British were his best friends. Feeling himself a guest in the duke's car, Cooper first held himself back from answering, but then said that it was his hope that Hitler would soon find that the British were his most implacable and remorseless enemies. The rest of the trip passed in silence.

Along the Polish roads the army and the people fled east, no lights showing on their conveyances, those on foot shuffling with their bundles, trucks piled high with gray shapes of sleeping figures, wheelbarrows with parcels pushed along, those who had dropped out lying under bushes and in ditches along the line of flight. One saw burning buildings, barracks, railroad stations. The dust rose in thick, choking clouds.

Sir Nevile Henderson went to Ribbentrop. He stood before him and read aloud: "I am to inform Your Excellency that, unless the German government are prepared to give His Majesty's government satisfactory assurances that the German government have suspended all aggressive action against Poland and are prepared promptly to withdraw their forces from Polish territory, His Majesty's government will without hesitation fulfill their obligations to Poland."

It was a warning, not an ultimatum, for there was no time limit named for German response. Ambassador Coulondre would in half an hour read out the same exactly worded statement to Ribbentrop, only the name of France substituted for that of His Majesty's government. Even Henderson's final bitter paragraph would be exactly echoed by Coulondre.

"I avail myself of this opportunity to renew to Your Excellency the assurance of my highest consideration."

SEVENTEEN

BY SATURDAY MORNING, twenty-four hours after the initial onslaught, the Polish army was effectively finished. The civil telephone system wires upon which they relied for their communications were yanked down by the advancing German tanks, and so their forces were unable to arrange to concentrate in any sizable manner. The Stukas screamed down on them. They formed in little groups and offered what resistance they could. It was hardly even a scratch upon the body of the force hitting them from three sides.

Typical were the activities of the Pioneer detachment of the Third Panzer Division of the German XIX Corps, which slew to the last man a large group of opposing Poles and lost but eight of its own number. A drop in the bucket, notable only for the name of one of the German dead: Platoon Leader Lieutenant Heinrich von Weizsaecker, son of the state secretary. The dead man's brother Richard came and sat grieving by the body for the night.* But what was one death, eight deaths, to forty-eight divisions, a million men?

Desperate rumors spread through the country. Six hundred British bombers had arrived in Warsaw and were leaving on missions against Bremen, Berlin, Cuxhaven. Hamburg was in ruins. The Germans were dumping crucifixes treated with acid to blister the hands of those who picked them up, they were dropping poisoned candy to kill children. A beautiful, blonde woman pilot led the airplanes, and the last thing many saw was her face in

---

*At this writing (1987) Richard von Weizsaecker is president of West Germany.

the cockpit of her plane, Lady Death with a spitting machine gun. The French infantry had taken Frankfurt. France and England were soon to unleash massive air raids on German cities. They would unload their bombs and fly on to Warsaw, where they would refuel for a return trip. That was why there was no gasoline. It was being held for them.

None of the rumors favorable or unfavorable were true. Reality itself was frightful for the Poles. The German planes attacked Warsaw in force, coming in at extremely low altitudes, almost appearing to skim the rooftops. People ran, clutching their heads, and dived into cellars, where the walls shook and flakes of white plaster flicked off. Outside fire engine horns sounded and women screamed. Fire blazed in the Muranow and Praga quarters, in the Smocza quarter and in Stare Miastro, the old town. White dust rose into the air and water no longer came from the tap. In the streets droshkas burned as the horses that had pulled them lay kicking in the traces. One found one's face contracting into a nervous, grinlike grimace and heard hysterical giggling coming out of one's mouth. The air was filled with the stifling smell of high explosives.

The capital was the main target but there were other bombing runs and strafing attacks, some of which appeared to have no thought behind them. Unimportant little towns with no military significance found themselves being hit. The flimsy houses blew up, leaving a fine cloud of dust and smoke lightly settling down on the ruins, while people who ran out into the streets were machine-gunned, as were peasants working in the fields. Even in the Dark Ages, thought the British reporter Clare Hollingworth, invaders let the land folk live. What was the sense of killing children, the girls to be buried with their little gray dolls, which no one dared to take away? It seemed random and purposeless, and some Polish officers reasoned that the Germans had lost their sense of direction or had useless maps.

But there was a reason: it was to panic and fatigue the entire Polish population and so prevent organized defense of any kind. The granaries packed with August's harvest burned, as did the stacked corn, and the fattened hogs dropped with machine-gun bullets in their bodies. By government order every shop in Warsaw that owned a radio had to keep its door open and the radio turned on so that it could be heard in the street. After an announcer let it be known that German planes were approaching,

the Polish military marches continually booming out were replaced by the opening bars of a Chopin nocturne, played over
and over every ten seconds. During a half-hour raid, calculated
the *Daily Mail* reporter Cedric Salter, the whole of Warsaw heard
the same sickening fragment one hundred eight times, *Ta-tum-
tum, ta-tiddle-TA, tum-tum-tiddley-um-tum*. It remained his deepest
memory of those days, how that sound drained his morale away.

"It is like a shooting party," gasped Ambassador to London
Raczynski. "We are the partridges and they are the guns." He
submitted to the British government: "The Polish government
recalls Article I of the Agreement on Mutual Assistance between
the United Kingdom and Poland, in which each Contracting Party
undertakes to give to the other Contracting Party, in case of
aggression, at once all the support and assistance in its power."

A Cheshire woman married to a Pole made her way through
shattered streets to the British Embassy in Warsaw. She found
cars filled with luggage in the courtyard, and silent people. She
went up to an officer. "Listen—your uniform—I can't help doing
this." The brilliant summer sun shone down upon them from
the cloudless sky. "I'm sorry," she said. "We're both English. Is
England coming in?"

He remained silent for a very long time. She could hear the
peasant carts creaking and the harnesses of the horses pulling
them as traffic went up the Avenue of the Third of May. "I don't
know," he said heavily. "There is no news. What do you expect
me to tell you? Nobody has told me."

The first trainloads of wounded were coming in from the
frontier, the wounded soon filling the hospitals, then lying on
the floors of museums, and in vestibules, corridors, courtyards
and palaces, and then in long rows along the platforms of the
station itself, where women came to tend them or at least offer
a cigarette and cup of coffee.

The Cheshire woman went there. "How are they fighting in
the West?" she heard men asking. "Are they bombing Germany?
Is England in?"

A Catholic, she told herself she could not go to the altar to
receive the sacrament in a Polish church. Not until England came
in. It was foolish, she told herself, unnecessary, it was self-
dramatization, but she would not go.

Parliament met in London. Henderson had told Chamberlain
from Berlin that the only solution seemed for Marshal Smigly-

Rydz to speak with Goering. The commander in chief of the Polish army should go to Berlin in the midst of what the Germans called a "counterattack with pursuit" but what the rest of the world called a shooting war. Calls were going back and forth from Paris and London to Rome. Perhaps Mussolini could do something.

But it was hopeless, Ambassador Attolico told himself in Berlin. He had seen Hitler two days earlier, just before the German forces moved in, and found him dazed and apparently almost in a coma, listening to inner voices and speaking in a half-dreamy voice.

"Too late," he said when Attolico spoke of mediation.

"Am I to understand that everything is at an end?" Attolico asked.

Hitler nodded. He was looking off into space as Attolico left.

To pick up the thread of conferences, proposals, counterproposals now when the Germans were in Poland and whole sections of Warsaw in flames—what, Attolico asked himself, were the odds? Lord Halifax held telephone conversations with Count Ciano. It was Italy, Mussolini, who had saved the world from war, after all, by being the inspiration for the Munich Conference just a year before.

Chamberlain's voice sounded as if it were thickening for a cold when he began his address to Parliament. What a strange man he had always been, reflected Sir Harold Nicolson, looking at the grim and drawn face. The prime minister began to talk about coordinating representations to be made to Germany with the French. He mentioned the possibility of Italian arrangements for a conference, and it seemed to Harold Macmillan that "a kind of shiver went through the House." For it sounded all too much like another Munich, with Poland playing the part of Czechoslovakia this time.

That was not in Chamberlain's mind, though Macmillan and the others could not know it. The prime minister realized, but could not face, that the game was up. He could not force from himself the last decisive, irrevocable, word. He palavered about, weak and formless, discussing what kind of time limit he and the French would contrive to present to the Germans. He had not thought, in those years of German belligerence, of economics or of British honor or markets or spheres of influence, but only of his cousin Norman in his grave under a Cross of Sacrifice along the former Western Front along with the one million others dead for king and country. He had thought and worked only for peace, and there were those who in later years would remember him as brave and big for that.

But it did not come through to the Parliament hearing him dither about technicalities when an ally to whom Britain had pledged its word had been under the most severe kind of attack, bombs and bullets raining down, for nearly thirty-six hours. When Arthur Greenwood arose, the acting Labor Party leader during the illness of Clement Atlee, a cry terrible for Chamberlain to hear greeted him:

"Arthur, *you* speak for England!"

Some said it was Robert Boothby who first shouted it, others Leo Amery, but many took it up and repeated it.

Speak for England, and Greenwood said he had wished to support the prime minister but instead must question and criticize. "Tomorrow we meet at twelve. I hope the prime minister then— well, he must be in a position to make some further statement and I must put this point to him: Every minute's delay means the loss of life, imperiling of our national interests—"

"Honor!" someone called.

"Let me finish my sentence," Greenwood said. "I was about to say imperiling our national honor."

They adjourned into a lobby so blacked out that when someone struck a match, it seemed to Nicolson like a beacon in the night. A group went to Churchill's flat in what Duff Cooper thought was a state of bewildered rage to watch their host put in a call to Ambassador Raczynski. "I hope—I hope that Britain will keep—will keep its . . ." Churchill said and broke down in tears.

Anthony Eden took the phone and told the Polish ambassador that their group was impatient for action and a war declaration. Razynski's Paris counterpart, Ambassador Juliusz Lukasiewicz, went to French foreign minister Georges Bonnet in the Quai d'Orsay to be told that talks with London were going on as to what action the Western countries should take.

"Talks, talks, talks!" Lukasiewicz burst out. "What's the use of talking? Poland needs action, and very swift action." Bonnet silently puffed on a cigarette. "It isn't right!" Lukasiewicz cried. "You know it isn't right! A treaty is a treaty and must be respected! You have no justification in delaying action! Or am I to assume that a French engagement is worthless? Am I to assume that your words are nothing but hollow sound? Do you realize that every hour you delay means further unimpeded attacks of the German air force on Polish civilian populations and death to thousands of Polish men, women and children?"

"Do you then want the women and children of Paris to be massacred?" Bonnet answered.

The summer heat broke with a ferocious and almost terrifying thunderstorm over London, almost Wagnerian, signaling the death of many things, thought Lady Diana Manners Cooper. Lord Halifax had walked that day with Lady Halifax and Sir Alexander Cadogan through the Buckingham Palace Gardens. The purple autumn crocuses were in bloom. The king had given him a key to the gates. Then Halifax had gone as spokesman to the House of Lords to tell his fellow peers of the government's position on arranging matters with France. His speech appeared to go down well, and he returned to his Eaton Square town residence to bathe and change into a dinner jacket. It was his wife's birthday and they were dining out.

The telephone rang. It was Chamberlain asking him to come to 10 Downing Street immediately. Halifax asked Geoffrey Dawson, editor of *The Times*, to take Lady Halifax to dinner. They went to the Savoy Hotel and he to the prime minister to find him in a state no one had ever seen before, entirely shattered, his nerves given out along with his policy of reason and understanding and goodwill, lost in the roar of the Stukas and Panzers and the scream of the bombs and machine guns in Poland far away.

A call reached Sir Alexander Cadogan as he was midway through his meal at home—he must come "at once, at once." He arose from the table and hurried to Chamberlain to find him with Halifax and Mrs. Chamberlain and Sir Horace Wilson. They gave him something to eat and then went to meet with a group of Conservatives who had arrived saying they would not leave until they told the prime minister that he must give the Germans an ultimatum, that England, and their civilization, could not survive otherwise. Chamberlain knew it.

With Cadogan and Halifax he talked on the phone with the French ambassador to England, Corbon, and with Premier Daladier and Foreign Minister Bonnet. While the conversations went on, the group waiting to speak to him seemed to Minister of Agriculture Sir Reginald Dorman-Smith to turn scruffy and slovenly in the humid heat and strangely more true than before to their individual ancestries—he himself, Dorman-Smith thought, more Irish, Secretary of State for War Leslie Hore-Belisha more Jewish. The prime minister called them in, Cadogan and Halifax in evening dress standing by, and they had at him with their views.

"Right, gentlemen," he said. Henderson in Berlin called the German Foreign Office to ask for a meeting with Ribbentrop at nine the next morning, September 3, Sunday.

"Really, you could receive the ambassador in my place," Ribbentrop told the German Foreign Office interpreter Paul Schmidt. "Just ask the English whether that will suit them, and say that the Foreign Minister is not available at nine o'clock." The message was given to the British and Schmidt went home for a few hours' sleep. It was four in the morning Berlin time.

In Washington President Roosevelt was holding a stag dinner after cocktails in the Oval Room. Poker would follow, dollar limit. That their leader played cards for money was sedulously concealed from the American public, but word had leaked out earlier in the year and the columnist Arthur Krock had let it be known that a display of bad temper by the President in March was due to poker games that saw him losing as much as $75,000 at a sitting. The men sat down to play. Secretary of the Interior Ickes told a joke about Senator Borah, and Roosevelt threw back his head and laughed. From time to time dispatches came in for the President, which he read at the table. The men played mostly seven-card stud with fives and tens wild, the President being the heaviest loser as he dropped around $35. Ickes won $53.50, he told his diary. At around eleven a dispatch came from London and the President read it and told the table, "War will be declared by noon tomorrow." The poker players got up at half-past midnight. At four in the morning the President took a call from Ambassador Kennedy in London, to whom Chamberlain had shown the speech he would be giving in two hours. "It's the end of the world, the end of everything!" Kennedy cried. The Dark Ages were returning, he told Roosevelt.

Bombs poured down upon burning Warsaw, and soon Rulka Langer got herself on a train fleeing the city. A German pilot saw the movement below him and came roaring down. The thunder of his engines shook the wooden carriages, and Mrs. Langer found herself on her knees crying, "We fly to your patronage, O holy Mother of God . . ." The explosions made her think her heart was about to burst. "Despise Thou not our petitions in our necessities." Her hands were shaking. "O kind, O sweet, O holy Virgin Mary . . ." Passengers were weeping all around her. "Have mercy upon us!"

Lord Halifax awakened in London knowing Henderson was about to meet with Paul Schmidt, and remembered a dream he once had. In it he was being tried for murder. Toward the end of the dream the jury brought in a verdict of guilty, and he was surprised at what a feeling of relief came over him. He had the same feeling now. If the struggle for peace was over, then it was over. Halifax felt himself somehow freshened for the new struggle that would replace the lost and finished one. He had dined the previous night, the night of his wife's birthday, at 10 Downing Street with Ivone Kirkpatrick, who became acting chief of the Central Department in the Foreign Office when William Strang had gone to Moscow for the negotiations with Molotov and then Voroshilov. The two men drank beer and laughed and joked. When Kirkpatrick mentioned that Joseph Goebbels had issued a proclamation forbidding Germans to listen to any foreign broadcasts, Halifax said Goebbels ought to pay people—or at least pay *him*—to listen to the stuff put out over the German radio.

Paul Schmidt awoke in Berlin and realized that he had overslept. He flung on his clothes and rushed off for the Foreign Office, jumping out of his cab and running into a side entrance when he saw Sir Nevile Henderson getting out of his car and going in the main door. Henderson came in. The men shook hands. Schmidt invited Henderson to be seated, but the ambassador declined and stood in the center of the room. Schmidt also remained on his feet.

"I regret that on the instructions of my government I have to hand you an ultimatum for the German government.

" 'More than twenty-four hours have elapsed since an immediate reply was requested to the warning of September 1, and since then the attacks on Poland have been intensified. If His Majesty's government have not received satisfactory assurances of the cessation of all aggressive actions against Poland, and the withdrawal of German troops from that country by eleven o'clock, British Summer Time, from that time a state of war will exist between Great Britain and Germany.' "

When he had finished reading out the statement, he handed

it to Schmidt. He said he was very sorry. Good-bye. Schmidt repeated the ambassador's sentiments and offered his own farewell. With the ultimatum Schmidt made for Hitler's New
Chancellory office. People crowded the room outside the office,
and he had trouble getting through. Hitler was sitting at his desk.
Ribbentrop stood by the window. Both looked at him. Standing
some distance from the desk, Schmidt read out the ultimatum.
When he ended, there was not a sound from his listeners. "Hitler sat immobile, gazing before him." He had not expected this
response. It was simply not part of his thinking. They had accepted German rearmament in the face of the Versailles Treaty
restrictions, an army and air force, they had accepted his reoccupation of the Rhineland, his taking of Austria, the Sudetenland, the rest of Czechoslovakia. "He sat completely silent and
unmoving."

He never had a childhood, he often had said, the aged and
crotchety father drinking too much and sometimes slapping him.
"Miserable urchin!" one of the old man's cronies remembered
him yelling at little Adi, years before in Linz on the Danube.
There followed the impoverished cold and hungry and lonely
years in Vienna and Munich after his mother's death and after
he left August Kubizek. Then the War and then the years of
struggle and finally Hindenburg making him Chancellor of the
Reich, and then the years of glory, Wagner mixing with Clausewitz, millions to adulate him and never a failure and never a
misstep, his intuition leading him on, he often said, like a sleep-
walker who never makes a false step. He always played for all or
nothing, he had told Hermann Goering.

"After an interval which seemed an age," Schmidt remembered, "he turned to Ribbentrop, who had remained standing by
the window.

" 'What now?' "

Schmidt went out to the anteroom. "In two hours," he said
to the people gathered there, "a state of war will exist between
England and Germany." Again there was complete silence.
Goebbels stood in a corner, downcast and self-absorbed.

"If we lose this war," Goering finally said, "then God have
mercy on us!"

It was glorious in England that morning, a wondrous day at
the beginning of an English September. The writer Vera Brittain's garden near Southampton was a royal glory of gold and

purple, jeweled, she thought, with the beauty of the butterflies. She sat with her children waiting to listen to the prime minister's radio address to the nation, due at eleven, when the ultimatum ran out. Immediately afterward he would leave Downing Street to address Parliament at noon.

The long-ago August of 1914 came into her mind when in a golden and cloudless summer of a sudden the curtain fell forever upon the world people had known. She had been at university then. There was a boy, Roland. They were together on his leaves. He had written he would soon be back for another. They had kissed each other, twice.

The day he was expected back there was instead a call from his young sister. Roland was gone. His things were sent on to his family, including the uniform in which he had died, horribly soaked with his blood. His father told the sister, hardly more than a child, to run into the garden and bury it. Roland's mother must not see. The girl dug a hole and put the uniform in, and from that moment on and for decades into the future could not see a soldier in military dress without feeling that she would begin to tremble.

Vera Brittain had a brother, Robert. He was a talented musician. He found his death with the British regiments sent to shore up the faltering Italians against a German-Austrian drive south against, she found when she visited it, a high and lonely mountain peak, where under the Cross of Sacrifice her brother and the others lay.

She put Roland behind her, and in 1925 married another man, Roland's people coming to the wedding, and he became in memory only her dream lover, gone while now she had a husband who had given her children. For Robert she never ceased to weep, never hearing music or going to a concert without imagining him beside her saying what he thought of the performance.

Chamberlain began to speak, his voice from her radio old, harsh, arrogant, but trembling. "You can imagine what a bitter blow it is to me that all my long struggle to win peace has failed. Yet I cannot believe there is anything more, or anything different, that I could have done."

Vera Brittain's little daughter Hilary looked out the window and saw a pony and the pony's dam. "Sweet foal!" the child cried and ran to look. She turned back to her mother listening to Neville Chamberlain on the radio. "Poor Mummy!" the child cried. She flung her warm, dimpled arms around her mother's neck. "Don't cry, Mummy! It'll be all right in the end, really it will!"

Before the prime minister ended his short talk Robert Dunbar, head of the Treaty Department of the British Foreign Office, walked from his office across Horse Guards Parade and to the Mall and then up the Duke of York steps and to Carleton House Terrace and into the German Embassy. Chargé d'affaires Eric Kordt was waiting. Dunbar handed him a piece of paper. "There it is, you know what it is," he said.

"Yes, I do."

At 9:00 A.M. His Majesty's ambassador in Berlin acting upon my instructions informed the German government that unless not later than 11:00 A.M. British Summer Time today, September 3, satisfactory assurance . . .

No such assurances having been received I have the honor to inform you that a state of war exists as from 11:00 A.M. today, September 3. HALIFAX.

The two men briefly discussed the safe passage home of members of the German diplomatic staff in London. "Good-bye," Dunbar said. He reminded himself not to add, "Good luck."

"Good-bye," Kordt said.

Air-raid alarms began to sound over London and over all of England, a high rising-and-falling wail. Neither Kordt nor Dunbar made any comment. The warbling cry of the screaming sirens reached Winston Churchill as he finished dressing to go to Parliament for the prime minister's speech at noon. He had interrupted himself to listen to the radio address. His collar was half buttoned on. He turned to his friend Brendan Bracken and said, "You know, Brendan, you've got to hand it to Hitler. The war's been on only a few minutes and here's an air raid already."

Mrs. Churchill came into the room and echoed him with a remark about German promptitude. Churchill went to look up at the sky, and his wife said they must go now to the air-raid shelter. He said he would not. She said he must set an example, and so he took a bottle of brandy and headed for the basement shelter, gazing at the street to see in imagination ruin and carnage, and vast explosions shaking the ground, buildings going down in dust and rubble, fire brigades and ambulances scurrying through the smoke beneath the drone of the enemy's planes.

Members of Parliament Sir Harold Nicolson, Leo Amery, Derek Gunston, Anthony Eden and Alfred Duff Cooper had been at Ronald Tree's home in Queen Anne's Gate listening to Chamberlain's broadcast, and were walking toward Parliament Square when the sirens came on. "They ought not to do that after what we have heard on the wireless," Amery said. "People will think it's an air-raid warning."

"My God," Nicolson said, "it *is* an air-raid warning."

"We had better make for the House," Eden said. "We still have time." They went on. "We're walking pretty fast, aren't we?" Gunston said.

A car driven by Sir Edward Spears stopped for them and they all piled in, Nicolson sitting on Amery's knees and Eden on his, and got to their destination to see that the crowd gathered outside Parliament had broken and was flying, Nicolson thought, like a flock of pigeons, running for shelters across the grass yard and up and down the surrounding streets.

All over England hands trembled and stomachs churned while lips moved in prayer. Some ran for shelter, others walked. One woman watched a neighbor ignore the screaming sirens to polish his car. "Rub, rub, rub," she thought to herself. "Now round the front again, unfasten the doors and rub their insides. Now the windows. Why doesn't someone yell at him that the whole world is going mad again? How can he just go along rubbing and rubbing a car which he may never use again?"

An army captain home from camp having a late breakfast said to his cat, "This is it," and continued eating until a frantic pounding on the door brought in a woman so upset she could hardly speak coherently enough to ask to use his telephone. She managed to explain that her children were at an aunt's house and she wanted to tell them to stay there until the raid was over. Her fingers trembled so that she could not dial, so he put through the call.

She turned to him when she finished. "And you," she said suddenly. "How can you sit there calmly eating eggs and bacon at a time like this?"

"Madam, what am I supposed to do? Do you expect me to rush out and repel German bombers with a knife and fork?"

Ten minutes later the all-clear sounded. Either someone had mistakenly turned on the central alarm that set off all the sirens, or the plane of the French assistant air attaché coming over the

Channel had been taken for the advance guard of a German air fleet. The people of England came from their air shelters, the members of Parliament to gather on the House's terrace in the sunshine and look at the barrage balloons before going in for Chamberlain's speech.

United States ambassador to France William Bullitt had picked up the prime minister's radio speech in the Paris Embassy. He listened in company with the junior diplomat Robert Murphy and the French newspaperwoman Genevieve Tabouis, "Cassandra" in her column, as much symbol as chronicler of the Republic of the 1930s, suspected secret agent, financial manipulator, arranger. The three remained entirely silent when Chamberlain stopped speaking. There was a drum roll and then "God Save the King" came from the radio. It was the end of France, Mlle. Tabouis said. Bullitt asked his subordinate to see her home.

Murphy drove her through a Paris strangely open and echoing, the streets empty now that so many had fled. Off to the east the colossal underground forts of the Maginot Line were filling up with men. During the early morning hours Order X had been put into effect, the evacuation on three hours' notice of all villages in front of or on top of the line. The people left and the Nied River floodgates were bashed down so that waters would cover fields that otherwise might offer passageways for German tanks. Church bells tolled as the country folk departed, using an itinerary planned in advance so that they would not clog roads reserved for troops coming up. None of the people protested, for the reason for the evacuation was clear: *They* were coming with *their* tanks.

Murphy halted his car before Mlle. Tabouis's home. All of France, it seemed to him, exuded the deepest gloom, from the highest official to the youngest messenger boy. He had seen how glumly the reservists went to the trains, many half-drunk and all sloppily turned out. There were no flags, no cheering, no bands.

"Tomorrow all this will be gone!" Mlle. Tabouis, Cassandra, said to him as they stood in her Boulevard Malesherbes of picturesque old buildings. "Our lovely Paris will exist no longer!"

She flung out her arms in despair as if, Murphy thought, already she stood among ruins. Her country's ambassador to Berlin was practically at that moment presenting a French ultimatum to Germany. It had taken a multitude of phone calls back and forth between London and Paris to decide when it would be presented and what time period it would call for, and the suspicion had arisen in more than a few places in England that the French would never hand in an ultimatum at all, but hope for an early conquest of Poland by the Germans so that Paris could regretfully declare that the matter was settled and there was no point in fighting.

"*My* country is at war *now* in fulfilment of *our* pledge to Poland," the member of Parliament Hugh Dalton said to Ambassador to England Corbin directly Chamberlain's radio address finished. Corbin threw his head back as if Dalton had struck him in the face.

Earlier Churchill had called and, in Brendan Bracken's words, talked to Corbin "as though he were an old washerwoman." If France ratted on the Poles, Churchill said, he who had always been a friend would be utterly indifferent to her fate. Corbin said there were technical difficulties involved in getting out an ultimatum and Churchill cried, "Technical difficulties be damned! I suppose you would call it a technical difficulty for a Pole if a German bomb fell on his head."

The problem the French faced was that they were afraid to give the Germans a war declaration before their advancing troops were all safely in the forts of the Maginot Line. It would be frightful to expose strung-out marching units to immediate air bombardment, argued the head of the army, General Maurice Gamelin, and so the ultimatum must have a time limit running out no earlier than four o'clock of the following morning, September 4. Gamelin's march orders called for complete investment of the forts by that hour.

Scientific-minded, elderly, more like a scholar than a soldier, armed with his charts and schedules, General Gamelin seemed irrefutable. But to wait that long, said Premier Daladier, meant to endanger the very life of France. For honor now commanded. The ultimatum would go through with a deadline for five that afternoon. It was the best he could do for him, Daladier told General Gamelin. A call was put through to Ambassador Coulondre in Berlin by the French Foreign Office official Alexis Leger. Coulondre asked if he should request an answer to the French Note of September 1 before handing over the ultimatum. Leger said he should. But what should he do, Coulondre asked, if the reply to the earlier Note was not entirely negative? Should he then give the ultimatum?

Leger said anything other than full compliance with France's September 1 request, that Germany cease operations at once against Poland and withdraw her troops, should be treated as a negative reply calling for delivery of the ultimatum. Foreign Minister Bonnet came on the line and confirmed what Leger had said. For such an act, Coulondre said, he must have confirmation by men with whose voices he was entirely familiar. Two officials well known to him repeated the instructions. Coulondre left for the Wilhelmstrasse. It was a little after half-past eleven.

Chamberlain came out of 10 Downing Street and got into his car for the short ride to Parliament. The last sounds of the all-clear had died away. His chauffeur stood waiting by the car. How drawn and tired the prime minister looked, Reginald Parker thought to himself. Normally Chamberlain politely greeted his driver, but as he came to the car only an unintelligible mumble came from his lips. Parker headed for the House of Commons.

A telephone rang in the Foreign Office. It was a German Embassy official, asking for Lord Halifax. But he was not available, the operator said. Was there someone else who could help? Perhaps some hope sprang up in her heart. It was the embassy's old black dog, the caller explained. For years he had been something of a London landmark, spending his days on the steps watching the world go by. It would be a difficult sea voyage for him back to Germany. Could Lord Halifax arrange a good home? Germany and England were at war, if only for moments, the operator thought. But at least something was left of normal human relationships and at least one kindly thought. She said she would get word to the foreign secretary. When she did, he arranged for the old dog's care.

As prayers began in Parliament, Coulondre was shown into the German foreign minister's office. Ribbentrop was not there, Baron von Weizsaecker, perhaps not yet informed of the death of his son, told the Frenchman. Coulondre asked if he himself was empowered to give a satisfactory reply to the French Note of September 1. Weizsaecker replied he was in no position to give a reply of any kind. Coulondre made as if to hand over the ultimatum but Weizsaecker refused to accept it, saying Ribbentrop would be there soon. They waited half an hour. Ribbentrop came in. Everything was England's fault, he said. Mussolini wanted peace and Germany also, and— "Do these remarks of His Excellency," interrupted Coulondre, "mean that Germany's answer to the French Note of 1 September is negative?" Ribbentrop replied that was the case. Coulondre handed him the ultimatum.

"If France attacks Germany she will be the aggressor," Ribbentrop said.

"History will be the judge of that," Coulondre said. He shook hands with State Secretary Weizsaecker and offered Foreign Minister Ribbentrop a slight bow.

"Everything that I have worked for, everything that I have hoped for, everything that I have believed during my public life, has crashed into ruins," Chamberlain said. The word "Poland" was not used once in his speech to Parliament. When he had finished, several members made brief supporting remarks and the session ended. It had taken thirty-four minutes. The members went out into the streets empty since Friday morning of children.

The radio reporter Edward R. Murrow told his audience in America that he did not know how to describe a city in which there were no youngsters shouting on their way home from school and none playing in the parks. He did not have, he said, the eloquence to describe the meaning of a London with no children. Churchill went to his apartment to take luncheon with his daughters, Sarah and Diana, and their husbands and his son, Randolph. At the end of the meal they opened a bottle of champagne. Churchill stood up and raised his glass and proposed a toast: victory. They signed their names on a sheet of paper dated September 3, 1939. In response to numerous calls, London's veterinarians opened their offices for people coming in to have their dogs put to sleep. "Outside the vets' surgeries the slain lay in heaps."

It was warm and sunny in Berlin, a hot and still afternoon. People gathered in cafés, and the parks were filled with babies in carriages and dogs on leashes. On the national radio network the Hamburg station orchestra was performing Liszt's First Hungarian Rhapsody when the music faded and a man's voice said: "The British government, in a Note to the Reich government, has made the demand . . ." and Germany learned it was at war. Newspaper specials, distributed free, appeared on the streets. People passing the British Embassy looked silently at the big canary-yellow stone building and the lion and unicorn.

In 1914, reflected Ambassador Henderson, they had come throwing rocks, breaking windows, howling abuse. He walked down an Unter den Linden that seemed to him filled with people all apathetic or gloomy and depressed, and went to a druggist's shop and asked for some codeine. The druggist said he could not dispense it without a doctor's prescription.

"I am the British ambassador," Henderson said. "If you poison me with your drug, you will get a high decoration from Dr. Goebbels."

It was a feeble joke, Henderson admitted to himself. But the druggist seemed to light up, and gave Henderson what he wished. How pathetic it all was, everything, Henderson thought. The waters had come over the bridge.

Unity Mitford had for days been sitting listening to the radio on the balcony of her new Munich apartment, where in her bedroom swastikas were draped down and Hitler's colored portrait rested on the table. She went out to eat at the Osteria Bavaria, where she had first met the Leader, and back to the balcony to listen to the bulletins and then the announcement. She spoke with a friend on the telephone and then took the phone off the hook while she wrote some letters. The receiver was still off the hook when in the slanted, lengthening afternoon shadows she went to Munich's Englischer Garten, the English Garden. There seated on a bench she took the 6.35 Walther pistol Hitler had given her when she told him about the hate mail she received from home, from England, pressed it to her right temple and pulled the trigger. Insensible, she lay by her bench until someone found her and called an ambulance. Unconscious and carrying no papers, she was not identified for some hours. Hitler's eyes filled when he was told. "You see, she was nothing but an idealist," he said.

Word of the British war declaration reached the retired British major general Adrian Carton de Wiart, who had been living in Poland, as he lunched in Lublin with a thirty-man military group that had just arrived from Alexandria via Romania with false passports depicting them as an "agricultural mission." At the news they changed into uniform and a cheering crowd, certain they were the vanguard of a giant British army, attended them as they boarded a bus for Warsaw. People hugged and kissed them as they got onto the bus quickly covered with flowers, but their hearts sank, for they knew they were all Britain would send. No one else in Poland knew it.

The telephone rang in the apartment of the Cheshire woman

and when her husband answered, a voice neither of them was ever to hear again said, "Is your wife there? Tell her it's all right. England is in." She had been earlier at a little chapel near her home, where she watched Poles weep and pray. "Lord," they sang, "what of Poland? So many years now, and so long!"

It came to her that like Jesus Christ Poland was being crucified for the world. She went with her husband and it seemed the whole of Warsaw to the British Embassy. Flowers were passed over heads to the struggling policemen holding back the people, to be put on a rising mound, a beautiful bank, before the railings.

"Long live England and Poland!" she heard people shouting. "We'll soon be in Berlin now!"

The *Daily Mail's* Cedric Salter estimated the crowd before the Embassy to number one hundred thousand people, all madly screaming for England. Ambassador Sir Howard Kennard had to come out on the balcony and wave in a self-deprecatory fashion. It seemed to Salter that this example of traditional well-bred modesty was exactly to the crowd's liking. They had become acquainted with it through the cinema. Men and women ran to kiss the hands of English men and women looking on. In Salter's eyes the ambassador appeared shamefaced and embarrassed by the noise and attention, as if he had been caught incorrectly wearing a white tie with a dinner jacket.

Foreign Minister Beck came and for ten minutes could not get through the wild crowd. So he and Kennard saluted each other across the sea of upturned faces. People were screaming, "God save England!" which came out as "Gott-safe-England!" One old man appeared to remember hearing something similar and with tears of joy running from his eyes grabbed Salter's hand and cried over and over, *"Gott straf England! Gott straf England!"**

The German planes were raining bombs on Poland. What was left of the shattered Polish army fled the rampaging German tank columns through oceans of dust. The attack plan worked out to the last detail by Chief of Staff Franz Halder, who hated Hitler and had thought of killing him, was working brilliantly. The Warsaw crowd in its masses went from the British to the French Embassy to sing there the "Marseillaise." Wolves were reaching for Poland's throat, thought the Cheshire woman as she watched the green lawns in which the French Embassy was set fill up with happy people, and out on the roads leading toward

*The German rallying cry of the Great War—"God punish England."

Germany the wells went dry and became mudholes; but the people told one another that France's great army would come to save them—hardly that General Gamelin would creep forward, take three of four unimportant border towns, abandon them, return to the Maginot Line and do no more.

From the French Embassy the Cheshire woman and her husband went to Simon i Stecki, a restaurant. The head waiter put next to her plate a little silk Union Jack on a silver stand. "For once," she told her husband, "I am going to enjoy the moment. After this, for long enough, we have only parting and sorrow to expect. I am going to make this last for another half hour."

Outside sirens screamed almost as if they were in her ears. The radio blared, "Alarm! Alarm! *Uwaga! Uwaga!*" She remembered it always, "Zone such-and-such . . . Zone another-and-another . . . Zone . . . Zone." The observation points strung out from the capital were reporting one by one German planes coming over them. The couple ate their luncheon. "Zone . . . Zone . . . *WARSZAWA! UWAGA! UWAGA! UWAGA! WARSZAWA! WARSZAWA!*" She heard what antiaircraft still existed starting to fire. They dropped Their bombs. The restaurant building near the Vistula trembled slightly.

In Winston Churchill's apartment the telephone rang. "I'll take it in the bedroom," Churchill said. His sons-in-law, Victor Oliver and Duncan Sandys, would soon be leaving to join their regiments. The door of the bedroom opened. Churchill came out. The fingers of both of his hands were spread on his chest. There were tears in his eyes.

"Tell me," Mrs. Churchill said.

"They have given me a job again. I am first lord of the Admiralty," he said.

In two or three hours' time he would walk into the rooms he had quit in such pain and sorrow in 1915 after the Gallipoli landing in Turkey had failed with unimaginable loss. It had been intended to force the Dardanelles and join the armies of the West with those of Imperial Russia, take the enemy in the rear and so end the stalemate of the Western Front of what had for so long been called the War and had now become the First War.

Churchill found at the Admiralty the same charts and the same octagonal table he had used so many years before. There before twilight came he was told that the first British casualties were recorded. WINSTON IS BACK, the Admiralty had cabled to all the Royal Navy ship and shore stations around the Empire and the world; but soon there came back the news that the liner *Athenia* en route to Canada from Glasgow had been sunk some two hundred miles northwest of the Irish coast. Oberleutnant Fritz Julius Lemp had been in the conning tower of his U-30 submarine when he saw the ship and took her for an armed merchant cruiser. He dived and fired four torpedos. He missed with two. The third misfired. The fourth took the ship in its Number Five hold against the engine room bulkhead. One hundred and twelve died, including sixty-nine women and sixteen children. The people sang "Roll Out the Barrel" as the ship went down, survivors said.

"I can't bear to think of those who lost their lives," Chamberlain wrote to the Archbishop of Canterbury that night. The day was coming when there would be losses that would make him place his forehead on the Cabinet table and keep it there, entirely silent, while the others waited, for ten minutes straight.

As twilight came on, King George spoke over the radio to his subjects. As Duke of York he had for years written in a diary each night. Then he had dropped making entries. He began writing again that day, remembering back to the first day of the other war, when he was an eighteen-year-old midshipman keeping the middle watch on the bridge of the *Collingwood* somewhere in the North Sea. His shipmates had been pleased, he wrote, that a war was upon them. "We were not prepared for what we found a modern war really was, & those of us who had been through the Great War never wanted another. Today we are at war again, & I am no longer a midshipman in the Royal Navy."

"In this grave hour," he said, sitting before a microphone on a Buckingham Palace table, his wife and daughters listening in another room, "perhaps the most fateful of our history, I send to every household of my peoples, both at home and overseas, this message, spoken with the same depth of feeling for each one of you as if I were able to cross your threshold and speak to you myself. For the second time in the lives of most of us we are at war."

He wore the uniform of an admiral of the fleet. His mother, the widowed Queen Mary, at Sandringham, had indicated she was coming to London, but he had told her he did not wish her in the zone of danger and asked her to go to Badminton in the West Country, where there was little possibility of German air attack. She was packing to go by auto the next day, with a stop for luncheon at Althorp with Lord and Lady Spencer.* She would live to attend her son's funeral, standing heavily veiled with the two other queens of her family: her daughter-in-law and her granddaughter.

"For the sake of all that we ourselves hold dear, and of the world's order and peace," King George said, "it is unthinkable that we should refuse to meet the challenge. We can only do the right as we see the right, and reverently commit our cause to God.

"May He bless us and keep us all."

Darkness came. Dressed in army field-gray and boots and with a gas mask and steel helmet slung over his shoulder and a re- volver at his belt, Adolf Hitler went in a cavalcade of five big Mercedes cars with armor plating and bulletproof windows to the Anhalt Station, where his special train, code-named *Amerika,* waited. Told that the Leader was coming, Erwin Rommel at Bad Polzin had his troops put on brassards reading "Führer's HQ," set up a security cordon and emplaced antiaircraft guns.

"Isn't it wonderful that we have such a man?" Rommel's wife had written him the day before. She had discussed the interna- tional situation with all her friends and the shopkeepers, and all agreed the Leader had done the proper thing in every regard. She had told everybody that he might soon be going to her hus- band on the Polish border. "All of them beg me to ask you to plead with him not to expose himself to unnecessary dangers. Our nation cannot possibly afford to lose him. One shudders at the very thought!"

Behind *Amerika* came two other specials: the Army General Headquarters, for soldiers, and *Heinrich,* for Himmler of the SS and the civilian officials. The last was formed of all kinds of spec- imens of the German rail system, Grand Ducal saloons and mod- ern signal coaches mixed with old wooden rattlers, one of whose Foreign Office occupants said that Charlemagne had traveled in it eleven hundred years earlier. The restaurant-car electric sys- tem was so weak that the men dined by candles stuck in bottles, some complaining it was as if they lived in the slums, while oth- ers said the situation was that of an elegant candle-lit dining room.

*Whose granddaughter would one day be in line to hold that position once held by Queen Mary.

Hitler would have perhaps left earlier for the Front but he had a social event to attend that day, attendance at which had made Ribbentrop half an hour late for his appointment with Ambassador Coulondre to receive the French ultimatum. It was a reception for the new Soviet ambassador to Berlin, Alexander Shkvarzev. After the affair and after seeing Coulondre, Ribbentrop cabled to the new ambassador's chief, Foreign Minister Molotov, that perhaps the time had come for the Russians to move their armies into one of the zones of influence given them by the secret protocol of the pact signed in Moscow. The two invading armies could then meet at the midway point on the body of dead Poland. Ten days had passed since Ribbentrop's agreement in the Kremlin with Russia's Vozhd, the Gensek; thirteen days since, the long half-twilight of the North's summer solstice coming on, Comrade Molotov (Mr. Molotov to the Westerners) had gone into the Gensek's office and emerged to give the German ambassador to Russia a letter signed by the Gensek and addressed to the chancellor of the German Reich, Mr. A. Hitler.

•

The photographer Cecil Beaton, who had taken his pictures of the queen in Buckingham Palace as the Guards officers shouted orders outside, and then gone to stay with Gertrude Stein, was back in England. His family had given up their flat and so he went to stay with a friend in Belgravia. As a young man the friend had lived in the same Dresden pension as Nevile Henderson when both studied German, and had taught the future ambassador the appreciation of Wagner's music. Gerald Tyrwhitt then, Lord Berners-to-be, he was a musician, painter and writer, rich, brilliant, a kind of eccentric eighteenth-century type English peer put to living in late August and early September of 1939 and reacting by coming to the conclusion that along with the world he was going insane. "Overnight Gerald grew old."

Cecil Beaton was about to step into one of his host's olive-green bathtubs on Sunday the third when the deaf old butler came and shouted, "The war's started." Beaton felt as if an electric current had run through him. Just before that moment he had visited his old home in suburban Hampstead. His dentist from childhood days still had an office out there. Everything seemed romantic and beautiful at the end of summer, and the appointment with the dentist did not take long, and so he went to where he had been brought up. Wistfully he noted how fine the flowers looked. The oak trees were flourishing.

Yet like every place from childhood, he reflected, everything seemed Lilliputian. Even the width of the sidewalk pavements seemed diminished. The trip to school had seemed when he lived in the house to be a long trek and an adventure. Now he saw it for what it was, a walk of but a few hundred yards. No one was living in his old house. Since he and his people departed, two other families had come and gone and a sign read PROPERTY FOR SALE. He rang the bell of the empty house and looked through the window at the parquet floor his family laid down so proudly. There were letters and circulars on it, popped through the slot by the postman. Beaton walked around back into the garden thinking that if a policeman appeared he would simply explain, "I've come back to see where I once lived."

He stood in the garden. Weeds were everywhere but he recognized the traces of happy days. "What a vast expanse this lawn once seemed, where Reggie practiced cricket in his cage of netting, where we had learned to putt." Here his sisters wheeled their doll carriages, here he took his first snapshots.

He picked a few roses from plants his mother had put in long ago, and drove away to present them to her. "A wild look came into her pale blue eyes." She seemed to recall the plants and the happy days. "And now the war." She grabbed for the blooms. "She became like an animal. She snatched the roses from my hands, crying in anguish, 'They're mine! They're mine!' and hurried to place the wilting remnants of a lifetime in a vase."

L'Envoi

In the first pages of his six-volume memoir of the events of 1939–45 Winston Churchill tells us that once Franklin Roosevelt asked him for a definition of those events.

"I said at once, 'The Unnecessary War,'" Churchill relates.

His viewpoint is at variance with that held by others. As early as 1933 Laurence Stallings, co-author of *What Price Glory,* co-authored a book titled with horrifying prophecy *The First World War.* Sir Nevile Henderson went to his grave saying the war of 1939 was like a Greek tragedy, predestined and unavoidable. Neville Chamberlain said everything that could prevent a war had been done, that he could not think of anything more that might have been done.

History has not completely decided between the two views, but leans toward favoring Churchill's analysis. Certainly Chamberlain's policy of appeasement will never find a defender in the person of any public official of the West. American actions in Korea and Vietnam and elsewhere all have their genesis in the events that followed the Munich Agreement of 1938. The very word "Munich" has become an instantly recognized definition.

It was remarkable how quickly the world of before-the-war vanished as soon as the first shots sounded. The concept that government cabinets and army leaderships should be composed of "vons" and second sons of lords, the hold of religion, the belief that a few nations clustered around the Mediterranean basin should be the rulers of the world, the concept that Communism was the coming salvation—these and a multitude of other convictions disappeared as quickly as did the rule that evening wear must be worn in the West End of London's nightclubs. The reader can fill in as replacing concepts whatever interests him or her— women's liberation, high technology, suffocating conformity, newly fascinating religious views, an emphasis on physical and mental health. All that is the modern world can be seen as resulting from what happened in the fields of western Poland, stubbly from the harvest, on September 1, 1939.

As quickly as that other world vanished, so also did those whose actions caused its disappearance. Hardly more than a year passed before Chamberlain and Henderson were dead. Within ten months, when France fell, all of that country's leadership was in the discard along with the British commanders Lord Gort and General Ironside, who spent the rest of the war haunting White-hall in search of a means to make amends for their eviction from the Continent. The end of the war found Hitler and Roosevelt dead and Churchill about to be relieved of his prime minister-ship. Only one man was where he had been at the beginning: Stalin.

On September 17, 1939, precisely two weeks after France and Britain went to war, Stalin's Red Army entered Poland, invited to do so by the Germans. For a year and a half the Russians stayed there, interning almost the whole of Poland's leadership class, eight thousand officers and a similar number of professors, engineers, politicians, noblemen. Apart from some four hundred men, none of the internees were ever seen again.

It came as a great shock to Stalin when the Germans turned against him in June 1941, for although he did not trust his clos-est collaborators, he had trusted Adolf Hitler. The shock of the German invasion of Russia immobilized him and for several weeks he seemed in a daze. Then he returned to himself and in time, after long retreat followed by long advance, his armies pushed to the suburbs of Warsaw. They halted there as the city's inhab-itants, encouraged by the Russians, rose in rebellion against the German occupiers. The Red Army remained in place as the Ger-mans slew the leading elements of the resistance, men and women who might have asserted Polish independence against Soviet rule. Then the Russians moved in and took Warsaw. They went on and took Berlin.

By then five million Polish civilians had perished. They joined in death some thirteen million civilians of other countries, and some seventeen million soldiers, sailors and airmen. (The figure was not far off from the figure of thirty million that Ambassador Bullitt had mentioned to President Roosevelt as the likely price of a second world war.) Stalin and the Red Army were supreme in Eastern Europe. Hitler had proved to be the most unsuccessful anti-Communist in history.

His great conquests did not change Stalin. He was the same as he had always been, quiet and mild as he conducted a new series of purges. At the end he was saying that Marshal Voroshilov and Foreign Minister Molotov were spies for the West. He died in 1953.

By then almost the last of those who dominated the headlines of 1939 were gone. The Polish leaders, Beck and the others, had within a few days of the first onslaught fled into Romania, where they lived as uneasy internees, half-prisoners and half-exiles, before dying as broken men. Unity Mitford never recovered from the bullet she fired into her head on the day Britain went to war against Hitler. After personally making himself responsible for her hospital expenses, the Leader arranged for her to be sent to neutral Switzerland, from where her parents took her home. An invalid, she lived for a few confused years and then died.

Joachim von Ribbentrop's performance at the Nuremberg war crimes trials astonished the world. Of all the defendants he seemed the most stupid and deluded. Almost gibbering, illogical, ignorant, he seemed an impossible person to have been foreign minister of a great power. Those who had known him before the war could hardly recognize him for the arrogant dandy he had then been. At the last minute, just before he was hanged for helping to bring the war, Ribbentrop returned to himself somewhat. He died with some dignity.

Hermann Goering told his intimates at Nuremberg that he was tempted to stand up to the victors of the war and their court and their trial and say: Kiss my ass. He came close to doing so. He declared over and over that he had never wanted the war. Condemned to hang, he took poison.

"The lamps are going out all over Europe. We shall not see them lit again in our lifetime," said British Foreign Secretary Sir Edward Grey when war came in 1914.

"Nothing will ever be the same again," Lady Diana Manners Cooper told her son when war came in 1939.

He had been right, and twenty-five years later she was right, too. In blood and pain there began that day the birth of the world we inherited.

Notes

(The numbers in the left-hand column refer to pages in this book; for references, see Bibliography beginning on p. 301.)

1. Stepped into the office of the general secretary: Deutscher, pp. 436–37.
1. Sun of Our Lives: Lyons, p. 185.
1. Drew up the chairs himself: I. D. Levine, p. 327.
1. "When Stalin says dance": Khrushchev, p. 301.
2. Inclined to agree with this comrade: I. D. Levine, p. 337.
4. Would appoint someone else to be the official widow: Khrushchev, p. 46.
5. Called home and shot: Medvedev, p. 193f.
5. "Then it would be your turn": Khrushchev, p. 307.
6. "Listen, give me someone for one night": Ibid., p. 104.
6. Existed in one room: Alliluyeva, p. 20.
6. "Everyone had a good time": Ibid., p. 31.
6. "My little sparrow": Ibid., p. 151.
6. "He couldn't go back": Ibid., p. 79.
7. "Tsar before God": Van Paasen, *Days of Our Years*, p. 107.
8. "Lenin's gendarme of the Revolution": So Butson titles him, p. 131.
9. Two of the five marshals . . . sixty out of sixty-seven corps commanders, etc.: Medvedev, p. 213.
9. Looked down upon the West's ambassadors: Strang, p. 175.
12. A well-worn joke: The pianist-statesman Ignace Paderewski is credited for its invention by Gunther, p. 391.
13. One hundred and seventy men: Watt, p. 44.
13. "I am no longer your comrade": Butson, p. 103.
14. "Make way for Poland.": Tabouis, p. 49.
15. Jewish situation in Poland: Nordon discusses this throughout his book.
15. Laundry to Paris in a coach: Sapieha, p. 62.
15. Carrot might be selected: Sapieha, pp. 61–62.
16. "Then there are the great powers": Eden, p. 105.
17. Horse equipages paraded: Adams, p. 66.
17. Chambers like drawing rooms: Ibid., p. 3.
17. Cavalrymen with drawn swords and hothouse atmosphere: Eden, pp. 187–88.
18. "Aren't you chic?": Beck, p. 88.
18. "But he is not Colonel Beck": Diana Cooper, pp. 227–28.

18. "Just let them try": Van Paasen, *To Number Our Days,* p. 308.
19. A "flexible cavalier. . . . A glint of fever": Gafencu, pp. 27–28.
20. People were suddenly different: Sapieha, p. 287.
20. "In autumn it will be lovely out there": Ibid., p. 293.
20. "Why did you get up?": Ibid., p. 291.
21. "You ask me how I feel about the French army": Namier, *Europe in Decay,* p. 39.
22. "Please invite": Ibid., p. 232.
22. "Hitler's birthday!": Cadogan, pp. 175–76.
22. "Easy rifle shot": Butler, p. 74f.
24. Cadets trained to defend: de Chambrun, p. 21.
24. The Maginot Line: Ibid., p. 48f.
25. "We were just too tired": Murphy, p. 36.
25. "There have been several Duchesses of Westminster": Flanner, p. 226.
27. On Stavisky: Shirer, *The Collapse of the Third Republic,* pp. 207–208.
28. On the riots: Ibid., p. 213f.; Knapp, p. 15f.
30. The winding sheet of the European race was woven, the Kingdom of Death, the damned would bring faggots to the stake: Schuman uses these phrases, and equally pessimistic ones, throughout his book.
31. "The newspapers fill me with despair": Gibbs, p. 51.
31. "We cannot stand the strain": Ibid., p. 112.
31. "The whole world is mad": Ibid., p. 201.
31. "We are, of course, all mad": Ibid., pp. 306–307.
31. "That is the astounding and alarming phenomenon": Ibid., p. 332.
31. "A new hospital for the wounded of the next war": Ibid., pp. 106–107.
32. On the cemeteries: G. Smith, *Still Quiet on the Western Front,* passim.
34. Chamberlain's early life is largely summarized from the opening chapters of Feiling.
34. "Your cap's crooked": Macleod, p. 20.
37. Her brother William Horace: H. A. Smith, pp. 2–3 and 64–68.
38. On Norman Chamberlain: Fuchser, p. 22.
39. "Nothing but immeasurable improvements": Ibid., p. 23.
40. "If I had not previously met": Macleod, p. 202.
40. On the edge of tears: Audax, p. 25.
40. Saved the country from bankruptcy: Fuchser, p. 76.
40. Spotted a gray wagtail: Gunther, p. 250.
40. "What he was like at home": Amery, p. 224.
41. MATCHES: Feiling, pp. 164–65.
41. "I want it to be said of me": Ferdinand Kuhn, Jr., in *We Saw It Happen,* pp. 188–89.
41. "I have no idea": Eden, p. 421.
42. "Awful, ghastly, dreadful": Wheeler-Bennett, p. 285.
42. "I never wanted this to happen": Ibid., pp. 293–94.
42. "You don't know anything about foreign affairs": Eden, pp. 501–502.
42. "On the whole I loathe Germans": Macleod, p. 206.
42. "A lunatic, half mad": Ibid.
42. "What a frightful bill": Ibid., p. 192.
43. "Stupid, so shallow": Ibid., p. 206.
43. "Did I tell you?": Feiling, p. 283.
43. "The one man to whom at this juncture": Fuchser, p. 76.
43. Was it to be taken literally?: Ibid., p. 75.
44. "My dear Kubizek": Kubizek, p. 273.
45. "Well, I have safely arrived": Ibid., p. 103.

NOTES

291

45. Gold and velvet overdone: Ibid., p. 104.
45. "What extraordinary eyes!": Ibid., p. 18.
45. "The whole of Vienna is awaiting you": Ibid., p. 140.
46. "He has no one else": Ibid., p. 126.
46. "Herr Hitler didn't leave anything": Ibid., p. 263.
47. "My youthful dreams": Ibid., p. 268.
47. "I should have recognized you anywhere": Ibid., p. 277.
48. "I will send for you": Ibid., p. 281.
48. "In that hour it began": Ibid., pp. 100–101 and 289–90.
48. Details of Hitler's career are summarized from G. Smith, *The Horns of the Moon*, which in turn derived from standard works: those by Bullock, Shirer, etc.
56. "The more exotic, the better": Zweig, p. 313.
61. "This last half hour": The German diplomat Erich Kordt is quoted by Namier in *Europe in Decay*, p. 231.
62. Only walking into their back garden: Lord Lothian is said to have coined the phrase.
63. The visit of Lloyd George: Schmidt, pp. 56–59.
64. The backgrounds of Eva Braun and Geli Raubal are described in all comprehensive lives of Hitler.
64. "Next to my wife": Pope, p. 131.
64. "The Walkyries' battle-cry": Sapieha, p. 118.
65. "Ordinary people in England": Pryce-Jones, pp. 119–20.
65. He gave her a 6.35 Walther: Ibid., p. 148.
65. "The most dangerous woman in Munich": Pope, p. 133.
65. "Bolshevism must be annihilated": Schuman, p. 241.
66. "The underworld in all nations": Ibid., p. 241.
66. "I had the Ural Mountains": Ibid., p. 241.
66. Anyone who went to Italy qualified as an international expert: Speer, p. 173.
66. Details on Ribbentrop are summarized from Schwarz.
67. "His idea of foreign policy is this": Irving, *The War Path*, p. 73.
67. The famous greeting to the king was alternately affirmed or denied by Ribbentrop. Sometimes he said he had slipped and saluted to cover his clumsiness. His wife said he saluted by order of Hitler.
67. "You are the very worst ambassador": Jan Masaryk, who sat next to Margot Asquith at the dinner, told Dalton of the conversation, and he printed it on p. 131.
67. "Even here one cannot escape": Schwarz, p. 67.
67. "So inept, so arrogant or so senseless": Nicolson, p. 304.
68. "Obsess him to the exclusion of all other considerations": Eden, p. 571.
68. Eden-Hitler meeting: The late Air Chief Marshal Sir William Elliot told the author of Churchill's remark.
69. Identified his wife as Her Royal Highness: Birmingham, p. 207.
69. "Berchtergarten, or whatever the place is": Fuchser, p. 92.
70. "The weather prophets are idiots": Kirkpatrick, p. 96.
70. "Shoot Gandhi": Ibid., p. 97.
71. "If we could sit down with the Germans at a table": Maisky, p. 68.
72. "The well-connected and the well-endowed": Connell, p. 95.
73. German army had forty-two generals: Götlitz, p. 42.
74. Boyishly enthusiastic about knight-errantry: Liddell Hart, p. 22.
74. "Good God, and the Führer kissed that woman's hand!": Höhne, p. 255.
74. "Marrying a whore": Shirer, *The Rise and Fall of the Third Reich*, p. 313.
75. "A lot of stinking lies!": Götlitz, p. 313.
75. The Schuschnigg-Hitler meeting and subsequent events in Austria are described in Smith, *The Horns of the Moon*, p. 102f.

78. Architectural plans: Speer describes them in many places in his book.
80. Chirp like birds: Nicolson, p. 347.
80. "No power on earth": Connell, p. 130.
81. "Did not promote cheerfulness": Dalton, p. 91.
81. "If we provoke Germany now": Nicolson, p. 346.
81. "War wins nothing, cures nothing": Feiling, p. 320.
82. "We pass no judgment here": Ibid., p. 321.
82. "An ancient historian once wrote of the Greeks": Ibid.
82. Eden's policy: Eden, p. 636.
83. "Go home and take an aspirin": Churchill, p. 250.
83. "In the end": Eden, p. 661.
83. Best to expect nothing from them but words: Feiling, p. 325.
84. "You damn fool!": Mosley, *On Borrowed Time*, p. 16.
84. "I watched the daylight slowly creep in": Churchill, p. 258.
85. "I send to you": Wheeler-Bennett, p. 76.
85. It seemed to both the king and queen: Ibid., p. 343.
86. "A Europe seething with fear and hatred": Kennan, p. 88.
89. "I am a soldier": von Hassell, p. 6.
89. A "criminal fool": Henderson, *Failure of a Mission*, p. 168.
90. He had almost drowned: Henderson, *Water Under the Bridges,* mentions it several times.
91. A good man and a good shot: Cowie, p. 31.
91. "Cretin" and drunkard: Irving, *The War Path*, p. 78.
91. "Specially selected by Providence": Henderson, *Failure of a Mission*, p. 3.
91. "Good, good!": Butler, p. 63.
91. "Animals, I presume?": Ibid., p. 64.
92. "This miserable pygmy race": Parkinson, p. 18.
92. "Is it not positively horrible?": Feiling, p. 357.
93. "Good man": Halifax, p. 197.
93. "Greatest thing ever done": Alfred Duff Cooper, p. 229.
93. Never get out of this alive: Wilson, p. 37.
93. The commonest little dog: Alfred Duff Cooper, p. 229.
93. "You would never notice him in a crowd": Macleod, p. 235.
93. "I have often heard of this room": Feiling, p. 366.
93. "This business of the Sudetenland": Mosley, *On Borrowed Time*, p. 38.
94. "Let me make it clear": Ibid.
94. "Look here, I am a practical man": Ibid.
94. "She will take the hero's way": Ibid., p. 40.
94. "Next time you come": Dalton, p. 179. Chamberlain told him and others of Hitler's remark.
94. Chamberlain had seen: Feiling, p. 367.
94. If Meissner could be so brutal: Pope, pp. 193–94.
95. "The alternatives are not between abject surrender and war": Parkinson, p. 29.
95. "An inhuman brute": Young, p. 51.
95. "On a two-wheeled bicycle": Tansill, p. 432. The prime minister made the remark to Lord Halifax.
96. "I am extremely sorry": Bullock, p. 228.
97. "I asked myself": Parkinson, p. 41.
97. "Like a barbarian": Mosley, *On Borrowed Time*, pp. 53–54.
98. The Wilson-Hitler meetings: Ibid., pp. 56–61, and Schmidt, pp. 104–105.
100. Bullitt meeting with La Chambre: Bullitt, pp. 297–98.
100. "How horrible, fantastic, incredible": Feiling, p. 372.
101. Felt tempted to make a last-minute coup: Götlitz, p. 338.

101. King George prayed, and Mrs. Chamberlain: Schuman, p. 415.
101. Branded as murderers: Nicolson, p. 365.
101. "We knew that precautions were of no avail": Diana Duff Cooper, p. 243.
102. "This is the Duce speaking": Shirer, *The Collapse of the Third Republic*, pp. 392–94.
103. "What can we do?": Götlitz, p. 338.
103. "Out of this nettle, Danger": Feiling, p. 374.
103. "If you have sacrificed my nation": Shirer, *The Rise and Fall of the Third Reich*, p. 411.
104. "Black as thunder": Kirkpatrick, p. 129.
104. The most horrible experience of his career: Young, pp. 50–51.
104. "If ever that silly old man comes interfering here again": Kirkpatrick, p. 135.
104. "It is always the English who are criticizing me": Brissaud, p. 124.
105. "Here is a paper which bears his name": Namier, *Diplomatic Prelude*, p. 41.
106. Only one other man before Daladier: Schuman, pp. 456–57.
106. "Instinctive revulsion": Lukasiewicz, p. 177.
106. No conqueror returning: Macleod, p. 268.
106. "I feel with God's help": Ibid., p. 270.
107. A quarter of a century had passed: Pope-Hennessy, p. 591.
107. "And this miracle": Alfred Duff Cooper, p. 243.
108. "Neville was born in Bethlehem!": Audax, p. 71.
109. "That damn Winston!": Mosley, *On Borrowed Time*, p. 95.
109. "Lead and we will follow!": Adamthwaite, p. 316.
109. "A dessicated stick, the king a moron": Bullitt, p. 310.
110. "It is difficult": Nicolson, p. 368.
111. "They are going to expel us from Germany": Mosley, *On Borrowed Time*, p. 109.
111. "Why, why?": Ibid., p. 108.
111. "The Jewish pig!": Ibid., p. 111.
111. "Do I need to tell you?": Ibid., p. 113.
112. "I have a personal knowledge of this piece of coast": Parkinson, p. 79.
112. "We'll kick him out": Mosley, *On Borrowed Time*, p. 124.
113. "Recalcitrant but well-intentioned": Boothby, p. 141.
113. *J'aime Berlin:* Gilbert and Gott, p. 51.
114. There were stories that the wife of Premier Georges Bonnet: Adamthwaite, p. 332.
114. "We are like people at the foot of a volcano": Fuchser, p. 125.
115. This represents a section: Horrocks, p. 62.
115. "Fatboy": Colville, p. 17.
116. "It was absolute murder": Young, p. 41.
116. "If one went in": Ibid., p. 46.
116. In twenty years of close association: Churchill, pp. 494–95.
116. "A rare, complex person": Young, p. 47.
118. "It's lies—all lies": Mosley, *Lindbergh*, p. 249.
118. "Build our White ramparts": Ibid., p. 251.
118. "This is a hell of a way": Whalen, p. 205.
118. "You can't expect me": Ibid., p. 210.
119. "That's what made the steam in him": Whalen, p. 381.
120. "Why do they waste good German bread?": Mosley, *On Borrowed Time*, p. 77.
120. "That's a bit much, surely": Ibid., p. 86.
121. "Wriggled like eels": Maisky, p. 86.
121. "Hurling long monologues": Speer, p. 81.
122. On the New Chancellory: Ibid., p. 150f.
122. Bearing the picture of the plane: Namier, *Diplomatic Prelude*, p. 59.

122. "The *Gauleiter* of Italy": Ciano, p. 53.
122. Kissed the hand: Connell, p. 86.
123. "How far apart we are!": Ciano, p. 10.
124. Stood for a long moment: Irving, *The War Path*, p. 180.
125. "With a thrush singing": Feiling, p. 396.
125. Goering had hinted: Parkinson, p. 103.
126. "Pariah or mad dog": Ibid.
126. Certainly logic indicated: Gafenco, p. 9.
126. "Very cheerful": Mosley, *On Borrowed Time*, p. 154.
126. "On every reasonable ground": Parkinson, p. 106.
126. "Cheerful," was the answer: Mosley, *On Borrowed Time*, p. 155.
126. "Almost suffocated in the late autumn": Namier, *Diplomatic Prelude*, p. 65.
128. Details of the Hacha visit: Schmidt, p. 122f.
130. "Kiss me!": Parkinson, p. 111.
130. "Don't worry, Father": Mosley, *On Borrowed Time*, p. 170.
130. Only time anyone saw him touch alcohol: Ibid.
132. "Anticipatory contempt": Churchill, p. 344.
132. "What has become?": Parkinson, p. 116.
133. Goebbels sent a notification: Irving, *The War Path*, p. 192.
134. Skin a parchment yellow: Nicolson, p. 393.
134. "Life is a complete nightmare": Cadogan, p. 173.
135. "Two flicks of the ash": Liddell Hart, p. 12.
135. Spoke only Polish: Dalton, p. 245.
135. "I will make the English swallow a devil's brew!": Brissaud, p. 133.
135. "Stones would cry out against it": Ciano, pp. 47–48.
135. "Unfaithful and treacherous": Ibid., p. 48.
135. "Insolence and duplicity": Ibid.
136. "Spiteful reaction": Ibid., p. 582.
136. "It would not be fair": Cole, p. 87.
137. "The other day": Ibid., pp. 129–30.
138. "I'll be back in the autumn": Langer and Gleason, pp. 82–83.
138. "The two madmen": Ibid., p. 88.
138. "Sermon to a mad dog": Ibid.
138. Goering said . . . Mussolini replied: Ibid., p. 87.
138. "So contemptible a creature": Ibid.
138. Most effective speech of career: Shirer, *The Rise and Fall of the Third Reich*, p. 471.
140. "He has sought to strike me a blow": Gafencu, p. 28.
142. "Only an affair of nuances": Ibid., p. 41.
142. "If it is really true": Hesse, p. 72.
143. "Even five-year-old children": German Foreign Office, *Documents . . .* , p. 387.
143. "Going through a deserted village in a taxi": *French Yellow Book*, p. 165.
144. "At the point of a bayonet!": Shirer, *The Rise and Fall of the Third Reich*, p. 464.
144. "We are not gathered here today": Mosley, *On Borrowed Time*, p. 271.
145. Danzig no longer a place: Ismay, p. 96.
145. "If you bring either or both of the children": Wheeler-Bennett, p. 37.
146. "My most onerous diplomatic labor": Bullitt, pp. 328–30.
146. Worked himself up into a rage: Ickes, pp. 617–18.
147. Required a flow of letters back and forth: Pogue, p. 434.
147. "They have crucified my husband": Ibid., p. 335.
147. "I have my handkerchief": Pope-Hennessy, p. 594.
148. Precautions accordingly taken: Halifax, p. 207.

148. "Nice young people": Wheeler-Bennett, p. 385.
148. "Daddy, oh, Daddy": Ibid., p. 384.
149. How democratic he was: Ickes, p. 654.
149. "My mother thinks": Wheeler-Bennett, p. 387.
149. *Exactly* the same as ours": Ibid., p. 389.
150. Roosevelt saw tears: *Franklin D. Roosevelt and Foreign Affairs*, p. 72.
150. Dear person dying in an upstairs room: Nicolson, p. 394.
150. "Just revert to mud and slime": Ibid., p. 404.
152. "There aren't any": Bethell, p. 32.
153. Just one solid, well-paved road: Van Paasen, *To Number Our Days*, p. 309.
153. "Happy people have no clocks": Weizsaecker, p. 189.
153. Two or three regiments of horse cavalry: Henderson, *Failure of a Mission*, p. 243.
154. "Natural haunt . . . maledict course": McKenna, p. 278.
154. "Confused by firsthand information": Ibid., pp. 220–21.
154. "So many great sides to him": Ibid., p. 357.
155. "Britain wants Hitler to be supreme": Ibid., p. 360.
155. "Cordell, what do you think?": Ibid., p. 361.
155. "I wish the senator would come down": Ibid., p. 362.
155. "I don't give a damn": Ibid.
155. Hull grew: Hull, p. 650.
155. "In view of the statement": McKenna, p. 362.
156. "What's the use?": Ibid., p. 363.
156. "Well, Captain": Ibid.
156. A moment desperately brilliant: Flanner, *Paris Was Yesterday*, p. 221.
157. Make the angels weep: Ibid., p. 219.
157. "I do not suppose": Diana Duff Cooper, p. 254.
157. "A child that has to die": Ibid., p. 252.
158. "Gone with the wind next year": Langer, p. 20.
161. "More threatening than ever": Schuman, p. 397.
162. "Band together and break Hitler's neck": Churchill, p. 365.
163. "My anthem": Eden, p. 76.
163. "Almost instinctive contempt . . . what amounted to a hatred": Cadogan, p. 53.
164. "I must confess": Feiling, p. 403.
164. "An intelligent rabbit": Halifax, p. 209.
166. Affection, now pity: Young, pp. 46–47.
166. "I trust no one, not even myself": Khrushchev, p. 307.
167. "Promising them an easy prey": Shirer, *The Rise and Fall of the Third Reich*, p. 477.
167. First time the Russian had called: *Nazi-Soviet Relations*, p. 1.
167. "Increasingly improved relations": Ibid., p. 2.
168. "Enough. Sign": Fischer, pp. 55–56.
168. One could cock an eyebrow: Strang, p. 165.
168. To Ambassador Sir William Seeds: Ibid.
169. "Which they dreaded more": Churchill, p. 362.
170. "Could afford to smile": *Documents on British Foreign Policy*, p. 89.
170. The newspaper predictions: Kee, pp. 200–202.
170. "Endless new palaver": Maisky, p. 157.
170. "If, Lord Halifax": Ibid., pp. 141–42.
170. "Why don't you go to Moscow, Edward?": Mosley, *On Borrowed Time*, p. 243.
171. "You little monkey": Dalton, p. 251.
171. "I do not think that this would help": Namier, *Diplomatic Prelude*, pp. 188–89.

171. "It was a rejection": Mosley, *On Borrowed Time*, p. 269.
171. "Nitwits and nincompoops!": *Documents on British Foreign Policy*, p. 119, and Mosley, *On Borrowed Time*, p. 269.
172. "Bursting through": Maisky, p. 144.
172. "Not entirely satisfactory": *Nazi-Soviet Relations*—Schulenburg's report to Berlin indicating Molotov said hardly anything else to the Anglo-French negotiators.
173. "Not become any easier": Strang, p. 181.
174. "We give them all they want": Cadogan, p. 189.
174. "Tiresome . . . mulish": Ibid., p. 191.
174. Two merchants haggling in a bazaar: Maisky, p. 149.
176. "Our air force leads the world!": Gafencu, p. 66.
176. "Our task is to isolate Poland": Allied Control Authority, pp. 391–92.
177. Molotov "most friendly": *Nazi-Soviet Relations*, pp. 5–6.
177. "Somewhat stubborn manner": Ibid., p. 7.
178. "The two ambassadors were surprised": Strang, p. 174.
178. "Colossal misunderstanding": Ibid., p. 181.
179. "Among our political merchandise": *Nazi-Soviet Relations*, p. 14.
179. "We will act": Shirer, *The Rise and Fall of the Third Reich*, p. 500.
180. "At best": *Nazi-Soviet Relations*, p. 34.
180. Observations of the British negotiators: Beaufre, pp. 97–98.
181. "Tranquil in his movements": Maisky, p. 166.
181. "It wouldn't be convenient": Ibid.
182. "From some minor German court": Beaufre, p. 104.
182. "Thank God that fellow will not participate": *Nazi-Soviet Relations*, p. 42. (The remark was reported to Berlin by a German informant.)
183. "I must insist": Beaufre, p. 110.
183. "I want a clear answer": *Soviet Peace Efforts on the Eve of World War II*, Part 2, No. 415.
183. "I want you to reply": Ibid.
184. "I think that Poland and Romania will implore you": Ibid.
184. "I understand your point of view": Beaufre, pp. 122–23.
185. "We risk the loss of our liberty": Ibid., p. 123.
186. "It would be important for us to know": *Nazi-Soviet Relations*, p. 36.
186. "We thought it expedient": Shirer, *The Rise and Fall of the Third Reich*, p. 505.
187. "Nervous, pathetic, almost shaken": *Documents on British Foreign Policy*, p. 691.
187. "If the slightest incident happens now": Ibid., p. 692.
187. "Could I pass on such a wish?": Ibid., p. 696.
188. Germany would crush them in forty-eight hours: Shirer, *The Rise and Fall of the Third Reich*, p. 508.
188. Ciano thoughts on Attolico: Ciano, p. 110f.
189. "I am prepared to make a short visit to Moscow": *Nazi-Soviet Relations*, p. 51.
190. "But is it possible?": Ciano, pp. 110–11.
190. "We want war!": Ibid., p. 582.
190. "No longer anything that can be done": Ibid., p. 119.
191. "Tear up the pact": Ibid., p. 125.
191. "You have been proved right": Schmidt, p. 132.
191. "In no case would the admission be agreed to": Shirer, *The Rise and Fall of the Third Reich*, p. 537.
191. "I do not admit": Shirer, *The Collapse of the Third Republic*, p. 460.
192. The doctor met a girl on the shore: Nordon, pp. 183–84.
193. On the Duke of York's Camp: Wheeler-Bennett, p. 397.
195. "Now I have the whole world!": Brissaud, p. 143. Additionally, Walter Hewel is quoted by Hilger, p. 300.

195. "Why should Ribbentrop want to see us?": Khrushchev, p. 127.
195. A swastika flag floating in the breeze: Schmidt, p. 135.
196. Withdrawn from Russian theaters: Krauchenko, p. 333.
196. Could not suppress a cry of surprise: Ribbentrop, p. 111.
196. A clear and unambiguous fashion: Ibid., p. 112.
197. "Things are going splendidly": Schmidt, p. 137.
197. "Don't you think?": Hilger, p. 304.
197. "I know how much the German nation loves its Leader": Nazi-Soviet Relations, p. 75.
198. "If England dominates the world": Ibid., p. 74.
198. "Such an imbecile": In his introduction to Ribbentrop's memoirs Allan Bullock cites an unnamed speaker.
198. A fit subject: Weizsaecker, p. 127.
198. Positively "pathological": von Hassell, p. 26.
199. On the photograph: Ribbentrop, p. 114.
199. A sign of his good mood: Khrushchev, p. 128.
200. "Do we have to conquer Poland?": Beaufre, p. 136.
200. "The locomotive whistle blew": Dallin, p. 53.
200. Admiral Drax did a little dance on the platform: Beaufre, p. 142.
201. "I have summoned you": Brissaud, pp. 144–45. Admiral Canaris took notes on Hitler's remarks.
201. "That displayed his impressive calves to considerable effect": von Manstein, p. 28.
201. "Here as a strong-arm man": Ibid.
201. "Cretins and half-idiots": Documents on British Foreign Policy, p. 257ff. The blunt word "Scheissegal" is in official papers toned down into "quite indifferent."
202. "The merry Chancellor's restaurant": Speer, p. 170.
204. "Unbelievable": Alsop and Kintner, p. 55.
204. "Political miracle for hundreds of years": Swing, p. 160.
204. "Greatest thing since Grant took Richmond": Rovere, p. 61.
204. "Oh, shut up!": Ibid., p. 64.
205. "We might or might not be destroyed": Ismay, p. 99.
206. "Surprise of a very unpleasant character": Schmidt, p. 142, called to Hitler to translate Chamberlain's remarks, found him silent and pensive.
206. Details on Henderson are from his two books, op. cit.
207. "Now it's a question of fighting with gangsters": Sapieha, p. 294.
209. "This idiot Henderson": Pryce-Jones, p. 228.
209. "Well, it's wonderful": Hastings, p. 101.
209. "Darling Head of Bone and Heart of Stone": Ibid., p. 103.
209. "If Poland whistles": Bethell, pp. 195–96.
209. "Only sitting-cases and corpses": Nicolson, p. 413.
209. Join his unit at once: Ibid., pp. 11–12.
210. Valentine sent to somebody's mother-in-law: Langer and Gleason, p. 189.
211. "I have the horrible feeling": Alsop and Kintner, p. 56.
211. "A great general": Beaton, p. 379.
212. Spoke in gentle, staccato expressions: Ibid., p. 375.
212. "Oh, no, no": Ibid., p. 379.
213. "Exceptionally good crops": Langer, p. 23.
213. "It's against human nature": Sapieha, p. 296.
213. "God's blessings": Langer, p. 7.
214. "Best solution would be": Ibid., p. 10.
214. Like children playing Indians: Sapicha, p. 301.
214. Had to get back to Warsaw: Langer, p. 29.

215. Jammed until five in the morning: Hollingsworth, p. 9.
215. "I'm old now": Langer, p. 34.
215. Eating in jammed restaurants: Sapieha, p. 283.
216. KEEP YOUR MOUTHS SHUT: Stipp, p. 121.
216. Been to a party: Karski, pp. 2–5.
218. At heart an artist: The footnote on Ambassador Kennedy's reaction is taken from *Franklin D. Roosevelt and Foreign Affairs*, p. 297. Kennedy offered his play on words in a letter to Secretary of State Hull.
219. Hitler-Coulondre exchanges: *French Yellow Book*, p. 303f.
220. Even slightly theatrical: Hofer, p. 191.
220. Von Rundstedt sat down for a meal: von Manstein, p. 31.
220. Eighty years behind the times: Liddell Hart, pp. 20–21.
221. "England and France are not needed": Karski, p. 7.
221. Like a knight donning his helmet: Edward W. Beattie in Riess, p. 132.
222. Given an escort battalion: Irving, *The Trail of the Fox*, p. 34.
222. Most people's idea of a professor: Bohlen, p. 114.
222. Not wish to be like a dance partner: Fermi, p. 397.
223. "I disagree with you": Weizsaecker, p. 206.
223. "It is enough to kill a bull": Ciano, p. 129.
223. "Now the prisoner of his own methods": Weizsaecker, p. 206
224. Hitler-Keitel exchanges: Brissaud, pp. 148–50.
225. "Ill-considered frivolity": von Manstein, p. 32.
225. "Peace is safe": Brissaud, p. 150.
225. "These generals who plot": Ibid., p. 168.
225. "With the least trouble": Gisevius, p. 371.
226. Invaded the dreams: Camus, p. 136.
227. "It's for Poland this time?": van Paasen, p. 506.
227. "In the long, tail-switching procession": Ibid., p. 507.
228. "Look, look at this": Ibid., p. 511.
228. "We scurried for shelter": Negri, pp. 390–91.
229. "Anytime?": Langer, p. 35.
229. "What's coming?": Ibid., pp. 46–48.
232. "I take the liberty": Lipski, p. 556.
234. "Like myself": *French Yellow Book*, pp. 311–12.
235. "Lived as a workingman in England": Dahlerus, p. 59.
237. "I do not know who I am": Kee, p. 287.
237. "Shouldn't like to have him as a partner": Dahlerus, p. 73.
238. Found him burning documents: Pope, p. 176.
238. Observations at the July celebrations: Ibid., p. 38f.
239. "Much better protection of the Führer": Pryce-Jones, p. 228.
239. "It looks so nice": Ibid., p. 229.
239. Meissner noticed his flower: Henderson, *Failure of a Mission*, p. 277.
239. "There are some snags": Irving, *The Trail of the Fox*, p. 35.
240. "We know the Poles": Dahlerus, p. 89.
241. "Let's drop the all-or-nothing game": Weizsaecker, p. 208.
241. AIR RAID SHELTER: Edward Beattie, Jr., in Riess, p. 132.
241. "Hold fast": Adamthwaite, p. 346.
241. "Where's the Pole?": Schmidt, p. 151.
242. "That's a damned lie": Ibid.
242. Did not know how to act: Ibid., p. 152.
243. "Cannot hand you these proposals": Ibid., p. 153.
243. "I do not like war": Lipski, pp. 569–70.
244. A shadowy figure: von Hassell, pp. 69–70.

245. "It is odd": Nicolson, p. 416.
245. A little self-conscious: Langer, p. 52.
245. "How unreasonable they are!": Dalton, p. 261.
247. "There is no point": Schmidt, p. 154.
247. "I'm inclined to believe": Irving, *The Trail of the Fox*, p. 35.
248. People strangely whispered: Langer, p. 55.
248. Along that border: Allied Control Authority, p. 242f.; Hochne, p. 345f.; Stipp, pp. 135–36.
248. "It's all very unimportant": Strzetelski, p. 78.
250. The pigeons soared up: Wegierski, p. 42.
251. "They're attacking!": Bethell, p. 4.
251. "This is Bill Bullitt": Alsop and Kintner, p. 1.
252. A strange and startling feeling: Roosevelt, p. 916.
252. "There flashed through my mind": Hull, p. 671.
253. A flood of profanity coursed out: Birchall, p. 355. Ibid.
253. "Keep smiling": Ibid.
253. "Here they are": Mass Observations, p. 297.
254. Did so through its radio station: Bethell, p. 4.
255. Battery ceased to exist: Karski, pp. 8–9.
256. "Dan would send me his car": Langer, p. 57.
257. Dark red walls: Wallace R. Deuel, in Riess, p. 141.
257. The world of 1939 is gone: Ibid., p. 142.
258. "He came close up to me": Dahlerus, p. 119.
259. She saw a group of people: Ziegler, p. 196.
259. "Hitler started on Poland this morning": Alfred Duff Cooper, p. 257.
260. When his wife told him: Diana Duff Cooper, p. 258.
260. "Well, I never!": Nicolson, p. 417.
260. One had to admire a man of such position: Ibid., p. 418.
260. "Nothing could be more dramatic": Ibid.
261. Came along and gave them a lift: Alfred Duff Cooper, pp. 258–59, and Diana Duff Cooper, p. 257.
262. The dead man's brother: Weizsaecker, p. 212.
263. Contracting into a nervous grinlike grimace: Strzetelski, p. 93.
263. Even in the Dark Ages: Hollingworth, p. 65.
264. The same sickening fragment: Salter, p. 35.
264. "Like a shooting party": Dalton, p. 275.
264. "Listen—your uniform": Anonymous, p. 33f.
264. *"Is England in?"*: Ibid., p. 40.
265. "A kind of shiver": Macmillan, p. 552.
266. *"You* speak for England!": Nicolson, p. 419, and Gilbert and Gott, p. 317.
266. "I hope—": Raczynski, p. 29.
266. "Talks, talks, talks!": Ball, pp. 27–28.
267. Signaling the death of many things: Diana Duff Cooper, p. 257.
267. "At once, at once": Cadogan, p. 212.
267. Scruffy and slovenly: Dorman-Smith in *The Times* (London), September 6, 1964.
268. "You could receive the ambassador in my place": Schmidt, p. 157.
268. Poker games that saw him losing: Ickes, p. 605.
268. "War will be declared": Ibid., p. 712.
268. "It's the end of the world": Alsop and Kintner, p. 68.
268. "We fly to your patronage": Langer, p. 106.
269. Remembered a dream he once had: Tansill, p. 554. Halifax related the dream and his feelings to Ambassador Kennedy, who wrote of the conversation to Secretary of State Hull.

269. Drank beer and joked: Kirkpatrick, p. 144.

269. Awoke in Berlin: Schmidt, p. 157.

270. "Completely silent and unmoving": Ibid., p. 158.

270. "If we lose this war": Ibid.

271. Horribly soaked with his blood: Clare Leighton's Preface in Brittain, *Chronicle of Youth.*

272. "Poor Mummy!": Brittain, *England's Hour,* p. 9.

272. "There it is": Ball, pp. 97–98.

272. "You know, Brendan": Fishman, p. 101.

272. To see in imagination: Ibid., p. 102.

273. "They ought not to do that": Nicolson, p. 421.

273. "We're walking pretty fast": Alfred Duff Cooper, p. 260.

273. Like a flock of pigeons: Nicolson, p. 421.

273. "Rub, rub, rub": Seth, p. 59.

273. "This is it": Ibid., pp. 59–60.

274. It was the end of France: Murphy, p. 27.

274. Church bells tolled: de Chambrun, p. 43.

274. "Tomorrow all this will be gone!": Murphy, p. 28.

275. *"My* country is at war *now":* Dalton, p. 269.

275. "An old washerwoman": Ibid., p. 271. Brendan Bracken told Dalton of the conversation.

276. He must have confirmation: Shirer, *The Collapse of the Third Republic,* p. 512.

276. Reginald Barker thought: Seth, p. 130.

276. Old black dog: Ibid., p. 140, and Ball, pp. 117–18.

276. "Do these remarks of His Excellency?": Seth, p. 132.

276. Did not know how to describe: Murrow, p. 22.

277. "Outside the vets' surgeries": Seth, p. 34.

278. "I am the British ambassador": Henderson, *Failure of a Mission,* p. 304.

278. "Nothing but an idealist": Pryce-Jones, p. 171.

278. They changed into uniform: Bethell, pp. 82–83.

279. "Is your wife there?": Anonymous, p. 49.

279. Traditional well-bred modesty: Salter, pp. 367–70.

279. *"Gott straf England!":* Ibid., p. 37.

280. A little silk Union Jack: Anonymous, pp. 55–56.

280. "I'll take it in the bedroom": Fishman, pp. 103–104.

280. WINSTON IS BACK: Churchill, p. 410.

281. When he saw the ship: Seth, pp. 171–73.

281. "I can't bear to think of those who lost their lives": Feiling, p. 419.

281. We were not prepared: Wheeler-Bennett, p. 405.

282. Luncheon with Lord and Lady Spencer: Pope-Hennessy, p. 596.

282. Mercedes cars with armor plating: Ball, p. 255.

282. "Isn't it wonderful?": Irving, *The Trail of the Fox,* p. 36.

282. Charlemagne had traveled in it: Schmidt, p. 160.

283. Beaton describes his trip and feelings on pp. 381–87.

283. In the same pension as the future ambassador: Henderson, *Failure of a Mission,* p. 252.

Bibliography

Adams, Dorothy. *We Stood Alone.* New York and Toronto: Longmans, Green and Co., 1944.

Adamthwaite, Anthony. *France and the Coming of the Second World War.* London: Frank Cass, 1977.

Allied Control Authority for Germany. *Trial of the Major War Criminals,* vol. IV, 1947.

Alliluyeva, Svetlana. *Twenty Letters to a Friend.* New York: Harper and Row, 1967.

Alsop, Joseph, and Robert Kintner. *American White Paper.* New York: Simon and Schuster, 1940.

Anonymous. *My Name Is Million.* New York: Macmillan, 1940.

Audax. *Men in Our Time.* New York: Robert McBride, 1940.

Ball, Adrian. *The Last Day of the Old World.* New York: Doubleday, 1963.

Beaton, Cecil. *The Wandering Years.* Boston: Little, Brown and Co., 1961

Beaufre, André. *1940.* London: Cassell, 1967.

Beck, Joseph. *Final Report.* New York: Robert Speller, 1957.

Bethell, Nicholas. *The War Hitler Won.* New York: Holt, Rinehart and Winston, 1972.

Birchall, Frederick T. *The Storm Breaks.* New York: The Viking Press, 1940.

Blumentritt, Günther. *Von Rundstedt.* London: Odhams Press, 1952.

Bohlen, Charles. *Witness to History.* New York: W. W. Norton, 1973.

Boothby, Robert. *I Fight to Live.* London: V. Gallancz, 1947.

Boyd, Louise. *Polish Countrysides.* New York: American Geographical Society, 1937.

Brissaud, André. *Canaris.* New York: Grosset and Dunlap, 1974.

Brittain, Vera. *England's Hour.* New York: Macmillan, 1941.

———. *Testament of Youth.* New York: William Morrow, 1982.

Bullitt, William, and Franklin D. Roosevelt. *For the President.* Boston: Houghton Mifflin, 1972.

Bullock, Alan. *Hitler.* New York: Bantam, 1958.

Bury, J. P. T. *France: The Insecure Peace.* London and New York: Macdonald and American Heritage Press, 1972.

Butler, Ewan. *Mason-Mac.* New York: Macmillan, 1972.

Butson, Thomas. *The Tsar's Lieutenant.* New York: Praeger, 1984.

Cadogan, Sir Alexander. *Diaries.* New York: G. P. Putnam's Sons, 1972.

Calder, Angus. *The People's War.* New York: Pantheon Books, 1966.

Camus, Albert. *Notebooks 1935–1942*. New York: Alfred A. Knopf, 1963.

Chambrun, René, de. *I Saw France Fall*. New York: William Morrow, 1940.

Churchill, Winston. *The Gathering Storm*. Boston: Houghton Mifflin, 1948.

Ciano, Galeazzo. *Diaries*. Garden City, N.Y.: Doubleday and Co., 1946.

Cole, Wayne. *Senator Gerlad P. Nye*. Minneapolis: University of Minnesota Press, 1962.

Colville, J. R. *Man of Valour*. London: Collins, 1972.

Connell, John. *The "Office."* London: Allan Wingate, 1958.

Cowie, Robert. 1977. *Nevile Henderson and the Chamberlain Government*. Ph.D. diss., Bowling Green State University.

Dahlerus, Birger. *The Last Attempt*. London: Hutchinson and Co., 1945.

Dallin, David. *Soviet Russia's Foreign Policy*. New Haven: Yale University Press, 1942.

Dalton, Hugh. *The Fateful Years*. London: Frederick Muller Ltd., 1957.

Deutscher, I. *Stalin*. New York and London: Oxford University Press, 1949.

Dietrich, Otto. *Hitler*. Chicago: Henry Regnery Co., 1955.

Documents on British Foreign Policy 1919–1939. Third Series, vol. VI. London: Her Majesty's Stationery Office, 1953.

Duff Cooper, Diana. *The Light of Common Day*. London: Rupert Hart-Davis, 1959.

Duff Cooper, Alfred. *Old Men Forget*. New York: E. P. Dutton and Co., 1954.

Eden, Anthony. *Facing the Dictators*. Boston: Houghton Mifflin, 1962.

Feiling, Keith. *The Life of Neville Chamberlain*. Hamden, Conn.: Archon Books, 1970.

Fermi, Laura. *Mussolini*. Chicago: The University of Chicago Press, 1961.

Fest, Joachim. *The Face of the Third Reich*. New York: Ace Books, 1970.

Fischer, Louis. *The Life and Death of Stalin*. New York: Harper and Brothers, 1952.

Fishman, Jack. *My Darling Clementine*. New York: David McKay, 1963.

Flanner, Janet. *An American in Paris*. New York: Simon and Schuster, 1940.

The French Yellow Book. New York: Reynal and Hitchcock, 1940.

Fuchser, Larry William. *Neville Chamberlain and Appeasement*. New York: W. W. Norton, 1982.

Gafencu, Grigore. *The Last Days of Europe*. London: Frederick Muller, 1947.

German Foreign Office. *Documents on the Events Preceding the Outbreak of the War*. New York: German Library of Information, 1940.

Gibbs, Philip. *European Journey*. New York: The Literary Guild, 1934.

Gilbert, Martin, and Richard Gott. *The Appeasers*. Boston: Houghton Mifflin, 1963.

Gisevius, Hans. *To the Bitter End*. Boston: Houghton Mifflin, 1947.

Görlitz, Walter. *History of the German General Staff*. New York: Praeger, 1953.

Gunther, John. *Inside Europe*. New York: Harper and Brothers, 1936.

Halifax, Lord. *Fullness of Days*. New York: Dodd, Mead and Co., 1957.

Harvey, Oliver. *Diplomatic Diaries*. London: Collins, 1970.

Hassell, Ulrich von. *Diaries*. Garden City, N.Y.: Doubleday, 1947.

Hastings, Selina. *Nancy Mitford*. New York: E. P. Dutton, 1985.

Henderson, Sir Nevile. *Failure of a Mission*. New York: G. P. Putnam's Sons, 1940.

————. *Water Under the Bridges*. London: Hodder and Stoughton, 1945.

Hesse, Fritz. *Hitler and the English*. London: Allan Wingate, 1954.

Hilger, Gustav. *The Incompatible Allies*. New York: Macmillan, 1953

Hofer, Walther. *War Premediated 1939*. London: Thames and Hudson, 1955.

Hollingworth, Clare. *The Three Weeks' War in Poland*. London: Duckworth, 1940.

Horrocks, Sir Brian. *A Full Life*. London: Collins, 1960.

Hull, Cordell. *Memoirs*, vol. I. New York: Macmillan, 1948.

Ickes, Harold. *The Secret Diary*, vol. II. New York: Simon and Schuster, 1954.

Irving, David. *The Trail of the Fox*. New York: E. P. Dutton, 1977.

————. *The War Path*. New York: The Viking Press, 1978.

Ismay, General Lord. *Memoirs*. New York: The Viking Press, 1960.

Karski, Jan. *Story of a Secret State*. Boston: Houghton Mifflin, 1944.

Kee, Robert. *1939*. Boston: Little, Brown and Co., 1984.

Kennan, George. *Memoirs 1925–50*. Boston: Little, Brown and Co., 1967.

————. *From Prague After Munich*. Princeton: Princeton University Press, 1968.

Khrushchev, Nikita. *Khrushchev Remembers*. Boston: Little, Brown and Co., 1970.

Kirkpatrick, Ivone. *The Inner Circle*. London: Macmillan and Co., 1959.

Knapp, W. *France: Partial Eclipse*. New York and London: Macdonald and American Heritage Press, 1972.

Kravchenko, Victor. *I Chose Freedom*. New York: Charles Scribner's Sons, 1946.

Kubizek, August. *The Young Hitler I Knew*. Boston: Houghton Mifflin, 1955.

Langer, Rulka. *The Mermaid and the Messerschmitt*. New York: Roy Slavonic Publications, 1942.

Langer, William, and S. Everett Gleason. *The Challenge to Isolation 1937–1940*. New York: Harper and Brothers, 1952.

Levine, Herbert. *Hitler's Free City*. Chicago: University of Chicago Press, 1973.

Levine, Isaac Don. *Stalin*. New York: Cosmopolitan Book Corp., 1931.

Liddell Hart, B. H. *The German Generals Talk*. New York: William Morrow, 1948.

————. *History of the Second World War*. G. P. Putnam's Sons, 1970.

Lipski, Josef. *Diplomat in Berlin*. New York: Columbia University Press, 1968.

Lukacs, John. *The Last European War*. Garden City, N.Y.: Doubleday, 1976.

Lukasiewicz, Juliusz. *Diplomat in Paris*. New York: Columbia University Press, 1970.

Lyons, Eugene. *Stalin*. Philadelphia and New York: J. B. Lippincott, 1940.

McKenna, Marian. *Borah*. Ann Arbor: University of Michigan Press, 1961.

Macleod, Iain. *Neville Chamberlain*. New York: Atheneum, 1962.

Macmillan, Harold. *Winds of Change 1914–1939*. New York: Harper and Row, 1966.

Maisky, Ivan. *Who Helped Hitler*. London: Hutchinson, 1964.

Manstein, Erich von. *Lost Victories*. Chicago: Henry Regnery, 1958.

Mass Observation. *War Begins at Home*. London: Chatto and Windus, 1940.

Medvedev, Roy. *Let History Judge*. New York: Alfred A. Knopf, 1971.

Moffat, Jay Pierrepont. *Papers*. Cambridge, Mass.: Harvard University Press, 1956.

Mosley, Leonard. *On Borrowed Time*. New York: Random House, 1969.

————. *Lindbergh*. Garden City, N.Y.: Doubleday, 1976.

Murphy, Robert. *Diplomat Among Warriors*. Garden City, N.Y.: Doubleday, 1964.

Murrow, Edward R. *This Is London*. New York: Simon and Schuster, 1941.

Namier, L. B. *Diplomatic Prelude*. London: Macmillan and Co., 1948.

———. *Europe in Decay*. London: Macmillan and Co., 1950.

Negri, Pola. *Memoirs of a Star*. Garden City, N.Y.: Doubleday, 1970.

Nicolson, Harold. *Diaries and Letters 1930–1939*. New York: Atheneum, 1966.

Nordon, Haskell. *The Education of a Polish Jew*. New York: D. Grossman Press, 1982.

Paasen, Pierre van. *Days of Our Years*. New York: Hillman-Curl, 1940.

———. *To Number Our Days*.

Parkinson, Roger. *Peace for Our Time*. London: Rupert Hart-Davis, 1971.

Pogue, Forrest. *George C. Marshall: Education of a General*. London: Macgibbon and Kee, 1964.

The Polish White Book. London: Ministry of Foreign Affairs, n.d.

Pope, Ernest. *Munich Playground*. New York: G. P. Putnam's Sons, 1941.

Pope-Hennessy, James. *Queen Mary*. London: G. Allen and Unwin, 1959.

Pryce-Jones, David. *Unity Mitford*. London: Weidenfeld and Nicolson, 1976.

Raczynski, Edward. *In Allied London*. London: Weidenfeld and Nicolson, 1962.

Ribbentrop, Joachim von. *Memoirs*. London: Weidenfeld and Nicolson, 1954.

Riess, Curt, ed. *They Were There*. New York: G. P. Putnam's Sons, 1944.

Roosevelt, Franklin D. *Personal Letters*, vol. II. . New York: Duell, Sloan and Pearce, 1950.

Rovere, Richard. *Final Reports*. Garden City, N.Y.: Doubleday, 1984.

Salter, Cedric. *Flight from Poland*. London: Faber and Faber, 1940.

Sapieha, Virginia. *Polish Profile*. New York: Carrick and Evans, 1940.

Schmidt, Paul. *Hitler's Interpreter*. New York: Macmillan, 1951.

Schuman, Frederick. *Europe on the Eve*. New York: Alfred A. Knopf, 1939.

Schwarz, Paul. *This Man Ribbentrop*. New York: Julian Messner, 1943.

Seth, Ronald. *The Day War Broke Out*. London: Neville Spearman, 1963.

Shirer, William L. *The Rise and Fall of the Third Reich*. New York: Simon and Schuster, 1960.

———. *The Collapse of the Third Republic*. New York: Simon and Schuster, 1969.

———. *The Nightmare Years 1930–1940*. New York: Bantam Books, 1985.

Smith, Gene. *Still Quiet on the Western Front*. New York: William Morrow, 1965.

———. *The Horns of the Moon*. New York: Charterhouse, 1973.

Smith, H. Allen. *The Compleat Practical Joker*. New York: Pocket Books, 1956.

Soviet Peace Efforts on the Eve of World War II. Part 2, No. 415. Moscow: Ministry for Foreign Affairs of the U.S.S.R., 1975.

Stipp, John, ed. *Devil's Diary*. Yellow Springs, Ohio: The Antioch Press, 1955.

Strang, William. *Home and Abroad*. London: Andre Deutsch, 1956.

Strzetelski, Stanislaw. *Where the Storm Broke*. New York: Roy Slavonic Publications, 1942.

Swing, Raymond Gram. *How War Came*. New York: W. W. Norton, 1939.

Tansill, Charles Callan. *Back Door to War*. Westport, Conn.: Greenwood Press, 1975.

Taylor, A. J. P. *The Origins of the Second World War*. New York: Atheneum, 1962.

Thirteen Correspondents of *The New York Times*. *We Saw It Happen*. New York:

Simon and Schuster, 1939.
U.S. Department of State. *Nazi-Soviet Relations.* Washington, D.C.: Government Printing Office, 1948.
Watt, Richard. *Bitter Glory.* New York: Simon and Schuster, 1979.
Wegierski, Dominik. *September 1939.* London: Minerva Publishing Co., 1940.
Weizsaecker, Ernst von. *Memoirs.* Chicago: Henry Regnery, 1951.
Whalen, Richard. *The Founding Father.* New York: New American Library, 1964.
Wheeler-Bennett, John. *George VI.* London: Macmillan and Co., 1958.
Young, Kenneth. *Sir Alec Douglas-Home.* London: J. M. Dent and Sons, 1970.
Ziegler, Philip. *Diana Cooper.* New York: Alfred A. Knopf, 1982.
Zweig, Stefan. *The World of Yesterday.* New York: The Viking Press, 1943.

Index

About the Author

GENE SMITH is a historian, horse fancier and writer with numerous books to his credit. He is the author of the bestselling biography of Woodrow Wilson, *When the Cheering Stopped*, as well as an award-winning biography of Herbert Hoover, *The Shattered Dream*, and a seminal dual biography of Generals Ulysses S. Grant and Robert E. Lee, *Lee and Grant*. He lives in Poughkeepsie, New York.